Teaching and Learning in the Early Years

Fourth edition

Edited by David Whitebread and Penny Coltman

 Routledge
Taylor & Francis Group

LONDON AND NEW YORK

Fourth edition published 2015
by Routledge
2 Park Square, Milton Park, Abingdon, Oxon OX14 4RN

and by Routledge
711 Third Avenue, New York, NY 10017

Routledge is an imprint of the Taylor & Francis Group, an informa business

First edition published by Routledge, 1996
Third edition published by Routledge, 2008

British Library Cataloguing in Publication Data
A catalogue record for this book is available from the British Library

Library of Congress Cataloging in Publication Data
Teaching and learning in the early years/[edited by] David
Whitebread, Penelope Coltman.—4th ed.
pages cm.
1. Early childhood education—Great Britain. 2. Early childhood
education—Curricula—Great Britain. 3. Language arts (Early
childhood)—Great Britain. 4. Learning. I. Whitebread, David,
1948– II. Coltman, Penny.
LB1139.3.G7T43 2005
372.210941—dc23
2014035564

ISBN: 978-0-415-72252-0 (hbk)
ISBN: 978-0-415-72253-7 (pbk)
ISBN: 978-1-315-85823-4 (ebk)

Typeset in Palatino
by Swales & Willis Ltd, Exeter, Devon

MIX
Paper from
responsible sources
FSC   FSC® C013056
www.fsc.org

Printed and bound in Great Britain by
TJ International Ltd, Padstow, Cornwall

DEDICATION

This book is dedicated to Dorothy Glynn (née Gardner), who was the professional tutor on David's PGCE course at Clifton College, Nottingham, during the academic year 1973–4. It was Dorothy who persuaded him to focus on the Early Years, and who was an inspiration to all her students with her deep love and enthusiasm for young children. She had been inspired, in her turn, by the work of Susan Isaacs. We thus like to think that we are continuing a long tradition of recognising that Early Years education must start with the needs and potentialities of the young child, and that this book will help to inspire others to continue it further.

CONTENTS

FIGURES

TABLES

CONTRIBUTORS

Amy Arnold has taught across the Early Years and lower primary phase. She has worked in a variety of senior leadership roles, including deputy headteacher, acting headteacher and local authority Early Years consultant. Her previous publications include *Stimulating Creativity and Enquiry* (Featherstone Bloomsbury, 2010), *Working with Parents* (with Roxanne Rutter, Featherstone Bloomsbury, 2011), and *Little Book of Multi-Sensory Stories* (with Kerry Agricole, Featherstone/Bloomsbury, 2013). Amy is currently teaching at the University of Cambridge, inspiring trainee teachers on the Early Years and Primary PGCE. Amy is passionate about making young children's learning meaningful, purposeful and irresistible. Amy is very excited to be embarking on her first headship in a Suffolk primary school.

Linda Bance began her career as a nursery nurse with musical skills. She was always the one who did the music whilst others shied away preferring to wash the paint pots. During the past 40 years she has pursued her work studying at Masters level at Trinity College of Music in both Early Years and music education and, through her writing, teaching, consulting and lecturing, Linda works full-time encouraging teachers, Early Years practitioners, musicians and families to use music-making as the perfect support to general development and well-being whilst at the same time celebrating music for music's sake. Recently, her work with PGCE students and generalist teachers and musicians has been highlighted as an inspiration in supporting the work of 'creative schools'. Linda is a visiting lecturer on the PGCE course at the Faculty of Education, Cambridge.

Miles Berry read History of Art at the University of Cambridge where he also undertook his PGCE. He specialised in the Early Years, with a particular emphasis on the use of technology to engage, inspire and record learning. His early career began in Cambridge where he taught in a nursery school and children's centre. He is now a reception teacher and technology curriculum co-ordinator at a South East London Prep School.

He has remained involved with the Faculty of Education at Cambridge and lectures their students in relation to the creative use of technology and lesson planning. Miles was also selected by the Cambridge Primary Review to carry out 'The Pink Project', which was designed to excite the imagination of children. In his spare time he is a keen amateur photographer – and photos for this book are his first commission.

Sue Bingham ran a nursery school in Bedford for ten years, following her training as a Montessori Early Years teacher in California and London. During this time she became interested in young children's emotional and social development and in how teachers could support this within their classrooms. For five years she was an Early Years adviser for Bedfordshire County Council and the Pre-School Learning Alliance in Luton, during which she engaged with a variety of settings, advising and coaching practitioners in best practice; more recently she was involved as a professional studies tutor on the Early Years & Primary PGCE course with the University of Cambridge, Faculty of Education. Sue completed a PhD at the University of Cambridge in 2012, focusing on how to measure young children's emotional regulation and how teachers can best support children's emotional and social development in the Early Years.

Helen Bradford is based at the University of Cambridge Faculty of Education where she coordinates the Early Years PGCE Professional Studies and English. With a teaching background in Early Years, she has written for a wide range of publications, particularly in relation to early language and literacy. Her current research interests centre on young children's perceptions of themselves as writers.

Helen Bromley was an outstanding infant teacher who went on to work at the Centre for Literacy in Primary Education and then became an Early Years consultant, delivering inspired inset sessions throughout the country, most particularly on play, communication, language and literacy. She contributed regularly to *Nursery World* and *Early Years Educator*. Her books include numerous contributions to the Lawrence Educational '50 Exciting Ideas Series', book-based reading games for CLPE and *Making Your Own Mark: Writing through Play*, published by BAECE in July 2006. Helen did her advanced diploma at Homerton College and was highly respected by those teaching it. She was also adored by students for her electrifying lectures. Helen died in December 2013 and is sadly missed.

Penny Coltman gained extensive experience teaching in both pre-school and key stage one settings in Essex. She now lectures in early education in the University of Cambridge Faculty of Education where she contributes to the Early Years and Primary PGCE course. Penny has worked with several major publishers on an extensive range of curriculum materials. Her research interests include the development of mathematical metalanguage in young children, and self-regulation in relation to the Early Years, including the extent to which encouraging classroom talk can support self-regulated learning. Penny shares the role of co-ordinator of the East Anglian regional Cambridge Primary Review Trust Network.

Kate Cowan worked as a nursery teacher in a Cambridgeshire Early Years centre for several years after completing her training at the University of Cambridge Faculty of Education. She is particularly interested in recognising and supporting children's diverse and creative ways of communicating, inspired by the Reggio Emilia approach and multimodal pedagogies in early education. She is currently completing a full-time PhD at UCL Institute of Education, University of London, researching multimodal methods for analysing video of child-initiated play in the Early Years.

Rebecca Dawkins has a BEd Hons in French and Early Childhood Education (3–8yrs). She has been teaching since 1989, primarily in the Early Years in Cambridgeshire. In her second year of teaching she set up a new nursery unit and is now a nursery teacher, foundation stage co-ordinator and science co-ordinator in an infant school. Rebecca was involved in the early research in 2001 for the Cambridgeshire Independent Learning (C. Ind.Le) project and has helped to support members in the second and third cohort of training. This led to a 'Certificate in Educational Enquiry'. She has also taken part in lectures and made presentations of her C.Ind.Le innovations, where her focus has been the importance of the learning environment and working closely as a team. Rebecca still teaches in Cambridge but teaches year one and is keen to continue the Early Years ethos of encouraging and showing children how to be independent learners and learning through drama and role play.

Mary Jane Drummond was, until her retirement, a lecturer at the University of Cambridge Faculty of Education, where she specialised in Early Years education and contributed to a variety of inter-disciplinary professional development courses. Her abiding interest is in children's learning; a third edition of her book *Assessing Children's Learning* was published by Routledge as a Classic Edition in 2012. She continues to work closely with Sightlines, a national network of educators inspired by the pre-schools of Reggio Emilia, northern Italy, and with Cambridge Curiosity and Imagination, an artists' co-operative organisation working with children and families to support their natural desires to create and explore. She is co-author of *First Hand Experience – What Matters to Children* (2005), a resource book for Early Years educators, and *Learning – What Matters to Children* (2008), which supports educators of children from birth to 11 years in thinking about learners, and what learners do: the 'verbs of learning' (both published by Rich Learning Opportunities).

Sue Gifford works in mathematics education with students and teachers at the University of Roehampton, having previously worked in London schools as a primary teacher and mathematics consultant. She has published on Early Years mathematics and young children with mathematics difficulties, including *Teaching Mathematics 3–5* (Open University Press) and articles in *Research in Mathematics Education*. Recently she worked with Nrich developing Early Years activities. Her current interests include Early Years mathematics, preventing mathematics difficulties and the use of manipulatives in teaching mathematics.

Jayne Greenwood has been a practising teacher since 1977. She has taught in a variety of Early Years and key stage one settings and currently works part-time as a teacher of year one children at a primary school in the London Borough of Tower Hamlets. Jayne is also a professional studies tutor on the PGCE course within the University of Cambridge Faculty of Education as well as teaching geography and design technology to Early Years trainees.

Natalie Heath qualified as an Early Years teacher in 2001, and completed a PhD in sociology of education concentrating on children's experiences of school choice. Since then, she has worked in a variety of foundation and key stage one settings and for the past seven years has also worked at the University of Cambridge Faculty of Education as a teaching associate, teaching a sociology of education paper to undergraduate Education Studies students. The paper encourages students to reflect on inequalities in education in relation to factors including gender, ethnicity, social class and poverty. She continues to lecture at the Faculty whilst putting her teaching career on hold to make the most of looking after her own little ones.

Kate Hemming graduated from Homerton College, Cambridge, in 1998 with a BEd (Hons) specialising in Early Years Education. She has nine years' experience teaching reception and year one in London and Cambridge. Her involvement in the C.Ind.Le (Cambridgeshire Independent Learning) project during 2003–4 gave Kate the opportunity to research the development of young children as self-regulated learners. Her particular interests through the project included peer tutoring and the importance of language acquisition in relation to independent learning.

Lesley Hendy is a former senior lecturer in Drama and Education at Homerton College, and a senior research associate for the University of Cambridge Faculty of Education. Before retraining as a drama specialist, she worked as a nursery and infant teacher and was a headteacher of a first school. Over the past few years she has specialised in drama for the Early Years and is the author of *Supporting Drama and Imaginative Play in the Early Years* (Open University Press, 2001). Since leaving Homerton she has been an educational consultant and has been working on the Expert Subject Group for English.

Holly Linklater has extensive experience as a class teacher across the primary phases, most of which had been based in the Early Years. Indeed, her PhD was a study of one of her reception classes in a large primary school in England, exploring how and why pedagogic choices and decisions were made and justified. It also includes lots of pictures of pirates. Holly has also accrued substantial experience in initial teacher education and supporting teacher research at the University of Cambridge and University of Aberdeen. Much of her research has focussed around developing understandings of inclusive pedagogy, which has involved working with teachers in the UK and internationally.

Patricia Maude has worked with children, trainees and teachers for many years, in schools, in Homerton College and latterly in the University of Cambridge Faculty of Education. She is now more widely known as an author and as a consultant in the UK and abroad. Her specialist areas are in young children's movement development and physical literacy and in enhancing the abilities of adults to ensure that children achieve their potential, confidence and enjoyment in all areas of their physical competence. Her most recent joint publication is _Teaching Physical Education Creatively_ (Routledge, 2014). She received an MBE for services to physical education in the New Year Honours, 2000.

Christine Parker has taught in primary, first and nursery schools in Sheffield, Leeds, Bradford and Peterborough for over thirty years. She had also worked in Karachi, Pakistan for two and a half years as an advisory teacher, supporting teachers in a wide range of settings to provide opportunities for active learning. Christine's research interests have included children's mark-making, parents' involvement in curriculum matters and the needs of emergent bilingual children. Most recently, as headteacher at Gladstone Primary School, Christine has led a leadership research project and the outcomes will be reported in her PhD thesis.

Harriet Rhodes was an Early Years teacher for twelve years before combining teaching with tutoring at the University of Cambridge Faculty of Education where she contributed to the Early Years Mathematics PGCE. Although initially trained as a secondary drama teacher, she navigated a course through the reception classroom, learning as she went. She believes in both the primacy of play and the development of independence as fundamental to effective Early Years practice. Now working as a lecturer at the University of St. Mark and St. John, Plymouth, Harriet delivers teacher training on the Early Years and Primary programmes.

John Siraj-Blatchford is an honorary professor at the University of Swansea, and an independent educational researcher and consultant. He is the director of research and development at the Land of Me and was previously employed at the University of Cambridge Faculty of Education, serving as an associate director of the ESRC Teaching and Learning Research Programme. His previous publications include _A Curriculum Development Guide to ICT in Early Childhood Education_ (Trentham Books, 2006), _Supporting Information and Communications Technology in the Early Years_ (Open University Press, 2003), and _Developing New Technologies for Young Children_ (Trentham Books, 2004). He currently co-directs early childhood ICT research projects in Wales and in Taiwan. Other recent projects have included contributing to the Equalities Review Report for EPPE 3–11, to C4EO reviews of family-based support for early learning and integrated children's services, and to UNESCO and OMEP work associated with early childhood education for sustainable development.

Nancy Stewart is currently working as an independent consultant and writer, following many years of working with children and families across sectors including schools, children's centres and private provision. She has worked in advisory roles in a local authority and at national level, and has been involved in producing national guidance materials (eg: *Development Matters in the EYFS*, DfE, 2012). She is particularly interested in the role of the adult in playful teaching and learning, early communication and language for thinking, and children's development as self-regulated learners.

David Whitebread is a senior lecturer in the Faculty of Education, University of Cambridge. He is a developmental psychologist and Early Years education specialist (having previously taught children in the four–eight age range for 12 years). His research interests are concerned with children's development and implications for Early Years and primary education, on which he has published numerous research articles, book chapters, and several books. He is currently directing research projects investigating the role of play in children's development of metacognition and self-regulation and their impact upon children's learning. Other research interests include insights from evolutionary psychology and neuroscience in relation to early childhood development. His publications include *The Psychology of Teaching and Learning in the Primary School* (RoutledgeFalmer, 2000) and *Developmental Psychology and Early Childhood Education* (Sage, 2012).

ACKNOWLEDGEMENTS

Cover photo: Miles Berry; Brunswick Nursery School Cambridge

Vygotsky's model of the 'zone of proximal development', Figure 1.1, is reproduced with permission from *Understanding Children's Development, 2nd edition* (p. 353) by Peter K. Smith and Helen Cowie, 1991, Oxford: Blackwell Publishers.

Bruner's nine glasses problem, Figure 1.2, from *Studies in Cognitive Growth* (p. 156) edited by J.S. Bruner *et al.*, 1966, New York: John Wiley & Sons Ltd is reproduced with permission from Jerome Bruner.

The growth of neural connections in the human brain, Figure 1.4, from *Mapping the Mind*, by R. Carter, 1998, London: Weidenfeld & Nicolson, is reproduced with permission from Malcolm Godwin.

In their art gallery contributions Monet's Water-lilies paintings inspired the reception class, Figure 3.4, and **In the art gallery, Year 1 displayed the work of Gaugin as if it was in his sitting room, hence the fire and his hat hanging on the wall**, Figure 3.11 are reproduced with grateful thanks to Jayne Greenwood and Debden C of E Primary School, Essex.

Milo's drawing, Figure 4.1, **Evie's drawing: A person will bring them yolk or chicken food. Peek a boob boo**, Figure 4.2, **Tayla's drawing: The chicks need a rainbow to help them to go to sleep**, Figure 4.3, **The fascination of developing chicks**, Figure 4.4, and **The growing chicks continue to provide valuable learning experiences**, Figure 4.5, are reproduced with grateful thanks to Amy Arnold and The Forest Academy, Brandon, Suffolk.

The children try out their ideas in breaking the ice, Figure 4.6, and **As gradually the chilly soft toy emerged, from a bag inside the ice shapes, the children were eager to warm him up and cuddle him**, Figure 4.7, are reproduced with grateful thanks to Amy Arnold and St Mary's C of E Academy, Mildenhall, Suffolk.

Children love to construct their own obstacle courses and are good at ensuring that they are presented with safe challenges, Figure 5.6, is reproduced with grateful thanks to Miles Berry and Brunswick Nursery School, Cambridge.

Early pre-verbal 'conversation', Figure 6.1, is reproduced with grateful thanks to Amy Coltman

Sharing a book as a stimulus to adult-child talk and discussion, Figure 6.2, is reproduced with grateful thanks to Miles Berry and Brunswick Nursery School, Cambridge.

Drawings of flying balloons: helping children to put their ideas into words, Figure 6.3, is reproduced with kind permission of Homerton Children's Centre, Cambridge.

Scott's first class register, Figure 8.1, **Scott's fire check register**, Figure 8.2, **Scott's Valentine's Day card**, Figure 8.3 and **Amelia's stamped, addressed envelope**, Figure 8.4, are reproduced with kind permission of Homerton Children's Centre, Cambridge.

Practising and consolidating learning, Figure 8.5, is reproduced with grateful thanks to Miles Berry and Brunswick Nursery School, Cambridge.

"Oh yes! My turn! My turn!", Figure 10.1, and all other figures in Ch. 10, are reproduced with grateful thanks to Sue Bingham and St Andrew's Montessori School, Bedford.

A beginning thrower, Figure 11.2 and **A beginning and advanced runner**, Figure 11.3, from K.M. Haywood and N. Getchell, 2001, Life Span Motor Development, 3rd edition (Champaign, IL: Human Kinetics) are reprinted with permission from Human Kinetics. These figures were originally drawn from film tracing provided by the Motor Development and Child Study Laboratory, University of Wisconsin-Madison.

Jack on a balance bike (aged 2), Figure 11.4, is reproduced with grateful thanks to Patricia Maude.

A 6 year old shows a mature kick, Figure 11.5, **Leaping**, Figure 11.6 and **'I am catching'**, Figure 11.7, are reproduced by permission of PCET Wallcharts Ltd., 27, Kirchen Rd., London, W13 0UD. Photographs are by Jan Traylen, 1994, from wall-charts entitled *Games Skills and Gymnastic Skills*.

Children are natural movers, Figure 12.4 and **Exploring the sounds that an instrument can make**, Figure 12.7, are reproduced with grateful thanks to Miles Berry and Brunswick Nursery School, Cambridge.

'Intelligent Materials' organised and displayed in the Nursery classroom, Figure 13.1, **Alex draws his magic trick**. Figure 13.2 and **A light projection of natural materials creates shadowy images**, Figure 13.3, are reproduced with grateful thanks to Kate Cowan and Histon Early Years Centre, Cambridge.

A spread from the 'Pink Project' book, Figure 13.4, is reproduced with grateful thanks to Miles Berry and Brunswick Nursery School, Cambridge.

Inviting curiosity: Why does the picture disappear when I stand here?, Figure 14.3, is reproduced with grateful thanks to Miles Berry and Brunswick Nursery School, Cambridge.

Exploring the properties of 3D shapes by stacking, Figure 15.2, is reproduced with grateful thanks to Miles Berry and Brunswick Nursery School, Cambridge.

The Land of Me, Figure 16.1, is reproduced with permission from Made in Me, 1 Rivington Place, London EC2A 3BA.

Noodlewords, Figure 16.3, is reproduced with permission from Noodleworks Interactive LLC.

Souptoys, Figure 16.5, is reproduced with permission from Souptoys Pty Ltd.

Baby Harvey with an heirloom in a timeline of his clothes, Figure 17.1 and **A satchel of treasures**, Figure 17.2, are reproduced with grateful thanks to Miles Berry and Brunswick Nursery School, Cambridge.

Marlene's postcard with writing in Czech "because Grandma does not know English", Figure 17.3 and **Concrete slabs/tiles with embedded objects selected**, Figure 17.4, are reproduced with grateful thanks to Holly Linklater and Mayfield Primary School, Cambridge.

Chopsticks and bangles; A wide range of resources from different cultures for children to explore, Figure 18.1 and **Putting out the fire: Role play areas allow the children to challenge assumed gender stereotypes**, Figure 18.2, are reproduced with grateful thanks to Miles Berry and Brunswick Nursery School, Cambridge.

PREFACE

When the first edition of this book was originally published eighteen years ago, it was noted that we found ourselves publishing at a time of critical importance for Early Years education in the UK and in other parts of the world as well. At long last the crucial importance of good quality Early Years education was finally being recognised. Research evidence that children's success in school and other aspects of their life can be significantly enhanced by quality educational experiences when they are very young was finally being taken seriously.

After the initial euphoria, however, the progress of early childhood educational provision has been anything but straightforward. Over the last couple of decades we have seen the transformation of educational administrative structures at national and local government levels, with increasing central control by government, decreasing control and co-ordination at local authority level, and increasing autonomy for individual schools. At the same time, there have been seemingly endless curriculum and assessment initiatives affecting the Early Years of education. There was a brief and very welcome establishment of a government Department for Children, Schools and Families, but this has now reverted back to the Department for Education. The promising *Every Child Matters* initiative has been phased out and in 2012 a revised Early Years Foundation Stage curriculum document was published, following the Tickell review. A positive outcome here was the establishment of the 'Prime Areas' of physical development, personal and social development, and communication and language, but unrealistic and developmentally inappropriate requirements in literacy and mathematics remain. The continued emphases on play, on personal, social, and health education, and on children's self-initiated activities have been hard fought for, and largely maintained, and continue to serve our zero- to five-year-old children well.

However, as was noted in 2007, the situation for five to seven year olds has continued to deteriorate. In 2012 we saw the publication of Robin Alexander's Cambridge

Primary Review, the most comprehensive independent review of primary education since the Plowden Report of 1967. Recognising that young children can best
build social skills, language, and confidence through planned playful activities
and talk with both adults and peers, a key recommendation of this review was that
the Foundation stage, with an active, play-based approach to learning, should be
extended to include 6 year olds. More radically, perhaps, the review included a suggestion regarding the feasibility of raising the school starting age to six, in the light
of research evidence, expert opinion, and international practice.

Sadly, the growing evidence of the damaging consequences of starting formal
learning too soon, particularly for children from disadvantaged backgrounds, continues to be ignored. Indeed, during the Gove administration, any respect for, or
consideration of, serious research was replaced by allegiance to the Secretary of
State's personal and misguided ideological beliefs. These viewed education as the
simple transmission of information, proposed that the quality of education could
be enhanced by increasingly draconian assessment and accountability regimes, and,
in the latest revision of the Primary National Curriculum, that children's progress
as learners could be enhanced by simply asking them to do more at younger and
younger ages.

The inevitable downward pressure continues: on Reception class teachers to teach
formal literacy and numeracy lessons to 'prepare' children for KS1, and on KS1 teachers to teach in inappropriately formal ways to prepare children for the six-year-olds'
phonics test and for learning the mountain of facts which now comprises much of the
KS2 curriculum, and so on. The resulting distortion of balanced, holistic, and playful
early learning experiences is a serious concern and has led a number of commentators to draw attention to the now worrying incidence of mental health problems even
among some of our very youngest children.

What is clearly the case, however, is that all these concerns and developments continue to endorse the need for an increase in the number of well-qualified Early Years
teachers with clear understandings about young children's development and their needs
as learners and as individual human beings. There are many calls, currently, for us to
give children back their childhood, to protect their time for unsupervised and unstructured free play time and to provide outdoor play spaces in natural environments. These
calls are well-supported by a range of longitudinal and other research studies linking
early play opportunities to beneficial academic and well-being outcomes.

Happily, despite all these concerns, it is the case that our young children are being
educated by teachers and other educators who are now better trained and more pro-
fessionally prepared than ever before. Thus, while the policy level landscape over
recent years has been largely unhelpful, we are heartened to witness the work of many,
many dedicated early childhood educators who, despite everything, continue to provide high quality learning environments for the young children in their settings and
classrooms. It is, of course, our intention and hope that this book will help to enhance
the quality of their preparation for, and professional development during, the endlessly fascinating and challenging task of educating three- to seven-year-old children.

The original impetus to produce this book arose from a perceived absence of published material written in a way which would interest and serve the needs of our Early Years and primary students. We wanted to produce a book that introduced and discussed general principles of Early Years education but, at the same time, showed how these translated into practical activities in the classroom. The book is intended to convey the strong research base related to children's learning and development upon which all good Early Years teaching must be founded. It is also intended to demonstrate that the best teaching of young children must have a strong element of fun and wonder and excitement.

All sound teaching of young children is based upon understandings about how young children learn, and the book begins with an analysis of current research in this area. Principles which derive from this research inform the subsequent sections of the book concerned with different aspects of Early Years teaching and the Early Years curriculum.

There follows a section on basic principles and approaches which discusses issues related to the organisation and management of the inside and outside Early Years learning environment. This is followed by a series of chapters concerned with play and language, the basics of Early Years education. A further section examines the wider curriculum of the arts, maths, technology and science, the social sciences, and physical education. Each chapter examines basic principles and illuminates them with inspiring, practical examples of classroom, outdoor, and out-of-school activities.

In this fourth edition, of course, there has been, yet again, extensive revision and updating in many chapters. There are brand new chapters addressing issues relating to assessment (Chapter 4), oral language and learning (Chapter 6), writing (Chapter 8), PSHE (Chapter 10), the teaching of music (Chapter 12), creativity (Chapter 13), time and place (Chapter 17) and embracing diversity and difference (Chapter 18). The chapters concerned with the organization of the Early Years classroom (Chapter 2) and with enterprise projects (Chapter 3) include significant new contributions. New, up-to-date, photographs illustrating today's practice, specifically commissioned for this edition, are included throughout.

The book is principally directed at Early Years trainee teachers, but it is also hoped that it contains material which will be of interest to the whole range of Early Years professionals and other adults concerned with the education of three- to seven-year-old children.

British nursery and infant education has long enjoyed an international reputation for high quality. This book is most of all a reaffirmation of this tradition, and an attempt to help maintain and improve the quality of the education offered to our young children.

David Whitebread & Penny Coltman
October 2014

CHAPTER 1

Introduction

YOUNG CHILDREN LEARNING AND
EARLY YEARS TEACHING

David Whitebread

There has traditionally been a strong association between understandings about child development and Early Years teaching. This book is written, however, at a particularly exciting time in this regard. The relationship between developmental research and the practices of teaching young children is currently a rich area of growth and development. This book is an attempt to distil the current state of knowledge about the ways in which young children (up to the age of eight) develop and learn, to show how educational principles derive from this, and to illustrate these principles with practical examples drawn from work in Early Years classrooms. In this introductory chapter I want to show how psychological research concerned with child development informs the principles of practice exemplified throughout the rest of the book.

There is a long tradition of ideas about children and their learning in Early Years education. In the nineteenth and early twentieth centuries these were largely developed by a number of outstanding and inspiring educators. Tina Bruce (1987) has provided an excellent review of the ideas of Froebel, Montessori, Steiner and others, derived Ten Common Principles of Early Years education and attempted to show how these relate to modern research. These principles emphasise the holistic nature of children's learning and development (as distinct from learning separated out into subjects), the importance of developing autonomy, intrinsic motivation and self discipline through the encouragement of child-initiated, self-directed activity, the value of first hand experiences and the crucial role in children's development of other children and adults.

As we shall see, many of these ideas have been reinforced by modern psychological research; they have also been extended and developed in interesting and important ways. Much of current thinking about children's learning has been influenced by the work and ideas of three outstanding developmental psychologists – Jean Piaget, Lev Vygotsky and Jerome Bruner – and so it is with their contributions that we begin.

Piaget

The first major developmental psychologist to influence classroom practice was, of course, Jean Piaget. His ideas were welcomed enthusiastically in the 1960s because they were a reaction to the 'behaviourist' view of learning current within psychology and education at the time, with which people were increasingly unhappy. The behaviourist view placed the child in a passive position, and viewed learning simply as a combination of imitation and conditioning by means of external rewards and reinforcements. This model works quite well as a way of explaining how you can teach parrots to roller-skate, but it is a woefully inadequate explanation of the range and flexibility of the achievements of the human child.

A huge amount has been written about Piaget's theory and its influence upon Primary education. Brainerd (in Meadows, 1983) and Davis (1991) provide good reviews of the impact on education. On the positive side, the most important contribution of Piaget's work was to alert educators to the child's active role in their learning, and the importance of mental activity (see Howe, 1999). Piaget showed how children actively attempt to make sense of their world and construct their own understandings.

On the negative side, Piaget's emphasis on stages of development appears to have been ill-founded and resulted in serious underestimation of the abilities of young children (see Wood, 1998). The work of Margaret Donaldson (1978) and many other developmental psychologists subsequently has demonstrated that Piaget's tasks (such as his famous conservation tasks) were difficult for young children for a whole range of extraneous reasons unconnected to the child's understanding of the underlying concept. These tasks were too abstract and did not make sense to young children, they over-relied on rather sophisticated linguistic competence, and they were embedded in misleading social contexts. Interestingly, one of the major areas of discovery as regards young children's learning in recent years has related to their peculiar sensitivity to these kinds of contextual factors. This is an issue to which I want to return later in the chapter and, as we shall see, it has important implications for Early Years teaching.

More recent evidence has suggested that young children arrive at school with many more capabilities than was previously thought and was suggested by Piaget. The pioneering work of Tizard and Hughes (1984) in the area of language, and of Gelman and Gallistel (1978) in relation to young children's understandings about number, are good examples here. Both suggested that children's abilities were being systematically under-appreciated by teachers, for much the same reasons as they had been by Piaget. In school, children were being faced by ideas or tasks taken out of any meaningful context and for no clear purposes, and they were finding them difficult. In the home environment, when the same ideas or tasks occurred naturally, embedded in real meaning and purposes, the same children understood and managed them with ease.

Vygotsky

Piaget has also been criticised for under-emphasising the role in children's learning of language and of social interaction with other children and with adults. The ideas of the Russian psychologist Lev Vygotsky have been an important influence in this area (see Smith, Cowie & Blades, 2011, Ch. 16, for an introduction and Moll, 1990, for an extensive review of educational implications).

Piaget had emphasised the importance of the child interacting with the physical environment, and his followers in the educational sphere argued that the role of the teacher should be that of an observer and a facilitator. The general view of this approach was that attempting to directly teach or instruct young children was a mistake. It was claimed that whenever teachers attempted to teach children something they simply deprived the children of the opportunity to discover it for themselves.

This view was partly a reaction against the simplistic 'behaviourist' model that children only learnt what they were directly taught. To some extent, however, it can be seen to have thrown the baby out with the bath water. More recent research inspired by the work of Vygotsky has argued that there is a much more central role for the adult, and, indeed, for other children, in the processes of learning. This role is not as an instructor delivering knowledge, however, but rather as a 'scaffolder' (a metaphor suggested by Jerome Bruner; see Smith, Cowie & Blades, 2011, pp. 553–569) supporting, encouraging and extending the child's own active search for understanding.

Perhaps the most significant idea within Vygotsky's model of human learning is that of the 'zone of proximal development', as illustrated in Figure 1.1. Faced with any particular task or problem, a child can operate at one level on their own, described as their 'level of actual development'. But they can perform at a higher level when

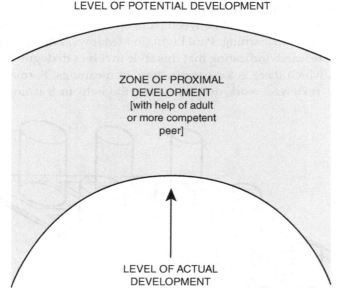

Figure 1.1 *Vygotsky's model of the 'zone of proximal development'*

supported or 'scaffolded' by an adult or more experienced peer, described as their 'level of potential development'. The 'zone of proximal development' (or ZPD) is that area of learning described by the difference between these two levels of performance or understanding. Vygotsky and his followers have argued, therefore, that children learn most effectively through social interaction, when they are involved in jointly constructing new understandings within their ZPD.

Bruner

This view has been supported by evidence of the significant role of language within learning. The work of Jerome Bruner has been influential in regard to this issue (see, for example, Wood, 1998, for a discussion of Bruner's ideas on language and thought). Bruner described language as a 'tool of thought', and demonstrated in a range of studies the ways in which language enables children to develop their thinking and perform tasks which would otherwise be impossible. In his famous 'nine glasses problem' (see Figure 1.2), for example, he showed that children who could describe the patterns in a 3 x 3 matrix of glasses (which were taller or shorter one way and thinner or fatter the other) were also able to transform the matrix (i.e. arrange the glasses in a mirror image pattern). Children without the relevant language to call on, however, were only able to reproduce the pattern exactly as they had seen it.

It is now widely recognised that providing children with a relevant vocabulary and requiring them to formulate their ideas in discussion is a vital element in helping children to develop flexibility in thinking and construct their own understandings about the world. This has led to the recognition that a certain style of interaction between adults and children, and between pairs or small groups of children, can be enormously beneficial to learning. Paul Light (in Meadows, 1983) provided an early useful review of research indicating that this style involves dialogue between adults and children in which there is 'co-construction' of meanings. Forman and Cazden (1985) similarly reviewed work demonstrating the help to learning provided by

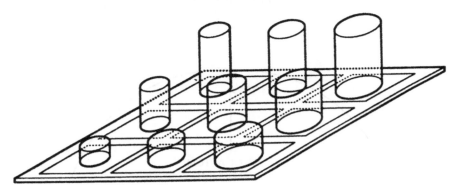

Figure 1.2 *Bruner's nine glasses problem*

collaboration and dialogue between children. The role of this 'dialogic' approach to teaching has continued to be a major area of research within educational psychology to the present day (for reviews, see Mercer & Hodgkinson, 2008; Smith, Cowie & Blades, 2011, pp. 553–569; Whitebread et al., 2013).

Jerome Bruner's other major contribution to our understandings about young children as learners is encapsulated in his phrase 'the spiral curriculum'. This is his view that, in principle, anything can be taught to children of any age, provided it is presented in a way which is accessible to them. Thus, having encountered a set of ideas at a practical level when they are young, they will use this knowledge to help them understand the same ideas at a more symbolic or abstract level when they are older. So learning is viewed as a spiral in which the same point is returned to and revisited but each time at a higher or deeper level. He demonstrated this by, for example, successfully teaching eight-year-old children to understand quadratic equations. He achieved this by providing them with the practical example of working out the area of rectangles (see Wood, 1988, Ch. 7, for a review of this work).

Bruner's view about the constraints upon children's learning is very much in line with a whole range of contemporary research. Piaget's earlier notion that children are limited in what they can understand by certain kinds of logical deficiencies in their reasoning powers has been largely dismissed. As Margaret Donaldson (1978) argued, research shows that adults make the same kinds of logical errors as children, and have difficulties with the same kinds of reasoning problems. Children's learning is now seen as being limited much more simply by their lack of experience and of accumulated knowledge. This makes it more difficult for them to see what is relevant in any new situation, and to see what is the best way to proceed. When this is made clear by the context in which a task is presented, however, children's potential for learning is phenomenal and often way beyond our normal expectations, as Bruner ably demonstrated.

The current view of the child as learner, therefore, is one which recognises their considerable appetite and aptitude for learning. However, it is also important to recognise the nature of children's limitations and their particular needs if they are to flourish. These needs are both emotional and intellectual. As we shall see, research evidence suggests that to become effective learners young children need love and security, and they need intellectual challenge. In the remainder of this chapter I want to examine these needs and their implications for educational environments. The chapter concludes with a brief look at emerging knowledge about the brain and some tentative thoughts about implications for Early Years education. Then, finally, lest we forget the importance of the enterprise upon which we are embarked, there is a short discussion of the evidence concerning the impact of quality Early Years education on children's later development. This final section links with Chapter 2, where the emerging theme of the young child as an independent or 'self-regulating' learner is more fully explored. For a fuller discussion of these ideas, the research behind them and their profound implications for Early Years practice, see Whitebread (2012).

The need for love and security

On the emotional side, in order to develop into effective learners within the school context it is clear that young children need love and security. An important element in the tradition of Early Years education has always been a recognition of the need to consider the whole child. Children's learning and intellectual development is inseparable from their emotional and social development. In their Early Years, as well as mastering fundamental skills and understandings, young children are also forming their basic attitudes to themselves as people and as learners. The basic attitudes they form at this stage have major implications for their future educational progress.

An enormous body of research evidence collected by developmental psychologists supports this view. High self-esteem and feelings of self-efficacy are strongly related to educational success, and low self-esteem and what has been termed 'learned helplessness' are equally related to educational difficulty. It is difficult to attribute cause and effect here, but there is clearly a positive cycle of mutual interaction between self-belief and achievement and, sadly, a negative downward spiral associated with self-doubt and failure. Rogers and Kutnick (1990) have provided a useful survey of work in this area and its important implications for teachers.

Essentially, there are three aspects to this. If they are to thrive emotionally and intellectually, young children need to feel love and self-worth, they need to feel emotionally secure and they need to feel in control.

Love and self-worth

Psychologists have investigated in considerable detail the ways in which the young child's sense of self develops in the first few years of life. From the earliest emergence within the first year of bodily awareness, and the recognition of the distinction between self and not-self, the young child's sense of self becomes rapidly differentiated. They develop a self-image of themselves as an individual, a self-identity of the sort of person they are and to which groups they belong (child, boy/girl, race, types of ability and so on), a distinction between their private and public selves (with an increasing number of roles within which they see themselves: son/daughter, sibling, friend, pupil), an ideal self to which they aspire, feelings of self-esteem and of self-worth.

In all this, a crucial element is the ways in which they are viewed and treated by significant others in their lives. The metaphor has been developed by psychologists working in this area of the self as a mirror. Children's views about themselves develop as a reflection of the views transmitted to them by others in social interaction. This has also often been referred to as the Pygmalion effect, after the famous play by Shaw. In the play a flower girl is treated by everyone as a lady (after some grooming by Professor Higgins) and so she starts to view herself as a lady, and becomes one. All the evidence suggests that children who develop positive self-images and feelings of self-worth are those who have been surrounded in their earliest years by unconditional love and emotional warmth (see Gerhardt, 2004, for a review of the

evidence of the impact of early emotionally warm relationships on brain development and healthy emotional development).

Their parents or other carers have transmitted to them very powerfully that they
are valued by others, and so they come to value themselves. These early experiences
also underpin the growth of emotional resilience and the ability to cope with stress.

Emotional security

Alongside positive attitudes to themselves, young children need to develop feelings
of trust in relation to their environment. The significance of feelings of emotional
security was first highlighted by Harlow's famous experiments in the 1950s with
baby monkeys. The initial experiments offered the babies a choice of two substitute
but inanimate 'mothers', one which was soft and cuddly and another which was
metal and hard but provided milk. The babies spent the vast majority of their time
cuddling up to the soft model. Perhaps even more significantly, Harlow discovered
that babies provided with a cuddly 'mother' of this kind became much more adventurous in exploring their environment than babies who were deprived this obvious
source of comfort.

In the 1950s, the view was advanced by Bowlby (1953) that the emotional security
needed by young children should ideally be provided by the biological mother or,
failing that, by one constant adult figure in the child's life. In his excellent review of
this and subsequent research, however, Rudolph Schaffer (1977) demonstrated that
care did not need to be provided by one particular adult continuously. Rather, the
quality and consistency of care emerged from research as the crucial factors in the
development of what are now referred to as 'secure attachments'. The quality of care
appears to be mostly a matter of how responsive the adult is to the child. The consistency of care is vital in giving the child a sense that their world is predictable. This has
two elements: first, that the same actions by the child produces the same response by
the adult, and second, that transitions between adult carers is handled carefully so
that the child understands the programme of events.

Young children's almost obsessive concern for fairness (with rules applied consistently) and their strong preference for routine can be seen as clear outcomes of their
need for emotional security. Their love of hearing familiar stories endlessly repeated
is possibly a manifestation of the same phenomenon. This need for their experience
to be predictable and to follow clear rules is very much linked to their need intellectually to make sense of their world, to which we return later. Emotionally, it is also
strongly linked to their need to feel in control, to which we turn now.

Feeling in control

We have probably all played that game with young children of a certain age where
the child performs an action, we respond in some way, and the child laughs (the
'dropping things out of the pram' game is a good example). Immediately the child

does it again, we repeat our response and there is more laughter. And so it goes on, and on, and on. The adult always tires of this game before the child does because the child is in the process of discovering something really wonderful. They are in control of their world, they can make things happen.

This feeling of empowerment is fundamental to children developing positive attitudes to themselves, and particularly to themselves as learners. Within modern developmental psychology there has been a huge amount of research about this aspect of emotional development and its relation to motivation. This research has been concerned with examining what is called 'attribution theory' because it is concerned with the causes to which children attribute their successes and failures. Where children feel that their performance is determined by factors within their control (for example, how much effort they put into a particular task) they will respond positively to failure and try harder next time, believing all the time in their own ability to be successful on the task. Where they feel that their performance is determined by factors outside of their control (for example, their level of ability, or luck) they will respond negatively to failure and give up, believing that they will not succeed however much they try. It is clear that such 'learned helplessness' is extremely damaging to children's development as learners.

This model of 'attributions' explains well how poor self-esteem can result in lack of motivation, which in turn leads to lack of effort and consequent poor performance, confirming the child's view of him or herself. The failing child thus becomes locked into a destructive self-fulfilling prophecy. In order to avoid this it is clearly vital that adults working with young children do everything in their power to give them the feeling of being in control.

Research on parenting styles is quite helpful here. Broadly speaking, researchers have found that it is possible to categorise parenting styles into three broad types. First, there is the 'autocratic' style, where rules are entirely constructed by the parent and enforced arbitrarily and inconsistently without explanation. At the opposite extreme there is the 'laissez-faire' style where there are no rules to which the child is expected to conform. Both these styles communicate low expectations to the child and a lack of responsiveness and consistency; children suffering under these kinds of regimes typically have low self-esteem and little emotional security.

The third style is what might be termed 'authoritative' or 'democratic'. Here there are rules to which the child is expected to conform, they are applied consistently and they are discussed and negotiated with the child. Under this kind of regime children typically have high self-esteem and feel in control.

Implications for the Early Years teacher

- Create an atmosphere of emotional warmth, within which each child feels individually valued
- Communicate high expectations to all children

- Praise and recognise children's achievements, particularly when they are the result of a special effort
- Run an orderly classroom which has regular classroom routines
- Always explain to the children the programme of events for the day and prepare them for transitions
- Put children in control of their own learning; allow them to make choices
- Exercise democratic control; involve children in decisions about class-room rules and procedures and enforce rules fairly
- Criticise a child's actions, but never the child.

The need for intellectual challenge

While it is clear that there is an intimate link between emotional and intellectual devel-opment, love and security on their own are not enough. Young children also need intellectual challenge. As we have reviewed, Piaget first argued, and it is now widely accepted, that children learn by a process of actively constructing their own under-standings. All the evidence suggests that a learning environment which helps children to do this will, not surprisingly, be one which challenges them intellectually and stimu-lates them to be mentally active. It also turns out to be crucial, once again, that the chil-dren are put in control. Such an environment will provide new experiences, embedded in meaningful contexts; opportunities for active styles of learning, involving children in problem-solving, investigations and opportunities for self-expression; and, perhaps most crucially of all, opportunities for learning through play.

Play

If we are to understand anything about the ways in which young children learn, we must understand first the central role of play. The distinction between work and play is entirely misleading in the context of young children's learning, for much of the evi-dence suggests that play is when children do their real learning (see Moyles, 1989). Children's language development, for example, is commonly associated with playful approaches and activities: making up nonsense words, verbal jokes and puns, silly rhymes and so forth are all much enjoyed and of great benefit.

It was Bruner, in a famous article entitled 'The Nature and Uses of Immaturity' (1972), who first pointed out the relationship across different animal species between the capacity for learning and the length of immaturity, or dependence upon adults. He also pointed out that as the period of immaturity lengthens, so does the extent to which the young are playful. He argued that play is one of the key experiences through which young animals learn, and also the means by which their intellec-tual abilities themselves are developed. The human being, of course, has a much greater length of immaturity than any other animal, plays more and for longer, and is supreme, of course, in its ability to learn.

The crucial aspect of human intellectual ability which enables us to learn so effectively, Bruner argues, is our flexibility of thought. Play, he suggests, is all about developing flexibility of thought. It provides opportunities to try out possibilities, to put different elements of a situation together in various ways, to look at problems from different viewpoints. He demonstrated this in a series of experiments (e.g., see Sylva, Bruner & Genova, 1984) where children were asked to solve practical problems. Typically in these experiments, one group of children was given the opportunity to play with the objects involved, while the other group was 'taught' how to use the objects in ways which would help solve the problem. When they were then asked to tackle the problem, similar numbers of children in the two groups were completely successful. However, the 'taught' children who failed to solve the problem gave up very quickly. By contrast, the children who had the experience of playing with the materials persevered longer when their initial attempts did not work, were much more inventive in devising a range of strategies to solve the problem, and generally came much closer to a solution. Crucially, while the 'taught' children appeared to be just learning, or failing to learn, one specific 'menu' to solve one specific problem, the children who played were learning far more generalisable skills and far more positive attitudes to problem-solving. They were, indeed, learning how to learn.

Observation of children at play gives some indication of why it might be such a powerful learning medium. During play children are usually totally engrossed in what they are doing. It is quite often repetitive and contains a strong element of practice. During play children set their own level of challenge, and so what they are doing is always developmentally appropriate (to a degree which tasks set by adults will never be). Play is spontaneous and initiated by the children themselves; in other words, during play children are in control of their own learning.

Mari Guha (1987) has argued that this last element is particularly significant. There are many examples in psychological research of tasks where being in control has turned out to be crucial for effective learning. Guha cites, for example, experiments concerned with visual learning in which subjects are required to wear 'goggles' which make everything look upside down. They are then required to sit in a wheelchair and learn to move safely through an environment. The results of such experiments show that subjects moving themselves around the environment (and having a lot of initial 'crashes') learn to do this much more quickly than those who are wheeled about safely by an adult helper.

The parallels here with Bruner's 'play' and 'taught' groups are striking. The implications for how we can most effectively help young children to learn are striking. A simple model which suggests that children learn what we teach them is clearly unsustainable. There is a role for the adult, however, in providing the right kind of learning environment, and this clearly needs to provide opportunities for play. Whenever a new material or process is introduced, for example, it is clear that children's learning will be enhanced if they are first allowed to play with them. When new information is being introduced, children need to be offered opportunities to incorporate this into their play also. As we discussed earlier, there is also a role for the adult in 'scaffolding' children's experiences within the learning environment, and various ways of participating and intervening in children's play can be enormously beneficial. Manning and Sharp (1977) have provided a very thorough and practical analysis of ways in which educators can, by these means, usefully structure and extend children's play in the classroom. For a recent review of the now considerable body of evidence of the importance of play for children's learning and development, see Whitebread et al. (2012).

New experiences

Anyone who has spent any time at all with young children, and attempted to answer all the questions they keep asking, will be well aware of their apparently insatiable curiosity. I am reminded of the manic robot Johnny 5, in the film *Short Circuit*, who continually and voraciously craves 'input'. Part of the notion of young children as active learners is a recognition of their compelling need for new experiences. Providing that they feel emotionally secure, as we have discussed, they will enthusiastically explore their environment and are highly motivated by novelty.

From the psychological perspective this is not surprising. It is one of the other distinguishing features of the human brain that it does, indeed, require a certain level of input. Unlike almost all other animals, we are very easily bored. Furthermore, if insufficient new information is being provided by the environment the human brain will provide its own amusement. Everyday, we all daydream. In extreme circumstances (for example, in sensory deprivation experiments where the subject is kept motionless in a completely dark, soundproof booth) this can result in powerful hallucinations.

Within psychological research, this kind of work has underpinned a well-established relationship, known as the Yerkes-Dodson law, linking an individual's state of arousal and their performance on a task. Too little stimulation produces boredom and too much stimulation produces anxiety. Both are dysfunctional in terms of performance on a task and learning.

Thus, while we need to ensure that children feel in control of their classroom environment, we also need to ensure that they find it a stimulating, exciting and motivating place to be. We must never underestimate young children's abilities to absorb new information and to cope with new ideas. They, for example, love being introduced to new vocabulary, especially if the words are long and/or difficult (e.g. tyrannosaurus, equilateral, strato-cumulus, etc.). Further, there is an age-related factor here, whereby typically our optimum level of stimulation decreases as we get older. The chances are, therefore, that if you as an adult are feeling really comfortable with the pace of events in a classroom, some of the children will be bored!

Meaningful contexts

The dominant model in contemporary psychological research concerned with human learning is that of the child as an active information processor. As such, the child attempts to make sense of, and derive meaning from, experience by means of classifying, categorising and ordering new information and relating it to what is already known. This inductive style of learning involving the identification of patterns and regularities from the variety of our experience is a very dominant aspect of human functioning. The astonishing facility with which children learn their first language by working out the rules for themselves (aided by a little 'motherese') is a good example of the power of inductive processes.

This search for patterns and regularities within the variety of experience has important implications for the ways in which young children make sense of new experiences. They expect to find pattern and regularity, and they expect new experiences to fit together in some way with what they already know. This was beautifully illustrated by an experiment in which young children were asked 'bizarre' questions, such as 'Is milk bigger than water?' and 'Is red heavier than yellow?' (see Hughes & Grieve, 1983). What happened was that the children answered the questions and did so in ways which illustrated their attempt to make sense of them in terms of the context in which they were asked and their own previous experience. Thus, they might reply that 'Milk is bigger than water because it's creamier' or 'Red is heavier than yellow because the yellow is a little plastic box and the red paint's got a big plastic box'.

As Hughes and Grieve point out, what the children were doing in response to these bizarre questions is what they do all the time when they are faced with new information or problems. It is for this reason that children's performance and understanding is always likely to be enhanced when tasks are presented in ways which help young children to make sense of them in the light of what they already know. In other words, tasks need to be placed in contexts which are meaningful to young children.

As we noted earlier, many of Piaget's tasks have been criticised precisely on the grounds that their meaning was not clear and in their attempts to make sense of them, children misinterpreted them based upon their previous experience. Donaldson (1978) reviewed a number of alternative versions of Piagetian tasks where an attempt had been made to place them in meaningful contexts and thus make their purpose more intelligible to young children.

For example, Piaget's famous number conservation task consisted of showing the child two equal rows of buttons (as shown in Figure 1.3, Part 1) and asking the child whether there are more white buttons or black buttons, or whether they are the same. One of the rows was then transformed by the experimenter (as shown in Figure 1.3, Part 2) and the question was repeated. Piaget found that many young children could correctly recognise that the first two rows contained the same number, but said there were more white buttons in the second condition. He concluded that these young children were overwhelmed by their perceptions and that they lacked the logical understanding of the conservation of number.

When this task was repeated, however, by a colleague of Margaret Donaldson's, the transformation of one of the rows of buttons was effected by a 'naughty teddy' glove puppet. In these circumstances many more young children were able to say that the two rows still contained the same number.

Donaldson concluded that the introduction of the naughty teddy changed the meaning for the child of the second question. This question is made sense of by the children in relation to the social situation and their own previous experience. When the adult transforms the pattern and repeats the question, this means to some children that their first answer was wrong and the adult is helping them to see the correct answer. In the amended version, the second question is a cue to check that the naughty teddy hasn't lost or added any buttons during his mischief.

The lessons for the Early Years teacher are clear. Young children do not passively receive the information we provide for them. They are engaged continually in a process of active interpretation and transformation of new information. If we want to help them to make sense of their educational experiences we must ensure that we place new tasks in contexts which will enhance their meaning for young children. This often means actively making links with what the children already know and

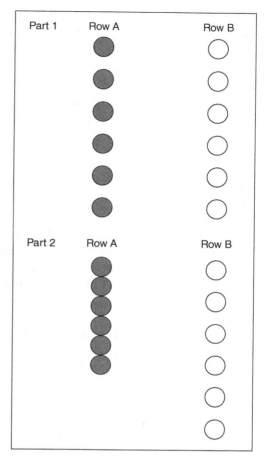

Figure 1.3 *Piaget's number conservation problem*

presenting the activity in the context of a story or game. As a consequence of children's limited symbolic understandings, it also means that hands-on experiences, where the children are gaining information directly through their senses, is always likely to be more effective. It is also a rationale for organising activities within the meaningful context of children's interests or a cross-curricular topic.

If children are to use their powerful inductive processes to find patterns and regularities in their experience it is also important to present the same ideas, concepts or processes in a variety of such meaningful contexts. Only in this way can children begin to disentangle what is relevant and what is irrelevant in relation to any particular idea. Children who are taught one way of carrying out a particular process are often left confused about the essential nature of the task. I have been told by young children that you cannot add together two numbers written side by side, you have to put one of them underneath the other. I also remember one of my own young daughters, on returning from a visit to the Science Museum, telling me excitedly about this machine she had seen (which sounded, from her description, like an internal combustion engine). When asked what she thought it was for, she replied that there was a lot of gravel all around it, so she thought it might be making that. Now that she has seen lots of machines in different contexts, she has induced that the gravel around museum exhibits is usually purely cosmetic.

Mental activity

An important feature of the human brain is that we all find enjoyment in mental activity. As we have discussed, it was Piaget who first drew attention to the fundamental relationship between mental activity and learning. The kind of mental activity we need for learning can be stimulated in two main ways, through problem-solving and self-expression. Both of these processes require us to restructure what we know and to make use of it in new ways. It is well established within modern developmental psychology that this kind of restructuring is required to integrate new information into our existing conceptual framework. In a very important sense, this is the essence of real learning.

Within a number of areas of research, the relationship between mental activity and learning has been clearly demonstrated. For example, within memory research, a range of research has confirmed what is known as the 'generation effect'. Information which has at least been partly generated or transformed in some way is always more memorable than that which has been simply received. It is for this reason that teaching spellings by providing anagrams from which the children have to generate the words is always more effective than simply giving a list of the words. Michael Howe (1999) usefully reviews a number of experiments which have demonstrated this point, and which suggest more active ways of presenting information to young children.

Problem-solving is fundamental to human intellectual functioning. It is part of our need to make sense of our experience and gain control over our environment. Robert Fisher (1987, 1990), amongst others, has argued that as educators we can most effectively harness the power of young children's abilities to learn by presenting new ideas and information as problems to be solved, or areas to be investigated, for purposes which are meaningful and real to the children. He has also produced excellent reviews of the justification and practice of this kind of approach within Primary education.

Within the purely cognitive sphere, however, it is also important because of the processes of cognitive restructuring involved. There is good evidence to suggest that the process of self-expression is important in helping children to understand and make sense of their experiences. The Vygotskian notion of learning through the co-construction of meanings in social situations (as reviewed by Light, in Meadows, 1983) and Bruner's notion of language as a 'tool of thought' are important here. In their explorations of young children's use of language in the home and school, Tizard and Hughes (1984) have presented evidence of children engaging in processes of intellectual search through talk. The kinds of meaningful dialogues with adults that are likely to stimulate this kind of mental activity, however, they found to be much more common in the home environment than in the school. They argue that as educators we must find means of developing quality conversations between ourselves and the children in our classrooms.

One way into this kind of activity which would appear to be well worth pursuing is that offered by the Philosophy for Children approach originally developed by Matthew Lipman and reviewed by Costello (2000). In essence, this approach consists of posing moral or ethical problems to children through the contexts of stories and then engaging them in philosophical debate about the issues raised. Children are encouraged to clarify their meanings, make explicit their assumptions, expose ambiguities and inconsistencies and so on. Exciting work has been done by using picture books with very young children (see, for example, Murris, 1992). Young children reveal impressive abilities to reason, argue and use talk to communicate meaning through this kind of activity, and develop a range of vital intellectual skills in the process.

One of the clear disadvantages of the classroom environment relative to the home is, of course, to do with the adult–child ratio. For this reason, it is also important to stimulate challenging talk between the children. As a consequence, a range of educators have urged the more extensive use of collaborative group-work in Primary classrooms (see, for example, Dunne & Bennett, 1990). As we reviewed earlier, research adopting a Vygotskian perspective (Forman & Cazden, 1985) has demonstrated the various ways in which peer interaction during collaborative group-work can enhance performance and stimulate learning. Requiring children to work in groups to solve problems, carry out investigations or produce an imaginative response in the form of writing, drama, dance or whatever is potentially of enormous benefit. Webb, Franke and Turrou (2012) have recently provided a review of the more recent evidence in this area and have reported their own research investigating the important role of the teacher in supporting productive groupwork in Early Years and primary classrooms. They conclude that the quality of children's explanations about their problem-solving and their level of achievement were highest when they engaged with each other's ideas (now commonly referred to as 'exploratory talk'; see Mercer & Hodgkinson, 2008), and where teachers modeled engaging with the children's thinking and explicitly communicated the importance of children interacting in this manner.

It is important to recognise that the value of self-expression is not limited to the medium of language. Requiring children to transform their experiences into various 'symbolic' modes of expression is likely to aid the processes of learning. When children draw, paint, dance, construct, model, make music and, indeed, play, they are engaged in the active process of making sense of their world in a way which is unique and individual to them, of which they are in control. The sheer vigour and enthusiasm with which young children engage in these kinds of activities is an important pointer to their significance.

Although I have attempted to separate out different elements in the psychological processes which relate to children's need for intellectual challenge, I must conclude by emphasising the powerful ways in which all these elements are of a piece. When children are playing, they are also nearly always problem-solving, or investigating, or engaging in various forms of self-expression. Play often helps children to place new information in meaningful contexts.

It is also important to recognise the ways in which intellectual challenge contributes to emotional or affective elements of children's development. It is no accident that humans find activities of the type we have discussed here immensely enjoyable. Adults at play, for example, are often enjoying the mental challenge of solving problems (crosswords, jigsaws, puzzles, games) or of expressing themselves (music, art, drama). With enjoyment comes concentration, mental effort, motivation and achievement. Self-expression is important in its own right because it builds upon and enhances children's sense of individuality and self-worth. A child who has experienced the excitement of finding things out for him or herself or of solving problems is learning to take risks, to persevere and to become an independent, self-regulating learner.

Implications for the Early Years teacher

- Provide opportunities for play of all kinds
- Provide vivid, first-hand, new experiences
- Place tasks in meaningful contexts: help children to make sense of new experiences by relating them to what they already know
- Introduce the same idea in a variety of meaningful contexts
- Organise tasks to stimulate mental activity: adopt problem-solving and investigational approaches wherever possible
- Provide opportunities for self-expression: when children have learnt something new, give them a chance to make something of their own from it
- Provide opportunities for meaningful, 'exploratory' conversations between groups of the children, and between the children and adults.

The brain and early education

I have referred here and there in this chapter to evidence about the ways in which the human brain learns and develops. Following the huge expansion of research in neuroscience during the 1990s – dubbed the 'Decade of the Brain' – we now know enormously more about brain functioning and development than we did even when the first edition of this book was published 18 years ago. Neuroscientists and educators are increasingly talking to one another and some commentators have rushed to justify particular educational arguments by reference to brain research.

At this stage, we need to approach neuroscientific evidence with a good deal of caution, however. Serious research into the brain is still very much in its infancy and the one finding about the human brain that is incontrovertible is that it is enormously complex. The possibilities for misinterpretation and oversimplification are legion. Talk of 'educating the left side of the brain' or the 'brain-friendly' classroom is dangerously premature.

However, a number of useful reviews have already been compiled of evidence which is of relevance to early education (Blakemore, 2000) and education generally (Byrnes, 2001). Such evidence as we have so far does, at least, seem to support a number of important, general positions in regards to early education:

- The brain develops and learns by forming vast numbers of connections between brain cells in 'neural networks'; this supports the inductive nature of human learning and its implications for experiential learning, play and meaningful contexts.
- The overwhelming majority of these connections are formed in the first few years of life (see Figure 1.4), causing the human brain, uniquely, to quadruple in size between birth and six years of age. Babies literally build their own brains, and the environments in which they do so are clearly significant.

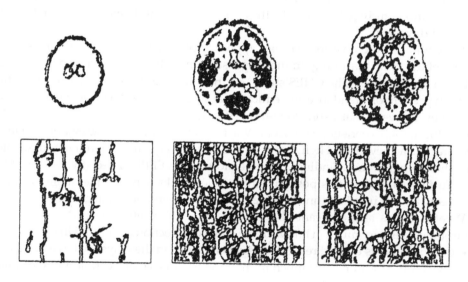

Neural connections are sparse at birth (left), but new connections are made at a terrific rate during infancy and by the age of six (middle) they are at maximum density. Thereafter they decrease again as unwanted connections die back. (right.) Adults can increase neural connections throughout their life by learning new things. But if the brain is not used the connections will become further depleted.

Figure 1.4 *The growth of neural connections in the human brain (from Carter, 1998)*

- Processing in the young brain is quite generalized. Specifically adapted regions gradually form over the first few years. Consequently, requiring young children to learn in ways which depend upon later emerging functions is futile and potentially counter-productive; there are important implications here for the introduction of formal, disconnected learning and of tasks involving the manipulation of symbolic representations such as letters and numerals.

As we learn more about the early development of the brain, it will clearly be of interest to Early Years educators. Those readers who wish to be better informed at this stage might like to look at Rita Carter's (1998) excellent and well-illustrated introduction.

The impact and nature of quality in Early Years education

It is now well established that a child's educational experience in the Early Years has both immediate effects upon their cognitive and social development and long-term effects upon their educational achievements and life prospects. Sylva and Wiltshire (1993) have reviewed a range of evidence which supports this position. This evidence includes studies of the Head Start programmes in the USA, the Child Health and Education Study (CHES) of a birth cohort in Britain and Swedish research on the effects of daycare.

To begin with, these various studies appear to produce inconsistent findings. Early studies of the Head Start programmes suggested immediate cognitive and social gains but little lasting effect. The CHES study, on the other hand, found a clear association between pre-school attendance and educational achievements at age ten. Further analysis, however, reveals that lasting long-term effects are dependent upon the quality of the early educational experience. Sylva and Wiltshire note particularly the evidence of long-term impact achieved by High/Scope and other high-quality, cognitively-orientated pre-school programmes. Findings from the more recent EPPE project (Sylva et al., 2004) have further supported this position, finding clear links between the quality of Early Years educational provision and a range of intellectual and personal gains.

What emerges as significant about these particularly effective early educational environments is very much in line with the kinds of directions indicated in this chapter. These environments offered real intellectual challenge in the ways we have discussed, with the adult educators very much in the Vygotskian role of 'scaffolding' the child's experience. Sylva et al. (2004) particularly identified, within the highest quality settings, the occurrence of episodes of 'sustained shared thinking' between adults and children. Within this kind of pedagogical approach, the child is put very much in control of their own learning. This theme of the central importance of encouraging young children to become independent or 'self-regulated' learners is one which we develop more fully in Chapter 2, when we look at the organization of the classroom environment.

In the High/Scope regime, for example, the central model of learning is the 'plan, do and review' cycle. Each child plans their activities for the session or the day in a small group with an adult educator. They then move off to carry out the planned activities, and later return to review progress again with their small group and the adult educator. This pattern builds in purposeful adult–child and child–child conversations which seem to Sylva and Wiltshire to be 'an embodiment of Vygotsky's notion of effective instruction within the zone of proximal development' (p.36).

This way of working also places the responsibility very much on each child for his or her own learning. What all the high quality Early Years regimes identified by Sylva and Wiltshire did was to help children develop what they term a 'mastery' orientation to learning and to themselves. This relates very closely to the emotional issues we discussed earlier in the chapter. Children in high quality Early Years environments developed feelings of high self-esteem, with high aspirations and secure feelings of self-efficacy. Such children grew to believe that, through effort, they could solve problems, understand new ideas, develop skills and so on. They felt in control of their environments and confident in their abilities.

The key roles of playful experiences and children's self-regulation abilities, and the dangers of too early formal teaching within early childhood education, have all been supported by a number of recent longitudinal studies. Marcon (2002), for example, demonstrated that, by the end of their sixth year in school, children whose pre-school model had been academically directed achieved significantly lower marks in comparison to children who had attended child-initiated, play-based pre-school programmes. In a second longitudinal study in the USA, McClelland et al. (2013) showed that key elements of self-regulation, namely attention span or persistence, in four-year-olds, significantly predicted maths and reading achievement at age 21 and the odds of completing college by age 25. The majority of this relationship was direct and was not significantly mediated by maths or reading skills at age seven. This is a clearly significant indication that an early emphasis on the teaching of literacy and numeracy is likely to be far less effective than a focus on supporting children to become self-regulating learners during their early childhood education.

These are some of the themes which this chapter has attempted to illuminate, and which permeate all the other chapters of this book. If we wish to provide quality learning environments for our young children, these need to be informed by understandings about how young children learn and develop. The rest of the present volume is dedicated to indicating how these understandings can be translated, imaginatively and reflectively, into the everyday practice of the Early Years classroom.

References

Blakemore, S.J. (2000) *Early Years Learning*. Report 140, POST (Parliamentary Office of Science & Technology).

Bowlby, J. (1953) *Child Care and the Growth of Love*. London: Penguin Books.

Bruce, T. (1987) *Early Childhood Education*. London: Hodder & Stoughton.

Bruner, J.S. (1972) The nature and uses of immaturity. *American Psychologist*, 27, 1–28.

Byrnes, J.P. (2001) *Minds, Brains, and Learning*. London: Guilford Press.

Carter, R. (1998) *Mapping the Mind*. London: Weidenfeld & Nicolson.

Costello, P.J.M. (2000) *Thinking Skills and Early Childhood Education*. London: David Fulton.

Davis, A. (1991) Piaget, teachers and education: Into the 1990s. In P. Light, S. Sheldon & M. Woodhead (Eds.), *Learning to Think*, London: Routledge.

Donaldson, M. (1978) *Children's Minds*, London: Fontana.

Dunne, E. & Bennett, N. (1990) *Talking and Learning in Groups*. London: Macmillan.

Fisher, R. (1987) *Problem Solving in Primary Schools*. Oxford: Basil Blackwell.

Fisher, R. (1990) *Teaching Children to Think*. Oxford: Basil Blackwell.

Forman, E.A. & Cazden, C.B. (1985) Exploring Vygotskian perspectives in education: The cognitive value of peer interaction. In J.V. Wertsch (Ed.), *Culture, Communication & Cognition*. Cambridge: Cambridge University Press.

Gelman, R. & Gallistel, C.R. (1978) *The Child's Understanding of Number*. Cambridge, MA: Harvard University Press.

Gerhardt, S. (2004) *Why Love Matters: How Affection Shapes a Baby's Brain*. Hove, Sussex: Routledge.

Guha, M. (1987) Play in school. In G.M. Blenkin & A.V. Kelly (Eds.), *Early Childhood Education*. London: Paul Chapman.

Howe, M.J.A. (1999) *A Teacher's Guide to the Psychology of Learning*, 2nd Ed. Oxford: Basil Blackwell.

Hughes, M. & Grieve, R. (1983) On asking children bizarre questions. In M. Donaldson, R. Grieve, & C. Pratt (Eds.), *Early Childhood Development and Education*. Oxford: Basil Blackwell.

Manning, K. & Sharp, A. (1977) *Structuring Play in the Early Years at School*. Cardiff: Ward Lock Educational/Drake Educational Associates.

Marcon, R.A (2002) Moving up the grades: Relationship between pre-school model and later school success. *Early Childhood Research and Practice*, 4 (1), pp. 517–530.

McClelland, M.M., Acock, A.C., Piccinin, A., Rhea, S.A. & Stallings, M.C. (2013) Relations between preschool attention span-persistence and age 25 educational outcomes. *Early Childhood Research Quarterly*, 28 (2), pp. 314–24.

Meadows, S. (Ed.) (1983) *Developing Thinking*. London: Methuen.

Mercer, N. & Hodgkinson, S. (2008) (Eds.). *Exploring Talk in School*. London: Sage.

Moll, L.C. (Ed.) (1990) *Vygotsky and Education*. Cambridge: Cambridge University Press.

Moyles, J.R. (1989) *Just Playing? The Role and Status of Play in Early Childhood Education*. Milton Keynes: Open University Press.

Murris, K. (1992) *Teaching Philosophy with Picture Books*. London: Infonet Publications Ltd.

Rogers, C. & Kutnick, P. (Eds.) (1990) *The Social Psychology of the Primary School*. London: Routledge.

Schaffer, R. (1977) *Mothering*. London: Fontana.

Smith, P.K., Cowie, H. & Blades M. (2011) *Understanding Children's Development*, 5th Ed. Oxford: Basil Blackwell.

Sylva, K., Bruner, J.S. & Genova, P. (1984) The role of play in the problem-solving of children 3–5 years old. In P. Barnes, J. Oates, J. Chapman, L. Victor & P. Czerniewska (Eds.), *Personality, Development & Learning*. Sevenoaks: Hodder & Stoughton.

Sylva, K. & Wiltshire, J. (1993) The impact of early learning on children's later development: A review prepared for the RSA inquiry 'Start Right'. *European Early Childhood Education Research Journal*, 1, pp. 17–40.

Sylva, K., Melhuish, E. C., Sammons, P., Siraj-Blatchford, I. and Taggart, B. (2004) *The Effective Provision of Pre-School Education (EPPE) Project: Technical Paper 12 – The Final Report: Effective Pre-School Education*. London: DfES/Institute of Education, University of London.

Tizard, B. & Hughes, M. (1984) *Young Children Learning*. London: Fontana.

Webb, N.M, Franke, M.L. & Turrou, M.C. (2013) Self-regulation and learning in peer-directed small groups. In D. Whitebread, N. Mercer, C. Howe & A. Tolmie (Eds.), *Self-Regulation and Dialogue in Primary Classrooms*. British Journal of Educational Psychology Monograph Series II: Psychological Aspects of Education – Current Trends, No. 10. Leicester: British Psychological Society.

Whitebread, D. (2012) *Developmental Psychology and Early Childhood Education*. London: Sage.

Whitebread, D., Basilio, M., Kuvalja, M. & Verma, M. (2012) *The Importance of Play: A Report on the Value of Children's Play with a Series of Policy Recommendations*. Brussels, Belgium: Toys Industries for Europe. (Downloadable from: http://www. importanceofplay.eu/IMG/pdf/dr_david_whitebread_-_the_importance_of_ play.pdf)

Whitebread, D., Mercer, N., Howe, C. & Tolmie, A. (Eds.) (2013) *Self-Regulation and Dialogue in Primary Classrooms*. British Journal of Educational Psychology Monograph Series II: Psychological Aspects of Education – Current Trends, No. 10. Leicester: British Psychological Society.

Wood, D. (1988/1998) *How Children Think & Learn*, 1st/2nd Ed. Oxford: Basil Blackwell.

Basic principles and approaches

CHAPTER 2

'Our classroom is like a little cosy house!'

ORGANISING THE EARLY YEARS CLASSROOM TO ENCOURAGE SELF-REGULATED LEARNING

David Whitebread with Rebecca Dawkins, Sue Bingham,
Harriet Rhodes and Kate Hemming

Amongst the many challenges and complexities involved in teaching young children is the recognition that, as truly 'active' learners, they do not just learn what they are taught; rather, they learn what they experience. The effective Early Years teacher, therefore, has to consider not only their own inter-personal style as a teacher, and not only the learning activities they will devise and provide for the children, but also the entire classroom environment and ethos within which they and the children will live and work.

It is always very sad to see the consequences of a poorly managed classroom: children standing around in queues waiting for a small amount of attention from the teacher; the children becoming over-dependent on adult support and unable to function without constant intervention; the teacher under constant pressure and frustrated that they never have time to do anything properly; equipment forever being lost in the general chaos – and so on. Lofty ideals about being child-centred, encouraging creativity and teaching the children to think for themselves all come to naught in such an environment.

This chapter contains outlines by four experienced and highly skilled Early Years teachers describing how they organize their classrooms. While a number of themes emerge from these descriptions, what is clear is that each of these teachers has thought very carefully and deeply about what they are trying to achieve for the children in their class, and how the environment they create supports this. A key theme guiding much of their thinking relates to supporting children in becoming 'independent' or 'self-regulated' learners. There are two very clear justifications for this approach. First, at the practical level, if the children are able to operate independently, taking initiative, setting their own goals, accessing resources as they are required, supporting and helping one another, working together co-operatively and so on, then this can release the teacher from the roles of traffic policeman, fire-fighter and general trouble-shooter, and allow him or her to spend more time in more educationally productive activities. Second, at a deeper educational level, there is now strong evidence to suggest that developing the skills of 'self-regulation', sometimes referred to in the psychological literature as 'metacognition', is crucial to becoming an effective learner. As we shall see, this development of young children as independent *learners* crucially depends on meeting the needs of young children discussed in Chapter 1 – the needs for emotional support and intellectual challenge.

There is now wide recognition of the importance of fostering self-regulation among young children, as attested by a number of publications (Featherstone & Bayley, 2001; Williams, 2003; Larkin, 2010; Whitebread & Coltman, 2011; Whitebread, 2014) and by official government guidelines. Since the original construction and development of the Early Years Foundation Stage, circulars and curriculum documents from various government agencies have offered a range of suggestions as to what independent or self-regulated learning might involve. In the most recent non-statutory guidance material, produced by Early Education (2012), and supported by the Department for Education, entitled *Development Matters in the Early Years Foundation Stage (EYFS)*, the list of 'Characteristics of Effective Learning' is perhaps the most developed version yet of such suggestions. On p.5 of this document, the following characteristics are listed:

Playing and exploring

- Finding out and exploring
- Playing with what they know
- Being willing to 'have a go'

Active learning – motivation

- Being involved and concentrating
- Keeping trying
- Enjoying achieving what they set out to do

Creating and thinking critically

- Having their own ideas
- Making links
- Choosing ways to do things

While a commitment to encouraging children to become self-regulating learners is very common amongst Early Years teachers, at the level of everyday classroom realities, however, there are a number of problematic issues. The need to maintain an orderly classroom, combined with the pressures of time and resources, and teachers' perceptions of external expectations from headteachers, parents and government agencies, can often militate against the support of children's independence. This is unfortunate and often counter-productive. The kind of overly teacher-directed style this tends to engender may create an impression of having 'covered' the curriculum, but is largely ineffective in promoting learning in young children, and does not help at all in the larger project of developing children's ability and confidence to become self-regulated and self-motivated learners.

There is also often, unfortunately, a lack of clarity as to the nature of self-regulated learning. Evidence from a study across the Foundation Stage and Key Stage 1 conducted by one of the present authors (Hendy & Whitebread, 2000) found that the Early Years teachers interviewed shared a commitment to encouraging greater independence in learning among young children, but held a wide spectrum of views about the essential key elements within it, and of their role in fostering the necessary skills and dispositions. There was a dominant concern, for example, with the purely *organisational* element of children's self-regulation, at the expense of any concern with cognitive or emotional aspects. Perhaps most worrying, however, was the finding that the children appeared to become more, rather than less, dependent on their teachers during their first few years in school.

In the early few years of this new millennium, David Whitebread worked with 32 Cambridgeshire Early Years teachers (including two of the teachers describing their classes here) on the Cambridgeshire Independent Learning (C.Ind.Le) Project (Whitebread et al., 2005; Whitebread & Coltman, 2011). This research has established that young children in the three–five age range, given the opportunity, are capable of taking on considerable responsibility for their own learning and developing as self-regulated learners, and that their teachers, through high quality pedagogical practices, can make a crucially significant contribution in this area.

From this work emerged four underlying principles for a pedagogy of self-regulation, which clearly relate back to the issues highlighted in regard to young children's learning in Chapter 1. These principles were as follows:

Principle 1: Emotional warmth and security

Classrooms which support children's growing confidence as learners and foremost characterised by emotional warmth, by mutual respect and trust between adults and children, and by structures which provide emotional support (for example, clear and consistently applied rules). This kind of emotional atmosphere gives young children the confidence to play creatively, to take risks emotionally and intellectually, and to persevere when they encounter difficulties. In the absence of this kind of support, many young children will remain timid and passive in their general demeanour in the classroom, will be unwilling to try out new or unfamiliar activities and will give up on tasks as soon as they encounter difficulties. Amongst many other things, to provide emotional warmth and security in the classroom environment, teachers can:

- provide a model of emotional self-regulation, talking through their own difficulties with the children;
- show that they appreciate effort at least as much as products;

- show an interest in the children as people, and share aspects of their own personal lives; and
- negotiate frameworks for behaviour with the children which are seen to be fair and supportive.

Principle 2: Feelings of control

Feeling in control of their environment and their learning is fundamental to children developing confidence in their abilities, and the ability to respond positively to set-backs and challenges. Human beings are, quite literally, control freaks. An early experiment carried out in California by Watson and Ramey (1972) involved the parents of eight-month-old babies being given special cots which came complete with attractive and colourful 'mobiles'. The parents were asked to put their babies in the cots for specified periods each day for a few weeks. In some of the cots the mobiles either did not move, or moved around on a timed schedule. But in other cots the mobile was wired up to a pillow, so that the mobile would move whenever the baby exerted pressure on the pillow. At the end of the experiment, the parents of the babies who had experienced these 'contingency mobiles' wanted to pay the research team large amounts of money to keep the cots because their babies had enjoyed these so much.

It is vitally important that teachers of young children allow sufficient flexibility in their classroom organization for children who have been inspired by a particular experience to pursue their interest. Allowing opportunities for child-initiated activities enhances children's sense of ownership and responsibility in relation to their own learning. Other practices which are helpful in giving children this feeling of control include:

- making sure that children have access to a range of materials for their own purposes;
- giving children the opportunity to make choices about activities;
- understanding that a beautiful teacher-made role play area or display may not be as valuable for the children's learning as one to which children have contributed; and
- adopting a flexible approach to timetabling which allows children to pursue an activity to their satisfaction, avoiding unnecessary interruptions.

Principle 3: Cognitive challenge

The third underlying principle of good practice which encourages self-regulatory and independent learning is the presence of cognitive challenge. Children spontaneously set themselves challenges in their play and, given a choice, will often choose a task which is more challenging than the task which an adult might have thought was appropriate. Providing children with achievable challenges, and supporting them so they can meet them, is the most powerful way to encourage positive attitudes to learning, and the children's independent ability to take on challenging tasks.

More generally, to promote this kind of cognitive challenge in their classrooms, teachers can:

- require children to plan activities;
- consider whether activities planned to be carried out individually could be made more challenging as a collaborative group task;
- ask more genuine open-ended questions that require higher order thinking, e.g.: 'Why?' 'What would happen if . . . ?' 'What makes you say that?' and
- give children opportunities to organize activities themselves, avoiding too early adult intervention.

Principle 4: Articulation of learning

Finally, it is clear that if children are going to become increasingly aware of and in control of their own mental processing, the processes of thinking and learning need to be made explicit by adults, and the children themselves need to learn to talk about and to represent their learning and thinking.

Building in to the regular practice within a classroom opportunities for the children to reflect upon their thinking and decision-making during and after activities is enormously advantageous in this regard. Other strategies which are effective in stimulating children to talk about their learning include:

- peer tutoring, where one child teaches another;
- involving children in self-assessment;
- making learning intentions explicit when tasks are introduced, or discussing them either while the children are engaged in the task or afterwards in a review session; and
- modelling a self-commentary, which articulates thinking and strategies; for example when solving a mathematical problem.

In the following accounts by four experienced and skillful Early Years teachers, many of these themes and principles can be seen to be brought to life through their classroom organizational practices.

A nursery class

The first account is from Rebecca Dawkins, who at the time of writing taught the nursery class in an infant school whose catchment area contains areas of reasonable affluence but also of relative economic deprivation. Perhaps partly in response to the characteristics of the individual children she receives into her class, what is noticeable in her account is the emphasis she places on the emotional climate of the classroom, and providing the children with a secure and supportive emotional environment. For many of the children, who are only three years of age when they join the class, this is of course their first significant experience which requires them to cope outside of the home. Making very strong links between the environment of the home and that of the classroom is a key and highly significant element of Rebecca's practice. As she was involved as a teacher in the C.Ind.Le project, the emphasis on supporting children to develop as independent learners is also clear, and she recognizes some ways in which this has influenced her practice.

Nursery ethos and classroom environment

For some of our children, nursery may be one of their first experiences they have away from home and their parents. It is therefore vital that we make the children's transition from home to school as smooth and enjoyable as possible.

A child once said to me, 'Our classroom is like a little cosy house!' She may have been referring to the classroom atmosphere or possibly the layout of the room – an area we will visit later. Our priority is to provide a homely, warm and calm learning environment.

Settling in . . . moving on

Our nursery is purpose built and is in the main building of the infant school. We have two part-time classes of 26 children. There is a full-time nursery teacher and a nursery nurse.

The beginning of the session is the most important time for us. It is a time when the children are invited to join both myself, the teacher, and the nursery nurse in a brief circle time. As the children come in with their parents they are greeted individually by name and encouraged to sit down facing into the circle. If a child is unsure or unsettled, the parents are invited to stay with their child for as long as they need. It is vital that the parent is involved in the settling-in process.

Circle time

The circle time becomes an intrinsic and valued part of the daily routine. The children gradually become more familiar with the pattern of the day and the circle time gives them the feeling of warmth and security and the opportunity to settle down.

Although it is brief, the staff have the opportunity to gauge how the children are feeling during the first few minutes of the session. They may be happy or sad, angry or excited, and we can respond immediately to their needs. Sometimes an upset child may need some quiet time away from the rest of the class on our comfortable armchair.

At the beginning of the year, when the children are new to the class, they say very little and lack confidence at speaking in front of a large group. Together, they are encouraged to say 'good morning' to staff members and the class and to respond to the register being called – even if they wave instead of speaking when their name is called! The children take great delight in taking the completed register to the school office.

Circle time provides an excellent opportunity for the staff to model a conversation. The nursery nurse and I engage in simple dialogue such as talking about the weather or what we are planning to do in the nursery today. The children observe us taking turns to speak and responding to simple questions. As they become more confident, we begin to involve them in the conversation. Through circle time, we are able to seek the views of the child in a protected environment and consult the children regularly about their attitudes, skills and knowledge.

Circle time helps the class to focus on the structure of the session and we make use of the situation to give a brief run-down of the programme of events during that session. During the second term, individual children are chosen to visit different areas of the room to describe what is available to the rest of the class.

Circle time may also take place later in the session. It provides an ideal opportunity to introduce an idea, concept or topical artifact. An object is sometimes placed on a small table in the middle of the circle to stimulate the children's curiosity and to encourage them to focus as they come in. This gives them a taster of what is to follow and a stimulus for discussion. The children are also given the opportunity, if appropriate, to pass the artifact around the circle and explore it using their senses.

The making of class rules: Why?

We have found that even the youngest children, who are just three years old, already have an awareness of what is right and wrong and the concept of fairness. The setting of class rules is a gradual but important process which evolves from one term to the next. During the first few weeks of term, we sit with the children and question what is important to them and what we as a class need to remember. These thoughts are scribed by the teacher on a big sheet of paper and are revisited for the next few days. Once everyone is satisfied with these rules, they are displayed in the classroom with accompanying photographs of the class to illustrate positive behaviour. The rules are constantly reviewed and adapted to suit the changing needs of the class and to include the outdoor environment. By setting the rules together, the children have immediate ownership of them. The rules help the class to establish a busy working atmosphere and to self-discipline from an early stage. The children can also enjoy their rights within clear boundaries. The photographs which accompany the class rules provide the children with a visual reminder of what is expected of them.

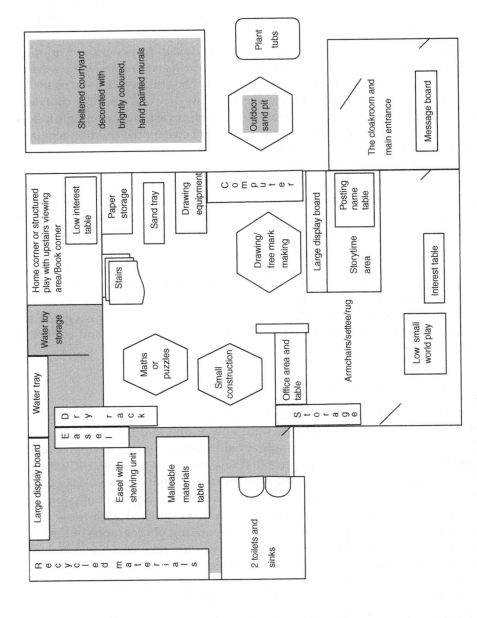

Figure 2.1 *Plan of Rebecca Dawkins' nursery classroom*

The organisation of the classroom and its resources

In order to make decisions and informed choices for themselves, the children need to be able to develop a sense of trust in the adults and peers with whom they work. To develop this sense of trust, they need to be familiar and comfortable with their surroundings both indoors and outdoors. Our classroom is organised into separate bays or areas (see Figure 2.1) with clearly labeled resources giving pictorial clues to the contents.

There are the following areas:

- Computer bay
- Office bay
- Interest tables
- Mini-world low tables
- Recycled materials bay
- Easel bay
- Construction area
- Comfortable area
- Story-time carpeted area
- Structured play area

Some areas are in a fixed position due to the need for power sockets; others, such as the structured play area, change each half term to suit the topic or by request from the children for more floor space. Many activities can be set up outside during dry weather. When the children are new to the class these areas are set up to invite them to explore freely. We have found that children enjoy revisiting activities, gradually in more depth. We are therefore not so hasty now to change resources. Sometimes the children request particular equipment for the sand and water tray and can access it for themselves. Over the past few years, and since being involved with the C.Ind.Le research, we have taken away some of the larger furniture to provide more floor space for the children to expand their play. Rather than having either carpet activities or table activities we have introduced lower surfaces which children can kneel at to play with mini-world figures or topic resources (see Figure 2.2). We have found that they revisit these small, quiet areas time and time again and seem to find them therapeutic. Perhaps their appeal comes from the fact that these areas are cosy, accessible and at child height.

The large floor-length display board near our carpeted area lends itself well to whole-group activities. The children have had the opportunity to fill a blank piece of backing paper with their mark-making or collage work. This two-week project gave the children (and staff!) the opportunity to choose a section of blank wall and fill it with their own creations. As the 'masterpiece' (named by the children) evolved, the children decided on a new rule that people should not be allowed to cover someone's design but should work around it (see Figure 2.3). Not one child out of 52 disobeyed the rule! Even tidying up the activity became a popular social event where the children learnt to collaborate as a team. Working on a grand scale encouraged the

Figure 2.2 *Exploratory play with topic resources*

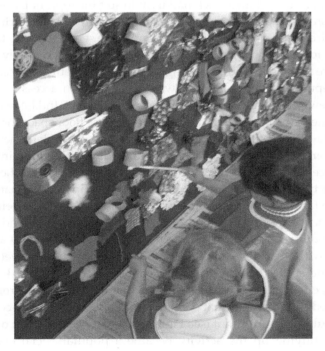

Figure 2.3 *Having time to negotiate*

children to be imaginative and take safe risks with their learning. Many interesting observations could be made about each child's social, cognitive and physical abilities. Afterwards, the display area became a viewing art gallery for the first half of the session, where children could come to admire and reflect. By providing resources and a simple structure we could gradually see the children becoming more independent thinkers and learners.

We have concluded that it is important to give the children both time and space to reflect on their ideas and thoughts and make sense of their experiences. It is sometimes so easy for us to jump in – albeit with good intentions – and distract the child from what he or she is planning to do and thereby change the outcome completely. The children need to absorb their experiences and tackle things at their own pace. Our miniature settees and armchairs have provided a comfortable, homely area where they can relax, rest, think . . . or even sleep! It is our role to nurture and encourage the children to take safe risks and to provide an appropriate environment for them.

As the year progresses, the children have more ownership of their learning and are capable of making good use of their time at nursery. They become more adventurous in their play, seeking out new experiences and making sense of the world around them. I feel very privileged to be a part of this.

Figure 2.4 *Having time to reflect*

Key points

So, Rebecca feels that it is important in her classroom to:

- Set clear rules and routines *with* the children and staff so everyone has ownership of them;
- Use circle time to bring everyone together as a 'family' group;
- Experiment with arrangement of the furniture (try some areas for kneeling, lying down standing and sitting);
- Give the children time and space to explore, reflect and relax; and
- Have clearly designated bays with clearly labeled resources.

A Montessori nursery

Our second account is by Sue Bingham, who is a fully qualified Montessori teacher who, when she wrote this account, ran a nursery within a private day school. What is interesting here is that while the Montessori philosophy is fully implemented in her classroom, including the use of the highly specialized equipment, and while the school serves a rather different clientele in terms of the children's home backgrounds, there are many clear commonalities between Sue's practice and that of Rebecca. Both have a strong commitment to the emotional and social well-being of the children, and to developing their independence. Both also make the purposes of different learning activities very explicit to the children, partly by organizing the classroom into clearly identified learning areas (although the nature of the areas is in some cases quite different, as Sue makes clear in her account).

It is interesting to note that Piaget was himself a great admirer of Montessori's work and it is possibly partly from her that he developed his view (as we reviewed in Chapter 1) that teachers of young children should be mostly observers and facilitators, rather than attempting to directly teach or instruct. It is important to recognize, however, that this does not lead at all to a version of child-centredness which allows young children free rein to do whatever they like. On the contrary, both Rebecca and Sue place great emphasis on classrooms with rules, and both have a clear idea of what young children need to learn. In the Montessori setting there is also a clear attempt to provide a range of prescribed 'child-friendly' activities which are specifically designed to support particular aspects of learning.

Introduction

There is a strong emphasis within a Montessori setting upon providing appropriately for the child's emotional and social needs as a basis for all their other learning. The physical layout of the rooms, the interaction with other children and adults and the curriculum content itself all reflect this central tenet. Although some of the equipment and materials seen in a Montessori setting are specific to this method of Early Years education, a focus upon a child's emotional and social well-being and learning is not of course limited to just this type of setting. Many teachers, in all sorts of educational establishments, coming from a variety of backgrounds with different training and experiences, believe and recognise that children are biologically 'pre-programmed' to learn, and that the best way they can support this learning is to provide a rich and appropriate environment and then to stimulate and encourage the children's natural appetite. In this section, we look specifically at how the physical environment, the quality and type of adult interaction and the content of one particular curriculum area come together within a Montessori setting to support a child's innate desire for independent learning and give him or her an emotional and social bedrock to underpin all other learning.

Background

From the very first Casa dei Bambini (Children's House) set up by Maria Montesssori herself in the slums of Rome in the early 1900s, the central pivot around which the rest of the Montessori philosophy and practice revolves is that the learning environment belongs to the children, rather than the teacher. Within our nursery of 32 children aged three to five years old, we have tried to bear this 'ownership' principle in mind at every decision point and reflect it in our everyday practice. It is a starting point which has implications that are not only physical, in terms of the layout of the rooms or the size of the furniture, or the fact that there is no visible teacher's desk, for example, but also shapes how we, as the teacher and staff, perceive our roles and how we interact with the children. We see ourselves as directing or facilitating the children's learning rather than 'teaching' them; we are part of the environment, rather than the centre of it.

It is sometimes difficult in today's society, which is frequently not just conscious of, but is actually restricted by, health and safety legislation, for young children to enjoy as much 'freedom' as they perhaps need within a setting. We want to give the children boundaries within which to explore and experiment at length – but in physical safety. One way to do this is not simply to remove the opportunities for children to learn how to do challenging things – such as cutting up food with a real knife, or banging nails in with a real hammer, for example – but to provide appropriately sized tools so that the child can hold and wield them effectively and then to provide plenty of opportunities for practising the necessary skills, initially supported by an adult, so that the child gains in confidence and is safe to manage the 'risk' by himself.

A second issue related to promoting a culture of 'freedom' within a classroom relates to behaviour. For most of the children in our nursery, this is their first experience of belonging to a group outside the family circle; their first opportunity to direct their own actions and behaviour without the constant presence of a parent. Clearly, different families have different ways and rules within their own homes, so an important part of what a child needs to learn as he comes into a new society

ROOM 1
TILED HARD FLOOR

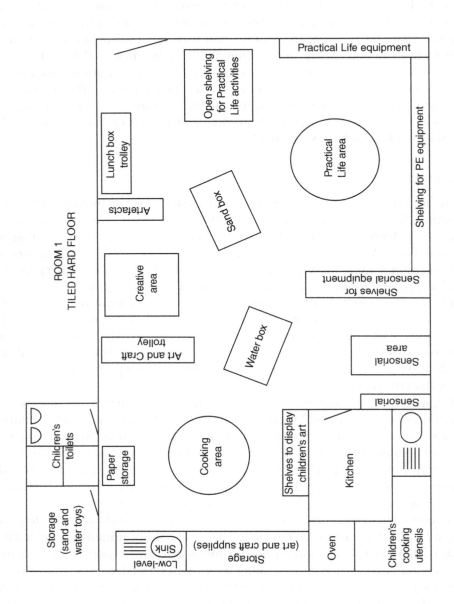

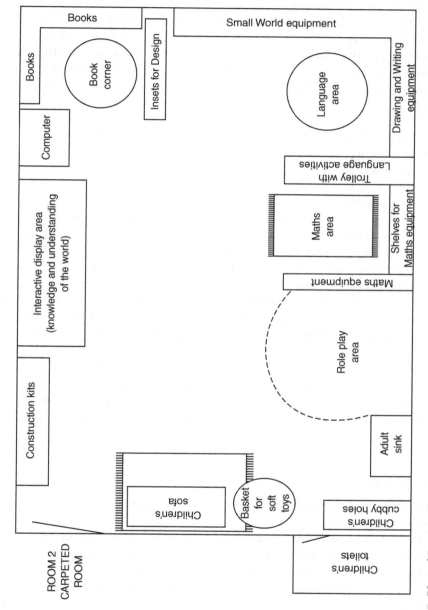

Figure 2.5 *Plan of Sue Bingham's Montessori nursery*

such as a nursery class is that the "rules" may be different here and that sometimes compromise will be needed!

We have found that it helps the children to understand and remember the 'rules' for nursery if they are part of discussions early in the academic year in which the children decide how they want their nursery to work. If children, even as young as the age of three have the opportunity to share ideas, air their own views and listen to those of others, they are more likely to see the sense in them and adhere to them. This needs to be gently but consistently maintained by all the adults. Of course, we try to frame the 'Ways We Do Things at Nursery' ideas as positively as possible, for example:

- We have gentle hands with our friends and with our things.
- We use walking feet inside.
- We use 'inside voices' in the classroom.

When the notion of 'compromise' is too abstract for our young ones, we also try to provide as many tangible reminders to the children that they can independently come to agreements with their friends about sharing and taking turns without recourse to an adult to sort out the problem. The trusty sand-timer is a very visible prop, encouraging children to sort out taking turns independently. In order to sort out turn-taking, two or more children agree to share the particular resource which they all want and then the sand-timer, which takes three minutes to empty, is turned over. While one child has a turn, the others wait for the sand to all trickle down before swapping over to the next child and turning the sand-timer over again to start the next turn. Other physical supports in our setting to promote the children's independent resolution of sharing include bracelets at the sand box and hats at the water tray. A limited number – usually four – placed near the box and tray indicate that there is only room for that number of children to play there comfortably. As a child comes to play, he puts on a hat or bracelet. If there are none left, a child will need to come back later for a turn.

The physical environment

In originally setting up our classrooms, we had several key objectives, which are outlined below.

The basic layout of the classrooms needed to be stable and constant; we felt that the children would gain a degree of security from knowing how to navigate themselves around the different areas of their environment. Within a traditional Montessori environment, these areas are the 'Practical Life' area, the 'Sensorial' area, the 'Language' area, the 'Maths' area, the 'Cultural' area and the 'Creative' area. In my classroom there is also an area for role play (see Figure 2.5).

Montessori was a pioneer in terms of the physical layout and furniture of the Children's Houses and we have tried to adhere to her principles. She had to have special furniture and child-sized cutlery and tools made – thankfully our society has become much more child-centred and the catalogues are full of low-level chairs, tables, shelving, book storage units and trolleys, for example, all at child height, enabling independent access to resources. This means that the children can select the resources they want without relying on an adult for direction or to physically reach or retrieve the materials. The child can place the resources where they want, using space at the tables or on the floor. A carpet tile is sometimes used by a child if he wants to define clearly the parameters of his workspace on the floor, indicating to others that they must not interfere with it while work is in progress.

Children need the security of a regular routine as much as a constant environment, so we try to keep activities with the same overall pattern every day as far as possible. Knowing that circle time comes first, followed by snack time and so on helps a child to feel that time is ordered and predictable, which imparts a sense of stability and security to the child.

The contents of each classroom area, however, need to be dynamic and constantly providing a challenge and stimulus for every child. Within the nursery we are lucky enough to have good storage facilities, so that new or different resources can be introduced when we observe that a child is ready for them, but in the meantime the shelves and floor spaces do not need to appear overly cluttered and unattractive. For aesthetic reasons we have tried to choose resources made of wood wherever possible and there is a schedule for their regular cleaning and maintenance. Resources are either placed directly on the shelves, which have little photographs of the materials pinned on them, indicating their normal position to the children as an aid at 'tidy up time', or they are placed in baskets or containers, again with small photographs attached to indicate the contents so that reliance on an adult is minimised.

The 'Practical Life' curriculum

Usually when a child comes into our nursery setting at the age of three, they are somewhat 'overwhelmed' by the range of activities on offer to them – either through feeling bewildered at having so much choice, or daunted at the prospect that they need to share the resources with other children! Experience has shown us that the Practical Life area is a good place for the adults to introduce a child to short, focused tasks with an obvious beginning and end, based on a skill and using equipment which is usually familiar in some way, similar to objects the child will have seen at home. The Practical Life curriculum is central to all others within Montessori philosophy and practice as it was designed to support the development of children's self-esteem and confidence first and foremost. Certainly, practical life skills are acquired by the child as they practise physical skills such as cutting (in cooking activities) or sawing (in woodwork activities), but it is the self assurance and positive attitude to tackling new tasks, the ability to persevere through the 'tricky bits' and the sense of accomplishment in completing the activities which form the primary learning objectives in this curriculum.

Caring for the environment

Much of the Montessori Practical Life curriculum focuses on helping a child to take care not only of his own personal physical needs (dressing and eating skills, for example) and his social needs, but also his environment, because as a child learns to master skills in his environment, such as tidying up, sweeping the floor or pegging up his own painting to dry, for example, he gains a degree of control over his world and his routines which can greatly enhance his self-esteem. We provide real tools, scaled down to fit a child's hand where necessary, not replicas made of plastic which cannot perform the required action. Over the years we have observed that the child more than rises to the trust and expectation shown by the adult in providing 'real' equipment for them to use in attempting a 'real' everyday task; rarely has a china plate or cup been broken as a child practises laying the table, or rarely has a child used the shoe polish inappropriately! Children within the nursery are encouraged to try a variety of everyday activities in caring for their environment, such as washing (dolls') clothes and pegging them out to dry on a line, sweeping the floor, polishing a mirror or some shoes and washing up. In each activity the secondary objective is to learn a practical skill which will be useful in life and the third objective is to strengthen and refine gross and fine muscles in preparation for pencil or paintbrush control, for example. The primary goal is to enable the child to master his or her sur-roundings and routines and thereby increase in self-worth. The sense of everyone in our little community contributing to a joint goal, namely that of looking after 'their' nursery, is also not to be underestimated.

Figure 2.6 shows a photograph of shelves containing some of the Practical Life resources available to the children. These include:

- table mats to enable the children to define their work-space;
- tasks to develop the pincer grip: a tweezers task, a spooning task, a lacing task; and
- tasks to develop fine motor control and independence: pots and jars for screwing on lids, stacking cups, table laying, pouring tasks with dry materials (e.g. lentils) as well as liquids.

Care of the self

Mirrors placed at the appropriate height encourage a child to notice what they look like and whether they need to wash their face or hands or brush their hair – thereby developing a sense of self-respect and attention to detail. In our nursery dressing skills such as buttoning, zipping and folding are practised when the child desires, using a range of special equipment to support their dexterity and self-confidence – there is nothing we like to hear more than someone saying 'No help thank you! I can do it myself' as we offer to do up a zip or shoe buckle! Opportunities for cooking are also important within our setting; we start with simple skills such as spreading – making sandwiches for our friends, for example – and go on to more complicated skills such as crumbling or creaming using appropriate tools. Again, the primary objective is not

Figure 2.6 *Practical Life resources in the Montessori classroom*

so much the physical dexterity which comes through practising such activities as the self-esteem and social prowess which a child experiences as they pass around the jam tarts which they themselves have made!

Grace and courtesy

Old-fashioned though this undoubtedly sounds, the principles behind the 'Grace and Courtesy' part of the Montessori Practical Life curriculum are timeless and equally applicable in non-Montessori environments. In working with children living in deprived areas, whose parents had had little or no education, Montessori observed the self-confidence which developed as a result of children feeling secure in the knowledge that they were learning the 'right way' to behave in certain situations. For example, she taught the children how to welcome and greet people, how to hold their knife and fork properly and even how to blow their noses appropriately! She stressed that although each child had the right to control his environment, there was an associated responsibility attached to this freedom and any potential negative impact on others must be minimised – so, in moving around the room, opening or closing a door, moving a chair from one place to another within the room, for example, the needs of others must be considered and the action must be performed gently and 'gracefully'. Nowadays, we probably take for granted the security which comes from knowing how to behave appropriately within a particular group of people, or, in other words, having what we might call appropriate 'manners' – but in our nursery we believe that there is still merit in supporting children's learning in this area to give them a social confidence.

Key points

The key points which emerge from Sue's account are as follows:

- The teacher's role is one of facilitator, rather than 'instructor'; children are not empty vessels to be filled up with knowledge by teachers.
- Risk taking is to be encouraged, not avoided. Life demands that we take risks – including emotional and social ones, so where better to learn how to do so than in a safe, caring environment amongst people we can trust?
- The attitudes and skills acquired through a Practical Life curriculum enhance a child's self-esteem above everything else.

A reception unit

At the time of writing, Harriet Rhodes taught a reception unit in a large urban two-form entry primary school. The overriding philosophy of the unit was based strongly on the High/Scope approach developed in the USA as part of the Head Start programme briefly reviewed in Chapter 1. This places a clear emphasis on children taking responsibility for their own learning and has been shown to strongly support the development of self-regulatory abilities. There is perhaps less direct emphasis on emotional support with these slightly older children, but there is still a very clear emphasis on making the classroom somewhere that the children feel is theirs. This is perhaps clearest in the approach to classroom display, in which the children have a clear role, and in the treatment and respect afforded to children's work in progress. Once again the classroom is designed to make the purpose of learning activities explicit. Having clearly designated areas for different aspects of the curriculum is a strong element in the High/Scope approach. Children's sense of autonomy is again supported by a continuing emphasis on making resources easily accessible.

The High/Scope approach

The development of the learning space for the children in the reception unit evolved over a period of years. This evolution was informed by a variety of factors but perhaps the most important was the continual development of the High/Scope philosophy which we built into the curriculum every day. During this time, children were able to 'plan', 'do' and 'review' their learning.

As a team of practitioners with a wide range of backgrounds, we had over the years accrued a strong sense of how we wanted our children to 'be' during their time in the reception class. We agreed that the promoting of children's independence and ability to think and talk about their learning transcended all other considerations. Therefore, it was important that the room would enable children to choose and freely access all the resources they required. Every box and drawer consequently had to be labeled with the name and picture of the contents.

Organisation of learning areas

An outline plan of the reception unit is presented in Figure 2.7. Over half of the room was vinyl floored so that children could use liquids and other messy items without concern. Although some of the room was strongly designated – the computers, construction/messy area and role play area were consistently in the same place – the majority of the classroom was 'open' and flexible rather than being 'zoned'. Although we were often tempted to remove some of the tables to create more space for floor activities, we resisted as we still felt compelled to have space for all children to be able to sit at tables at the same time. As the classroom was large enough to accommodate all children sitting comfortably in a circle on the floor, this seemed the best option.

The expressive arts and wet area

The wet area was extended to enable a large table for construction (junk modeling, play-dough making etc.) to be in place. The scale of the table (which could accommodate up to 12) was important as it allowed children to think 'big', see each other's ideas and work collaboratively. A large crate for junk modeling resources was alongside, often overflowing with a range of attractive materials contributed by the children's families. Also in the wet area were a painting easel and trough for wet or dry materials, the contents of which were changed regularly depending on topic or the requests of the children. We decided to invest in a large cabinet with many plastic trays of differing sizes to accommodate string, ribbons, sequins, feathers, fabrics and many lovely craft materials. This attracted children who did not necessarily choose to express themselves in three dimensions but who were excited by different textures and colours. The nearby cupboards all contained obvious tools and basics such as paints, glues, brushes, pallets, clay, play-dough ingredients, scissors, sellotape etc., which the children were able to access.

Interactive displays

The interactivity of displays became more important as we developed our practice. Two learning walls were developed – one for maths, one for language/literacy. Children were able to use a range of materials to stick on to the walls, and could write on the displays and in this way exemplify their thinking. This obviously offered many opportunities for us to interact with children and assess their understanding.

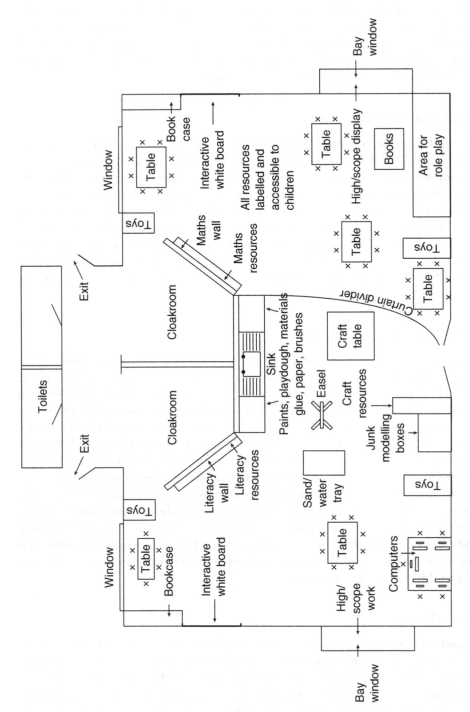

Figure 2.7 *Plan of Harriet's Reception Unit classroom*

There was a variety of 'maths objects' (multilink, Cuisenaire, set rings, counters, rulers, sorting animals) which the children could stick to the wall with blue tack, as well as whiteboards to write on. Next to the maths wall was a portable wooden 100-square (blank on the reverse) which was in constant use as the children became more and more interested in 'big numbers' and place value. We also displayed two large number lines placed prominently on the walls at either end of the room – both from 0–30. The significance of the line extending to 30 was to represent the number of children in the class; this enabled us to refer to it during registration, calculating dinner numbers, absentees etc.

The role play area

The role play area was updated often with the children's input. They were consulted about the type of space they would like and were encouraged to contribute items as part of the philosophy of involving them in decision-making and fostering their ability to see projects through to conclusion. They were encouraged to make the role play space themselves. Within that space there would always be opportunities for children to alter the environment or make some impact on it. So they were able to change the displays, move the furniture, write on the laminated signs and so on.

The High/Scope approach meant that children would often have pieces of work, pictures, models etc. unfinished at the end of sessions. Initially, we asked the children to put their creations in inconspicuous places overnight so that they could resume work the following day. Eventually we had a brainwave and decided to devote two large windowsills (situated at both ends of the room) to displaying the work-in-progress along with the finished articles. The High/Scope windows were a means of showcasing children's thinking and displaying their talents. They were encouraged to find, choose and write a label for their work and, if possible, record a little about it. This signaled the value we attached to their play and underlined the importance of it.

Reviewing and reflecting on learning activities

The children were encouraged to find and use cameras to photograph their activities during play which would be uploaded to the interactive whiteboard and used during the 'review' part of the session. This again conferred a status on their activities and was a means of promoting reflective and evaluative thinking. The daily opportunity for children to listen, talk, and frame questions for each other enabled these skills to develop to such a degree that by the end of the year, the children could run their review with no adult input.

So, in a way, the room was made to fit the curriculum rather than the other way around and, although it did not always look tidy or ordered, it was, hopefully, an enabling space which fostered independence and encouraged creative exploration.

Key points

For Harriet, the key points to bear in mind when organising a reception classroom are as follows:

- It is important for children to contribute to the environment of the classroom, so that they develop a sense of ownership of it.
- There should be a good deal of flexibility in classroom organisation to meet the current interests and learning needs of the children.
- Resources need to be easily accessible to children, so that they can learn to plan and make decisions about their activities.
- Children should be encouraged to pursue their interests and persevere with activities over increasingly long periods of time; their work-in-progress should be valued and respected.
- Children should be supported to record their activities to enable reflection and review.

A Year 1 class

Our final account is from Kate Hemming, who at the time of writing taught a Year 1 class in an independent school. She was also a teacher involved in the C.Ind.Le project. While the school is independent, and the children in her class came from relatively affluent home backgrounds, she shared the common difficulties currently being experienced by all Year 1 teachers nationally, of managing the children's transition from the play-based curriculum of the Foundation Stage to the very much more directed approach required in Key Stage 1 of the National Curriculum. Kate's account is particularly interesting in this respect, as she taught reception classes for a number of years before she moved to Year 1. What she managed to achieve with great skill, as is clear in her account, is to bring the best of her Early Years practice and modify it advantageously to this slightly older age group (who, it must be remembered are still just five or six years of age and in many European countries would still be in kindergarten). She shows how the requirements of a more formally academic curriculum can be met, while still allowing the children a good deal of control over their learning. Like Harriet, she also emphasizes flexibility, so that she is constantly monitoring provision in her classroom to ensure that her organizational arrangements are supporting the children's learning. Like all the other contributors to this chapter, Kate also emphasizes the value of consulting the children about classroom rules and organizational decisions; this not only involves the children and gives them a sense of ownership, but also often results in far better decisions.

Kate's classroom

I teach a Year 1 class in a large independent school. My teaching experience is based firmly within Early Years education. On moving from teaching reception to Year 1,

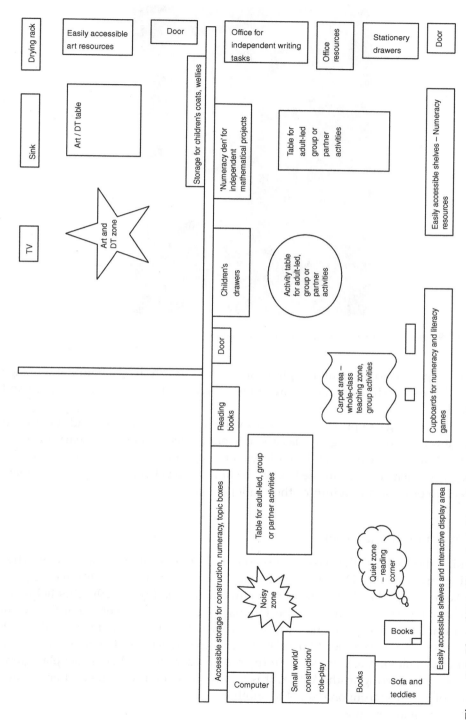

Figure 2.8 *Plan of Kate Hemming's Year 1 classroom*

Figure 2.9 *Independent use of the whiteboard by Year 1 children*

the challenge was to bring all my philosophies and insight in the Foundation Stage into a more demanding and potentially more restrictive Key Stage 1 curriculum and timetable.

Whilst teaching reception, my practice evolved as I experimented and researched different ways of organising my classroom to encourage independent learning. Now teaching Year 1, it is clear that the children, although more confident and capable of self-regulated learning, continue to crave a supportive yet challenging environment in which to practise and reinforce their independence.

The layout of the classroom

Planning the layout of the classroom is an important part of providing a supportive learning environment. The layout is changed as the needs of the children evolve.

I like to 'zone' the classroom into distinct areas (see Figure 2.9). This helps the children to feel secure with the expectations of their environment, e.g. if they want a quiet time, they know that the reading corner is the place to go for relaxation. Of course, there is always scope to overlap, for example, when construction play is generated from enjoying a 'story sack' in the reading corner or when a role play game inspires some writing in the 'office'. It is vitally important to value and encourage fluidity of learning from one 'zone' to another.

My classroom always has:

- a reading corner – with story sacks, non-fiction, fiction and poetry books;
- an 'office' to encourage independent writing or artwork with resources such as different textured paper, pens, envelopes, telephones and diaries, and blue tack to display work on the wall;
- a numeracy corner with calculators, number lines, shapes and dominos;
- a role play or 'small world' area; and
- space for construction activities – and a space to display the items made.

All other classroom resources are easily accessible and the children know that they are able to use them to support their learning. They include cubes, whiteboards, scissors, glue, magnetic letters and dictionaries (see Figure 2.9).

Planning for independence

In Year 1 it is essential to build upon the children's Foundation Stage experiences where sustained periods of learning are encouraged. My timetable has been adapted to support the transition from reception to Year 1. Rather than diving straight into a distinct literacy and numeracy hour, during the autumn term the timetable has been rewritten to allow whole mornings of either literacy or numeracy. This enables the children to enjoy extended learning opportunities within a familiar structure and timescale. For example, throughout the morning there may be two adult-led activities, group problem-solving activity, construction, role play, ICT, a creative activity and sand or water play – all linked to the literacy or numeracy objective but with scope for independent exploration. The emphasis is on free-flow within the classroom; the aim is that all the children will have experiences of all available activities throughout the day.

This way of working has been immensely rewarding for the children. I feel it enables them to have more control over their learning, knowing they can develop their activities with greater autonomy. It certainly helped the children to settle in their new environment and it has given me the opportunity to support children's initiative through spontaneity.

Issues that I consider whilst planning the environment for independent learning

Is each style of activity designed with a specific independent learning objective?

If so, make these explicit to the children so that they understand your expectations e.g. for a collaborative group work objective, 'I am really hoping to see you working as a group and listening to each other in the role play corner' or, for a peer-tutoring objective, 'You played this game yesterday, can you teach it to two more children? You will need to make sure that they understand how to play.'

Once the children are confident, they may be able to work out what the focus might be for the activity and could set the objective for the rest of the group.

Consider the space available

Is there enough carpet/table space for the children to utilise in a construction activity? I involve the children in the planning of the space. Discussions about why certain resources are placed in specific areas encourage the children to think about the way they play with them and the types of learning involved. When setting up a classroom office or numeracy workshop, I ask the children which resources they would need and then ask them to arrange them in the designated area themselves. The children made a list, as a group, of required resources, e.g. number lines, calculators, dice, counters and clocks.

Of course the planning of the space is a lesson in independent learning in itself: I can observe the children negotiating with each other, making decisions and problem solving. Having ownership of their environment and knowing that they have control over their learning empowers children and results in meaningful learning experiences.

Think about the time constraints

Have all the children been given enough time to evolve their learning?

Balance the needs of the individuals

Think about how you group children – those who are more confident independent learners can support others. Children learn so well from observing others. Use the children to scaffold and guide their peers. This reinforces independent learning at all levels.

Consider appropriate adult intervention

Be confident enough to sit back and observe the children's learning, but know when to step in to move the activity along.

Above all: Be flexible!

Working with young children requires immense flexibility. Flexibility is demanded from the environment as the curriculum changes and the children mature. In order to maintain a challenging yet supportive learning environment we need to be flexible enough to recognise that changes need to take place. Knowing when to intervene and move the learning forward is vital.

Assessment and regulation within the learning environment

Discussing thinking and learning with young children is rewarding and is an essential part of developing independence. The environment needs to be supportive in order for the children to extend their higher order thinking without fear of failure. It is important to model this type of thinking for young children and to engage them (either as a class or as individuals) in genuine conversations about their learning. Observe the children talking to each other about their learning, listen in to self-commentary and challenge the children to explain to you about what they have found out.

Key points

So, for Kate, the key points to consider when organizing her Year 1 classroom are as follows:

- In Key Stage 1, build on the children's experiences from their Foundation Stage environment and aim to mirror some of the key features in terms of freedom of choice of activities, space and time.
- Involve the children in the planning of the environment, thereby developing the children's sense of ownership of their learning. This includes devising and sharing explicit independent learning objectives.
- Encourage flexibility and freedom: consider the flexibility of the environment (allow the layout of your classroom to evolve throughout the year), the timetable, children and adults and the impact this flexibility has on developing independent learners and practitioners.
- Provide a supportive and nurturing environment where discussions about learning are valued by adults and children.

Conclusions

Within cognitive developmental psychology over the last 30 years or so there has been a very considerable body of research evidence related to the development of children as independent learners. Within the psychological literature this has been variously characterised as 'learning how to learn', 'self-regulation' (Schunk & Zimmerman, 1994) and 'metacognition' (Metcalfe & Shimamura, 1994), all of which are concerned with children's developing self-awareness and control of their own mental processing. What has emerged is a body of research and theory which suggests that it is this aspect of development which is crucially responsible for individual differences in children's development as learners (Whitebread, 2014).

The term 'metacognition' was first coined by Flavell in the late 1970s (Flavell, 1979), and arose from his studies of memory development. Since then, the crucial significance of an individual's ability to monitor and regulate their own cognitive activity has been demonstrated across a wide range of human development. Indeed, in a review of the extensive literature in just the first decade of research, Wang, Haertel and Walberg (1990) concluded that metacognition was the most powerful single predictor of learning. The more recent meta-analysis of the relative effectiveness of educational interventions in the UK produced by Higgins, Kokotsaki and Coe (2011) similarly ranks the support of metacognitive and self-regulatory abilities as one of the most powerful means of enhancing young children's development as learners.

In its application to education, work in this area has been inspired by the socio-cultural tradition founded on the work of the Russian psychologist Lev Vygotsky (1978, 1986), some of whose key ideas we reviewed in Chapter 1. He lived in the first three decades of the last century and died tragically young. But he produced a set of ideas about children's learning which have inspired many developmental psychologists, particularly in the last 20–30 years, to explore the social and cultural origins of children's learning. For Vygotsky, the development of children's learning was a process of moving from other-regulation (or performing a task while supported by an adult or peer) to self-regulation (performing a task on one's own). Crucially, research stimulated by these ideas has shown that a key characteristic of a good supporter or 'scaffolder' (to use Bruner's metaphor – see Wood, Bruner & Ross, 1976) is the ability to sensitively withdraw support as the child becomes able to carry out the task more independently, or to take over more of the regulatory role for themselves (for an excellent review of work in this area, see Schaffer, 2004).

In recent research in this area there has been the recognition of metacognitive processes in very young children. In the early work on metacognition, some writers argued that it is a late-developing capability. However, this very quickly became an untenable position, as it became clear that early research methodologies were systematically under-estimating the abilities of young children. In a very comprehensive overview, Bronson (2000) demonstrates that the development of metacognitive and self-regulatory processes is fundamental to the whole range of young children's psychological growth. She lists work with children concerned with the development of the regulation of arousal, of emotional responses, of adaptive control of behaviour in familiar settings, of problem-solving and of motivational patterns. She goes on to describe in detail extensive research which has explored the emotional, prosocial, cognitive and motivational developments in self-regulation throughout the different phases of early childhood.

Our experience in Early Years educational settings clearly accords with this body of research. Throughout all the fieldwork and subsequent training courses associated with the C.Ind.Le project, whenever a teacher moved to give young children more responsibility for their own learning, or allowed them to be more involved in decisions regarding the running of the classroom or the organization of the curriculum, these teachers were always deeply impressed by the response from the children, and have seen the benefits for the children's motivation and learning very quickly.

When they enter school, the vast majority of young children are voracious in their enthusiasm for life and for learning and, sadly, for many the experience of schooling diminishes rather than supports these appetites. Education has become, for too many of our children, something which is done to them, rather than with them. We hope that some of the ideas in this chapter will help readers to make the educational experience in their classrooms one which genuinely supports young children's development as confident and self-regulated learners.

Pointer for organizing the Early Years classroom

Themes which emerge from all four accounts concerned with organization of the Early Years classroom to support independent learning:

- Think carefully about the children's transition from their immediately previous environment into the world of your classroom.
- Involve the children in decisions about class rules and organization.
- Make the resources the children will need accessible to them, so that they can make choices and decisions.
- Organise your class to provide a range of different spaces and learning environments which have clear and explicit purposes (this may involve getting rid of some of the chairs and tables!).
- Support the children in pursuing their own interests and ideas, developing their own ways of carrying out tasks, reflecting upon their own learning and taking responsibility for it.
- Be reflective about the organization of your classroom and be prepared to be flexible and make changes in the interests of the children's learning.

If you would like to know more about the C.Ind.Le project you can access further details, downloadable versions of publications and an order form for the CD-based training resource produced by the project team at: http://www.educ.cam.ac.uk/cindle/index.html

References

Bronson, M.B. (2000) *Self-Regulation in Early Childhood*. New York: The Guilford Press.

Early Education (2012) *Development Matters in the Early Years Foundation Stage (EYFS)*. London: Department for Education.

Featherstone, S. & Bayley, R. (2001) *Foundations of Independence*. Featherstone Education.

Flavell, J.H. (1979) Metacognition and cognitive monitoring: A new area of cognitive developmental inquiry. *American Psychologist*, 34, 906–11.

Hendy, L. & Whitebread, D. (2000) Interpretations of independent learning in the Early Years. *Internat. J. Early Years Education*, 8 (3), 245–52.

Higgins, S., Kokotsaki, D. & Coe, R (2011) *Pupil Premium Toolkit: Summary for Schools*. London: Sutton Trust. Retrieved from http://www.suttontrust.com/research/toolkit-of-strategies-to-improve-learning/

Larkin, S. (2010) *Metacognition in Young Children*. London: Routledge.

Metcalfe, J. & Shimamura, A.P. (Eds) (1994) *Metacognition: Knowing about Knowing*. Cambridge, MA: MIT Press.

Schaffer, H.R. (2004) The child as apprentice: Vygotsky's theory of socio-cognitive development. In H.R. Schaffer, *Introducing Child Psychology*. Oxford: Blackwell.

Schunk, D.H. & Zimmerman, B.J. (1994) *Self-Regulation of Learning and Performance*. Hillsdale, N.J: Lawrence Erlbaum.

Vygotsky, L.S. (1978) *Mind in Society*. Cambridge, MA: Harvard University Press.

Vygotsky, L.S. (1986) *Thought and Language*. Cambridge, MA: MIT Press.

Wang, M.C., Haertel, G.D. & Walberg, H.J. (1990) What influences learning? A content analysis of review literature. *Journal of Educational Research*, 84, 30–43.

Watson, J.S. & Ramey, C.T. (1972) Reactions to response-contingent stimulation in early infancy. *Merrill-Palmer Quarterly*, 18, 219–27.

Williams, J. (2003) *Promoting Independent Learning in the Primary Classroom*. Buckingham: Open University Press.

Whitebread, D. (2014). The importance of self-regulation for learning from birth. In H. Moylett (Ed.), *Characteristics of Effective Learning: Helping Young Children Become Learners for Life* (pp. 15–35). Maidenhead: Open University Press.

Whitebread, D., Anderson, H., Coltman, P., Page, C., Pino Pasternak, D. & Mehta, S. (2005) Developing independent learning in the Early Years. *Education*, 3-13, 33, 40–50.

Whitebread, D. & Coltman, P. (2011) Developing young children as self-regulated learners. In J. Moyles, J. Georgeson & J. Payler (Eds.), *Beginning Teaching: Beginning Learning: In Early Years and Primary Education*. Maidenhead: Open University Press.

CHAPTER 3

'My mum would pay anything for chocolate cake!'

ORGANISING THE WHOLE CURRICULUM: ENTERPRISE PROJECTS IN THE EARLY YEARS

Penny Coltman, David Whitebread and Jayne Greenwood

There is no doubt that the last few years have been ones of considerable change and turmoil in education, and particularly in the Early Years. During the last decade or two, we have had the introduction of the National Curriculum, the renewed emphasis on early literacy and numeracy, and the persistent tightening of the 'standards' and accountability agenda (through the publication of Ofsted reports and league tables). This has all resulted in well-documented and considerable downward pressure on Early Years practitioners to teach young children more formally before the research evidence indicates that it is developmentally appropriate, as we reviewed in Chapter 1. However, with the Tickell review (Tickell, 2011) and the publication of the revised EYFS (DfE, 2012), the dust has settled somewhat, and a clearer picture is emerging which is, at least for the moment, not incompatible with Early Years principles. For example, the establishment of communication and language, physical development, and personal, social and emotional development as the 'prime' curriculum areas within the EYFS, and the relegation of literacy and mathematics to the status of 'specific' areas, is a clear victory for the research evidence regarding early childhood development and learning.

And, of course, the re-statement within these documents of the primacy of play in early learning is key. As we discussed in Chapter 1, the decline of opportunities for playful learning in the Early Years, and throughout the primary years, has been a major cause for concern. Early Years educators have always understood the importance of playful contexts and activities in young children's learning. However, as has been recorded in a number of studies and reports (see Ofsted, 1993; Bennett, Wood & Rogers, 1997), the effective structuring of playful activities to ensure maximum benefit for young children's learning and development requires considerable thought and planning. This chapter sets out to illustrate one particular approach which has been shown to be a particularly powerful way of combining playful learning with a number of important principles which should guide the content and organisation of the Early

Years curriculum. These principles derive from the evidence about children's learning, and from the collective experiences and views of Early Years educators, as discussed in Chapter 1. Despite the dangers, it is our belief that the National Curriculum, even in its unfortunately content heavy form at Key Stage 1, is not necessarily incompatible with these principles, but they should guide the way it is taught and managed.

Principles for an Early Years curriculum

As we reviewed in Chapter 1, for the Early Years curriculum to be effective and appropriate, it needs to take into account young children's needs as learners. As we argued there, to learn effectively, young children need a curriculum and a style of teaching which provides them with emotional security and feelings of being in control. Young children need a curriculum which starts with what they understand and can do already, and helps them make sense of their world by providing them with meaningful tasks, which require their active engagement, and which give them opportunities to express their understandings in a variety of media, principally through imaginative play and talk. Young children's natural curiosity can be stimulated to help them learn effectively by providing novel first-hand experiences and opportunities to explore, investigate and problem-solve.

From these understandings we have derived four principles which we believe should guide the organisation and management of the Early Years curriculum. These principles are as follows.

Young children's learning will be enhanced when:

1   the content of the curriculum is **'meaningful'** to them and related to their existing knowledge and interests;
2   they are **active participants in their learning** rather than just passive recipients; they should have opportunities to make their own decisions about their learning;
3   they are encouraged to indulge their natural inclination to engage in **imaginative play** related to significant life experiences; and
4   they are **emotionally secure** because there is continuity and good communication between the worlds of home and school.

Enterprise Projects

These principles clearly support an integrated, topic-based approach, and this can be carried out in a whole variety of ways. In the remainder of this chapter, however, we want to demonstrate one kind of approach which seems to embody these principles in a particularly powerful way. This approach consists of what has been termed 'Enterprise Projects' (see DES, 1990, for a general review of this kind of work in primary schools). In essence, these consist of using some kind of adult 'enterprise' or place of work as a starting point, and enabling children to explore and investigate it, partly by carrying out a similar kind of enterprise themselves.

Over a period of five years, the authors carried out an Enterprise Project each year with classes of young children ranging from Reception to Year 2. These have been focused on a bakery, puppet theatres, a newspaper, a museum, and a fashion show. The details of some of these projects have been reported elsewhere (Coltman & Whitebread, 1992; Whitebread et al., 1993, 1994, 1995). This chapter also describes an additional whole school art gallery enterprise event carried out more recently. What follows is a description of these projects and an analysis of the ways in which such projects provide a powerfully effective curriculum for children in the Early Years, particularly in relation to the four principles identified above.

All the projects involved the following basic elements:

- a visit to a local workplace to find out, by a variety of means, about the kinds of work carried out and the people who worked there;
- the children engaging in a related, small, real enterprise of their own, which involved research, planning, production, advertising, accounting etc.;
- opportunities for the children to represent their experiences for themselves in a variety of ways, through talk, play, drawing, modelling and writing; and
- a fixed 'end point' in the form of an event towards which children could work and to which friends and families could be invited.

Learning through 'meaningful' work

The first principle is concerned with the extent to which the content of the curriculum is 'meaningful' to young children and related to their existing knowledge and interests. This also relates to the links between home-based styles of learning, which are informal and for real purposes, and school-based styles of learning, which sometimes suffer by comparison by being formal and purposeless from the child's point of view. Research in relation to both language (Tizard & Hughes, 1984) and mathematics (Hughes, 1986) has demonstrated that most children find the informal, 'real' world of the home and the community a much more conducive environment for learning than the artificial and, from the child's point of view, 'meaningless' tasks of traditional schooling. This has led to a developing new pedagogy which emphasises the importance of children within school carrying out tasks for 'real' purposes within the context of real-world situations and problems (see, for example, Hall, 1989, in relation to language and Atkinson, 1992, in relation to maths).

This 'authenticity' was established within the Enterprise Projects we carried out in a number of ways:

- *The localness of the workplaces* visited gave them a meaningfulness to the children through familiarity. The local newspaper was taken by many of the children's families, many had already visited the local museum and some of the children's friends and relations worked at the local bakery. The art project was initiated by visits to a local art gallery and an exhibition of the work of amateur artists at the town library.

- *Projects related to the children's interests* (e.g. the bakery mainly made Christmas puddings; the puppet show gave them an opportunity to re-enact one of their favourite stories (Cinderella and Snow White were chosen, somewhat adapted to give everyone a part!); the contents of the newspaper they produced contained items of interest to them: reviews of latest children's films, a fashion page complete with

House for sale. 5 bedrooms.
Dining room. Conservatory.
2 toilets. Kitchens. Large
pond in garden. Quiet area.
Good Price.
£80,000.

A lovely house with a large garden.
Close to the shops. Near to a school.
It has 1 main bedroom and a lounge.
1 roof garden and your own little
parking space next to the house.
Price £40,000.

This house has 2 bedrooms.
1 pool. Room under stairs.
Double glazing. Double bed.
A vase of flowers. It's a
bargain.
Price 70,000.

1 bed. home. Ballet room.
Disco room. 1 big bathroom
and a nice size kitchen.
Swimming pool and stable.
Come soon.
Price £100,000.

Figure 3.1 *The children advertise their own houses for sale*

photographs of 6–7 yr. old 'models' (an interest later developed in the fashion show project), Aunt Sherry's Problem Page (Dear Aunt Sherry, my brother is a pain in the neck!), and a page of Houses for Sale (the children's own houses, drawn and described by them – see Figure 3.1); the museum set up by the children exhibited artefacts provided by themselves, their families, village friends and the school and focused on the history of the school and the village.

A wide range of opportunities for learning through 'real' work provided:

• *Writing for real purposes*: the children wrote scripts, programmes, posters, price lists, guidebooks, official invitations to special guests, press releases, a whole newspaper, and, most excitingly as it turned out, a range of business letters. These included letters accompanying the donations to charities, but also letters to local businesses selling advertising space in the class newspaper, bids for an Arts Grant to support the puppet theatre companies, and for sponsorship for the class museums and the fashion show (see Figure 3.2). All these letters received formal and entirely business-like replies which were much treasured by the children.

Back to the Past Museum Company.
(a division of Class 4 enterprises).

27.1.94.

Dear Sir,

Please may you consider sponsoring our posters for our Back to the Past museum. We estimate the cost will be about 10 pounds. Your company logo will appear on all posters and we anticipate a large crowd of people attending.

Thankyou for your kind attention.

Yours Faithfully,

Matthew Paddick,

(Company Secretary.)

Figure 3.2 *Writing for real purposes: Matthew writes applying for sponsorship*

- *Real maths*: a lot of book-keeping and accounting, of course (see Figure 3.3), but also measuring ingredients for refreshments when parents and friends were invited in for the grand launch or opening; handling real money when children sold tickets, postcards, programmes etc.; setting out the seats in the 'auditorium' for the puppet shows, with tickets corresponding to numbered seats; measuring and making patterns and costumes to fit for the fashion show; making decisions about what to charge for various items in all the projects.

- *Genuine economic transactions*: real money was used throughout; all costs were charged, but all the projects managed to make a good profit! The children were confronted with the simple realities of costs, prices, consumer preferences, profits and losses throughout the projects. Our records are full of fascinating discussions we held with children, particularly when they had to make decisions about pricing, for example. How much profit was it fair to make? What price would people pay for a newspaper? Children had to use their real-world knowledge to help them solve these problems. On one occasion a child volunteered that his mum would pay anything for chocolate cake!

- *Work roles and processes emulated authentically*: work roles were made explicit to the children. To help with this process, for example, badges for 'cook', 'market researcher', 'editor', 'museum guide', 'designer' and so on were often worn by the children when they carried out these roles. Processes seen by the children on visits were emulated in ways which made them as real as possible. Good examples of this would be the cataloguing procedures developed during the museums project, the computer booking system developed during the puppet theatre project, the operation of a real telephone by the children during the newspaper project on which they took calls to a 'tele-sales' service, and computer aided design for T-shirts in the fashion show.

Children being 'active' learners and empowered to make their own decisions

Our second principle concerns children being active participants in their learning, rather than just passive recipients, and having opportunities to make their own decisions about their learning. An 'active' style of learning is an intrinsic aspect of Enterprise Projects because the children are actually experiencing adult activities first-hand, and not simply being told about them. What goes along with this is that we must always be open to the children taking the initiative. A good example of this was a poster designed by one of the children. This was done in the evening at home, inspired by a day of designing the role play area to accompany the fashion show project, and proudly brought into school the next morning. On another occasion, during the puppet theatre project, a child on her own initiative brought into the class a large cardboard box which had contained her family's new washing machine. She explained that this was to be made into a puppet theatre. The provision of opportunities for imaginative play is also an important aspect of this 'active' involvement of children, and we will come on to this in the next section.

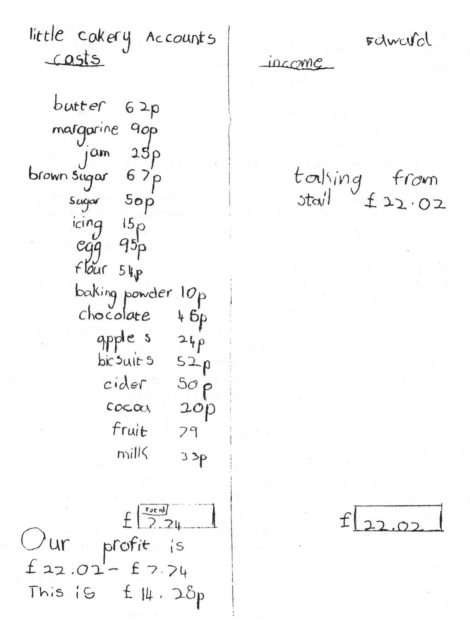

little cakery Accounts   Edward

costs   income

butter 62p
margarine 90p
jam 25p
brown sugar 67p
sugar 50p
icing 15p
egg 95p
flour 54p
baking powder 10p
chocolate 46p
apples 24p
bicsuits 52p
cider 50p
cocoa 20p
fruit 79
milk 33p

talking from
stall £22.02

£ [Total] 7.24

£ [22.02]

Our profit is
£22.02 - £7.74
This is £14.28p

Figure 3.3 *Real maths: Edward's cake stall accounts*

In the case of the whole school art gallery project, school council style class repre-
sentatives were elected in order to overcome the potential difficulties involved with
'pupil voice' when working with a large number of children. The focus of the prelim-
inary gallery visits was to learn about what is involved in putting on an exhibition
and displaying art work to best effect. As a result of these visits, children fed back

to the committee two important issues that they wished to include in their own gallery: (1) the works of art in the exhibitions visited were numbered and catalogued in a booklet for visitors to read and find out about each exhibit; and (2) the gallery had a gift shop that visitors passed through on the way out of the exhibition and children were excited by this.

What is significant here, however, are the opportunities Enterprise Projects offer, because of their intrinsically open-ended and problem-solving character, for children to take decisions and so develop feelings of empowerment. Tizard and Hughes (1984), among others, have pointed out how so much of what happens between adults and children in the home is child-initiated, whereas this is very much not the case often in the classroom. The consequent loss of feelings of control, self-efficacy and self-esteem for the young child can be very damaging. Research has consistently shown that self-esteem is whittled away by the difficulties many children face in relation to school learning. The strong relation between self-esteem and school achievement is well documented.

All the projects were set up in such a way as to allow the children considerable opportunities to make decisions and develop a real feeling of ownership and empowerment. The children made choices collectively about such matters as the name of the cake stall they set up and ran, which story to do as a puppet play, how to spend the profit made by their enterprise and so on. Individually and in small groups they made a whole range of sophisticated decisions – about what to charge for postcards on sale in the museum 'shop', about the content and layout of their page in the class newspaper, about how many tickets to print for the puppet show, what information to include in the programmes and so on. Many of these decisions involved considerable research and discussion. The mechanism of company board meetings was also used within some of the projects as a way of helping the children to review progress and discuss and plan the work still to be done.

In the case of the whole school art gallery project, each class was presented with a brief to include a study of one artist or art mode with the children's own representations of this; and work in another medium e.g. clay, sculpture, photography, etc. Each class set about selecting their artist and the medium they wished to work in. The brief was interpreted in different ways, making for interesting variations. Some classes looked at just one painting and represented that while others looked at a range of work from the chosen artist.

While, of course, they had their plans for the projects, the teachers involved always attempted, as a further way of empowering the children, to respond to and support initiatives coming from them. This is sometimes referred to as the 'dead bird' model of the curriculum, because children are inclined to bring in this kind of fascinating object, and the skilful Early Years educator has always made the most of such opportunities. But it is a feature of the curriculum which has been under threat from the pressures of the National Curriculum, and which it is desperately important that we preserve.

There are numerous examples of this from all the projects, but let us just mention two from the fashion show. Sometimes occasions arise because children, stimulated

Figure 3.4 *In their art gallery contributions, Monet's water-lilies paintings inspired the reception class.*

by their involvement in the project, bring in items with rich possibilities. During the fashion show project, a child arrived one day with a box full of Victorian hats, and the whole day was given over to examining them, finding out about how they were made, what they were made of, who wore them. Pictures were drawn, the children made their own Victorian hats, and so on.

Other occasions arise when an activity introduced by an adult is developed by the children in unexpected ways. An example of this arose when, as part of the fashion show project, an activity was introduced involving drawing a 2D scale drawing of the catwalk. This activity, which was planned to take about an hour, lasted for two days, as the children transformed it into a 3D modelling activity. Having completed the 2D drawing, children began to add stand-up proscenium arches, which needed buttresses. Then they raised the catwalk plans onto box bases to show the height, added model pot plants, audiences on seats and delightfully accurate paper puppets of themselves in costume (initially on straws, but later on strings to facilitate twirling). With their models complete, the children then gave miniature performances of the show to a tape of the music.

Opportunities for imaginative play

This last example leads us very well into our third curriculum principle. Once again, as was reviewed in Chapter 1, there has been renewed interest in the ways that children's natural playfulness, usually given full rein in the home but very much curtailed within the school context, enhances the quality of their learning. Learning through play supports the strategies developed under the previous two headings. It helps children to derive meaning from their experiences. One of the main factors in the efficacy of play is also its self-directedness; play gives children control over their own learning.

The play corner in the classrooms during the projects was transformed into an imaginary cake shop, a practice puppet booth, a box office, a newspaper office, a museums office (see Figure 3.5), gift shops or exhibition guide production offices and a boutique. These were designed and largely built by the children, and played in to the point

of destruction. During the puppet theatre project, for example, following the visit to the theatre, some of the children suggested that they turn part of the classroom into a box office. The teacher set about discussing with the class how they would go about rearranging the classroom to accommodate this. Tables were moved, chairs piled up, and carpets rearranged. A table was needed for the booking lady, a door for people to walk in, somewhere to display the puppets, a noticeboard for the posters, and so on. When the general environment of the box office had been created, discussion followed of what was needed to equip it. A telephone was installed, a computer, paper, pencils, pens, diary, tickets and a telephone book. From then on throughout the project there were always children in the box office busily taking telephone calls, writing messages, issuing tickets, taking

Figure 3.5 *Role play: the museum office*

money, making programmes and posters, putting up notices and signs and generally becoming thoroughly involved in the exciting new world of theatre management!

This kind of play was engaged in by the children throughout each of the projects with energy and enthusiasm. As the projects developed it was notable the extent to which new elements of the project, and new information which had been made available to the children, was incorporated in their play.

Integrating the worlds of school and community

The final feature of the projects was the extent to which the divisions between the school and the outside adult community were broken down. As we have discussed, there is an important aspect of this to do with styles of learning, but continuity and good communication between the worlds of home and school is also a vital component in providing young children with emotional security in the classroom.

There were a number of aspects of this attempt at integrating the worlds of school and adult community within the projects:

- the children visited an adult place of work, and often one where adults they knew worked; our observations of the adults explaining their work to the children suggested this was an intense and satisfying experience for both parties;
- adults visited the classroom to explain their work to the children, and also to work alongside the children with their enterprises; this also, of course, supported the authenticity of the children's enterprises (see Figure 3.6);

Figure 3.6 *Adults working alongside the children: the local museum warden discusses one of the class's collection with Sam*

- in the art gallery project, classes worked with an artist or art teacher from the local secondary school who supported the project and gave it a good start. These workshops demonstrated skills which gave inspiration and helped children to develop their ideas;
- the children interacted with adults in the local community in a business-like manner (formal letters requesting sponsorship, selling advertising space, inviting local dignitaries to open the Grand Launch, giving interviews to the local press about the projects, etc.); and
- the projects generated an enthusiasm which led to an enormous involvement of the parents and the wider community in all kinds of ways – loaning resources (exhibits for the museum), helping with making (puppets, costumes, cakes), helping with research (important people being interviewed for the newspaper, and as a source of local history for the museum), attending the Grand Opening or Launch, providing expertise (photographs of the children as models for the fashion page, and the village policeman setting up a mock robbery, both for the newspaper), offering sponsorship, providing ideas and moral support.

The involvement and enthusiasm of the children and of the local communities for these enterprise projects has been particularly rewarding. An atmosphere of real teamwork was generated in which young children, parents, teachers and community shared the pleasure of co-operative purpose and achievement. The museum exhibitions, for example, were so popular that when they were taken down in school they had to be immediately remounted within the local museum which received large numbers of interested visitors, many of whom purchased some of the postcards designed and made by the children (see Figure 3.7). The video of the fashion show quickly sold out, with copies being sent as far away as the Orkneys and northern Norway!

Planning and Assessment

Carrying out the kind of projects with young children described in this chapter can be an enormously rewarding and effective way of organising and developing the curriculum. As with any high quality teaching, however, it depends vitally upon detailed planning based upon careful assessments of the children's needs and abilities. We therefore need to conclude with some remarks about these crucially important aspects of the Early Years educator's work.

Progression

The topic-based approach to the curriculum has commonly been criticised because of the lack of progression in activities. One argument for teaching a more subject-based curriculum has been that it enables concepts and skills to be introduced and then built upon more systematically. It is, however, perfectly possible to build progression into the activities within a topic, given careful task analysis and planning. As part of

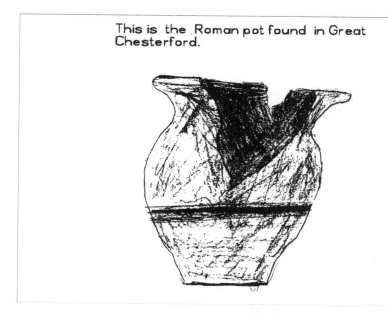

This is the Roman pot found in Great Chesterford.

Figure 3.7 *Alexander's postcard, one of half a dozen which sold like hot cakes at the local museum*

the planning for the kind of Enterprise Projects described in this chapter, for example, it is important to analyse the planned activities in terms of different areas of the curriculum (see Figure 3.8). This ensures a good range and balance of skills is being addressed. It also leads on to an analysis of the nature of the skills and understandings to be taught. That the activities are placed in the meaningful context provided by the topic or project, however, enhances the children's understandings about their purpose and thus supports rather than detracts from the real progression in learning. Here are a couple of examples from the fashion show project:

Letter writing

- **Introduced** with letters to Father Christmas (not part of the project), which were chatty, informal, and concluded with 'love from...'
- **Developed** within the project with formal, thank you letters to some people from Marks & Spencer's children's clothes department who had been into school to talk to the children about the design process; these letters had a more formal layout with the school address, proper indentation, the date, began with 'Dear Sir' and concluded with 'Yours sincerely . . . ', but the content was very straightforward.
- **Concluded** with formal letters with more complex content; these involved applying for sponsorship, inviting special guests to the fashion show, sending a charity donation (to Radio Cambridgeshire's Send-a-Cow appeal on this occasion!) and so forth (Figure 3.2 is a good example of this stage); invariably replies were received to these letters, also written very formally.

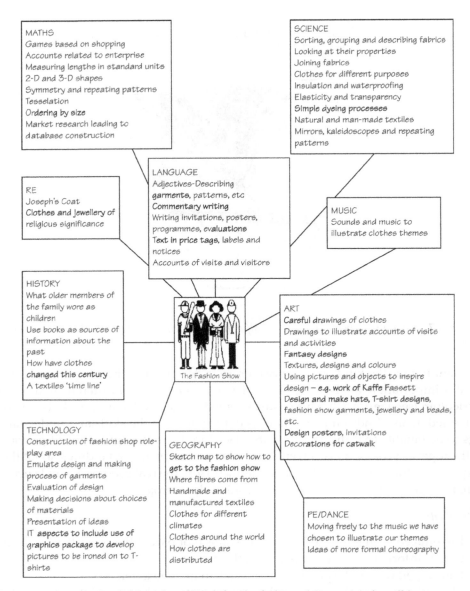

MATHS
Games based on shopping
Accounts related to enterprise
Measuring lengths in standard units
2-D and 3-D shapes
Symmetry and repeating patterns
Tesselation
Ordering by size
Market research leading to
database construction

SCIENCE
Sorting, grouping and describing fabrics
Looking at their properties
Joining fabrics
Clothes for different purposes
Insulation and waterproofing
Elasticity and transparency
Simple dyeing processes
Natural and man-made textiles
Mirrors, kaleidoscopes and repeating
patterns

RE
Joseph's Coat
Clothes and jewellery of
religious significance

LANGUAGE
Adjectives-Describing
garments, patterns, etc
Commentary writing
Writing invitations, posters,
programmes, evaluations
Text in price tags, labels and
notices
Accounts of visits and visitors

MUSIC
Sounds and music to
illustrate clothes themes

HISTORY
What older members of
the family wore as
children
Use books as sources of
information about the
past
How have clothes
changed this century
A textiles 'time line'

The Fashion Show

ART
Careful drawings of clothes
Drawings to illustrate accounts of visits
and activities
Fantasy designs
Textures, designs and colours
Using pictures and objects to inspire
design – e.g. work of Kaffe Fassett
Design and make hats, T-shirt designs,
fashion show garments, jewellery and beads,
etc.
Design posters, invitations
Decorations for catwalk

TECHNOLOGY
Construction of fashion shop role-
play area
Emulate design and making
process of garments
Evaluation of design
Making decisions about choices
of materials
Presentation of ideas
IT aspects to include use of
graphics package to develop
pictures to be ironed on to T-
shirts

GEOGRAPHY
Sketch map to show how to
get to the fashion show
Where fibres come from
Handmade and
manufactured textiles
Clothes for different
climates
Clothes around the world
How clothes are
distributed

PE/DANCE
Moving freely to the music we have
chosen to illustrate our themes
Ideas of more formal choreography

Figure 3.8 *Analysis of planned activities for the fashion show project by subject*

Tessellation

- **Introduced** by looking at patchwork patterns on fabrics and tessellating squares, rectangles and hexagons of different patterns; all these shapes tessellate with themselves in any orientation.
- **Developed** by looking at pattern-cutting for various shapes which tessellate when the shape is rotated, e.g.: T-shirt, sock, skirt (see Figure 3.9).

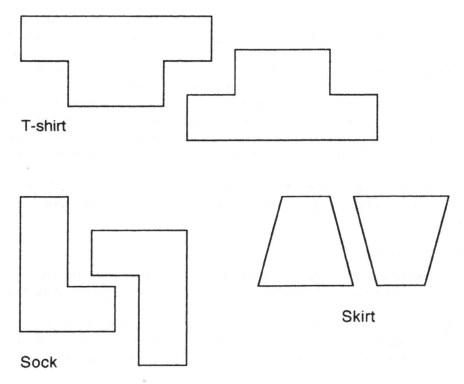

Figure 3.9 _Tessellating T-shirt, sock and skirt patterns_

- **Concluded** by looking at real dress-making patterns which did not tessellate and attempting to fit them onto rectangles of fabric in the most economical way (i.e. fitting in the most patterns with least waste, as we had seen at the clothes factory we visited).

Assessment

Early Years educators have always placed great emphasis on making careful observations and assessments. In order to make assessments of an individual child's understanding or level of skill it is important to plan activities which will enable the extent to which a child has made the new understanding or skill their own to be seen. This involves another kind of progression, from _structured or closed activities_ to introduce the new skills or concepts, developing on to more _open-ended activities_ which give the child opportunities to use what they have learnt in their own innovative ways.

It is entirely possible to build this kind of progression of activities into Enterprise Projects. The meaningful context, furthermore, provides a real purpose to the activities, and the child's real level of skill or understanding can be much more validly revealed than when they are carrying out an activity simply for its own sake, where the child's motivation and understanding of the requirements of the task are sometimes open to question. More open-ended activities reveal a child's thinking and abilities much more clearly than closed tasks, particularly of the 'Blue Peter' variety where all the child has to do is follow instructions. They also provide children with opportunities to express themselves, to gain feelings of ownership, and to have a more memorable first-hand experience. This is, of course, often what is happening, as we have reviewed, when children engage in imaginative play related to significant new experiences, and their play can be an important source for observations and assessments for this reason.

Within the Enterprise Projects many of the activities were planned with this kind of assessment in mind. Here are two examples, both from the fashion show project:

Measuring materials for costumes

- **Structured or closed activities** in which the children were taught various techniques for measuring themselves, including the use of appropriate measuring units and instruments.
- **Open-ended activities** where the children were required to use their measurements of themselves to measure out materials so that their costumes would be the right size; choice of method of measurement left to the children.

Emergent writing

- **Structured or closed activities** in which the children were taught the names of different garments, how to write out sizes, amounts of money, addresses and so forth.
- **Open-ended activities** in the role play area, the Clothes 'R' Us boutique, including, for example, the provision of an order book in which children, role playing as shop assistants, could write out orders taken from other children role playing as customers (see Figure 3. 10).

Differentiation

Having planned for a progression in the children's understandings and skills, and made assessments of their responses to the various activities, it is, of course, vital to differentiate the activities so that each child can succeed at an appropriate level. There are numerous ways in which this can be done, and once again this needs to be planned. Here are some suggested means of doing this and some examples from the Enterprise Projects:

- **Outcome:** perhaps the simplest form of differentiation is to set up an activity so that the requirements are the same for all the children, but it is so open-ended that they can respond at their own level. *Examples*: designing a poster, making a model catwalk (see also Figure 3.11).

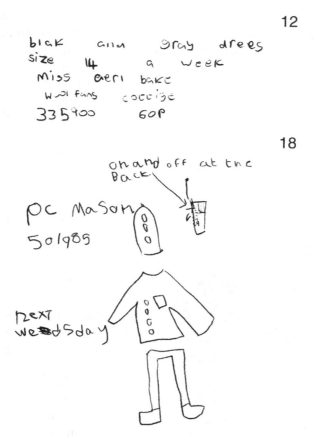

Figure 3.10 *Writing in the role play area as a means of assessment: orders placed in the Clothes 'R' Us order book*

- **Support**: once again, the requirements can be the same, but the level of the outcome needs to be similar, so this common level of achievement is reached by means of variable levels of adult support. *Examples*: making a costume, baking a cake.
- **Recording method**: the activity may be the same for everyone, but the children may be required to record what they have done in more or less sophisticated ways. *Example*: a science activity on the qualities of different textiles recorded by sticking samples of the textiles on paper, by drawings, or by descriptive writing.
- **Complexity**: finally, the children may be given tasks to do which are all related to the same skill or concept, but which are at different stages in the progression of work planned. *Example*: mapwork related to the destinations of different garments made at the clothes factory involving activities at three levels: (1) countries located on world map and drawings of garments attached; (2) journey of garments to Hong Kong investigated and a list made of the continents they travel through; and (3) journey of garments through the UK to the port investigated; compass directions, road numbers and towns travelled through recorded.

As suggested above, differentiating the presentation and demands of a task by these means should lead to its successful completion by every pupil. In planning for this, one approach is to think about the various 'sub-tasks' involved and to then view them in reverse order. It is the actions needed to complete the task – the fastening of the final button on the coat – which children must be encouraged to complete without aid, however small this step may be. Once that step is mastered, the starting point for the task can be moved back until the child is managing all the steps from start to finish.

Thus, in writing a story there is little joy for a child with difficulties in meeting the differentiated expectations of a teacher by managing the scribing of 'Once upon a time' – and no more. It is the satisfaction of writing ' . . . and they all lived happily ever after' which offers the real sense of achievement. The learner has independently added the last piece of jigsaw, and hence has ownership of the completed puzzle.

Figure 3.11 *In the art gallery, Year 1 displayed the work of Gauguin as if it was in his sitting room, hence the fire and his hat hanging on the wall*

Conclusion

Within education there is growing interest currently related to developing more experiential, problem-solving approaches to teaching and learning across the curriculum (Fisher, 1987, provides a good review of work in primary schools). We have attempted to show that Enterprise Projects can provide an excellent basis for this kind of development. There was an intensity of 'real' learning for the children within these projects which was very special. The enthusiasm with which the children, their teachers, parents and other members of the local communities still recall the projects, in some cases now after several years have elapsed, is a testimony to their significance for all who participated in them. We have attempted to demonstrate in this chapter that such projects form an excellent basis for organising an appropriate and effective Early Years curriculum. Through this kind of project it is possible to meet the needs of young children. They arrive at school confident and expert learners in the informal context of their home environment.

Through the kind of curriculum organisation proposed here they are enabled to make the transition to becoming equally effective and assured in the environment of the school.

Pointers for organising the Early Years curriculum

- With thought and imagination, it is possible to organise the Early Years curriculum in ways which are compatible with the demands of the National Curriculum, and with our understandings about how children learn.
- Young children's learning will be enhanced when:

  1 *the content of the curriculum is* **'meaningful'** to them and related to their existing knowledge and interests;
  2 they are **active participants in their learning** rather than just passive recipients; they should have opportunities to make their own decisions about their learning;
  3 they are encouraged to indulge their natural inclination to engage in **imaginative play** related to significant life experiences; and
  4 they are **emotionally** *secure because there is continuity and good communication between the worlds of home and school.*

- These principles can be embodied powerfully within Enterprise Projects.
- The success of this model of curriculum organisation depends upon:

  1 *clearly identified* **progressions** of related activities;
  2 **assessment** of children's level of understanding or skill using **open-ended activities**; and
  3 **differentiation** of activities, so that each child can succeed at an appropriate level.

References

Atkinson, S. (Ed.) (1992) *Mathematics with Reason*. London: Hodder & Stoughton.

Bennett, N., Wood, E. & Rogers, S. (1997) *Teaching through Play*. Buckingham: Open University Press.

Coltman, P. & Whitebread, D. (1992) The little bakery: an infant class develops EIU. *Economic Awareness*, 5, 1, 3–9.

DES (1990) *Mini-Enterprise in Schools: Some Aspects of Current Practice: A Report of HMI*. London: HMSO.

DfE (2012) *Statutory Framework for the Early Years Foundation Stage*. London: HMSO.

Fisher, R. (Ed.) (1987) *Problem Solving in Primary Schools*. Oxford: Basil Blackwell.

Hall, N. (1989) *Writing with Reason*. Sevenoaks: Hodder & Stoughton.

Hughes, M. (1986) *Children and Number*, Oxford: Basil Blackwell.

Ofsted (1993) *First Class: The Standards and Quality of Education in Reception Classes.* London: HMSO.

Tickell, C. (2011) *The Early Years: Foundations for Life, Health and Learning.* London: DfE.

Tizard, B. & Hughes, M. (1984) *Young Children Learning.* London: Fontana,

Whitebread, D., Coltman, P. & Bryant, P. (1994) Project file: A class museum. *Child Education*, 71, 12, 27–34.

Whitebread, D., Coltman, P. & Farmery, J. (1993) Project file: A puppet theatre. *Child Education*, 70, 6, 31-8.

Whitebread, D., Coltman, P. & Davison, S. (1995) Project file: Infant newshounds. *Child Education*, 72, 1, 29–36.

CHAPTER 4

'When the chicks hatch, a man will come and bring them yolk to eat'

ASSESSMENT IN THE EARLY YEARS

Amy Arnold

Early Years educators are ready, clipboard in hand, pencil sharpened and ready to go, but what is it they are looking or listening for? What do they see? How are children demonstrating their understanding? How can children's learning be extended and built upon?

Early Years educators monitor children's development to inform their day-to-day teaching and to allow them to report learners' achievements. They use formative assessment, where the emphasis is on planning the next steps to be taken with a child, and summative assessment to provide a snapshot of the child's achievements and abilities at a particular stage. In doing this they have made assessment all-embracing, attempting to build a picture of the 'whole child', believing that 'the process of assessing children's learning – by looking closely at it and striving to understand it – is the only certain safeguard against children's failure, the only certain guarantee of children's progress and development' (Drummond, 1993, p. 10).

Throughout this chapter we will look closely at the skills and understanding young children are demonstrating when they are engaged in a variety of experiences, and how their individual learning could be developed and enhanced.

Learning in action and making assessments

Educators are adept at using a variety of questions for different purposes. Early Years pupils benefit from questioning that will allow them to articulate *their* ideas. Only then can this information be used in teaching that is targeted to develop learning. The following transcript highlights how questioning, peer discussions and observation can be used to make assessments and lead into planning for teaching and learning for different children. This transcript looks at a group of Reception children independently expressing their current ideas and understanding, through close observation and exploration of the life cycle of a chicken.

Throughout the transcript, we will look at how questioning, observation, peer discussions and children's recordings can help educators to make ongoing formative assessments of individual children.

Background

To provide first-hand, real life opportunities for discovering and investigating, the Reception class had received an incubator and eggs from a specialist company, Hens for Hire.

The eggs and equipment were introduced to the class and factual information was shared with the children about the eggs and what was happening inside the eggs. Many early discussions were had about how the eggs were different from eggs in the supermarket, even though they looked the same. It caused a great deal of hilarity when the children discovered that if you had this type of egg at home you could end up with a chick and not a yolk. As one child excitedly shared, 'If the farmer didn't sort them out we would have a little chicken walking around in the pan!'

A small group of children were gathered at the incubator, looking and chatting about the current happenings inside. Other children visited and joined in with discussions and moved on to other playful activities, but the small core group remained at the incubator.

(P = visiting practitioner)

P: Wow! What's in here? [Pointing to the dome shaped incubator]
Hollie: Baby chicks!
P: Oh, where are the chicks?
Hollie: They are inside. Inside the eggs, we can't see them.
Milo: They eat yolk, the chicks will hatch out when all of the yolk has gone.
Evie: They use their little beak to crack the egg. [She mirrors small beak movement with her fingers]

[P places her hand gently on the outside of the incubator.]

Hollie: It's warm, to help them not die.
Ruby: Because it will be freezing and freezing and they might die straight away.

The children were instantly regarded as the experts; as a result merely of the practitioner placing a hand on the incubator children were eager to share their understanding of the temperature and the importance of this. Taking the back seat and allowing children to take on the role of expert proved they were able to confidently and competently share their recently acquired knowledge of both the equipment and the happenings inside the eggshell.

The conversation shifted from the observations of the incubator, as children began to refer to their own unique previous experiences of chicks and chickens as a point of reference for sharing and making links to their ideas.

Taylor: The cockerel lays the eggs. On Peppa Pig the cockerel is called Neville, he is really noisy and the song goes with a peck, peck, peck. [Sung in an upbeat cheery voice with hips swaying]

Ruby: You buy chocolate eggs at Easter, so they will hatch out then.

But what happens next?

Questioning and discussing predictions about unknown future events requires higher order thinking and more abstract thought which goes beyond the concrete here and now. This can allow practitioners an insight into the thought processes and minds of individual children, and, of course, the chance to make formative assessments, whilst establishing different starting points and ways in to teaching and learning for different children.

Nutbrown (2011, p. 140) highlights how young children do not think in discrete subject areas. 'In reality, young children do not think in subjects, or "areas" of learning for that matter. Neither do adults. Human beings think in terms of situations, puzzles, problems to be solved, and questions to be answered: it is the same for adults and children alike.'

As the conversation moved into thinking about what the chicks may need when they hatch, the rich opportunity for peer discussions and learning became powerfully evident.

P: I wonder if the chicks will need anything when they hatch . . .

Evie: When the chicks hatch, a man will bring them yolk to eat.

Evie was actively drawing on her existing knowledge of the current stage of the life cycle; she knew that the chicks are eating the contents inside the eggshell and used this knowledge as a platform to predict what may happen after hatching, actively making links between the concrete and abstract.

In English schools the curriculum documentation for Early Years provision identifies three characteristics of effective learning:

- playing and exploring
- active learning
- creating and thinking critically (DfE, 2012).

This example provides evidence of how Evie was able to think critically by having her own ideas and was able to make links to her prior understanding.

Milo had very clear and firm ideas of what the chicks would need when they had hatched. He confidently shared that:

Milo: They will need food – little seeds.

Listening to Milo, Evie refined her original prediction and added:

Evie: They might need chicken feed – no that's when they are big, they would need chick food and water to drink.

After closely watching the eggs and listening to the ideas of her peers, Tayla joined in the conversation.

Tayla: The chicks could have a rainbow to help them go to sleep, because babies have those in their rooms and it helps them to sleep.

Tayla demonstrated that she was able to draw upon her previous experiences and understanding of new life, to make predictions and links between ideas. All three children went on to discuss where you could or couldn't get a rainbow from and if it was possible to catch a rainbow. Tayla brought the conversation to an agreed conclusion by stating that, 'Chicks can have a picture of a rainbow next to them when they hatch.'

Milo, Evie and Tayla all chose to record their ideas of the things that the chicks may need when they hatch, and these can be seen in Figures 4.1, 4.2 and 4.3 respectively.

Listening and discussing ideas with their peers, as stimulated by the educators' wonderings, was enough to trigger new pathways of thought and build upon their individual and original ideas; it provided the opportunity to compare their own ideas to the ideas of others. Children were able to reflect and review their ideas, offer additional further information to explain their thoughts or build upon their original ideas taking into account the thoughts and contributions from class friends. Talking with and listening to friends can give children the valuable and rich opportunity to combine their collective thoughts and learn from and about one another.

Being a participant observer, watching and listening proved vital for understanding the links children made to their own lives, their prior experiences and how they formulated and justified their ideas. Observing the children recording their representations of what the chicks may need after they hatch provided a myriad of opportunities for making assessments across a range of learning and development areas.

While considering the use of questioning and discussion in obtaining evidence for formative assessment, it seems sensible to go further and to consider how both children's recordings and observations of children actively engaged can be used in combination with questioning and discussion to build a more comprehensive profile of an individual learner.

Milo (Figure 4.1) gave a running commentary as he was drawing his ideas. 'They need food, little seeds, somewhere nice to sleep, like hay. Oh and they need to be safe, here is a fence.' Milo had a clear understanding of some of the things newly hatched chicks may need. By including the need for chicks to be safe he

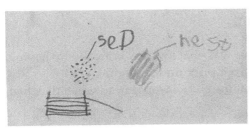

Figure 4.1 *Milo's drawing: The chicks will need food – little seeds*

showed a higher level of cognition as he began to move beyond the basic needs of food and water and considered the need for comfort with a nest and protection with a fence.

Evie (Figure 4.2) was able to link her prior knowledge and understanding to make links with her ideas. She was confident to communicate in writing and chose this method independently. Her recording could provide evidence of her ability to apply her phonetic knowledge at that given time, as well as providing ideas for engaging her in future learning experiences.

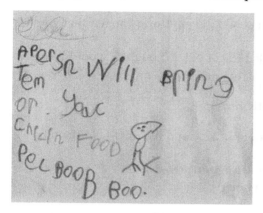

Figure 4.2 *Evie's drawing: A person will bring them yolk or chicken food. Peek a boob boo*

Tayla (Figure 4.3) showed that she was an empathetic learner, able to consider the 'invisible' basic needs of new life. She was confident with her decisions and able to take on board ideas of others, and provided a clear rationale of her ideas, as evidenced in her idea of the chicks needing a rainbow.

Returning to the Reception class a few days later, over half of the chicks had hatched and many more were trying hard to break out of their shells.

Figure 4.3 *Tayla's drawing: The chicks need a rainbow to help them to go to sleep*

Milo was very keen to share with me what had been happening:

Milo: More eggs have hatched [pointing to chicks]. They had to peck on the inside of the egg to get out.
P: Wow! How exciting! When they hatched did anything happen that you did not expect?
Milo: One was really weak and struggled to get out. I thought it would be easier for them.

Milo pointed to a chick which was currently hatching.

Milo: Look, this one is trying to come out but he can't. We can't help them as we could hurt them.
P: Is that the same as the weak chick which surprised you?
Milo: No, it was black, this one is more gooier!

Tayla came past and looked closely inside the incubator. She observed closely and asked:

Tayla: Why are they eating the shell?
Milo: Because they haven't been fed yet.

One chick finally broke free from the shell and flopped onto the floor of the incubator. The group of children that had gathered were relieved and cheered that he had safely hatched.

P: Wow! How does the chick look?
Tayla: With his head and eyes. [!]

Tayla's response indicated that this question could indeed be interpreted in different ways; as the chick looked red, bloody, sticky and slimy it was wrongly assumed this may be what the children may refer to in their answer! This question would have benefited from being a more open question, or an enabling statement such as:

- I wonder how the chick may be feeling . . .
- It looked like that could have been hard work for the chick . . .
- I can see lots of different colours.

Evie and Archie joined the group and conversation flowed:

Evie: Yesterday that one was in the shell, I thought it might hatch today – it has made a bigger hole though.
Archie: It's pecking all of the stuff [shell] off.

The practitioner then asked Evie and Archie:

P: Did anything happen when the chicks hatched that you did not expect?

Evie: That one is a bit laying down and its bum is a bit red there. I wasn't expecting them to have a red bit like that.

Evie: The yellow ones are the girls and the brown ones are boys – Joshua told me.

Archie: At night time they tried to crack it open. They are out of the shells and going around the incubator.

The children continue to spend a great deal of time closely observing the hatching process and the behaviour of the newly hatched chicks over the next few days.

Listening to children's responses to questions which allow them to share their own ideas gives educators the knowledge to plan the next steps for children's learning and development, designed to ignite, excite and instil a love of learning and build on what they have already discovered.

The cycle of assessment, with the each individual unique child at the centre, highlights the cycle from observation to assessment to planning the next steps. The following experiences are just a snapshot of how Milo, Evie and Tayla's future learning experiences could be planned to follow on from the observations, discussions and responses given.

Milo demonstrated an in-depth knowledge and understanding of the process of hatching and the needs of chicks. He was firm in his ideas and able to communicate this using expressive language, often with a sophisticated vocabulary ('One was really weak and struggled to get out'). Milo's fascination with the natural world, his interest in non-fiction texts and his clear understanding of the chicks could be utilised to extend his learning through playing with knowledge. Working with

Figure 4.4 *The fascination of developing chicks*

a practitioner and other children to produce 'Top Trump' cards for chicks could involve discussions on rating categories such as cuteness, strength and size. This would provide a meaningful context in which to apply and extend his receptive and expressive language and vocabulary, and a fun and playful context to discuss, negotiate, plan, set rules and fulfil his thirst for knowledge of the natural world. Information sources could be used to research information, distilling and communicating snapshots of information. This could be extended to include a set of Top Trump birds or animals.

Evie enjoyed talking with and to others; she was confident to communicate in writing and chose to do so independently. She gathered information from those around her and used this to influence her own ideas. Capitalising on Evie's chatty nature, her ability to listen to others to gather information along with her confidence in communicating through writing could lead seamlessly into a reporting role within the classroom. Evie could be guided to use recording equipment to interview adults and peers to gather updates and information on the chicks. This information could be used to produce press releases for *Chick News*. Skills such as questioning, distilling information, expressive language, problem-solving and writing could be developed through this genuine, purposeful learning opportunity.

Tayla's empathetic nature, her ability to make links with her prior experiences and clear enjoyment of songs gives practitioners invaluable information for providing future learning opportunities. Tayla's thoughtful nature could be explored further through the creation of small world habitats and the provision of additional materials and resources to allow her to add her own touches, such as rainbows near where animals sleep. I wonder what other thoughtful ideas she may have in mind? Creating and giving purpose and meaning to children's learning adventures could open some of their most original and creative ideas. Perhaps a letter from the caretaker expressing his concerns that the chicks find it a little too quiet in the evening when the children have all gone home and he is not sure what to do? Carefully listening to and observing children sharing their thoughts and ideas are essential for facilitating learning and development. Would Tayla perhaps create lullabies with soft musical accompaniment to play to the chicks at night time?

Nutbrown (2011, p. 137) reminds us that 'Meaningful experiences are the essence of a respectful and challenging curriculum.' The experience of observing the life cycle of a chicken gives a strong purposeful backbone to the curriculum which can be continued and extended over time. Indeed, a return visit several weeks later discovered children actively and proudly sharing the latest developments in chick world as the snapshot of the child-initiated conversations below shows:

Milo: Look, they need a red light now. [Pointing to the chicks, most of them are sitting getting warm by the little red light]

Evie: The girls are all yellow, the yellow ones look fluffier than the brown ones. There's a baby mum chick in there.

Milo: It's obviously a girl chick that is older.

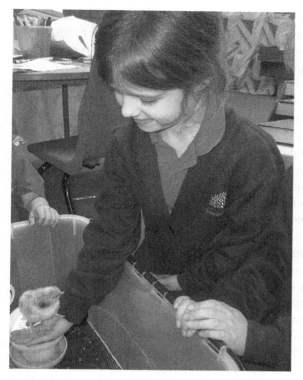

Figure 4.5 *The growing chicks continue to provide valuable learning experiences*

Observing and listening to young children sharing their original and unique ideas really is a privilege, and the buzz of reflecting with colleagues, planning the next exciting steps in the children's journey of learning, setting up irresistible experiences, observing and facilitating children as they uncover and discover the world can be heartwarming. The following snippet, really made me smile!

Evie: I put my finger at the hole and it pecked at it; it didn't hurt.

P: Wow! That's exciting. I wonder why the chicks came to peck you.

Evie: They thought I was a branch!

Of course, the meaningful and memorable experience of watching the chicks hatch does not just end when they leave the building. The continuation of learning experiences through the making of wider connections can add another dimension to children's learning and provide continual assessment opportunities. This could be planned for in a myriad of ways, including cooking involving eggs, making information leaflets or videos on how to care for chicks and, of course, finding out about 'grown up' chickens.

Assessment for learning in the Early Years

The findings of Black and Wiliam (1998), later developed by Shirley Clarke's work with thousands of primary school teachers (2001), provide a series of strategies for developing effective formative assessment. Key strategies for Early Years educators are considered below.

Child self-assessment

Involving children in the assessment of their own learning can provide the missing jigsaw piece when completing the full picture of a child's individual achievements and attainment. Self-assessment by learners, 'far from being a luxury, is in fact an essential component of formative assessment' (Black and Wiliam, 1998, p. 10).

Positive pupil attitudes to learning experiences are clearly essential if motivation is to be maintained, self-esteem is to be enhanced and learning progress is to be made. Many children's enjoyment of assessing their own performance is enhanced if they feel they can convey how they feel about the activities they are undertaking, as well as commenting on their progress. One way that self-assessment can be encouraged is through the educator modelling the process of commenting on a task.

Where learning activities and experiences are introduced or set in the context of a problem to solve or someone who needs help and advice, young children's learning has a real purpose and meaning. Giving children a genuine reason to share and report their learning and findings can support children to reflect on and share their new learning. For example, reporting back to Percy the Park Keeper about the roofing materials that would be best at keeping the animals inside his shed dry can give children a greater sense of accountability to report back their findings and discoveries. Purposeful learning experiences permeate across all areas of learning and can allow children richer opportunities to consolidate their discoveries, new vocabulary, understanding and learning in a variety of contexts.

Drawing out the children's experiences, ideas, findings or creations enables them to reflect on their learning and discoveries. A key worker can facilitate, scaffold and support children's reflections by involving them in collating their own records of learning – perhaps by sticking in photographs, drawings or their mark-making. Indeed, it is noted by the Standards and Testing Agency (2013, p. 10) that children should be part of the assessment process: 'Accurate assessment will take account of a range of perspectives including those of the child, parents and other adults who have significant interactions with the child'.

Sharing learning intentions

Educators understand the necessity of defining clear learning objectives in order to ensure that both teaching and assessment are focussed. However, it is also essential that these 'learning intentions' are shared with the children, in terms that help them to make sense of the purpose of the task. To enable children to feel a sense of success and begin to self-regulate their own learning needs, they need to be clear about any specific instructions relevant to their investigations or tasks and what the learning objective looks like in practice.

Feedback, marking and individual target setting

Feedback for very young children will inevitably be oral and as immediate as possible to the learning in which it relates. Written feedback can be introduced as the children become increasingly able to interpret symbols (using strategies such as thought bubbles or shapes recognised from whole-class or group guided activities, such as stars or wishes) and to read familiar comments used by the educator.

There are, however, several important principles that should be applied to all feedback, some of which relate to target setting.

Feedback needs to be provided as promptly as possible, and for young children this can often mean during the course of an activity. It needs to be positive, reflecting on success in relation to the learning intentions of the task. Stating the next achievable target should also be part of the purpose of the feedback. Obviously, with young children any targets will need to be stated in very simple terms and will be revisited during future learning activities which also actively make links back to children's prior learning. This is where recording of assessment information is so important, as no educator can expect to hold essential 'next steps' for all children in his or her head. Equally important, however, is the view of assessment as a sampling process, whereby the focus shifts from child to child and from one area of the curriculum to another. It is impossible to give detailed feedback and targets to all children for all work undertaken, just as it is impossible to engage all pupils in self-assessment for all tasks.

Adjusting teaching to take account of learning

There is an intimate and unbreakable link between effective teaching and effective planning and assessment. The three together form a cycle of action that should lead to the curriculum being increasingly refined for the child.

When working with Early Years children it is vital that the assessments and subsequent changes to the curriculum consider the whole child. A child who is assessed as having weak fine motor skills may be unable to complete a practical activity but may have the conceptual understanding to follow what is happening. At such times, the careful matching for both skills and understanding can lead to more enjoyable and successful learning.

The learning environment

The learning environment is crucial in enabling children to actively demonstrate their skills and understanding through playful and exciting learning experiences, giving educators the chance to carry out insightful and purposeful observations and therefore make accurate assessments. Creating opportunities for observation and assessment should, therefore, form part of the planning for and design of the learning environment, Does the learning experience look inviting? Will children find it irresistible and impossible to keep their hands off it?

Icy explorations

On a chilly February morning, a class of Reception children had experienced a slippery journey to school. A well timed and realistic 'interruption' from a teaching assistant altered and engaged the children in the change that had happened in the outdoor environment. A class discussion on ice and melting occurred naturally as the children instantly took the lead in finding out where an unusual ice trail led. They discovered some very

Figure 4.6 *The children try out their ideas by breaking the ice*

large ice shapes – with something strange inside them! Had something become trapped?

Children's ideas on how to retrieve the mystery objects were captured through note observations, photographs and video clips; some of these were instantly recorded on an ipad using a digital assessment program. The careful planning and resourcing of the outdoor learning environment resulted in the children being enthused, excited and buzzing with ideas on how to melt the ice, along with equipment and resources to instantly test out their ideas, which ranged from smashing the ice with sticks or stamping on it to using hot water to melt the shapes and release the cuddly toys trapped inside.

Thus the teacher's observation of the children discovering strange and unusual icy trail in the school's outdoor area led to powerful investigating, allowing educators to gauge and assess children's understanding of melting and freezing.

The indoor environment allowed the same opportunities as outside but on a smaller scale, with smaller mystery items inside and a variety of tools and objects which could potentially be used to melt the ice. Educators responded to the children's ideas and made adjustments to the learning environment to support the class's emerging and developing ideas, for example by bringing in a small oven on wheels to test if the ice would melt in the oven and providing fluffy material to make the ice hot. The learning environment was designed to allow instant observations and assessments to be made as the children developed their understanding of melting.

> Children must have access to a rich learning environment which provides them with the opportunities and conditions in which to flourish in all aspects of their development. It should provide balance across the areas of learning. Integral to this is an ethos which respects each child as an individual and which values children's efforts, interests and purposes as instrumental to successful learning.
>
> Standards and Testing Agency (2013, p. 9)

Figure 4.7 *As the chilly soft toy emerged gradually from a bag inside the ice shapes, the children were eager to warm him up and cuddle him*

Making holistic assessments

Children are constantly learning and developing through everyday experiences across all elements of their lives, including their home, community and educational settings. Working closely with parents by having open, honest and frequent dialogue with them about their child enables all parties to look more closely, deeply and holistically at individual children's achievements and learning preferences.

In 1930, Susan Isaacs recognised the importance of children's interests out of their school or setting by saying that 'it is the twentieth century world in which most children, and certainly those in this group, are interested – the world of motor-cars, engines, aeroplanes, gramophones and the wireless' (p. 23). Now, in the twenty-first century, things have advanced and progressed. Wireless has a whole new meaning, technological advances are moving at an astonishing pace, and children's lives are filled with devices which allow them instant connectivity to the world: they may well have experienced motion-sensor games, voice-activated commands and almost certainly some form of touch-screen technology. However, whilst children's interests may have advanced, the level of influence and the importance of schools and settings building on children's out-of-school interests remains the same:

These tools of use and pleasure surround them in the street and the home, in picture books and illustrated papers and in the talk of grown-ups and older children. They are part of these children's immediate and concrete world, which it is the business of the school to illuminate and simplify their understanding.

(Isaacs, 1930)

Children's young minds are buzzing with images, thoughts, questions and ideas about their experiences. Instinctively, they will seek to play out these experiences to help make sense of their world and to make connections with previous experiences.

Amber and the animals

The following example is an observation of Amber, who is aged four years and six months, playing with a selection of small-world animals. Amber had independent access to several baskets of small-world animals, pebbles, stones and miniature logs, which she carefully selected independently.

Amber talked to herself, and the animals, as she played.

'Good seals. This one is the mummy, this one is the daddy.' [Arranges seals on two pebbles]

[Moves the polar bear into the seals' zone] 'The polar bear doesn't have a mummy or daddy, so the seals are looking after him – they all live together.'

'The polar bear has been poptin. It's ok polar bear, come on this rock.'

'The horse can't live on the pebbles, we don't have grass. Horse you will have to go over there.'

[Amber stroked and reassured the polar bear] 'It's ok, it's ok.'

This very brief snapshot of Amber playing demonstrates her empathetic nature, along with her understanding that horses need grass. It left the observer wondering about the word 'poptin'. Open-ended questioning from the practitioner resulted in the identical repetition of the word with the added explanation from Amber that 'he was poptin because the seal looks after him'; whilst it sounded very much like 'popped in', this did not make sense in the flow of her play. After chatting with Amber's mum and briefly sharing details of her thoughtful animal play and exciting new word, Amber's mum was able to explain that they had visited a farm where a young calf had lost its mother during childbirth and had been 'adopted' by the workers who were bottle feeding it! Clearly, Amber was testing out the new vocabulary, 'adopted', in her play, whilst making sense of her new experiences.

Parents hold the key to piecing together children's achievements, learning and development and can enable educators to make holistic assessments. Recognising parents' role as their child's first educator from the very beginning can ensure that parent voices are heard, and an open, honest and genuine relationship is forged, with the child's well-being and happiness at the core. As Hurst and Lally have commented, 'Assessment of young children must cover all aspects of a child's development and must be concerned with attitudes, feelings, social and physical characteristics . . . Learning is not compartmentalised under subject headings for young children (1992, p. 55).

Pointers for assessment in the Early Years

Many Early Years educators show clear ability and commitment to assessments that involve the whole child. The following points are, we believe, central to effective assessments in the Early Years:

- Be aware of the wide variety of opportunities for formative assessment.
- Plan for and take time to listen to and observe children.
- Appreciate that discussion holds the key to much effective assessment.
- Involve children in collating their records of learning.
- Feed assessment information into planning for future teaching.
- Imaginative activities lead to open-ended exploration and greater assessment opportunities.
- The learning environment should be planned to allow for assessment opportunities.
- Regarding children as experts allows children to lead their learning and educators to make valuable observations.

References

Black, P. and Wiliam, D. (1998) *Inside the Black Box: Raising Standards through Classroom Assessment.* London: King's College.

Clarke, S. (2001) *Unlocking Formative Assessment: Practical Strategies for Enhancing Pupils' Learning in the Primary Classroom.* London: Hodder & Stoughton.

Department for Education (2012) *Statutory Framework for the Early Years Foundation Stage.* London: HMSO.

Drummond, M.J. (1993) *Assessing Children's Learning.* London: David Fulton Publishers.

Hurst, V. and Lally, M. (1992) Assessment and the nursery curriculum. In G. Blenkin and A. Kelly (Eds.), *Assessment in Early Childhood Education.* London: Paul Chapman, pp. 69–92.

Issacs, S. (1966) *Intellectual Growth in Young Children.* London: Routledge.

Nutbrown, C. (2011) *Threads of Thinking.* London: Sage.

Standards and Testing Agency (2013) *Early Years Foundation Stage Profile Handbook 2014.* Available at www.education.gov.uk/assessment.

Further reading

Featherstone, S. (2011) *Catching Them at It! Assessment in the Early Years*. London: Bloomsbury.

Swaffield, S. (2008) *Unlocking Assessment*. London: Routledge.

Whitebread, D. (2012) *Developmental Psychology and Early Childhood Education*. London: Sage.

CHAPTER 5

'This is the best day of my life! And I'm not leaving here until it's time to go home!'

THE OUTDOOR LEARNING ENVIRONMENT

Christine Parker

Observation: play in the nursery garden

Jason and Jack are playing in the nursery garden. Jason runs up to Jack. Jack says, 'You're the monster.' Jason runs away and says, 'I'm not the monster, I'm not.' They enter the willow tunnel and sit on the tree stumps. Jason asks, 'How shall we get out?' and squeezes through a gap in the willow tunnel. Jack suggests, 'Let's go to the park'. Jason responds, 'This one here?' and points to the climbing pod. As they pass the sand pit, Sophie offers Jason some sand cake. He says, 'No thank you', and the two boys run off to the climbing pod and follow one another along the climbing ropes. Jason looks at a loose tree stump and says, 'Me need this', and attempts to move it. Jack helps him and then tries to move an even bigger tree stump. He says to Jason, 'I can't move it. Can you help?' but Jason responds, 'No, it's too big for me.' They both return to the sand pit and observe the other children making sand cakes. Jason goes off to the resource shelf and returns with a large bucket and a plastic scoop. He fills the bucket with sand using two hands to lift each full scoop. Jason asks, 'Where's some water for me?' Jack replies, 'There's a bucket.' Jason picks up the bucket of sand and struggles to carry it to the bucket of water.

In this observation, a three-year-old child decides whether he is a monster or not, finds out how to escape out of a willow tunnel, follows his friend's suggestion to go to the park, exercises on climbing ropes, tests out his muscular strength, takes cues from other children around him and asks meaningful questions – all in minutes.

Jason's key worker noted, 'Jason demonstrated high levels of involvement (Laevers, 1994), interacts effectively with his peers, displays lots of collaborative play, shows independence in accessing resources and engages in imaginative play.' I would like to add: Jason enjoys a physical challenge.

The purpose of this observation is to highlight the value of outdoor play. It has now been widely acknowledged (QCA, 2000, p. 25; Garrick, 2004; Edgington, 2004, p. 2) that young children need access to the outdoors in their Early Years, in both pre-school and primary school. Children benefit from developing their play and learning in environments where they can move from the indoors to the outdoors, and vice versa, freely. Currently, more children have access to the outdoor environment in reception classes, but an increasing number of Year One children also do so. *Continuing the Learning Journey* (QCA, 2005) supports the provision of frequent opportunities for outdoor play.

We know the outdoor environment offers young children an abundance of play and learning opportunities. But how can we capture their engagement and fascination for the outdoors? This chapter is an attempt to support Early Years educators to:

- appreciate how the outdoor learning environment enhances and extends children's development and learning;
- define the areas of provision;
- observe and plan for the outdoor learning environment;
- provide practical solutions to the organisation of the outdoors;
- be inspired and motivated to ensure the outdoor environment is embedded in the Early Years curriculum.

How the outdoor learning environment enhances and extends children's development and learning

Emotional development

For many young children, the daily opportunity to access the outdoors impacts on their levels of well-being (Laevers, 1994). Some children prefer to be outdoors; it makes them feel better about themselves and become more adventurous and playful in their learning (as discussed in Chapter 1). Having different types of spaces enhances their emotional development: having a place to hide, to be quiet and sometimes alone, is equally as important as sharing the joy of the outdoors with others. In considering our mental health, we know the appreciation of the outdoors supports our emotional and spiritual development (Jenkinson, 2001, pp. 34–36, pp. 100–101).

Social development

Children learn most effectively within a social context (Vygotsky, 1978, pp. 89–91). The outdoor environment offers many opportunities for children to share their play and learning with another child, a group of children, an adult or all adults present outside. Children's outdoor play and learning has the potential to support complex narrations within social dramatic play; to support planning, preparing and enjoying the outcomes of growing vegetables, herbs and fruits; and to support time to meet, discuss and enjoy each other's company.

When Early Years educators find that children's superhero role play challenges the boundaries of acceptable behaviour, the children can learn to identify their rules for this type of play and learn to protect each other. At Caverstede Early Years Centre, the rules, identified by the children, were:

- Outside – not inside;
- You don't hurt anybody;
- No fighting;
- Just battling swords together, not on someone's body;
- Play with children who want to join in; if they're busy they might want to play later;
- Don't push anybody;
- Tell your friends the rules.

Physical development

Having the space and freedom to practice running, jumping, climbing, balancing, lifting, carrying, transporting, pushing, pulling and swinging ensures children's healthy physical, mental and intellectual development. Experiencing physical challenge is a

Figure 5.1 *A child who loves to be active and loud has the opportunity to be energetic within a space in which these qualities are appreciated by others.*

risky enterprise but is essential in supporting and developing the child's own sense of what is safe and what is not. As Early Years practitioners, it is our role to provide situations that will help children to deal with testing the surface, judging whether the ladder will wobble or daring to explore a dark space behind a hedge.

Continuous daily access to PE equipment enables children to develop their skills to throw and catch, retrieve, and handle a range of tools with skill, agility and confidence. Children's fine motor skills are also appropriately enhanced and developed through gardening activities, role play dressing-up, and the provision of mark-making materials and equipment to use with natural materials. Children have a wonderful fascination for mini-beasts and learn to handle creatures with care and respect.

Sensory integration is well supported through the provision of different surfaces on which to move. It is the normal neurological process our brain uses in order to organise sensation in our everyday lives. We receive information from our senses, including the movement senses. This information tells our brains about balance, movement, gravity and what our muscles and joints are doing. We know we need to provide different surfaces and a range of physical experiences to support each child's sensory integration. In the nursery garden children experience walking, running and jumping, on grass, concrete pathways, bark chippings, Astroturf, rubber surface, gravel, logs and wooden pathways; there is also a change in gradient. These experiences enable the children to feel comfortable about accessing other learning opportunities.

Figure 5.2 *Climbing a ladder to explore a different view of the willow tunnel*

Intellectual development

Children relish the grandeur of the problems they need to solve outdoors. How do we transport this pile of leaves, these large blocks or these wooden planks? How do we save the planet when we're superheroes? How can I make this fit? How can I make the water flow in the direction I want? Through the children's exploratory and imaginative play, they have problems to solve, roles to negotiate, knowledge to acquire, much to remember, and many questions to ask. Earlier in this book David Whitebread explains Bruner's description of language as a 'tool for thought' and the child's need for meaningful social contexts in which to learn, as identified in Vygotsky's work. The outdoors provides endless opportunities for the children to express their thoughts and learning and to share these with other children and adults. Some children are more confident and relaxed when they are able to express themselves outside.

At Caverstede Early Years Centre, we created a bog garden. The children were highly involved in this project, and demonstrated lines of enquiry through their questioning:

- 'Will we wake all the plants up?'
- 'Can we splash in the bog garden?'
- 'Will the birds come?'
- 'Do spiders crawl really fast?'

Figure 5.3 *At Caverstede Early Years Centre the children planned and created a bog garden with their key workers' support*

- 'Can I ask about the butterflies?'
- 'Do seeds die because they are not planted properly?'
- 'Do worms make the plants nice?'

The bog garden also inspired list-making, as shown in Figure 5.4.

The science curriculum has the potential to be fully supported through quality outdoor provision; enhancing and providing challenges. There are key scientific themes to explore outside, such as, change, weather, seasons, properties of materials, growth and living things. Close observation is key to developing scientific investigative skills.

Defining the different areas of provision for the outdoor learning environment

It is as important to define the different areas of provision in the outdoor environment as it is to define the areas of the classroom. As Early Years educators we need to

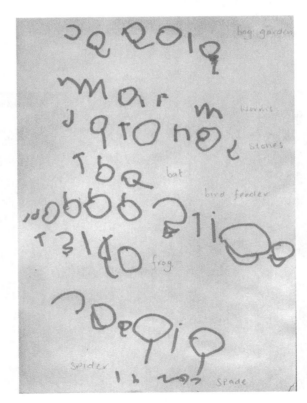

Figure 5.4 *A list of what was required for the bog garden, including the creatures that may visit*

ensure we have given time to considering what is appropriate and beneficial outdoor provision. Helen Bilton explains,

> For the outdoor area to be a learning and teaching environment, it cannot be left as an empty space. It has to be treated in the same way as a classroom and what is provided in the outdoor area and where activities are positioned all need careful consideration.
>
> (Bilton, 2002, p. 36)

My own experience as a nursery teacher and head teacher and my reading of a range of literature (Bilton, 2nd ed., 2002; Garrick, 2004, pp. 66–67; Bradford Education, 2000, pp. 8–9; Ryder Richardson, 2006, pp. 2–10, p. 46) led me to consider the organisation of the outdoor environment under a number of areas of provision. I see these areas of provision as being continuous; that is, they are available daily and a consistent level of provision is maintained. The areas of provision I identified were:

- The natural environment: wildlife and vegetation
- Gardening
- Physical challenge and sensory integration
- Role play
- Transporting materials
- Natural materials
- The construction site
- The creative arts
- Meeting places

Bilton (2002, p. 41) suggests versatile resources that allow a whole range of learning opportunities and outcomes. This continuous provision is then further enhanced following observations of the children's play and learning and identification of development and learning needs for individuals, groups of children and the whole class.

The natural environment: wildlife and vegetation

The National Curriculum, in England, becomes subject based for children aged five and above, beginning with Key Stage One. Key Stage One science supports children's knowledge and understanding of the living world – and what better place to develop children's acquisition of key concepts than outside? Outside we can inspire and motivate children to investigate mini-beasts, bird life and small mammals. Scientific investigations can be well-supported by core stories in literacy sessions. In this way we can make meaningful links in the children's learning between science and literacy, for example through *The Very Hungry Caterpillar* (Carle, 2002).

The children at Caverstede Early Years Centre take full advantage of the shrubs and we always ensure that it is possible to tunnel through. The shrubbery allows children to have small enclosed private spaces and also inspires wonderful imaginative play.

Good planting provides children with a wealth of learning about plants (Bilton, 2002, p. 61). Considerations may include planting that supports children's sensory development: our herb garden is a constant reference for both children and adults, and contains plants of different heights and leaf types which flower at different times, shrubs that children can hide behind and trees that provide much needed shelter.

Gardening (vegetables, fruit, herbs and flowers)

Provided that it is well-supported by an interested adult, gardening offers great potential in developing knowledge and understanding of sustainability, and in giving children first-hand experience of what it means to grow your own food. In Margaret McMillan's open-air nurseries of the 1920s, she emphasised the provision of a herb garden and kitchen garden (Bradford Education, 2000). Growing food is a strong seasonal experience and has the potential to develop a sense of belonging to a community.

It is essential to provide gardening tools that allow the children to be successful in their efforts. In small restricted areas good use of unusual containers can be made, for example, tyres. From experience, I advocate retaining an area for digging, allowing children to immerse themselves in the mud. The children soon learn that one area is for freer exploratory play and another is for the specific purpose of growing food.

Figure 5.5 *Preparing the bed for the herb garden*

Children are keen to make waterproof labels and to inform others that this is not a place to dig!

The recommendation is to start small and and let it grow! Again, there are endless opportunities for cross-curricular links in literacy, numeracy, creative development and physical development. The garden inspires interest in stories. For example, *The Enormous Turnip* includes references to numeracy and comparisons of size and weight, and children growing their own turnips and other vegetables can create pictures as well as re-enacting the stories. Physical development can be enhanced through opportunities to pull and push, just like the characters do in the story.

Physical challenge and sensory integration

As previously stated, the outdoor environment provides children with great opportunities for physical challenge on a daily basis and to meet their sensory integration needs. Children benefit from learning to ride two-wheelers, climb up ladders, roll down hills, balance along logs and planks, swing freely, walk on different surfaces and experience impact safely.

At Caverstede, PE equipment is part of the continuous provision. The expectation is that the equipment will be used for the purpose it is designed for. Balls and bats, hockey sticks, goal posts, bean bags and hoops are all accessible.

Figure 5.6 *Children love to construct their own obstacle courses and are good at ensuring that they are presented with safe challenges*

Figure 5.7 *Meeting physical strength challenges by pushing a tree stump up the slide*

Role play

If as a young child you want to be a police officer or a fire-fighter, what better place than outside, where you have the time and space to develop your narrative? It makes sense to extend active role play outside where children can make a lot more noise than indoors. Role play, often strongly influenced by real-life experiences, becomes more involved where children are able to recreate a sense of time and place. They can walk to the 'shops', run to the 'emergency' and visit several relatives. Superhero play can be supported in ways that are non-threatening but provide children with a wonderful release of energy and sense of purpose.

Transporting materials

Young children frequently demonstrate an interest in transporting materials (Athey, 1990). In the classroom this can cause anxiety due to a lack of space and resources. Opportunities for transporting can be well-supported outside, and the more real the experience, the greater the levels of involvement and learning – for example, the provision of wheeled vehicles to transport leaves in the autumn.

Natural materials: water, sand, mud, rocks and pebbles

The exploration of natural materials is a messy business and so it is easier to provide outside. With suitable clothing, the whole experience can be so much more meaningful – for example, the provision of all-weather suits allows children to physically immerse themselves. Kernow Woodland Learning is a woodland project in

Cornwall (Callaway, 2005) which supports the need for children to experience the outdoors in all weathers. One project aim is to 'encourage children to respect the outdoors: diverse weather conditions, the beauty and forms of nature and the changing seasons' (Callaway, p. 3).

Observations in the sand pit show us the opportunities for parallel and social play: great cooperation is required to fill all the containers. The provision of a range of graded containers enhances the quality of play and there are more opportunities to make those important comparisons of weight, size and capacity. Rigging up a pulley adds a scientific dimension to children's play and learning.

Natural materials enhance the quality of the children's small-world play. Children's imaginary miniature worlds enables them to empathise, create narratives and share understandings. Play with natural materials inspires imaginative play on both a small and life-size scale.

The construction site

Combining sand and water often naturally leads to an interest in building. The opportunity to build on a large scale offers children a real challenge and a great sense of satisfaction. Large materials such as planks, tyres and crates require a large space and the opportunity to construct for a purpose.

Nutbrown explores notions of children's rights in *Children's Rights and Early Education* (1996) and asks whether children's privacy is respected. She refers to aspects of communication, but it is also important that children have the opportunity to have a private space where they can be undisturbed by an adult. We can supervise with sensitivity.

Figure 5.8 *Concocting magic spells*

Figure 5.9 *Constructing dens for private meetings*

The expressive arts and design

The expressive arts can be developed outside in exciting and innovative ways. There are places to do large-scale artwork and to explore sound and music, and outside areas can be designed for performance.

Inspiration from past and living artists can be introduced in a way that is meaningful for the children. Andy Goldsworthy inspires sculptures using collections of natural materials, allowing children to explore the visual elements of pattern, space, shape, colour and texture. Jackson Pollock's artwork can be fully explored outside where children can experiment splattering paint and admire their efforts on a larger scale than that restricted by the indoors. Children delight in making marks with large paintbrushes and containers of water and with large pieces of playground chalk. The provision of art materials can enhance the development of construction and role play, to include drawing maps and plans.

It is important to provide opportunities for outdoor art that are also soothing and calm. For example, children will respond to the provision of watercolour paints by exploring colour and the effects that can be made with watery paint running, mixing and blending.

Children enjoy experimenting with music outside where organised sound provides a different experience. Visiting musicians have played in our nursery garden and the children are able to respond spontaneously, moving their bodies to the rhythms and melodies.

Core stories (Barrs & Ellis, 1998) such as *The Gruffalo, We're Going on a Bear Hunt* and *The Billy Goats Gruff* are greatly enhanced by being presented outside. The children will then initiate their own narratives when adults have modelled the story-telling process.

Figure 5.10 *An adult modelling watercolour painting to encourage care and attention to detail*

Meeting places

The outdoor environment has the potential to offer children spaces where they can be alone in a safe and secure place, as well as special places to meet. These places include under a willow dome, in a tunnel in a hedge, in a wooden shed or in the sand pit. Children congregate and socialise. These are places where children's role play will be initiated – children will travel to 'Spain', 'the moon' and 'the shops down the road'.

Analysis of our observations is the key to providing well-informed planning to further enhance and extend the children's development and learning. We now move onto planning the outdoor learning environment.

Observing and planning for the outdoor learning environment

Observing children outside

Why do we need to observe children outside? If we truly value children's outdoor play and learning then we have to give it equal status in terms of the need to highlight, capture and document the children's development and learning – we cannot leave this to chance because then it will not happen. There are challenges because of the weather, so photographs, using digital cameras, come into their own. Here are two examples:

Observation one

> Joshua is in the reception class and it is the autumn term. He has built a tall tower using the large plastic bricks. Joshua decides to use the sticky labels that have been provided to record the corresponding numeral; he sticks one onto each brick. He refers to the number-line that has also been provided for when he is writing numerals above 10. Joshua focuses on this activity for 20 minutes.

The space outside has given Joshua the confidence to engage in a numeracy activity which he otherwise would not have self-selected.

Observation two

> Carl is putting the doll on the slide and sliding it down. He slides down after it. He transfers the doll to another slide and again follows it down. The plastic slide allows him to go fast. 'Wheeee!' he yells.

> He picks up a scooter nearby and scoots around in a circle. He comes back past the doll on the floor, slowing to look at it. He scoots on and stops by an adult who is talking about moving on to the next school. He appears to listen, but keeps moving the scooter in a circle around a bush. The conversation shifts to 'friendships'. Carl makes facial expressions including smiling.

> He leaves his scooter and twizzles in three circles.

> Carl says to his peer, 'You got hiccups?' He chases his peer around big bush.

Figure 5.11 *Joshua numbering bricks*

Carl's displayed need for movement, possibly rotational schematic play, evidences a desire, interest and appreciation in social interaction. Carl dips in and out of it, beginning to create social situations imaginatively with the doll to re-enforce and 'prepare' himself for real social interactions.

Planning the outdoor learning environment

Planning the outdoor learning environment is a dynamic process that has to evolve over time. It deserves frequent revisits in order to monitor the quality of play and learning that is occurring for the children (Bilton, 2010).

In creating plans for the outdoors, it is important to give serious consideration to the precise experiences and learning opportunities desired for the children. The areas of provision need to be clearly defined and understood by everyone involved. Matching the areas of provision to the potential development and learning is a key process to revalidate the value of outdoor play and learning and ensure a shared understanding is embedded.

The examples in Tables 5.1, 5.2 and 5.3 respectively show a long-term plan, an extract from a medium-term plan and an overview of the nursery garden during one week (the short-term plan).

Provide practical solutions to the organisation of the outdoors

To be inspired and motivated by the outdoor environment, and to give it value, Early Years educators need to acknowledge that there can be barriers to quality provision. Below is a brief summary of the common difficulties and barriers that may be experienced.

- Safety issues/supervision/adult expectations/sun safety/rules and boundaries
- Storage/time to set up
- Access/restrictions due to design of building and size of area
- The weather (inclement weather can be discouraging, particularly for some adults, but generally is not discouraging for children
- Adult attitudes towards children playing outside, or not sharing our understanding of the value.

Holding onto the vision is vital! Do not be discouraged. The outcomes are of great benefit to the children. Table 5.4 provides some solutions to these common dilemmas.

Table 5.1 Long term planning: continuous provision

Outdoors

The outdoor area provides the opportunity for active learning across the whole curriculum, allowing children to access varied learning experiences.

Learning experiences/activities

Personal, social and emotional development

- Sharing and taking turns with equipment
- Working on collaborative projects
- Developing independence
- Being excited by the outdoor world and being motivated to learn

Communication, language and literacy

- Exploring mark-making, using large and small equipment
- Making and using signs such as road signs
- Using fiction and non-fiction as a starting point
- Making and exploring sounds
- Talking, negotiating and communicating ideas

Mathematical development

- Counting
- Number games
- Matching numbers and numerals
- Looking at and making patterns and shapes
- Measuring and problem-solving
- Comparing quantities

Knowledge and understanding of the world

- Investigate, observe, explore and compare using a range of resources, including ICT
- Building and constructing on a large scale

Physical development

- Developing gross motor skills and spatial awareness
- Developing fine motor skills
- Becoming aware of and talking about changes

Creative development

- Making large murals
- Making mobiles
- Making music and dances in all weathers
- Setting up role play areas, with suitable clothing

Adult role

- Recognizing, valuing and building on children's interests
- Sensitive intervention
- Modelling of skills
- Sharing of information
- Asking challenging questions
- Engaging in play alongside children
- Providing additional resources as appropriate
- Supporting close and accurate observations

Resources

Suggested resources could include:

- Selection of wheeled toys to ride and push and pull

- Gardening equipment
- Mark-making equipment (large paintbrushes, playground chalk)
- Throws, tents, tunnels, clothes airers, washing lines and pegs
- Bubble solution and bubble wands
- Wellies
- Guttering, pipes, funnels, water tray, set of small trays
- Skipping ropes, various balls, basketball net, goal
- Large wooden blocks
- Easel/chalkboard
- Sand and water toys
- Selection of small-world equipment
- Resources to support role play, e.g. emergency services, the construction site
- Art resources to support large scale painting and sculpture
- Resources for outdoor music and sound-making
- Items for movement play
- Toolbox and workbench
- Selection of reclaimed materials
- Trampoline, balancing boards, stilts, seesaw, plastic barrel
- Selection of natural resources

Fixed resources:
- Climbing frame/equipment
- Picnic table and benches
- Play house, kitchen
- Swings and slide
- Tyres and inner tubes
- Storage

Planned areas:
- Areas set up as they might be indoors e.g. sand, water, paint, role play
- A space large enough for children to run, skip and jump
- A designated area for wheeled toys
- An appropriately resourced climbing and balancing area
- A quiet area
- A free-digging and exploration area
- A garden area

Key prompts/questions
- What's happening here?
- What's going to happen next?
- Seasonal changes
- Large movement: speed, direction, type and quality of movement
- Mathematical concepts: area, measurement, quantities
- Scientific concepts: 'change', 'living things', 'growth'

Vocabulary
- Words to describe weather, questions to support exploratory play, correct vocabulary for vegetation, wildlife, mini-beasts. Words to describe movement and speed: run, skip, jump, hop, crawl, roll, leap, twist, turn, fast, faster then, fastest, slow, slower than, slowest, rapid, swift
- Vocabulary to support imaginative role play

Table 5.2 Medium-term plan: autumn 2: cultures, festivals and celebrations

Area of learning: PD

Aspect: Movement

Notes/comments	Learning priorities (B-3, FSCG)	Adult-initiated	Resources
	A healthy child *Growing and developing* • Being active, rested and protected • Gaining control of the body A competent learner *Healthy choices* • Discovering and learning about his/her body *Being imaginative* • Imitating, mirroring, moving and imaging • Express themselves with action and sound • Are excited by their own increasing mobility and often set their own challenges • Move spontaneously within available space • Respond to rhythm, music and story by means of gesture and movement • Can stop • Move freely with pleasure and confidence • Move in a range of ways, such as slithering, shuffling, rolling, crawling, walking, running, jumping, skipping, sliding and hopping • Use movement to express feelings • Adjust speed or change direction to avoid obstacles	• Listening to music from other cultures • Video of cultural dance and celebration • Moving in response to music, vibration and visual stimuli, e.g. firework dances, jumping, spinning, bouncing, in response to poems, percussion, signing and clapping; banging, stamping, jumping, and marching to African drums; moving fast and slow, turning, twisting to Indian music; Jabadeo movement play to range of music. • Moving and chasing with ribbon and floating materials. • Party music and games: statues, dancing. • Children preferred sensory integration techniques, e.g. the swings crashing. • Finger rhymes. • Floor play: mark-making, stories, sand tray.	Videos e.g. • Cultural dancing • Ballet • Ice skating • Swings

	Enhanced provision	References
• Negotiate space successfully when playing racing and chasing games with other children • Go backwards and sideways as well as forwards • Experiment with different ways of moving • Initiate new combinations of movement and gesture in order to express and respond to feelings, ideas and experiences, • Jump off an object and land appropriately • Move with confidence, imagination and in safety • Manage body to create intended movements • Combine and repeat a range of movements • Sit up, stand up and balance on various parts of the body • Demonstrate the control necessary to hold a shape or fixed position • Mount stairs, steps or climbing equipment using alternate feet • Manipulate materials and objects by picking up, releasing, arranging, threading and posting them • Show increasing control over clothing and fastenings • Move with control and coordination • Travel around, under, over and through balancing and climbing equipment	• Space and opportunities created indoor and outdoor for movement to music and sound • Scarves/heavy and light material • Percussion • Display photographs of children moving • Stimulus pictures: fireworks, dancing, athletics, sport, wind pictures, climbing, parachuting	• Birth to 3 framework • Foundation stage curriculum guidance • 'Every Child Matters' outcomes: enjoy and achieve; make a positive contribution; economic well-being • Continuous provision document • Nursery garden document • Sensory integration booklet • Schema leaflet • Jabadeo plan • Firework poems • Link with CD • Music and PD • Movement 2

Table 5.3 Short-term plan: nursery garden

Continuous provision: Week beginning ....

Art	Mark-making	Sand	Water	Tactile
A group of boys gained a lot from creating 'splats' like Jackson Pollock's art. They dropped sponges loaded with paint from a height and became proficient in knowing how forcefully you should aim the sponge.	Luke and Aaron looked at sheep as they made marks. Luke said, 'I'm doing down and across there.' (He pointed to the △.) Aaron said, 'Mine is round. Now it's along, look.' (He made curves and wiggles.)	Jay and Daniel used the boats in the sand, making tracks, talking about oceans and docking.	It was raining and the undercover was leaking. The children lined up buckets to catch the rain from the leaks. The group of children observed the rain filling up the buckets. Once full, they emptied the buckets.	Aaron, Corben, Ben and Rosie were smelling, touching and tearing little bits off herbs. Rosie said, 'I've smelled that before.' Ben and Aaron know the different names of herbs.
Reflections	**Personal, social and emotional development**	**Communication, language and literacy**	**Mathematical development**	**Construction/blocks**
Lots more 'hide and seek' going on. Could develop as a focus. We have managed to go for walks with all children over lunch on two different days. The second day we linked up with the Ladybird class. The children enjoyed looking at and collecting leaves. The walk was a significant marker in the day to those staying all day.	• Being able to express feelings • Knowing when to ask for help • Striving for responses from others • Growing awareness of self • Feeling safe and secure and demonstrating a sense of trust • Having an awareness of, and showing interest in, cultural and religious differences • Having a positive self-image and showing that they are comfortable with themselves • Making connections between different parts of their life experience	• Communicating meaning • Creating and experimenting with one's own symbols and marks • Beginning to bring together hand and eye movements to fix on and make contact with objects • Using action, sometimes with limited talk that is largely concerned with the 'here and now' • Using talk to connect ideas, explain what is happening and anticipate what might happen next • Using language to imagine and recreate roles and experiences • Drawing lines and circles using gross motor movement	• Making patterns, comparing, categorising and classifying • Noticing changes in groupings of objects, images or sounds • Gaining awareness of 1–1 correspondence through categorising belongings • Showing curiosity about numbers by offering comments or asking questions • Using mathematical language in play • Showing an interest in shape and space by playing with shapes or making arrangements with objects	A group of children placed the wooden reels in a line. They then stepped on each reel, counting as they stepped on each one, 1 to 8. Increased interest in the blocks as builders start laying bricks. Children are using sand and scrapers to mix and spread cement. Alfie said, 'These are the bricks. I'm going to build with them. All round the edge. It's finished.' Den building; groups frequently initiate constructing enclosures with roofs.

Literacy	Physical development	Knowledge and understanding of the world	Creative development	Equipment
Songs and singing filtering through into all aspects. Children are singing on the spinning board, climbing frames and along the pathways. They could distinguish between a number and a letter. Manjeet found lots of letters 'M'.	• Gaining control over the body • Imitating, mirroring, moving and imaging • Are excited by their own increasing mobility, setting their own challenges • Using tools and materials for particular purposes • Exploring malleable materials by patting, stroking, poking, squeezing, pinching and twisting them • Responding to rhythm, music and story by means of gesture and movement	• Developing competence and creativity • Are curious and interested in making things happen • Are interested in others and their families • Realising that tools can be used for a purpose • Expressing feelings about a significant personal event • Beginning to try out a range of tools and techniques safely	• Exploring and discovering • Exploring and sharing stories, songs, rhymes and games • Creating and experimenting with blocks colour and marks • Showing an interest in the way musical instruments sound • Responding to sound with body movement • Beginning to describe the texture of things • Beginning to differentiate colours • Working creatively on a large and small scale	Slides: The children are exploring friction. They have noticed that they travel at different speeds depending on what clothes they are wearing and how they lifted their legs. Hills: The children are enjoying rolling down hills. Tom copied the more confident children.
Role play	Digging	Natural world	Music/sound	Climbing/sensory
Children from all three classes participating in 'waiting for the bus/train' (trolley) and paying for the ticket	We emphasised the appropriate use of different tools	A group of children were collecting stones and placing them on the floor of the tree house. One child said, 'Put the eggs in the tree house.'	Rhythmic play and sequential visual clues coming to the fore – e.g. marching, banging drums and placing stepping stones. Children following each other in a line. Sequence of activity has a beginning and an end.	Rosie and Alice instigate a turn-taking game on the spinning board. They were singing 'Sandy Girl' then choosing the next one to have a go.

Table 5.4 Practical solutions to common problems

Common dilemma	Practical solutions
Safety/ rules and boundaries	• Confidence-building amongst the team • Ensure all risk assessments are in place and are revisited • Visit other settings/schools where staff are confident with outdoor safety • Ensure everyone knows the safety policies and procedures • Involve the children in discussions about playing safely • Invite the children to decide on their rules for outdoor play
Storage and time	• Plan to acquire appropriate storage over time; set achievable goals • Look at good examples in other settings/schools • Involve the children in transporting resources • Build up the availability of resources as everyone becomes more confident • Identify provision that can remain in site, particularly natural materials/the garden – and add to the vegetation
Access	• If you are in a school, negotiate for the classroom with the best access to the outdoors
The weather	• Weather boxes • The weather is a great learning resource which supports the Foundation Stage and the Key Stage One curriculum
Attitudes	• Find a like-minded colleague! • Documentation of the children's play and learning and extends our confidence to demonstrate to the children, their families and colleagues the value of the children's achievements • Whole-team involvement in developing policy and procedures • Shared learning and understanding • Information booklets to support policy

Be inspired and motivated to ensure the outdoor environment is embedded in the Early Years curriculum

Provision for early childhood education has embraced the potential of the outdoor environment for many years. I am often inspired by the work of the pioneers of nursery education. The first open air nurseries were opened in the 1920s by Margaret McMillan, who was a strong advocate for the benefits of outdoor play. She provides advice that remains current. Here she explains the benefits of providing a kitchen garden and apparatus in the garden.

Kitchen Garden. Here vegetables for the table should be grown. Potatoes, cabbages, parsnips, beetroot, parsley, onions, radishes, carrots, rhubarb and marrows. They are needed as part of the children's food, and nothing trains the mind and fills it with wholesome memories better than the carrying out of all this work in their sight, and with their help. Even the toddlers want to help. They follow our gardener, Mrs Hambleden, down the paths, and into the drills; and very early and without formal teaching of any kind they learn to know the names of things. 'Where is the beetroot?' visitors say, 'Where are the parsnips?' and the three-year-olds walk to the right bed or point to the right place.

Apparatus in the garden. This is always very simple, and is often improvised. A student leans a plank for instance against a box or seat, and up this plank our little ones go. At first holding a hand on each side, then letting go one hand, and at last walking up and down alone, always, it is true, watched and prevented, but allowed to go alone!

(McMillan, 1919)

The adult's role in supporting children's development and learning outside goes far beyond supervision. We do need to ensure there is adequate cover, but it is paramount that we show the children we are just as interested in their outdoor learning as we are in their indoor learning.

Pointers for the outdoor learning environment

In the Early Years, the outdoor learning environment:

- enhances and extends children's development and learning;
- should include a range of areas of provision;
- requires careful observation and planning; and
- should be embedded in every area of the curriculum.

References

Athey, C. (1990) *Extending Thought in Young Children: A Parent–Teacher Partnership.* London: Paul Chapman.

Barrs, M., & Ellis, S. (1998) *The Core Booklist.* London: Centre for Language in Primary Education.

Bilton, H. (2002) *Outdoor Play in the Early Years: Management and Innovation,* 2nd ed. London: David Fulton.

Bilton, H. (2010) *Outdoor Play in the Early Years: Management and Innovation,* 3rd ed. London: David Fulton.

Bradford Education (2000) *'Can I Play Out?' Outdoor Play in the Early Years.* Bradford: Bradford Education.

Callaway, G. (2005) *The Early Years Curriculum: A View from Outdoors.* London: David Fulton.

Carle, E. (2002) *The Very Hungry Caterpillar*. London: Puffin Books.

Edgington, M. (2004) The outdoors curriculum. *Nursery World*, 2 September 2004.

Garrick, R. (2004) *Playing Outdoors in the Early Years*. London: Continuum.

Jenkinson, S. (2001) *The Genius of Play: Celebrating the Spirit of Childhood*. Stroud, Gloucestershire: Hawthorn Press.

Laevers, F. (1994) *The Innovative Project: Experiential Education 1976–1995*. Leuven, Belgium: Research Centre for Early Childhood and Primary Education, Katholieke Universiteit Leuven.

Nutbrown, C. (1996) *Children's Rights and Early Education: Respectable Educators – Capable Learners*. London: Paul Chapman.

Qualifications and Curriculum Authority (QCA) (2000) *Curriculum Guidance for the Foundation Stage*. London: DfES.

Qualifications and Curriculum Authority (QCA) (2005) *Continuing the learning journey*. Norwich: QCA.

Ryder Richardson, G. (2006) *Creating a Space to Grow: Developing Your Outdoor Learning Environment*. London: David Fulton.

Vygotsky, L. S. (1978) *Mind in Society: The Development of Higher Psychological Processes*. Cambridge, MA: Harvard University Press.

Play and language

CHAPTER 6

'Listen to my idea!'

COMMUNICATION AND LANGUAGE
IN THE EARLY YEARS

Nancy Stewart

Some very young children swim confidently in the sea of language around them. They can listen attentively to a story, understand a question posed to them and – perhaps even more importantly – pose their own question clearly in their minds. They verbally negotiate different points of view in play, and explain their own ideas in some detail. Their skilful use of language will underpin their learning across all areas of an Early Years curriculum. For Early Years educators, supporting all children to develop such rich communication and language should be high priority.

Crucial elements of language development have already taken place by the time a child enters a nursery or school. We are born to be communicators, with the earliest roots of language laid down even before birth and then fostered within early interactions with caring and attentive people. A newborn baby recognises the voices of its parents following months of hearing the muffled sounds of speech in the womb, and in the early days of life prefers listening to the human voice over all other sounds and already recognises the rhythms, tunes and vowel sounds of its native tongue compared to other languages. Babies also instinctively seek out eye contact and gaze at faces with rapt attention. These inborn patterns of behaviour support rapid connections with the people who provide the care and attention a baby needs, and lead to a phenomenal amount of learning about communication and language during the Early Years of life.

But while babies are primed to develop language, not all children receive the opportunities in rich communication environments that enable them to learn crucial skills. A famous study of language use in the home (Hart & Risley 1995) estimated that by the age of three children in language-rich families had heard over three times as many words as in low-talk families, as well as eight times as many encouraging comments from their parents. Unsurprisingly, this gap in language experience showed up in children's vocabulary and amount of talk by the age of three. Recent UK research (DfE 2011) confirms not only the differences in children's early communication and language experiences, but also the impact on their later learning. The quality of a child's communication environment – over and above the socio-economic factors which are associated with levels of language development – was found to predict a child's expressive vocabulary at age two. And children's language development at age two was seen to be very strongly associated with their success on entering primary school.

Many learning opportunities involve talk, so it's easy to see why being able to communicate effectively with words underpins success at school. The important area of literacy clearly rests on a base of spoken language, since reading and writing are essentially the recording and retrieval of language into and from a printed format. If children have a limited vocabulary or difficulty in comprehending complex sentences that are said to them, they will struggle to obtain meaning from what they read. If they cannot use talk to put ideas into words, to recall an event, tell a story, or explain their thinking, then their skills as writers will be similarly limited.

The importance of early communication and language, however, goes far beyond its link to literacy. Language supports children's social development, and interacting with others is a central plank of how we learn. Children need to be able to talk about their feelings, ideas, intentions, and strategies in order to make friends and to be confident contributors in a social scene. Emotional regulation is also enhanced when feelings are put into words. Children whose language is well-developed as toddlers, for example, are better able to cope with feelings of frustration and anger at the age of four (Roben, Cole & Armstrong 2012). Across all areas of learning, children benefit from a richly-developed vocabulary, such as using mathematical language confidently. They also need to draw on the particular role of language in enabling us to be good thinkers – to hold abstract ideas in our minds, to pin down a concept, to follow a logical train of thought, and to consider how to solve problems in all areas of learning.

From communicating to using language

We communicate in many different ways, and only some of these involve language. Facial expressions, gestures, sounds, signs, actions, drawing, and music can all send a message about feelings, intentions and ideas. The crucial point about communication is that it involves transmitting something from one mind to another, so it always requires a receiver of the message who interprets what has been expressed to make a meaning in his or her own mind.

Language is a uniquely human, sophisticated, symbolic way of communicating. It rests first of all on understanding that we can have an exchange with others, so the more experience children have of the many forms of communication the more readily they will add language to their repertoire. When babies and young children recognise that someone is tuning into and responding to the signals they send, it stimulates renewed interest and enthusiasm for communicating. There is no point in sending out a message if no one is listening. This is why the early 'chat' with

Figure 6.1 *Early pre-verbal 'conversation'*

babies, copying each other's sounds and facial expressions in a back-and-forth 'conversation', is such an important precursor to developing language. The baby may not understand what you are saying – though there is evidence that by six to nine months babies are already building understanding of words (Bergelson & Swingley 2011) – but they will be picking up the rhythms of social turn-taking in a call-and-response fashion (see Figure 6.1).

Babies and young children also need to hear plentiful models of talk. As you chat about what you are doing, simply narrating everyday activities, the child not only has plentiful opportunity to hear the particular sounds used in the language but also picks up the rhythms and intonations of phrases and the structures of different types of sentences. As well as living in a sea of language about what is happening in the here and now, songs, the lilting repetition of nursery rhymes, and the language of books also provide strong language models that support children to tune into language.

It is important that this rich language experience is available to children early in life. The developing brain is particularly sensitive to language sounds in the first years of life, and, while we are born able to become fluent speakers in any language, we gradually lose our early sensitivity – so that if we learn a new language later in life we would never speak like a native. If you've ever listened to a speaker in another language and tried to work out how many separate words were spoken, or tried to repeat accurately what was said, you will appreciate the complexity of the job facing young language learners.

Spoken language enters our ears as a steady stream of sound rather than neatly broken into words, and the child has to learn to pick out the syllables from the rhythm, and to notice individual sounds and combinations of sounds which signal where syllables and words start and stop. Since everyone's voices are different, the ways they say the same word are not exactly the same. In order to tune into language and notice patterns in the sounds, the listening baby's brain needs to 'chunk' similar sounds and begin to consider a particular range of sounds to be the same. At the same time, the brain gradually loses the ability to discriminate other sounds not used in the language. This process needs a lot of examples to work from, and the more opportunity to hear language used, the better phonological awareness develops.

Children also need to develop the ability to produce speech sounds, and to use the voice with controlled pitch and volume. This complicated skill also requires practice, and babbling babies and young children playing with voice sounds are developing control over the production of air to generate sound, which is then shaped by all the muscles of the tongue, mouth, lips. Very young children may be understood most of the time by people who know them well, but often sound unintelligible to others. By the time they are three years old, most children will be generally understood by unfamiliar people, but typically some of the more difficult speech sounds and blends of consonants are not fully mastered until a child is five or six years old. It is important not to confuse the clarity of speech with a child's language development – the mechanics of the sound production are less important than the ability to use language well, and children can be made self-conscious and become reluctant to speak if adults focus on the sounds instead of what children are saying to us.

Then, with everything in place – with a child enjoying warm and responsive interactions with others, listening to and perceiving the sounds of language around them, and purposefully producing voice sounds – the child moves into using language. This enormous feat requires the mental ability to symbolise; to understand that a word which is no more than a random set of sounds, totally unconnected from what it refers to, can stand for an object ('cat'), an action ('run'), or an abstract idea ('more').

It takes two

This leap into language depends on another mental ability which develops in the first years of life. We can only understand words once we begin to recognise that someone else is using the language code to mean particular things, so we will be able to understand each other. We have to move beyond our own awareness to understand something about the mind of other people. Knowing that other people have a different mind and know and think differently from ourselves is known as theory of mind, and some aspects are not likely to be in place until a child is four years or more. But the early understanding of the point of view of others is crucial to developing language.

At first, babies can pay attention to only one stimulus at a time – perhaps to an object, or to the intriguing face of someone who is making interesting noises and expressions. Once children begin to be aware of the awareness of the other person, they can engage in episodes of joint attention. At this stage a baby or toddler will look where someone has pointed, and the adult can supply the word for the object that is pointed out. The next stage is where the child takes charge by using eye gaze and then finger pointing to direct the attention of the adult, checking back to see whether they are looking. It's almost as if the child is saying, 'And what is that? Tell me about it!' Studies consistently find that children who spend more time in episodes of joint attention in the first and second years of life develop larger vocabularies, and are more successful in their later learning. So we come back again to the importance for language learning of the adult who interacts with the child, stimulating his or her attention, providing the words, and responding readily to the child's signals.

Children are learners with inborn developmental patterns which spur them onward. But in all areas of development and learning the dimension that an adult brings to a child's experience can either enhance or limit how well the child progresses. The influence of another person is never stronger than that seen in the quality of the adult's behaviour as a communication partner. Language develops in the context of interaction, so the adult's skill in using strategies which support talking together is crucial. Just as it's not possible to learn how to play the piano just by listening to great pianists, learning to use language well is not just about listening to others – you have to have a go for yourself. Sadly, too often talk in Early Years settings and schools is centred around the adult who does most of the talking and steers the discussion, with the child primarily cast as the listener or expected to supply the words the adult is looking for. In this situation, children are missing out on practice at finding the words to express their own ideas and thoughts. Adults need to be expert listeners in order to support children to become effective speakers. There are also particular strategies that skilful adults can employ to offer appropriate scaffolding of children's early use of language, to model and support the next stage.

When we seek to understand and support children's developing language there is a tendency to focus our attention on the expressive language a child uses. But what a child says is actually the end result of groundwork in other areas, without which effective language use will be limited. Adults can be a positive influence in each of these aspects, so understanding the foundations of language and providing the conditions for each element to develop is necessary in order to support all children as well as to give target support to children who are having difficulty.

Listening and attention

In order to take part in communicative exchanges and to learn about the sounds and words of language, children need to focus their attention and listen. During the first years of life children develop the ability to purposefully focus their attention rather than being distracted by any new stimulus, until eventually children can listen effectively even while they are occupied with something else – for example, they can continue building a model while being involved in a conversation. Until that point, there are many ways to support children to focus their attention in order to listen.

To support children's listening and attention, set the scene by reducing unnecessary visual and sound distractions. To create a communication-friendly environment, practitioners use calm colours, avoid over-exuberant displays, turn off background music or TV, and ensure there are quiet spaces available for talk.

Skilful adults also interact in ways which support listening and attention. First of all, establishing contact for communication is key. Adults need to be face-to-face with the child, on the child's level. From about six months onward, children pay close attention to reading adults' lips to help them focus on the specific sounds being made. At all ages it is easier to maintain focus on communicating with someone who is facing you rather than someone who towers over you or turns away, talking at you while doing something else. For children who are not able to focus their attention easily, using the child's name to gain their attention before speaking to them prepares them to listen. Using a lively voice, gesture and facial expression also supports children to listen, which is why adults instinctively use a higher-pitched, lilting voice when speaking to babies and small children. In a group situation it is helpful to supplement calls to attention with sound signals such as a bell, and visual signals and clues.

Activities can be arranged to support listening and attention. Working one-to-one or in small groups supports listening far more than large group sessions. High-interest activities set the scene and enable children to focus. Specific activities give practice in listening and attention, such as games that include listening and waiting for a signal, like peek-a-boo, Jack-in-the-box, ready-steady-go, Simon says, and activities that involve careful listening such as a listening walk, passing sounds around the circle, copy my sound, listening to voices on tape.

Children learn through imitating, so it is important for adults to model being a good listener. Adults can also explicitly draw attention to good listening, including looking and thinking about what they hear. Children can be encouraged to listen to each other, for example by reminding them to look at the speaker: 'Let's all let Cara see our eyes, so she knows that we're listening.'

Understanding

Children's comprehension of spoken language is often given little direct attention, perhaps because knowing exactly what a child understands isn't easy. A child's difficulty with understanding language can easily be masked in the early stages, since it is possible to rely on other forms of communication. Children can gather quite a bit from the context, from gestures, from facial expressions and from what they see others doing, even if they don't understand the words or can't follow the whole sentence. Any concerns about a child's understanding can be checked out by asking them to follow instructions at an appropriate level (for example, without giving clues through gestures, say 'Where's the ball?' to a two-year-old when looking at a picture of a few objects; or 'Get some scissors and then come to the blue table' to a four-year-old). Once we are aware of a child's level of comprehension, we can pitch our language at the right level for the child so they aren't left behind in discussion and can take part effectively.

Children's receptive vocabulary – the set of words which they understand – develops before they begin to use the words to talk. At this early stage, language becomes an exceptional means to unlock the door to more powerful thinking. Imagine you are a baby using your senses to explore a straw hat. You feel its rough texture, you hear the scratchy sound it makes when you bend it, you see its golden colour and perhaps even taste it. You find it has similarities to the wicker ball in your treasure basket. But the adult tuning into your exploration in an episode of joint attention highlights the word 'hat', using it several times in a clear way. So what is 'hat' – rough, scratchy, golden? Later you encounter a red, woolly object that the adult also labels 'hat', but it has no sensory information in common with the object already associated with 'hat'. Then the connection dawns on you, and you recognise that what they have in common is their function, the fact that they both go on your head. You have been lifted out of the here and now of sensory knowledge, and given a tool to grasp an abstract idea. You can also begin to play with this idea in imaginative ways, since it is not tied to the physical world. You can now put a cup on your head and say 'hat!' You are on your way to being an abstract, flexible, creative thinker.

Words help children to understand categories, and to think carefully about what does and does not define belonging. Why is every man not called 'Daddy'? Why is the four-legged furry creature with a tail and a bark not called 'cat'? Descriptive words such as 'big', 'heavy', and 'fast' sharpen children's awareness of comparing different features, while using richer tier-two words – such as 'galloped', 'thundered', 'scampered', 'darted', 'zipped', or 'sprinted' – will help children think of running with greater discrimination. Words for emotions help children to identify and begin to understand the waves of feeling 'angry', 'sad', 'excited', 'worried', and so on.

Language comprehension also requires the ability to make sense of the way words are put together in phrases and sentences. The order of words makes a difference to the meaning, so 'Tommy chased Becky' is the opposite of 'Becky chased Tommy'. Understanding the way more complex sentences are built to combine ideas, using structures involving 'if', 'and', 'but', 'then', 'because', is essential to follow a train of thought.

Hearing a rich vocabulary and different kinds of talk – everyday chat, discussion and negotiation, poems and rhymes, narrative and nonfiction texts – is crucial for children to continue to develop their understanding of words and sentences, which is a precursor to being able to use these themselves.

An effective technique to support children's understanding is to simply describe what babies and children are showing interest in and what they are doing in their activities, which helps them to link objects and actions to words. In making this running commentary, it is important to follow the child's lead and to use language on the right level for the child. In general, a child will be able to grasp the meaning of sentences that are one word longer than those the child uses him or herself. So pre-verbal children need to have one word highlighted among the more general commentary provided, by repeating and emphasising the single word to help it to stand out for the child. A child who uses single words is ready to understand two-word phrases emphasised by your intonation and stress. Again, using a lively voice and supporting what is said with visual clues – gestures, objects, pictures, or signs – supports comprehension.

It takes several seconds for children to mentally process what they hear and make sense of what you might mean, so don't rush on too quickly. Leave pauses, and use repetition of key words and phrases to give the child time to process the language.

The meaning of new words becomes clear to children when the word occurs repeatedly, in different contexts, so a focus on new and interesting words will help adults to look for chances to use it. For example, a child may choose a 'shiny' star to glue on his collage, and later there may be opportunities to describe the doll's shiny eyes, or how the bucket looks shiny when it is wet. Providing real objects and props for children to handle, which reflect what they hear about in stories and for them to use to re-enact stories, will also help make the link between a new word and its meaning.

Expressive communication

We come now to considering the child as message-giver, rather than message-receiver. It's important to understand this area of communication and language broadly covers all aspects of a child's expressive communication, and not just to think about 'speech' which refers to the production of sounds, or even to talk alone. Some children with particular needs may never speak, but can learn to express themselves effectively using signing or other alternative or augmented methods.

Children can be effective communicators from the beginning, and can use sounds and gestures to communicate their needs, feelings, and interests. A baby several months old who lifts his arms when he sees a parent is saying, 'I want to be picked up,' and a baby who points is saying, 'Look at that' or perhaps 'I want that'. It's up to the responsive adult to do the required work to meet the communicating child in the middle and work out the message.

Toddlers rapidly begin to use single words, and by about age two begin to put words together into two-word sentences. Children use the rules of the language they have discovered: for example, they use word order correctly so they say 'dog get ball', not 'ball get dog'. They also show that they are forming general rules about language, and apply them by analogy to other words – so children who say 'sheeps' or 'goed' are showing good logic about how the language works. When a child makes mistakes in language usage, rather than correct it directly adults can acknowledge what the child says, but then use the correct form so the child notices the difference: 'Yes, there are two sheep,' or 'Oh, they went, did they?'

One of the ways language becomes a powerful tool for children is through talking aloud to themselves. This private speech, where they narrate their own activities, is an important way that children begin to become aware of their own thoughts and regulate their own behaviour. Beyond all the practical uses of language, such as asking for what they want, children can move into many more sophisticated purposes which support their thinking and learning. They ask questions to seek information or explanations, they recount an experience or create a narrative which helps them to make sense of their experiences, they use talk to pretend and so develop their imagination and flexible thinking, they describe plans and so become more purposeful in their intentions, they give explanations which help them to think things through. Children can begin to use emerging talk for such rich purposes when adults support them well by tuning into and responding to the child's communicative intentions.

A shorthand description of the conditions that support children's developing language use is: *Someone to talk to, and something to talk about.* The listener is someone who is interested, and also is skilful in supporting language growth. Having something to talk about requires a learning environment that stimulates a response through fascinating resources and involving experiences.

The physical space of the learning environment that supports children to talk will have features of good Early Years provision, such as open spaces that children can use flexibly, accessible resources that are clearly marked and can be combined in different ways, inviting book areas, role play areas, comfortable light, limited noise, and smaller intimate spaces. The outdoor environment should equally be organised to support communication – Early Years practitioners who improved their outdoor environments have sometimes been surprised to hear the rich and purposeful talk that bursts forth from some children who have communicated very little indoors.

The role of the adult as the communication partner, however, is both more subtle and more powerful than the environment. It can be relatively straightforward to plan and organise a physical environment. But how we communicate with others is a personal style that includes long-established habits. Developing skills of effective interaction may require critical awareness of how we respond to children and the degree of respect and real fascination we demonstrate for establishing a two-way communication. It may mean changing a view of the adult as the leader in children's learning to seeing the children as active thinkers who are engaged in their own learning and benefit from sharing the process with the adult as a partner.

Communication partner

Expert communication partners are aware that almost everything is a communication and language opportunity. Although there are times where a child's silent concentration should be valued and not interrupted by adult talk, the adult can still be taking note of the child's interest in order to talk about it after the moment of intense concentration has gone. Most often, a companionable interaction can be a language-learning experience and adults who keep that in mind will be strong supporters for children's developing talk.

Talking with children in ways which support their language development begins with being a good listener. This means tuning in to all the ways children communicate, and responding to the child's gestures and expressions as well as what they say. It requires making the effort to try to understand the child's intentions – ideas and feelings which are being expressed – rather than jumping to conclusions or steering the exchange to where the adult wants it to go. Ordinary conversation about what the child is interested in is the ideal ground for supportive language exchanges. When the adult follows the child's lead by talking together about the child's current activity or preoccupation, the child is motivated to try to put ideas into words.

When the adult offers a comment or question, it is essential to then give the child time to think rather than rapidly following up with a question or statement that cuts off the child's train of thought. It can take several seconds for the child to process what was said, consider their answer, form it mentally into words, and then give a verbal response. Maintaining an interested expression while waiting patiently will give the child encouragement to put their thoughts into words.

Closed questions with limited choice of response clearly mean the adult is leading, and offer children little room to express themselves. Even open questions, however, can put the adult in charge of the agenda. In a balanced conversation, nobody likes to feel they are responding to a barrage of questions. If you ask me 'What is that piece going to be?' when actually I'm interested just in the process of gluing pieces into the spaces on my page, I am not encouraged to engage with you. If instead of a question you make a comment, such as 'That piece looks a bit wrinkly,' I might respond 'It will fit here, though. I can press it flat in this space.' In general the 'five-finger' rule is a good guide: offer four comments (fingers) for every question (thumb).

Within the conversation, adults can offer children a bridge to the next level by expanding just beyond what the child currently does. This sort of language support is in line with Vygotsky's concept of the zone of proximal development. By acknowledging the child's comment and reusing it in an expanded form, the adult pitches a model at just the right level for the child to begin to assimilate it. Here are some examples of **expansions**:

Child: 'Big bus'
Adult: 'Yes, it is a big bus. It's a big red bus.'
Child: 'We go shops. Me and Grandma.'
Adult: 'Oh, you went to the shops with Grandma.'

Rather than directly drawing attention to language errors either in pronunciation or grammar, **recast** the child's comment in the correct form. This immediate contingent

Figure 6.2 *Sharing a book as a stimulus to adult–child talk and discussion*

model helps children to notice the error and make the correction without discouraging their efforts to talk. For example:

Child: 'Look at that heckilopter.'
Adult: 'The helicopter's blades are zooming around!'

The adult also has a role to play in encouraging children to talk for many different purposes – to recount, to explain, to negotiate, to tell stories, to wonder. As well as providing opportunities for each of these in the continuous provision and routines, specific language learning activities can be planned. Some activities have been found to be particularly effective in building children's expressive language, such as dialogic book talk where a book is used not for a literacy purpose but as a prompt for children to discuss their own thoughts and responses to the book (see Figure 6.2). Other approaches include talking-tables or conversation-stations, both planned opportunities for children to have one-to-one or one-to-two discussions about things that interest them.

Partnership with parents

However rich a communication environment a setting can provide, it is much more effective when it builds a joint approach with parents. Some settings share top tips for interaction, boxes of resources to encourage conversation at home ('chatter boxes'), or story sacks, and enjoy joint activities focussed on play and talk. The many ways of building parent partnerships can make an enormous difference to children's outcomes when focussed specifically on communication and language both at home and in settings.

Toddler talk

A day nursery linked to a children's centre established a baby–toddler environment, where the linked spaces provided more room and enabled continuity of key person, who remained with a child up to the age of three. The close relationships that developed enabled the key person to be sensitively aware of children's early communication.

One day the practitioners had brought into the setting a few coloured helium balloons for the children to play with. Luke, aged 17 months and just steady on his feet, was enjoying holding onto the ribbon of one of the balloons and shaking it vigorously up and down. Sharon, his key person, said, 'Shake, shake', and copied his action. Luke smiled broadly and shook even harder. Suddenly the ribbon slipped from his grasp, and the balloon floated rapidly to the ceiling. He looked at Sharon with an expression of surprise and alarm. She mirrored his look of surprise, and said, 'It's gone **up! Up!**', as she gestured upward with her arm. Luke reached upward toward the balloon, but the ribbon was beyond his reach. 'It's up high! Shall we get it?', Sharon asked. 'I'll reach **up**.' When she stood to reach it, Sharon saw that the end of the ribbon was just out of her reach. She stretched and said, as she looked at Luke, 'Oh, no, it's way **up high.** I'll have to jump.' She jumped and caught the ribbon, which she handed to Luke. He held it a moment and then let it go again, grinning and pointing up. 'Ah', said Sharon, acting surprised. 'It's gone **up!**' Luke started bending his legs and suddenly lifting his trunk – like a jump without his feet leaving the ground. 'Shall I jump?' asked Sharon. '**Jump!**' she said as she retrieved the balloon again. This sequence was repeated a few more times, and Luke began joining in with the word 'Jah!' and doing his version of a jump. Later Sharon noticed that as Luke played with a toy digger he paid close attention to how he could move the claw arm, and she commented on what he was doing while taking the opportunity to use key words in this new context: 'Oh, it goes **up**. And down. And **up**. And down.'

The setting planned time every day for nursery rhymes in key groups. Each key person had a bag containing finger puppets linked to familiar songs, and children were invited to choose the puppet for the song they wanted to sing. Staff were aware that the repetition helped the children to become familiar with language and to try out in song some phrases that they would not manage otherwise. Sharon decided to add 'The Grand Old Duke of York' to their familiar songs, and Luke took part eagerly in bobbing up and down. The setting didn't use taped versions of songs which could not allow any adjustment for the children's pace, so instead the staff always sang the songs, watching for the children's responses and encouraging them to join in where they could. Sharon took the opportunity to slow down and emphasise the words 'up' and 'down'.

The next week another child brought a balloon from their birthday to the nursery, and Sharon was delighted when Luke looked at her and said, 'Jah!' as he made his linked movement. 'Yes,' Sharon said, 'we **jumped** for the balloon!' And she joined in with Luke, jumping and saying, '**Jump, jump!**'

From moons to balloons

Nursery children had been singing 'Hey Diddle Diddle', and looking at the illustration of the rhyme in a big book. What follows is a discussion drawing on their experiences, theories and interests, where children listen to each other and put their own ideas into words. Their teacher was interested in the importance of dialogue among children, and developing her skills in supporting thinking conversations. She used strategies of open questioning and referring back to children's ideas, encouraging them to extend their thinking. It is notable that the children responded to each other without the adult mediating each contribution.

A discussion among nursery children aged three to four, following the singing of 'Hey Diddle Diddle'

Millie: I went in my caravan in night time once, and I looked up at the moon . . . it made my eyes swell.

Olivia: On Saturday I saw the moon. We were still at Grandma's house. It was round and none of it was half. (*comparing with the crescent illustration in the book*)

Tom: I didn't see the moon.

Adult: Can cows really jump over the moon? (*reflecting on the illustration*)

Jasmine: No, 'cos the moon's not real.

Fin: Cows can't fly. Cows haven't got wings so they can't fly. Birds have wings.

Charlie: One time Mummy and Daddy and Ned and me went in the car in night time from Nana's.

Adult: What is the moon? (*If not real, then what is it?*)

Louis: It's round, it's a circle.

Charlie: Sometimes it goes like that (*draws a crescent moon in the air*) with a pointy bit at the end.

Olivia: I think the moon might be round. I think it's made from golden.

Fin: The moon is right high up.

Adult: What is it made of? (*expand on theory of 'made from golden'*)

Millie: Gold!

Tom: Soft . . . soggy soft.

Ben: Hard, just hard.

Boo: I think it's made of water.

Charlie: Tiny water.

Ben: No! It's made of silver . . . silver yellow.

Tom: I haven't got a clue!

Adult: Why does it change shape? (*Refer back to circle/crescent*)

Charlie: I know 'cos every day sometimes it changes shape.

Louis: 'Cos it turns to a circle and it turns to a long shape.

Ben: When it's winter days it changes shape.

Tom: 'Cos it does . . . it's that much skinny.

Adult:	How did it get there? *(Offering a new question to consider)*
Ben:	It stays up there and it's till night time and in the morning time the clouds cover over it.
Charlie:	Sometimes I see the moon in the morning time.
Louis:	Me too!
Boo:	I got a caravan, and I got into bed and opened the curtains and I saw the moon and it was orange.
Jasmine:	I just saw the moon when it was light.
Boo:	I think a bird lifted it up.
Ben:	If the bird put it up there it would fall down! It stays up there and in the morning it disappears . . . 'cos maybe when it's autumn it disappears.
Louis:	You know, it comes up by the high hill, 'cos the sun comes up by the high hill, too.
Ben:	Space men can fly and buttlerflies. I know how we can get up . . . if Buzz Lightyear was near!
Louis:	I have a better idea, use a parachute with fire.
Ben:	No, 'cos a parachute goes down, down, not up and up!
Louis:	I know how we get there – a rocket!
Tom:	With a spoon and fork and a pumpkin, the pumpkin has to jump on to the spoon and fork and fly to the moon.
Charlie:	Wallis and Gromit went to the moon. They made a real big rocket . . .
Millie:	No! they made a big rocket and painted it orange and lived in it.
Charlie:	No! . . . I was saying . . .
Ben:	I know you need a rocket. You go to the airport to get a plane, but the plane doesn't go to the moon, it goes to a city. You have to go to the rocket landing place. I know – we could go up in the air if we made something.
Louis:	If we had metal we can make a rocket and I can drive a rocket, 'cos do you know, little boys can drive rockets.

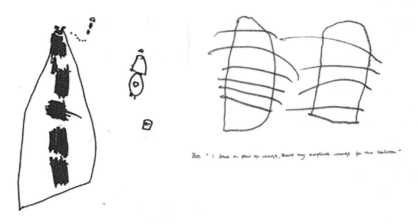

Figure 6.3 *Drawings of flying balloons: helping children to put their ideas into words*

In subsequent sessions the teacher continued to re-offer to the children strands of their previous conversations. She opened the next conversation with 'I've been thinking about flying. I wonder, what things can fly?' From there the discussions over a period of two weeks ranged through rockets, birds, wings, how to make something that would fly, and finally exploring the jet propulsion of a released balloon and whether they could find a way to make it fly straight. The children drew pictures of their ideas, which helped them to be clear about their thinking as they attempted to put their thoughts into words. The drawings were annotated with the children's comments so they could revisit these to support later discussions (see Figure 6.3).

Reviewing learning in a reception class

A reception class had an extended session of child-initiated activity each day, with open access to a richly resourced indoor and outdoor environment. As they were setting off, the children were asked to describe briefly what they were going to do, with many following up on the previous day's activities with other children. The teacher said to a few children, 'I would like you to review for us today.' One of these was Thomas, who was returning to his work on making a ship. The teacher circulated among the children, dipping in here and there to join in. With a group of girls who were building towers from cartons outside, she asked whether they would also like to review today and they said they would.

Thomas had a stick as a mast for his ship, which he wanted to tie to the sides of his ship. He had cut several lengths of string, but when he tried to tie them on he found they weren't long enough. The teacher asked him first to describe the problem.

'It's not long enough,' Thomas said. 'But I held it up and measured it.'

'Why do you think that might be?' asked the teacher. 'Why isn't it long enough now, when it was long enough when you held it up?'

Thomas considered carefully, and then said, 'Because the tying used up the string.' His teacher encouraged him to talk about how he might work out the right length to cut his strings, to include extra for tying.

An hour later the class gathered before lunchtime for review time. In twos and threes children stood up to demonstrate and talk about what they had been doing. When it was Thomas's turn he first showed his ship with a brief description. The teacher then asked the children, 'Is there anything you want to ask Thomas about his ship?' The children were used to asking questions about the process, since this had been consistently modelled by the teacher. They asked Thomas: 'Did you have any problems when you were making it?', 'Why did you decide to use that wood?', 'Are you going to change anything on your boat?', and Thomas replied appropriately to each of their queries.

Pointers for communication and language in the Early Years

Babies and children are born to communicate and develop language, but they need opportunities in communication-rich environments in order to learn crucial skills. Early Years practitioners can provide sensitive and skilful support through interactions and environments which enable children's communication and language abilities to flourish.

Young communicators, speakers and listeners need:

- warm, reciprocal interactions with caring and attentive people;
- opportunities to communicate through expression and gesture as well as with the voice;
- models of language, including chatting about everyday activities, songs, nursery rhymes, and books;
- an environment which supports listening and attention in calm, quiet spaces;
- adults who support understanding by using language at the right level, along with gesture, lively voice, repetition, and visual clues;
- something to talk about – stimulating resources and experiences which invite engaging communication;
- someone to talk to – a listener who is interested and takes time to discover what the child wants to express; and
- support for moving their language onward, through strategies to sharpen and expand language structures and vocabulary.

References

Bergelson, E. and Swingley, D. (2011) 'At 6–9 months, human infants know the meanings of many common nouns.' *Proceedings of the National Academy of Sciences (2012) 109 (9)*, 3253–3258. Doi: 10.1073/pnas.1113380109. Available at http://www.pnas.org/content/early/2012/02/07/1113380109.abstract

DfE (2011) *Investigating the Role of Language in Children's Early Educational Outcomes.* www.education.gov.uk/publications/eOrderingDownload/DFE-RR134.pdf

Hart, B. and Risley, T.R. (1995). *Meaningful Differences in the Everyday Experience of Young American Children.* Baltimore: Paul H. Brookes Publishing Co.

Roben, C., Cole, P.M., and Armstrong, L.M. (2012) 'Longitudinal Relations among Language Skills, Anger Expression, and Regulatory Strategies in Early Childhood', *Child Development* (2013) 84 (3), 891–905.

Further reading

Bond, M. and Wasik, B (2009) 'Conversation Stations: Promoting Language Development in Young Children.' *Early Childhood Education Journal*, 36 (6), 467–473.

Dockrell, J.E., Bakopoulou, I., Law, J., Spencer, S. and Lindsay, G. (2012) *Developing a Communication Supporting Classrooms Observation Tool*. Department for Education Research Report DFE-RR247-BCRP8.

Dockrell, J.E., Bakopoulou, I., Law, J., Spencer, S. and Lindsay, G. (2012) *Guidance On Completing Communication Supporting Classrooms Observation Tool*. Available at http://www2.warwick.ac.uk/fac/soc/cedar/better/cscobsvtl/guidance.pdf

Wasik, B. and Bond, M. (2001) 'Beyond the Pages of a Book: Interactive Book Reading and Language Development in Preschool Classrooms.' *Journal of Educational Psychology* 93 (2), 243–250.

The Every Child a Talker materials (*Guidance for Consultants and Lead Practitioners*) can be found at http://www.foundationyears.org.uk/category/library/national-strategies-resources/page/3/

CHAPTER 7

'It is only a story, isn't it?'

INTERACTIVE STORY-MAKING IN THE
EARLY YEARS CLASSROOM

Lesley Hendy

Children are born as storytellers. We have an innate need to tell, act out and listen to stories in order to shape our lives and give them meaning. As Bettleheim (1991) reminds us, 'Today, as in times past, the most important and also the most difficult task in raising a child is helping him to find a meaning in life.' Children's story-making is often hurriedly dismissed as either being appealing but rather shallow or lacking in coherent construction and limited in meaning. But as Engel (1999, p. 3) suggests, 'Children's stories can be vital to us as parents, teachers and researchers because they give us insight into how children of different ages experience the world, and how a specific child thinks and feels.'

One of the initial activities that can be observed in the behaviour of early childhood is the ability to play in the 'as if'. When you ask a group of adults what games they played as children, they often reply, 'mummies and daddies', 'doctors and nurses', 'cowboys and Indians', 'shops', 'hairdressers' and so on. All these games require children to substitute the real for the fictional; the play is about working 'as if' you were someone else, somewhere else, doing something else. This ability to use 'pretend play' begins before nursery age and often continues into puberty and sometimes beyond.

Children actively engage in story-making from as early as 12 months old. They are able to use 'pretend' play to act out their stories either by themselves or with others. Small children at play will often speak their thoughts aloud and provide actions to support them. As their lives change, the stories of their lives change accordingly. Many parents and teachers have experienced the 'make-believe' tea party or the imaginary friends.

It could be said that the beginnings of drama can be found in these early types of story-making activities. These stories are 'played out', and the 'scripts' children use come from their experiences. Drama as used in early education, however, concerns the making of meaning rather than the making of plays. Young children are not creating 'roles' in the theatrical sense but enter these 'pretend' situations as themselves. As Hendy and Toon (2001, p. 22) state, '"Pretend" play could be described as children engaging with a series of different behaviours and events. It is about trying out ideas, motivations and reactions to events in make-believe situations.' Pretend play, in this regard, has a very important role in a child's development. The introduction of the National Curriculum sadly brought about a decline in 'pretend' play and especially the role play area as an integral part of the curriculum. It is hoped that the establishment of the Foundation Stage will reverse this trend.

The phrase 'role play' is a problematic term. It is often used to describe what children are doing in 'pretend play'. There are inconsistencies and individualised understandings of the term 'role play' that make it complicated. In the theatrical sense the actor who is in 'role' has to take on board all of the characteristics of the character they are playing. They need to know about a character's past history, emotions and relationships with others. When young children engage in 'role play' they play as 'themselves' being a doctor, nurse, shopkeeper, etc. They take on the generic nature of a 'role' as they are not able at this stage to play a fully rounded character. I prefer to describe young children who are engaged in 'fantasy play' as using their 'pretend self'. We are not asking them to 'act'.

As schooling progresses, personal response through play and pretend-play is often regarded as unreliable and self-indulgent. By adulthood the wonderful spontaneity and creativity found in small children has been replaced by feelings of inadequacy and social foolishness. Mention the word 'drama' to gatherings of trainees or practising teachers and a perceptible apprehension travels through the group. 'I hope she isn't going to make us get up and do something' or 'I'm not making a fool of myself' are common comments often heard at the beginning of drama courses. For many, the memory of reading Shakespeare around the class or participation in performance requiring the learning and delivering of lines has caused their adult misgivings.

In the last ten years or so, business and industry have rediscovered the use of role play as an important constituent of management training. There are now few courses in which there is not an element of role play used for team-building or the exploration of difficulties in groups, or as a means of engaging in problem-solving and decision-making. These are precisely the things that the good Early Years specialist wants to encourage in her children's learning and development.

In this chapter, I shall outline some ways in which drama in the Early Years can be used as an effective learning medium, from adult intervention of play in the 'home/ role play corner' to actively making stories with children. I shall also discuss the use of drama strategies as a way of providing time for reflection and widening experience within story-making. In doing so I hope to ease anxieties about drama and provide Early Years educators with a strong rationale for including drama as a teaching tool within the planning of the curriculum.

Why drama is important in the Early Years

As an integral part of the natural development of children's play, pretend-play offers us a ready-made medium in which we can engage with our children. Through the 'as if' (i.e., the ability to function in an imaginary environment), children are given a different viewing point from which to consider, discover and make meaning of the world.

However, 'pretend-play' as a feature of child play needs careful examination. We need to be aware that small children function in the 'as if' in two distinct ways. The first is *socio-dramatic play* in which they act out 'scripts' from their real lives and the second is *thematic-fantasy play* where they create story from their imagination. It is important we provide opportunities for both, as each requires a different mode of thought.

It was Bruner (1986) who first defined these two ways of thinking. His 'paradigmatic' mode, which he described as being involved with logic, sequencing and the ability to be analytical, can be detected in the socio-dramatic play of 'homes', 'hospitals', 'offices', etc. Bruner's 'narrative thinking, on the other hand, can be found in the creativity and construction of 'make-believe' events found in thematic-dramatic play.

The inclusion of dramatic activity in Speaking, Listening and Learning at Key Stages One and Two (Core Learning in Literacy) would appear to be for the encouragement of purposeful language. Some significant research has shown the importance of role play in the development of early language (Sylva, Bruner, and Genova, 1976; Hutt, 1989; Kitson, 1994) and an OFSTED report *First Class* (1994, p. 8) indicated that where 'drama and role play were used effectively' there appeared to be 'better overall standards in literacy'.

In spite of this, the use of drama should not be seen as exclusive to the development of language. The socio-dramatic aspects of 'pretend' play should be extended across the curriculum and used in any circumstances that require children to describe and communicate their findings and observations. All aspects of the curriculum can be enhanced when children are given a fictional 'as if' context in which to discuss and communicate what they know. They will need to use their logical and analytical abilities in 'as if' contexts that require natural laws to apply. The 'narrative' skills provided by thematic-dramatic play will develop creative thinking and strengthen work in the other arts.

Drama work, as well as giving opportunities to explore the curriculum in different ways, can also provide the teacher with the opportunity for group activity that involves social interaction and the exchange of ideas. Through such activity the core skills as identified in the Foundation Stage literature can be addressed. Children pose and solve problems, reason, make decisions, use numeracy, engage in communication, extend their personal, social, and emotional skills, and use their knowledge and understanding of the world. There are also opportunities to develop creativity and physical ability.

By bringing into the classroom the dimension of action, drama enhances learning through the use of PEOPLE–SPACE–TIME. Through the creation of a fictional world, children are given the opportunity of being who they like, where they like, and when they like. For example, they could enter a fictional world, as themselves, trying to find solutions to such matters as how to clean up their village as part of a project on the environment. They might be mice trying to reach the moon in order to see whether it is really made of cheese as part of a topic on the sun and moon. They could be a group of servants worried about the disappearance of Snow White or, alternatively, farmers trying to work out how you can remove milk from a broken down milk tanker. The use of fictional contexts puts children in control, casting them in the role of 'experts'. By making use of their existing language, experience, motivations, and interests, the teacher can intervene in the play to bring new shape and fresh ways of looking at things. These opportunities provide the teacher with a wide range of potential contexts otherwise unavailable in the normal classroom situation.

The overall purpose of drama as a way of learning should be to effect change, which may occur in a number of ways. For example, it may, bring about:

- a change in the level of knowledge and understanding;
- a change in ways of thinking;
- a change in attitude;
- a change in the expectation of what pretend-play can offer;
- a change in existing language; and
- a change in awareness and the needs of others.

There may also be a change in the relationship that exists between language use and the control of knowledge. By providing opportunities for children to set the agenda and to learn about things that interest them the teacher has access to a wider curriculum. This can be achieved even within the constraints of existing curriculum requirements.

The general characteristics of drama as a learning medium can be described as:

- a method of teaching that helps present information and ideas within a different form of communication (sometimes children are the experts, the teacher the one who needs to be taught);
- a means of giving children some control over their learning, thereby giving them greater access to knowledge and ideas (children are given opportunities to choose the problems that have to be solved and the decisions to be made);
- a method of giving children a fictional situation in which they can respond outside the structure of the ordinary classroom (the shy child is given a context in which to act as someone else);
- an alternative means of describing and communicating which allows pupils to bring their own knowledge about the world into the classroom (children with specialised knowledge such as fishing or horse-riding are able to make a fuller contribution);
- a method of learning that allows pupils and teachers to function as equals; and
- a method of providing a 'need to know' which can heighten the learning that has taken place or will take place back in the classroom (children often want to research into something that has arisen within a story).

If drama activity is about anything, it is about the learning and turning-points in life. Such moments can cause the participants to reflect on their actions and to re-think some of their ideas from within a safe environment. To sustain the action the players have to use both their factual and subjective knowledge. They will also be introduced to new material, both factual and objective, that they can use to help them solve problems and take decisions. This is where the teacher plays such a crucial role. As Readman and Lamont (1994, p. 16) reflect:

> It is the responsibility of the teacher to:
>
> - resist any assumptions about the kind of role(s) children might adopt;
> - select content areas which reflect genuine cultural diversity;
> - enable children to adopt roles which challenge any stereotypes;
> - offer children opportunities to work collaboratively.

Out of the home corner

In the Early Years classroom the most obvious place for a teacher to introduce new ways of using the 'as if' is in the home/role play corner. Home/role play corners in the classroom are usually the province of children only and sometimes it is important to allow the children to play alone, but there are other times when an adult could enter the fantasy situation and play alongside them.

Knowing when and how to intervene constructively, without the children feeling the teacher is intruding, takes sensitivity and watchfulness. Initially, just passing by and engaging in short conversations in role will help build trust. On a recent visit to an infant classroom in which the teacher had set up a seaside cafe in her home corner, I was encouraged to buy chips and join a complaint about the lack of salt and vinegar!

When you gauge that the children are ready to accept you, an adult, into their 'make-believe' world, more time can be spent with them in their home/role play corners. By dropping the word 'home' and renaming it the 'role play' area, many more possibilities become available. Role play corners should be seen by the children as more than just places for dressing up and pushing the doll's pram; a home corner can confine the activities to socio-dramatic play only. By providing different types of environment, the children are given scope to engage in both socio-dramatic and thematic-dramatic play.

The creation of a role play area could involve the class making things to go in it and might require knowledge of number and shape, making things, or the use of IT. Often, sterile play comes from the fact that the children have had no input into the design or management of the area.

Intervention by adults

Having joined the children at play and adopted a pretend persona within their make-believe, we can both initiate or respond in order to facilitate learning. Each intervention by the teacher varies the learning opportunities and the possible learning outcomes (Baldwin & Hendy, 1994). It is particularly effective if the teacher identifies and makes use of learning opportunities that arise naturally and are offered by the children themselves. It is important for children to feel some ownership of the story and that their contributions to the dramatic play are valued. The teacher may enter the story as the patient or the customer but they must treat the 'doctor' or 'dentist', 'travel agent' or 'greengrocer' with the same respect as if it were real life. This will help to develop the shared fiction in a more open way, and as other children hear the conversations they can be encouraged to join in. The teacher's intervention will also help the child in role to become more committed to his or her part in the fiction. By using this approach, we are able to indicate to the children that their dramatic play is valued and highly regarded. We communicate that it is important to us and is a respected form of activity.

Types of role play area

Role play areas do not always have to represent familiar locations: any place and any time is possible. Some examples might be:

- places that take children back in time, such as castles, sailing ships, pirate ships, or old houses; these begin to give small children a sense of the past;
- time travel settings, such as a space ship or a time machine;
- fairy-story places, such as the Three Little Pigs' brick house, Little Red Riding Hood's cottage, Cinderella's kitchen or the Seven Dwarves' house; and
- places of the imagination, such as the all-green room, the upside-down room, or the room of dreams.

All these possibilities develop children's speaking and listening and allow exploration of other areas of the curriculum. What we choose to provide for our children will determine the learning opportunities we can exploit.

By entering children's dramatic play in this way, we are able to build up trust and commitment. We are able to add dimensions that children are usually unable to sustain for themselves. The ideas can be extended later when bigger group or whole-class drama is undertaken. Our interventions can add the dimension of persistence and consequence; what children do and say can be challenged, questioned, and analysed, not just by the adult but by the children themselves.

The Greek word for drama means 'living through' and the action of the drama needs to be lived through by players using 'make-believe' to create the setting for their pretend existence. Within this fantasy world, it is important that all agree to take part and share the same action. Adults must be careful never to begin in role without telling the children that they are doing so. Saying 'Can I play?' informs children of our intentions. All the players must employ knowledge they have brought with them from their real lives to help them in the pretend world. Life experience and factual knowledge are applied in an active way, frequently providing a genuine 'need to know'. It is important that children and adults are always aware that they are playing – they must be able to 'hold two worlds in their head at the same time' (Readman & Lamont, 1994, p. 27). All should be aware that at any time the 'make-believe' can cease, which paradoxically creates the safety. Vygotsky described this ability to live in these two worlds as the 'dual affect' (1986). Aristotle also described this phenomenon as 'metaxis' – the real world and the fantasy world of the drama coming together in the mind of the player.

Drama helps children to communicate in a more significant way and allows them to think more deeply about the consequences of their actions. The random 'play' shooting of the playground, for instance, can be challenged – shooting hurts people, and this can be explored. Also, drama allows children to have new experiences and to test out their reactions in a 'safe' environment. Children are repeatedly asked to interpret the actions of others, often in unfamiliar ways, and are given the opportunity to replay, change, and reflect upon different parts of the action.

Using improvisation as the medium for dramatic activity

The term *improvisation* as the medium for dramatic activity often appears in documents and books. Within most groups of students and Early Years educators there is some common understanding as to what this term means but less understanding of how it works. It can best be defined as an active method of working which requires both children and teachers to enter a fictional world in which – sometimes as themselves and sometimes as other people – they will be able to:

- explore human relationships and behaviour;
- have a first-hand experience of events and ideas;
- have a genuine need to talk and listen; and
- solve problems and make decisions.

In this fictional world, both dialogue and non-verbal action between participants is made up as the situation proceeds, as with ordinary conversations and actions in real life. The group does not have a pre-written script that is learnt, spoken, and acted. Through the fictional context, the dialogue and non-verbal action can be steered to include anything the teacher or the children want to discuss or explore. This activity is known as 'continuous improvisation' as it carries on as long as all participants are able to sustain it. Drama in the classroom uses elements that are also to be found in theatrical action: human relationships and situations driven by tension and suspense caused by complications in the plot linked through place and time, using movement and language.

It is very difficult to sustain continuous improvisation for long periods of time. Young children can quickly become disengaged from it either because they feel their contribution is not being heard or they become absorbed in their own story-making. Maintaining improvisation with very large groups may not be easy and, with ever increasing class size, drama needs to be carefully planned and organised.

Drama strategies/conventions as a tool for planning

A drama strategy/convention is a structuring device that helps the teacher focus the children on certain aspects of the story being made. Over recent years, the use of drama strategies/conventions has become an important aspect of drama planning and structuring. A teacher can interrupt the story by using a drama strategy/convention to:

- help build a shared environment (Are we all in the same wood? What common understanding do we have about circuses? As we look at the island what do we all see?);
- move the plot on through teacher narration if the story is not going anywhere or has become rather circular in its development; and
- look at something that has happened so as to help build group identity about the dilemma - this stops children's insatiable desire for 'what happens next'.

In some instances the group can go back and re-run a section which might be leading the children somewhere they do not want to go. 'Unlike real life', as one student observed, 'you can re-wind and change what has just been done.'

Some useful drama strategies/conventions that work with Early Years children

Most good books on educational drama contain descriptions and uses for drama strategies. The books I personally have found most suitable for work with Early Years children are Baldwin and Hendy, 1994; Readman and Lamont, 1994; Woolland, 1993; Neelands, 1990; and Toye and Prendiville, 2000.

Teacher-in-role is possibly the drama strategy/convention most familiar to educators. This is a very powerful tool as it allows the teacher to enter the fictional world alongside the children and to structure the story from within. When first introduced to this strategy, teachers-in-training can find the prospect of entering into the context with the children rather daunting; organising the action from the outside seems a much safer option. Those who are willing to undertake teacher-in-role and participate fully in the story-making find that this is one of the most effective and adaptable roles they can employ. To engage children in a known story, use the drama strategy/convention **My Story.** Here, the teacher tells, in role, the story of his or her predicament e.g. Mother Pig cannot find her children, the Park keeper has lost all the animals, the Sandman's grandchild doesn't know where to find the right sand.

Other strategies/conventions include:

- **Still-image:** the group or smaller groups take up a pose to construct a picture to describe what they want to say.
- **Continuous role play:** all the children are involved in creating the story by taking on the role of a generic group, such as farmers, office workers, friends of the three pigs, or children who know how to fly.
- **Circle-time:** the whole group gathers in a seated circle to discuss events and make group decisions. This is a useful device for calming and controlling the group.
- **Collective role play:** several children take on the role of one character and support each other in what they say.
- **What can you see?** Each child describes an environment, an event, or a person to build a group image; this is more suitable for Key Stage One.
- **Thought-tracking:** individuals say aloud what they think and feel about an event, character, or idea. This is more suitable for Key Stage One.
- **Small-group work:** a small group of children is asked to create a small scene, with or without dialogue, to show what might have happened during an event or what might happen if an idea is carried out (again, this is more suitable for Key Stage One).

Planning dramatic activity

By using the elements of theatrical action, improvisation, and drama strategies/conventions, teachers have the tools to plan and structure story-making. The dramatic activity is based on creating a context for improvised situations to take place, which can be enhanced by the use of other dramatic strategies when needed. As has already been suggested, using drama for educational purposes is about making meaning for children, rather than making plays.

The structuring of the story-making must provide a strong dilemma (tension and suspense) from which the children can build belief; in other words, something must happen to engage their interest. The children need to be able to enter the role behaving 'as if' it were so. To work, the activity must provide enough stimulation for the children to have a common willingness to 'suspend disbelief'.

Young children possess an innate ability to understand the structuring of stories. They instinctively know that once the story of the drama has started something is going to happen (Hendy, 1995). They know that the protagonists in the story will come across complications and dilemmas that have to be solved: Red Riding Hood meets a wolf who wants to eat her, the Three Little Pigs are chased by a wolf intend on destroying their homes and eating them. These dilemmas are strong and life threatening. This does not mean to say that all drama must be about life and death situations. But something must be happening that creates a powerful tension to hold interest and create contexts in which new knowledge and understandings can take place.

Choosing the context

Choosing the context is an important factor in the planning for interactive story-making. Well-known children's stories are a good basis for starting, as they often have interesting settings that capture the imagination of small children. Having selected the context it is worth identifying some of the learning areas that could be explored as the story develops. Stories set in woods or the outdoors might lead to environmental issues or aspects of knowledge and understanding of the world. Stories set indoors might provide a context for communication, language and literacy, problem-solving, reasoning, and numeracy.

After the theme has been selected, key learning areas should be identified. These can be universal ideas such as:

- How do we find out about what people are like?
- How do we deal with people who are different?
- How do we deal with the things that frighten us?

Or the learning can be more curriculum based, such as:

- How do we describe similarities and differences between materials? (Knowledge and understanding of the world)
- How do we design something which will carry us on the wind? (Problem-solving, reasoning, and numeracy)
- Can we recount a story from our past? (Communication, language, and literacy)
- How should we treat these new people that we have found? (Personal, social, and emotional development)

To answer some of these questions, the story can be structured – through the use of improvisation and drama strategies/conventions – to explore key learning areas. Using 'the Sandman' as an example (see detailed plan in Table 7.1), the universal question from this story might be 'How do we cope with difficult problems?'

Table 7.1 Interactive story-making session planner: using a nursery rhyme, 'The Sandman Comes'

The Sandman comes

The Sandman comes.

He brings such pretty snow-white sand

For every child in the land

The Sandman comes.

Learning objectives
Speaking, listening and responding

- enjoy listening to and using spoken language and readily turn to it in play and learning
- sustain attentive listening, responding to what they have heard with relevant comments, questions or actions

Drama

- explore familiar themes and characters through improvisation and role play
- adopt appropriate roles in small or large groups and consider alternative courses of action

Learning intentions	Planning	Making the story
To encourage attentive listening	Teacher as herself teaches the nursery rhyme and makes contract with the children	Gather children into sitting circle. Teacher reads the nursery rhyme 'The Sandman Comes' and teaches the children to say the rhyme. Teacher asks 'Who is the sandman? What does he do? When does he come? What does he bring?' Encourage answers. (Set up the story by making the contract) Tell the children they are going to make a story together. Teacher tells the children she will leave the circle and when she comes back she will pretend to be the novice 'Sandman' who comes every night and they are to be children who can't get to sleep.
To provide information to set the context for the story	Teacher uses 'T-I-R' and 'My Story'	You are a novice 'Sandman' who comes every evening with the snow-white sand and you sprinkle the magic sand into the eyes of little children to make them sleep. You are very new because your grandfather, who has been the Sandman for many, many years, wanted a holiday from flying around the world every night, and he has asked you to take over while he is away. What he didn't tell you before he left on his long, long holiday is where vou go to get the snow-white sand. You have run out and you have come to the children to ask for their help

To use language to imagine and create roles and experiences	**Continuous improvisation** to build the context	Children prepare with T-I-R to get ready for their journey. T-I-R asks 'What do we need to take with us? How long will it take to get there?' Children will provide answers and solutions to the problems set. T-I-R assesses the options and decides the most likely solution with the children. Begin the journey.
To develop communication and social skills	**Continuous improvisation** to create the tension	The journey could take you anywhere. T-I-R should bear in mind you are looking for places where sand can be found. Keep asking questions such as 'Where can we find beautiful white sand?' 'Has anyone been on a beach lately?' 'How will I know it is the right sand? The stuff my Grandpa uses.'
To develop problem-solving and reasoning	**Circle-time** to reflect and re-engage	Periodically take time out by gathering in a group to discuss what has happened and what is going to happen. Discuss actions and decisions.
To develop personal and emotional skills	**Still image**	To restart the story, ask children to take up position as if in a photograph of what they were doing just before they were called into the circle. Ask them to close their eyes and think about how they feel about the journey. Ask the picture to come to life and very slowly ask children to find a friend and whisper how they feel to their partner.
To work in small or large groups and consider alternative courses of action	**Continuous improvisation** to develop the story and build to an acceptable conclusion	Allow the story to develop, following the children's ideas until you reach an acceptable conclusion. In the case of this story, the children should return home and the apprentice Sandman should sprinkle the sand in the children's eyes and they finish all going to sleep.

The teacher needs to decide whether the story-making is going to be used to develop 'paradigmatic' or 'narrative' thinking. Stories that involve children pretending to be in familiar surroundings can be effective vehicles to introduce information or assess their ability to problem-solve, reason and use numerical understanding, communicate with each other, and work together socially. Such stories could be termed 'home' stories, as they are based in reality and all the activities are controlled by natural laws; in other words, there is *no magic*. Such interactive stories are a useful way of helping young children learn more about their world.

Fantasy stories, on the other hand, have a different feel and are rooted in the imagination. This kind of drama work can extend children's narrative thinking and imaginative powers, allowing the possibility of all worlds and ideas, however bizarre and extraordinary. The planning must take into consideration the children's willingness to:

- adopt the 'pretend';
- make-believe with regard to actions and situations;
- make-believe with regard to objects;
- maintain the make-believe verbally;
- maintain the make-believe through movement;
- interact with the rest of the group; and
- keep to the structure and the rules of playing.

Teachers must also plan with a commitment to their own participation in mind. Children are not able to engage in effective learning through drama unless the adult has:

- a genuine desire to work in this medium;
- an eagerness to enter the child's world, to believe in what they are doing and to take their work seriously;
- an understanding of how improvisation and drama strategies function and can be used;
- knowledge of the learning potential of any particular story together with ability to keep this to the fore;
- techniques to introduce problems for the group to solve;
- the willingness to take risks; and
- the willingness to work beside the children and allow the group to make decisions.

Making the contract

It is important that before engaging in interactive story-making both children and adults enter into a contract which makes clear the plan of action – the expectations and the responsibilities of how to proceed when the story-making has begun. As has already been advised, never begin a story until all participants know what they are expected to do.

Some examples of active story-making

Working with a modern children's story

A trainee teacher recently decided to use Nick Butterworth's *After the Storm* as the basis for her drama. This story is set in a wood in which a storm has taken place and the animals have been left homeless. It provided a richness of learning possibilities she could explore with her reception class, and the class topic was 'animals' so this story fitted well into the overall curriculum planning.

She began to examine her areas of learning. The wood setting would allow her to test out the children's knowledge of trees and animal habitats, work that they had already undertaken in the classroom. She wanted to discover how much knowledge the children had of life processes and living things. She wanted to see whether she could introduce some information about shape, space, and measures as the children, in their role as animals, started to think about the design of their new homes. Design and making would be a strong feature of the story. Knowledge and understanding of the world could be discussed as the children made observations about their damaged habitat. By asking the children to remember what it was like before the storm, and sequence events before they heard the great wind, she hoped to increase their sense of the past. Gradually, through careful planning, she was able to build up the learning potential inherent in the story.

Throughout she was keen to let the 'animals' tell their own story, but by participating herself, in the role of a water rat, she was able to question, pose problems, and expand their understanding. Almost immediately the children introduced 'tension' by introducing the idea of wolves. These animals were never seen but were present throughout, driving the 'animals' to find a new home quickly before they were eaten. Not having the right tools or materials also became a major problem and slowed up progress on the new homes. Rescue came in the role of Wise Owl, a character again introduced by a child, who invited all the animals to his home in the tree and gave them tea.

Most of the story was created through 'continuous improvisation', but the trainee introduced some other strategies to increase reflection and commitment. At the very beginning, the children were asked to stand quietly in a circle and look at the tree. The trainee went round to each child in his or her role as an 'animal' and asked what could they see. Gradually the children built up a group picture of the tree fallen in the wood. She then asked each of them to go and rescue something from his or her home. The children returned to the circle and showed the others what they had rescued and what it meant to them. Many of these items were then used in the story. At the end of the story, each child was asked to pretend to be a photograph (still-image) of his or her animal standing outside its new home. She subsequently read them the story and it became a big favourite with the class.

Working from children's ideas

When working from children's ideas, the teacher has to be able to 'think on her feet' and to seize learning opportunities as they arise. Such work is ideal for building group cooperation and extending children's ability to solve problems and to take decisions. This does not mean that there is no previous planning involved but the planning will be of a more fluid nature, predicting beforehand what learning could be achieved if certain situations arose. With experience, teachers can engineer situations whatever line the story is taking. The following example comes from a story developed by a vertically-grouped class who had been working on the theme of castles.

The session commenced with circle-time. The children sat together with the adults and decided where they were, who they were, and what they were doing. They wanted to be servants to a King and they were to be preparing a grand banquet. To start the action in a controlled manner each child was asked to enter the story space and take up a pose of the job they were doing (still-image) as if someone had painted a picture of them. When all the children were assembled, the action began.

The story began slowly with all the children 'acting out' mixing and peeling and roasting, etc. In my role as a new servant, I asked for jobs to do and was told where everything was. I created problems by not doing my work well and was helped by the other servants. From this I learnt a great deal about the children. Their knowledge of food preparation was very good and we had a long discussion about the best way to cook the potatoes. I asked questions about what I thought I knew about cooking and checked whether I was correct. In this instance, the children were the 'experts' and I was the novice.

Before long, the first major complication, the one that changed the course of the story-line, occurred. A child shouted 'fire' and immediately we were running about trying to put out the flames. This was an opportunity to talk about the dangers of fire: How did it start? What happens when you get too near the flames? How do you deal with burns? Having dealt with this complication, another arose. A second child told us that it was not the servants' carelessness which started the fire but a dragon the King had locked in the dungeon for burning people. The dragon was now crying and her tears had put out the flames.

As we sat down amongst the ruins of the King's banquet, we discussed how we could help the sad dragon. Could we trust her not to burn us? How do you learn to trust people who have done you harm? Was the dragon really fierce or was she just afraid? Why might she have been burning villages and people before she was captured? After the discussion each 'servant' was asked to say aloud what they thought and felt about the dragon (thought-tracking) and the bravest were dispatched to release her from her prison. Questions in such stories are endless and can lead to many learning opportunities of a kind that are difficult to discuss in normal classroom situations, as they do not necessarily arise.

To describe all the events in this story would take too long here; suffice to say, some ninety minutes later the dragon had been taken home to her babies and the 'servants', complete with cooked banquet, returned to the castle to feed the King. Many areas of the curriculum were covered including problem-solving, reasoning, and numeracy (How big will we need to make our magic carpet to hold all the servants and the dragon? How can we measure the length of the dragon without a tape measure?); knowledge and understanding of the world (Do dragons eat the same things as people? How fast do we need to run to get our magic carpet to fly? Where in the world do dragons live? What sort of terrain will we be walking through if we land in the mountains?); and creative development (Let's make up a quiet song to sing to the dragon's baby to make her sleep).

The stories made up in this way are very special to children. I always make the point at the end to tell children that no-one has ever heard this story before, it is new and it belongs to them. By writing these stories into book form they can make their own popular addition to the book corner.

Making use of a fairy-story

Through the employment of teacher-in-role, the teacher became the mother of the Three Little Pigs and asked the children in role as the little pig's friends to help her find them. By placing the context (the who, where, what, and when) outside the events in the story already known by the children, the teacher gave herself more scope for exploration. It avoided the sometimes unproductive 'acting out' of a familiar story. The children's knowledge of the original story helped them create a sequence of events, but more like detectives piecing together evidence on their journey.

The story began with circle-time, when the teacher told the children who she was going to be. She said that when she returned to the circle she would be in role as the mother of the Three Little Pigs and that they, the children, would be some of the pigs' friends. She asked them to close their eyes while she went out of the circle.

On returning she began to tell them about her children and how worried she was as they had been away for a very long time and she had received only had one letter since they had left home. She reached into her pocket for a letter (which she had prepared earlier). She read it to the children. The letter said, 'Hello Mum, We are fine. We have built a house made of straw and we are very proud of it. We have heard there is a wolf about so we will take care.' She asked the children questions about wolves and what they are like. Should she be worried? Should she go and look for them? Would the children like to join her?

In small groups they drew maps of the landscape around the pigs' home using pictures and symbols to represent different places. These maps were used on the journey. Questions were asked about the locality: Which way did they go? Did they go north, south, east or west? Did they go over the hills or through the woods? The path through the woods was chosen. As it grew dark, they thought about a shelter for the night. Where will be the best place? How will they protect themselves from the wolf? Where will they find something to eat?

As the session progressed, the children's interest was sustained by the teacher in her role as mother. By introducing challenges and problems through effective questioning and leading discussion, and by allowing children to direct the story and make it their own, she was able to exploit much of its learning potential. Through skilful use of drama strategies she created moments of reflection on events, people, or ideas when and where they are needed.

The session ended as it had begun, in a circle-time. The pigs had been found, the wolf was vanquished, and all the participants were ready for bed.

Drama as a time saver

Contrary to popular thinking, teaching through drama is not a drain on precious classroom time. Through working in this active way teachers are given a powerful method of teaching and learning which is not always available in other forms of classroom organisation. Learning by doing, through the use of this interactive method, encourages the retention of information. Recently a seven-year-old was able to tell me, in great detail, the events of an interactive story she had made two years previously in her reception class. Through the different modes of thinking and talking which story-making promotes, children are able to articulate what they know. With careful planning and structuring, drama, in the form of interactive story-making, provides a time-saving method of introducing children to new learning, challenging their assumptions and ideas and testing their existing knowledge within different contexts. This type of activity makes a significant contribution to children's social, emotional and cognitive development in their Early Years.

Pointers for Early Years drama

Some points to remember when using drama in the Early Years classroom:

- story-making is a natural activity in early childhood;
- drama in education is about making meaning, rather than making plays;
- drama is a useful teaching tool across the curriculum and not exclusive to speaking and listening;
- the teacher, as well as the children, must be willing to suspend disbelief and participate in the 'as if';
- planning for drama is strengthened by the effective use of drama strategies;
- the context of the story must contain interesting complications and dilemmas;
- the context of the story should provide powerful learning situations; and
- by its nature, drama is an efficient and time-saving method of introducing new learning or testing old knowledge.

References

Baldwin, P. and Hendy, L. (1994) *The Drama Box*. London: Harpers Collins.

Bettleheim, B. (1991) *The Uses of Enchantment: The Meaning and Importance of Fairy Tales*. Harmondswoth: Penguin.

Bruner, J. (1986) *Actual Minds, Possible Worlds*. Cambridge, MA: Harvard University Press.

Butterworth, N. (2011) *After the Storm*. London: HarperCollins.

Engels, S. (1999) *The Stories Children Tell*. New York: W.H. Freeman.

Hendy, L. (1995) 'Playing, Role playing and Dramatic Activity', *Early Years* 15 (2), 13–22.

Hendy, L. and Toon, L. (2001) *Supporting Drama and Imagination Play in the Early Years*. Buckingham: Open University Press.

Hutt, C. (1989) 'Fantasy Play'. In S.J. Hutt, S. Tyler, C. Hutt and H. Christopherson (Eds.), *Play, Exploration and Learning*. London: Routledge, pp. 99–116.

Kitson, N. (1994) 'Fantasy Play: A Case for Adult Intervention'. In J. Moyles (Ed.), *The Excellence of Play*. Buckingham: Open University Press.

Neelands, J. (1990) *Structuring Drama Work*. Cambridge: Cambridge University Press.

OFSTED (1994) *First Class*. London: HMSO.

Readman, G. and Lamont, G. (1994) *Drama: A Handbook for Teachers*. London: BBC Education.

Sylva, K., Bruner, J., and Genova P. (1976) 'The Role of Play in the Problem-Solving of Children 3–5 Years Old'. In J. Bruner, A. Jolly, and K. Sylva (Eds.), *Play: Its Role in Development and Evolution*. Harmondsworth: Penguin.

Toye, N. and Prendiville, F. (2000) *Drama and Traditional Story for the Early Years*. London: Routledge.

Vygotsky, L. (1986) *Thought and Language* (revised by A. Kozulin). Cambridge, MA: MIT Press.

Woolland, B. (1993) *The Teaching of Drama in Primary School*. London: Longman.

CHAPTER 8

'I can write . . . on my own!'

WRITING IN THE EARLY YEARS

Helen Bradford

Overview

This chapter describes a range of experiences that enable young children to become confident, motivated writers. Taking a developmental approach, it is built on the premise that children do not wait until the beginning of formal instruction to explore the features of writing. They are already experimenting from a very early age, before they begin to use the alphabetic principle of letter-sound relationships and despite the fact that the writing produced might not be conventional from the perspective of an adult. Young children are constantly exposed to print in the environment in which they live; they see adults writing both at home and in their Early Years setting and formulate their own hypotheses about how the print world works. They use their emergent knowledge and understanding to experiment, exploring the creation of meaning on paper and on the computer screen as they gradually develop their awareness of the functions and forms of writing. A key focus of this chapter is to raise awareness of the role of the Early Years educator in building on children's emergent writing skills and so to scaffold the steps to conventional writing.

Developing writing

Children begin to explore the features of writing from a very early age. They do so with the intention of creating meaning before understanding of the alphabetic principle has developed, and despite the fact that the writing produced is not conventional in that it cannot be read by an adult (Bradford and Wyse, 2010; 2013). Early experimentation of this kind is known as emergent literacy (Teale and Sulzby, 1986; Hall, 1987). Emergent literacy theories explore the reading and writing behaviours of young children that precede and develop into conventional literacy. In relation to writing, emergent literacy is characterized by two key premises: (1) as a set of practices that young children who have had relatively little experience of writing engage in, and (2) as incorporating an element of growing metacognitive awareness in young children, perceiving them as active enquirers into the nature and purposes of literacy (Wray, 1994; Jacobs, 2004).

Intentionality is a characteristic of the writing process which recognises that children are already making planned organisational decisions about their writing and that they write with an expectation that the graphic signs they make will make sense. Harste, Woodward and Burke (1984) discovered that children as young as three display intentionality within their early attempts to write. Goodman (1986) and, more recently, Lancaster (2003) argue that children as young as two engage in writing tasks for a wide variety of reasons and that most have begun to use symbols to represent real things.

Marie Clay (1975, p. 15) argued that by examining children's earliest attempts at writing we are provided with a 'rich commentary on [children's] . . . learning about print', learning which is 'encapsulated in their accumulated attempts to write'. To this end, Rowe's (2003) analysis of children's unconventional texts suggests that young children's authoring processes are not qualitatively different from those used by older writers. Several other studies such as Harste, Woodward and Burke (1984) and Wray (1994) make a case for adults and children alike using similar cognitive processes in terms of the decisions they must make when confronted with a writing task. Writing involves choosing from a range of possible actions, which in turn implies a degree of conscious awareness of potential alternatives. Pahl (1999) argued that children will interpret things according to the information and resources to which they have access at the time and according to what is currently salient in their thinking. In other words, children will simply make use of what they know. In this respect it is inexperience that determines their ability to write conventionally, rather than the strategies they use when they approach a written task. Jacobs (2004, p. 18) describes such strategies as 'temporary scaffolds' which will be gradually refined as children begin to understand more about the writing process.

Understanding children writing: Scott

Research built on sociocultural theory shows that children's earliest discoveries about written language are learned through active engagement with both their social and cultural worlds (for example, Compton-Lilly, 2006). By living and participating in an environment in which others use print for various purposes, children infer the semiotic and functional nature of written language (Purcell-Gates, 1996). Literacy development will occur wherever literacy practices are occurring; thus children begin to learn about reading and writing initially in their homes and communities through interacting with others in reading and writing situations. It therefore follows that children arrive at their Early Years setting with at least some knowledge and understanding of the function and purpose of writing. A small-scale study (see Bradford and Wyse, 2013) investigating the writing behaviours of a group of six children aged between three and four years old found that all had meaningful perceptions of themselves as writers. The children also attributed meaning to their writing in spite of its unconventional nature. Listen to what Isla, at the age of three years and six months is telling us below:

Isla: I can write.
Helen: Can you write?
Isla: On my own.

This was Isla's perception of herself as a writer; despite the fact that the only conventional writing she could produce at the age of three years and six months was her name.

The following short case study of another of the participant children, Scott, is characterized by several key points outlined in the theoretical section of this chapter. Scott demonstrates how he uses what he knows about writing to create meaning through his explorations; how he uses what he knows to produce texts; and how he draws on his hypotheses about how the print world works. Finally, the case study reveals how Scott's writing experiences at home impact on his approach to writing in his nursery setting.

At the start of the study, and at the age of three years and four months, Scott was just beginning to show an interest in letters. He referred to all letters as numbers and would ask, 'What does that number say?' whilst pointing to a letter. Scott regularly observed his mother writing shopping lists at home and liked to write his own list on his own piece of paper alongside her. He preferred to use blue biro pens to write with at home, probably because he observed his parents writing with these. He knew where to access the necessary tools for writing at home. He had a drawing table with pencils, crayons and paper, but also referred to the breakfast bar in the kitchen as 'the office'. Scott clearly associated the breakfast bar with writing. It had a telephone, pad and pen and one stool, and was where his parents would observe him writing lists. He would tell them 'I'm in my office'. He copied writing behaviour modelled by his father who sometimes worked from there, for example making 'notes' on a pad whilst he 'spoke' on the phone. When he wrote he held the pen very carefully and made very deliberate marks on paper. He was interested in signs when out with his parents and recognised the phoneme /s/ for Scott and /r/, the initial letter sound in his younger brother's name.

The four-month period of the study saw Scott's perception of himself as a writer develop. He began, however, with a clear understanding that print conveyed meaning. As at home, Scott had a preference to use a biro in the nursery to write with. Soon after the study began, he was observed role playing taking the class register. His register consisted of a clipboard, a plain piece of A4 paper clipped to the clipboard and a biro. Clipboards were accessible to the children and usually had pencils attached to them with string, however Scott would deliberately find one without a pencil so that he could choose to use a biro instead ('I had to find something else', he once explained). The nursery nurse in the classroom suggested he create his register that day by looking at the children's name cards on the name board. He did, pointing to each card and appearing to check names against his clipboard (see Figure 8.1).

In Figure 8.1, the first two letters (N and A) were written by the nursery nurse for him. Scott continued to take a class register on a daily basis for a while. Another day

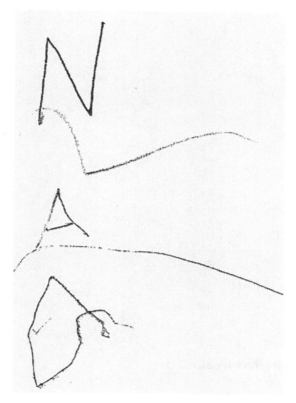

Figure 8.1 *Scott's first class register*

he requested everything he needed to take it and continued to do so for most of the one-and-a-half hour indoor session, mainly working alongside the nursery nurse who was doing formal observations of all the children, and who was also using a clipboard and a pen. He carefully watched her writing and copied her mannerisms and writing behaviour. For example, he would look at a peer, then look to the name board to 'find' their name before noting it down on his register. Finally, he reported that there were nineteen children in the nursery that day. He then decided to dress up as a fireman and did a safety fire check against his register (see Figure 8.2).

As at home, Scott had identified an area of the classroom that he associated with writing activity. Coincidentally, the writing area in the classroom was also called the office. Four months after the study began, Scott wrote his name conventionally for the first time by following the letters on his name card in the correct order. He then added some "kisses" (his explanation of the marks beneath his name) at the end. He was extremely proud of his card and writing (see Figure 8.3).

There is a considerable difference between the example of Scott's writing in Figure 8.3 and the marks he made four months previously to represent his fire check register. Scott's perception of himself as a writer changed over the period of the

Figure 8.2 *Scott's fire check register*

Figure 8.3 *Scott's Valentine's Day card*

study as his confidence grew. He showed an increasing awareness of some of the conventions of writing as well as how print conveyed meaning. He began to develop his knowledge and understanding of how individual sounds and letters could be put together to make words with a particular focus on his own name. By the end of the study he could write his name conventionally supported by an adult and using his name card. His perception of writing was that it was something to be enjoyed, something that he could do, something that could usefully communicate meaning and something that would be appreciated by others.

The role of the Early Years educator

For writing to become part of a child's communicative repertoire they need to be in an environment that allows them opportunities to write (Dyson, 2001). Writing behaviours emerge when children have access to writing materials, see models of writing and observe people writing. In addition, it is important that the Early Years educator is able to look at and identify what children know about writing as opposed to what they do not know; in this way next steps in terms of appropriate activities and challenges can be planned. How the Early Years educator responds to children's writing is crucially important in developing confidence and positive perceptions of its value and purpose. Asking children, for example, 'What did you write?' or 'Can you read what you have written to me?' or 'Who have you written your letter to?' are examples of how to use the vocabulary of writing. Questions such as these serve to validate young children's efforts at meaningful communication via print. Noting the context, as in the case of Scott's fire check register, is also important when observing children writing. Context gives meaning, purpose and understanding to children's explorations. Modelling writing within the setting or classroom and incorporating handwriting (both the Early Years educator's and the children's) within displays, in addition to labels created using computer-generated text, will both support and encourage children to see the possibilities.

Creating a vibrant writing environment

Early years educators need to create an emotional environment in which children can take risks, explore and be adventurous in their endeavours to write. Children should be provided with opportunities to choose and decide on their own reason for writing in addition to supporting them to write in response to a stimulus. Writing areas are features of Early Years settings and classrooms, from the nursery into Reception and Key Stage One. In the Key Stage One classroom, where there is perhaps no dedicated writing area, another option is to provide opportunities to write within a role play area. Creating opportunities for writing outdoors is another option across the whole Early Years age phase: writing labels for seeds planted in the garden, for example, or writing menus and taking orders from customers in an outdoor café in the summer. A dedicated writing area will provide time and space for children to experiment with a range of writing materials. Providing relevant materials following real-life experiences will further support children to experiment and develop their expertise as writers. For example, following a December visit to the postbox to post Christmas cards made and written in the setting, nursery children were provided with a range of cards and envelopes to access independently in the writing area. One penny stamps were also included as a resource. A display incorporating photographs of the children writing their Christmas cards in the setting, and following them en route to the postbox and back again in small groups, was located adjacent to the writing area.

Figure 8.4 shows what Amelia did following her visit to the postbox.

Amelia knows a lot about how to address an envelope! She had observed an adult addressing her original Christmas card envelope to her parents at her home address prior to visiting the postbox. She had been invited to stick the stamp on the envelope before carrying it herself to post it; note the careful placing of the stamp on her envelope here. Amelia she is using what she knows about writing, which includes being able to write the first two letters of her name, to address an envelope to her daddy. She had just written him a letter. Once she had placed her letter inside the envelope she went to post it in the setting postbox.

Materials

There are many materials that could be provided for an indoor or outdoor writing area; however perhaps not all at once! What is provided may be determined to some extent by children's recent experiences, or by a current topic or theme. This list is by no means exhaustive and the possibilities are many and varied.

- Unlined paper – assorted sizes, shapes, colours, textures and types
- Cardboard – assorted colours, textures and thicknesses

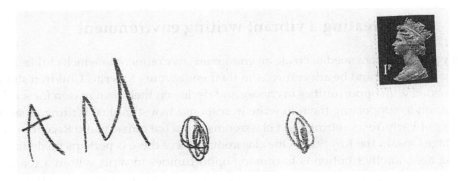

Figure 8.4 *Amelia's stamped, addressed envelope*

- Music paper, graph paper, lined and plain
- Pads, notebooks, envelopes (used and unused) and stamps (real, to the value of 1p)
- Clipboards, whiteboards and blackboards
- Post-it notes and labels (sticky, luggage)
- Address books, diaries, registers and spiral-bound notebooks
- Ready-made books – zigzag, stapled and staple-less

A range of tools can also be provided:

- A range of writing tools of different thicknesses – felt-tipped pens, markers, crayons, writing pencils, coloured pencils, biros, whiteboard pens and chalks
- Pencil sharpeners
- Stampers and ink pads
- Staplers
- Hole punchers
- Rulers and scissors
- A range of fixing materials – sticky tape, glue, glue sticks, stapler, paper clips, treasury tags, masking tape, string, and wool

In order to further enhance the writing environment, include:

- Examples of environmental print – notes, timetables, adverts, leaflets, junk mail
- Message and display boards/communication pockets (at child height for children to use independently)
- Name cards and number lines
- A mark-making/writing trolley with a variety of equipment that can be used both indoors and outdoors. Or fill plastic, portable trugs with writing equipment, either chosen by the educator or the child to carry outside.

Writing experiences

Some possible indoor writing experiences are:

- Creating/taking the register
- Name writing – to label a painting, for example, or writing in a card
- Recording significant events or appointments in diaries and calendars Recording phone numbers and addresses in a telephone/address book
- Writing recipes and ingredients for a cooking activity; provide scales, clocks and timers to record weight, volume and time
- Taking handwritten messages to the school office
- Recording feelings using pads/paper and pens in a quiet area
- Providing writing opportunities in the role play area, e.g. shoe shop – filling in slips and order forms, shoe sizes on boxes

Participating in outdoor literacy activities means that as children get older they do not come to see writing and numbers as indoor 'work' tasks. Some possible outdoor writing experiences are:

- Put pads, paper and books in a playhouse
- Put clipboards, paper and envelopes in a gazebo
- Create maps from huge sheets of paper and fat felt pens
- Let children write or paint on a picnic table covered in large sheets of paper
- Lay rolls of paper on the floor
- Provide writing opportunities in a role play area, e.g. a builders' yard where children can fill in slips and order forms, draw their architectural designs and have opportunities for recording, counting, measuring, calculating and quantities.

The role of play in supporting young children's writing development

Play is important for early learning for many reasons. All of us learn best when we want to do something and are least likely to learn when we are being made to do something that does not interest us. Children are naturally drawn to play experiences and many concentrate for long periods in their self-chosen play. Play therefore offers children the chance to explore and learn at their own pace and stage of writing development; it offers children the chance to be in control and to feel competent within relevant, meaningful and open-ended experiences – for example writing with a real purpose and without fear of 'getting it wrong'. Through play, children are able to meet their own needs and make sense of their world. Play, as we have seen from the example of Scott, can provide children with opportunities to mark-make, effectively laying foundations for the later use of symbols such as letters and numbers to represent ideas. Play encourages creativity and imagination; it offers children the opportunity to consolidate learning (see Figure 8.5). Finally, children's play enables Early Years educators to observe them at their highest level of competence and to see, understand and accommodate their ideas, concerns and interests.

Play is an important vehicle for providing meaningful contexts through which children can explore print independently. Bromley (2006, p. 7) argues that 'in play children mimic adults' writing habits for their own ends.' One of the challenges for Early Years educators is therefore to arrange the most appropriate physical environment to support and include writing experience, including maximizing opportunities to incorporate writing into play. Neuman and Roskos (1997) investigated young children's literacy activity within play settings specifically designed to reflect authentic literacy contexts for them. The study further acknowledged the role peers can play in a child's literacy development. From observations and taped conversations, evidence was found to suggest that more expert play partners, through their more capable demonstrations of 'pretend' play such as how to post letters in a Post Office, appeared to teach their less skilled peers, increasing their knowledge of the environment.

Role play areas provide generous and varied opportunities for incorporating writing within play. One Early Years educator created a Jack and the Beanstalk themed role play area with her reception class for example. The area was the giant's castle at the top of a beanstalk that wound around the top of the castle. The children wrote letters to Jack, on green beanstalk leaves, in their role as Jack's mother, asking him to collect specific items for her from the castle, such as the golden eggs. The children put the letters in a postbox in the role play castle. The Early Years educator then attached the letters to the beanstalk after school each day for the children to

Figure 8.5 *Practising and consolidating learning*

find and read the following morning. This provided opportunities for discussion and acknowledged the credibility of the children's writing, encouraging others to write knowing that their letters would be valued in the same way. Another role play area created that year was based on the story of *Handa's Surprise* by Eileen Brown. The role play area became Handa's home in her village and included her basket with all her fruit. Dressing up clothes were provided so that the children could role play Handa's journey to see her friend Akeyo. They were able to go outside to do this in the reception outdoor area, having been taken on the journey initially by the Early Years educator who strategically placed the animals in the story along the way. The children then drew maps of their journey once back in Handa's home, labelling the animals encountered on their journey and the types of fruit they had taken from her basket.

Children writing in the Early Years and into Key Stage One: Boys, girls and superheroes

Children's interest in writing needs to be ignited. This can be done using a range of inspirational stimuli. Stimuli that might be used include visual images (for example pictures, photographs and film); music; children's literature; artefacts; first-hand experiences, including school trips; writing warm-ups; writing games; role play and drama; talk before writing; and story boxes and bags. Children need to understand why they are being asked to write and the creative Early Years educator will develop meaningful contexts for writing that include a sense of audience and purpose. Early years educators should never underestimate the value of talk for writing. Significant elements of current approaches to the teaching of writing incorporate talk as a crucial precursor to successful writing (see, for example, Fisher, Jones, Larkin and Myhill, 2010). Talk enables and allows children to explore their ideas ahead of writing, to use and develop new vocabulary, and to consolidate thinking. In this way, talk scaffolds children's learning in order for them to (eventually) be able to sustain independent writing.

There has traditionally been an issue with boys and writing, particularly in relation to their motivation to write. In the Introduction to the Boys and Writing Project carried out by the Centre for Literacy in Primary Education (2003–2005), two reasons were put forward for the difference between boys' and girls' achievement in writing:

1   Boys have an unwillingness to write, stemming from lack of confidence and motivation.
2   Boys lack a 'way in' to writing that they are familiar with, or do not feel they can succeed.

Research further suggests that it is not simply the setting context that plays a role in boys' attitudes and perceptions, but also the wider context of community, family and culture (Bearne, 2002; Younger and Warrington, 2005; UKLA, 2004). Bearne also describes a 'fear factor' that is evident in boys' writing which prevents some boys from taking risks in their writing, so causing them to make less progress. The Raising Boys' Achievements in Writing project (UKLA, 2004) developed a model for an extended approach to teaching writing which required specific attention to a combination of drama and/or visual approaches. Within the context of the project, this model proved highly successful in raising boys' achievements in writing. The work of the project also had beneficial effects on boys' writing across the wider curriculum, and gave boys more positive attitudes towards themselves as writers. This has led to further research projects, for example that of Bhowanji, Lord and Wilkes (2008), who investigated the impact of engaging boys (and girls) to write through using a multimodal approach in the classroom. Their project includes case studies of groups of children as young as six years old. Outcomes of the project included boys' greater engagement, motivation and more positive attitudes to writing.

All writers write best when they write from within about what they already know. It is important, therefore, for the Early Years educator to discover and tap into children's interests in order to find a way in to create positive and purposeful writing experiences. Meaningful contexts will resonate and inspire children to share the knowledge they already have, to develop new knowldge and to be able to set that knowledge down in words, whether handwritten or typed. A theme such as superheroes will, however, be sure to appeal and there is now a range of texts available that crosses the gender divide in this area. A small selection of these are listed below.

- *Traction Man is Here!* by Mini Grey. Traction Man is an eponymous superhero whose daring adventures are played out in the imagination of the young boy to whom he belongs. The adventures take place in the context of the boy's everyday family life at home.
- *Eliot Jones, Midnight Superhero!* by Anne Cottringer and Alex T. Smith. Eliot Jones is a young boy who one day saves the earth from a giant meteor.
- *Super Daisy and the Peril of Planet Pea* by Kes Gray and Nick Sharratt. Daisy saves the earth from a collision with Planet Pea and prevents peas being served with every type of food imaginable.
- *Superworm* by Julia Donaldson and Axel Scheffler. Superworm saves insects and small animals from Wizard Lizard.
- *Superhero ABC* by Bob McLeod. Learning letter sounds from A to Z. Written and illustrated in comic strip style. Both male and female superheroes feature.

Shared writing

The effective teaching of writing for the Early Years age phase requires input with individual children, the whole class and small groups of children.

Shared writing is a term used to describe a whole-class writing experience designed to form a bridge between the Early Years educator demonstrating the writing process to children and their independent writing. Three levels of shared writing provide a range of opportunities for educators to model effective strategies, to explicitly teach a skill or approach and to draw children into the process through questioning, talk, drama and other response activities. The first of these levels is demonstration. Here, the teacher is the 'expert', modelling how to write a particular genre of text or a particular feature, giving a running commentary on what they are doing, and why. The second is scribing. The children are included in the composition and the educator scribes their suggestions to create a shared piece. Examples of suggestions might include word choices, sentence construction, characterisation and editing. In relation to superheroes this might include, for example, appropriate vocabulary to describe a particular superhero. The third level is supported writing. The Early Years educator gives responsibility for word choices or a sentence to the class. Children work in pairs with whiteboards and hold their whiteboards up for the Early Years educator to see.

Guided writing

Guided writing is a small-group approach involving six children at a time grouped on the basis of ability and need. Guided writing normally follows on from shared writing and addresses the specific identified writing development needs of each group, with a specific focus at whole text, sentence or word level. Guided writing may be used to both simplify elements of the shared writing session for less confident writers and to extend shared writing to challenge more able writers. During a guided writing session the children work with the Early Years educator for a period of up to twenty minutes. A guided write might include a general focus such as understanding the concept of a sentence. The objective in relation to superheroes might therefore be for the children to write a sentence to describe what power they would have if they were a superhero. Alternatively, the focus of the guided write might be more specific to a particular genre, for example use of descriptive language when writing a story. Superheroes fall within the realm of fantasy and creating a list of descriptive vocabulary to incorporate within a superhero fantasy story will serve to scaffold, support and motivate the children in their later independent writing.

Further ideas for superhero writing

- Create an interactive display to include key texts and dressing-up items such as superhero masks that the children have made alongside their superhero character profiles.
- Further develop cross-curricular links with science. Which material would be best for a superhero costume to protect him or her from the rain? Which material would be best to protect his or her eyes from the light? Test a variety of materials and record the results.
- Create a story/comic strip about a made-up or existing superhero.

Here is another inspirational resource to support the theme of superheroes: http://www.teachprimary.com/learning_resources/view/pie-corbetts-superhero-resource

Conclusion

Learning to write conventionally takes time. Children begin to explore the functions of writing before they arrive at their Early Years settings and there is therefore a degree of knowledge and understanding already established upon which Early Years educators can build. These early experiences are important in relation to future conventional writing development. Writing is hard work; it is therefore task of the Early Years educator to create exciting and inspirational activities that motivate children to see writing as purposeful and relevant. It is important to get to know the children that we teach in order to inspire them, through meaningful contexts, to write.

Pointers for writing in the Early Years

Young writers need:

- to perceive themselves as writers;
- an environment in which they are perceived as writers, where their writing is valued whatever their stage of development;
- an environment to write in which provides exciting, interesting and real purposes for writing;
- to have ownership of their writing;
- to have some choice over what they write about;
- to have experiences which link writing with talking and reading; and
- to see adults writing.

References

Bearne, E. (2002). *Making Progress in English*. London: Routledge.

Bhowanji, P., Lord, B., and Wilkes, C. (2008). *'I Know What to Write Now!' Engaging Boys (and Girls) through a Multimodal Approach*. Leicester: UKLA.

Bradford, H., and Wyse, D. (2010). Writing in the Early Years. In D. Wyse, R. Andrews, and J. Hoffman (Eds.), *The Routledge International Handbook of English, Language and Literacy Teaching*. London: Routledge.

Bradford, H., and Wyse, D. (2013). Writing and Writers: The Perceptions of Young Children and Their Parents. *Early Years* 33(3), 252–265.

Bromley, H. (2006). *Making My Own Mark – Play and Writing*. London: Early Education.

Clay, M. M. (1975). *What Did I Write? Beginning Writing Behaviour*. Portsmouth, NH: Heinemann Educational Books.

Compton-Lilly, C. (2006). Identity, Childhood Culture, and Literacy Learning: A Case Study. *Journal of Early Childhood Literacy* 6(1), 57–76.

Dyson, A. (2001). Writing and Children's Symbolic Repertoires: Development Unhinged. In S. B. Neuman & D. K. Dickinson (Eds.), *Handbook of Early Literacy Research*. NY: The Guildford Press.

Fisher, R., Jones, S., Larkin, S., and Myhill, D. (2010). *Using Talk to Support Writing*. London: Sage.

Goodman, Y. M. (1986). Readers' and Writers' Talk about Language. In C. Pontecorvo, B. Burge and L. B. Resnic (Eds.), *Children's Early Text Construction*. NJ: Lawrence Erlbaum Associates.

Hall, N. (1987). *The Emergence of Literacy*. London: Hodder & Stoughton.

Harste, J. C., Woodward, V. A., and Burke, C. L. (1984). *Language Stories and Literacy Lessons*. Portsmouth, NH: Heinemann Educational Books.

Jacobs, G. M. (2004). A Classroom Investigation of the Growth of Metacognitive Awareness in Kindergarten Children through the Writing Process. *Early Childhood Education Journal* 32(1), 17–23.

Lancaster, L., (2003) Moving into Literacy: How It All Begins. In N. Hall, J. Larson, and J. Marsh (Eds.), *Handbook of Early Childhood Literacy*. London: Sage.

Neuman, S.B., and Roskos, K. (1997). Literacy Knowledge in Practice: Contexts of Participation in Young Writers and Readers. *Reading Research Quarterly* 32(1), 10–32.

Pahl, K. (1999). *Transformations: Meaning Making in a Nursery*. London: Trentham.

Purcell-Gates, V. (1996). Stories, Coupons and the TV Guide: Relationships between Home Literary Experiences and Emergent Literacy Knowledge. *Reading Research Quarterly* 31(4), 406–428.

Rowe, D. W. (2003). The Nature of Young Children's Authoring. In N. Hall, J. Larson, and J. Marsh (Eds.), *Handbook of Carly Childhood Literacy*. London: Sage.

Teale, W., and Sulzby, E. (1986). *Emergent Literacy: Writing and Reading*. Norwood, NJ: Ablex.

UKLA/Primary National Strategy (2004). *Raising Boys' Achievements in Writing*. Leicester: UKLA.

Wray, D. (1994). *Literacy and Awareness*. London: Hodder & Stoughton.

Younger, M., and Warrington, M. (2005). *Raising Boys' Achievement*. Research Report 636. Leicester: UKLA.

CHAPTER 9

'What's that dog thinking, Mrs Bromley?'

PICTURE BOOKS AND LEARNING TO READ

Helen Bromley

Supporting young children with their development as readers should be an exciting prospect for all those working with children in the Early Years: building on the knowledge of reading that they bring with them, sharing well-loved favourite texts, introducing and discussing new authors and titles, and, most of all, watching the children's excitement grow as the world of the reader opens up to them (see Figure 9.1).

Figure 9.1 *The excitement of reading!*

My own memories of school reading are not exciting. I can vividly recall being sent to the headmistress' study to read some of my *Happy Venture Reader* books (Schonell, 1958–) to her. Although I can remember Dick, Dora, Nip and Fluff, it is not with any particular affection. They are remembered more as distant relations who had to be tolerated, rather than as good friends. The books with which I formed the closest ties had been introduced to me at home, courtesy of the local library: *Little Bear*, *Fox in Socks* and many others. This was in the late '50s. Since then there has been an explosion in the publishing of books for children, providing educators with a rich and varied selection to use in the classroom.

Liz Waterland (1992) talks about the difference between 'free range' and 'battery' books. The former are those written by authors and illustrators who have had freedom to carefully choose and compose their books from the imagination, whilst the latter, the 'battery' books, are products of a factory-type approach to literature: 'There is a hint of unnatural practices, of confinement and restriction...even a suggestion of the mechanical and the automatic' (pp. 160–161).

Books as children's friends

In order to explore this difference further, I will return to the analogy of friendship. Children need friends that they can interact with time and time again; they need to share the good times and the bad. Books described as 'free range' – that is, high quality, multi-layered texts – provide such opportunities. Amelia, aged four, sat with a copy of *The Teddy Robber* every morning before school for six months, just as she might have depended on one child for friendship. She read it over and over again, taking great comfort in its familiarity and the happy ending. Eventually, she was able to make other 'friendships', but in times of stress she always returned to *The Teddy Robber*. Developing favourite texts is a key experience that all young readers should have, and is closely linked to the development of tastes and preferences.

Brooke, whose Aunt had recently died, took the book *Granpa* home, not for herself but for her mum. As she explained to me, 'It's so mummy will see that everything will be all right in the end.' An example of one friend helping another, and an example of how the youngest children can develop an understanding of how reading can support all of us. I have used many reading schemes during my career and cannot recall examples of any which would have provided such support. 'Battery' books do not provide the sort of friends that stick around for long. They are with you for a short period of time, before you leave them and move on to the next. Lasting ties are not encouraged.

One of the important parts of friendship is the shared conversations that can exist. With your friends you laugh, cry and build a collection of joint memories, whilst all the time finding out more about yourself. Children's literature can provide such experiences. Alyck took *Owl Babies* home repeatedly because he thought that Bill, the baby owl, was so funny. Other young children that I have taught enjoyed *Owl*

Babies because they felt that 'missing their mum' is legitimised in the story, and they strongly identified with Bill.

Children need friends that will help them learn without fear of failure and with the knowledge that risk taking is a worthwhile activity. Friends encourage you to 'have another go', whether that is trying to ride your bike without stabilisers or reading *Each, Peach, Pear, Plum* for yourself. Books such as those I have mentioned invite re-reading because they offer opportunities to see the familiar and unfamiliar juxtapositioned in such a way as to make you want to read them again and again – just like visiting an old friend, but playing a new game. Texts constructed especially for the teaching of reading may not provide such friendly support, especially if reading does not come easily. It is often difficult for children to recognise themselves in the text (or illustrations) and there may be no chance of trying out a new game until you have mastered the old one.

There is no doubt that the best friends are those that grow and change with you, not just those that were suitable for you when you were five or eight. This is also true of children's reading material. As C.S. Lewis wrote, 'No book is really worth reading at the age of ten which is not equally (and often far more) worth reading at the age of fifty' (1982). Look at the books that you use in the classroom as if you were looking for friends. If you do not find them interesting and want to get to know them better, then why should the children? This is not to deny that there will be differences in opinion and in taste, but it's a good place to start.

I hope that, encouraged by the adults with whom they work, children can develop a rich collection of good friends, to be remembered with affection and pleasure, friends who teach them that reading is a pleasure for life, not a series of hoops through which they must jump. This chapter intends to introduce activities for using meaningful texts with children that have been successful in my own Early Years classroom. It is not intended to be a definitive list of suggestions. Far from it! I hope instead that people will try one (or all) of the ideas out for themselves and be inspired to go on to discover more.

What young children need to learn about reading

It is important to accept that young children already know much about reading when they enter our classrooms. The activities outlined in this chapter, therefore, are designed to allow children to demonstrate what they already know, as well as educating them in new lessons about reading. Henrietta Dombey (1992, pp. 12–15) summarises the lessons that she feels children need to learn about reading; this is an abridged version of her list:

Attitudes

- Pleasure and satisfaction: to see books as a powerful source of enjoyment, information and understanding.

- Confidence: a firm belief that they will learn to read.
- Concentration and persistence.
- Toleration of uncertainty.
- Tentativeness: a readiness to correct error.
- Reflexiveness: a readiness to look with a certain detachment at what they can do and have read, and at what they need to learn.

Knowledge and strategies

Children need to understand

- That the text is the same on each re-reading and that the marks on the page tell you what to say.
- That language is composed of separable words.
- The conventions of the English language system.
- That words are made up of individual letters.
- The rules of English spelling.
- A reliable sight vocabulary.
- How to use their knowledge of the world and the content of books to aid word identification.
- How to use the information from the pictures [as in Figure 9.2].
- How to use all these various devices together – orchestration.

I feel that the best way for children to learn these vital lessons is through the provision of a variety of rewarding experiences, provided by an educator who is enthusiastic about reading. Some lessons will, by necessity, be more explicit than others, but

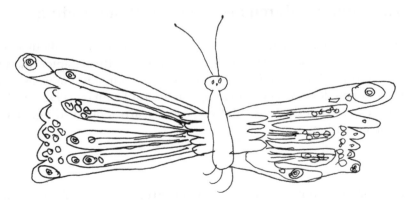

HaNNaH andrstas The words Becos of The Piclets.

Figure 9.2 *Using information from the pictures*

all will be crucial to the development of the children as readers. There is not room within this chapter to document all the ways in which it is possible to support the emergent reader, but the activities outlined below show a variety of meaningful contexts in which most, if not all, of the above lessons could be learned, both implicitly and explicitly.

Big books

The theory behind using Big Books is well documented. Holdaway (1979), for example, working in New Zealand in the 1970s, looked at children who were already reading when they came to school in order to find out what had made them successful. Many of the children had favourite stories that were read to them repeatedly. Gradually, the children were able to take on more of the reading for themselves, firstly by remembering the text and eventually being able to match words and phrases to the known text. Big Books were devised as a way of making stories available to a wider audience. Holdaway noted that all of the children were able to be successful at their own level with this approach. Large groups were able to be involved in the shared reading of a familiar text; such books provided a shared context for discussion and made it easy for all the children in a class to focus on the chosen text.

A favourite Big Book in my reception class was *This Is the Bear*. The children already knew the text extremely well, having heard the small version read out many times. The text rhymes and has marvellous pictures, features which help support the developing reader. Using this story in its outsize version helped the children to learn both explicit and implicit lessons about reading. Each time the big book is used, a similar format can be followed:

- Look closely at the cover. Find features such as title, author, illustrator, publisher and publisher's symbol. If this is done on a regular basis, then the children will pick up the vocabulary surrounding books and authorship very quickly. They then use these terms for themselves, quite naturally.
- Have a look at each page, ignoring nothing. Some books contain beautifully constructed endpapers and in some case these tell part of the story (as in *Farmer Duck*, for example).
- Look for dedications. To whom would the children dedicate a book?
- What initials would they use?
- Do the cover and the preceding pages tell the reader anything about the story that is to follow?

Developing comprehension skills

The teacher can then follow one of several paths. Skills of prediction and authorship can be encouraged by reading the story part of the way through and asking the children to decide what happens next. To extend this activity, ask the children to justify their reasons for suggesting particular outcomes. This provides an excellent opportunity for formative assessment of their ability to make deductions and create their own hypotheses.

Alternatively, the story can be read to the children, not necessarily without interruption, but with as little as possible, so that the children can get the most meaning from the story. This will be the first of many readings, so there will be plenty of opportunities for discussion. The idea is not to encourage passive listeners – an audience powerless to interrupt the reading instructor – but rather to encourage the children to join in and to question what they see and what they hear. This is more effective, however, when the children have heard the whole story through once and have a shared context for discussion.

There are many ways in which big books can be used to stimulate discussion. One of the most effective ways I have used is to organise the children into small 'talk groups' and ask them to devise questions to ask about the story. This gives all children some opportunity to be involved in discussion about the text, and provides a safe context for talk for those who prefer not to speak in front of a large group. It also promotes close scrutiny of the text in a collaborative way, providing an ideal opportunity for children to discuss their reading and learn from one another.

Looking at features of print

As well as promoting comprehension skills, big books can be used to look carefully at features of print.

- Choose a particular letter. How many of this particular letter can the children find on one page or on a double-page spread?
- Can they find any shorter words within longer words, such as 'is', 'in', 'the', or 'and'?
- Can they find two words with similar endings? (This is particularly useful in a rhyming text.)
- How many capital letters can they see? Whereabouts do they appear in the text?
- Introduce the children to the notion of the silent letter. Can any of these be found?
- Use the children's own names as a basis for the print search. Can Jodie find any words beginning with J? Can Matthew find 'at', 'the' or 'he'? My experience has shown that children especially enjoy the activities that involve their names and quickly learn features of not only their own, but also other people's names.
- Children can also be encouraged to devise similar questions of their own, so that this can become an independent, as well as an adult-led, activity.

Obviously, there is far more to becoming a critical and highly motivated reader than studying metalinguistic features of print! As educators, we want children to know that reading is pleasurable and that there is much to be gained from the re-reading of old favourites. Again using big books, it is possible to demonstrate all of this to children and, at the same time, allow them space to air their opinions and perceptions about the books that they are reading. This is achieved by a combination of teacher questioning and, most importantly, providing the opportunity for the children to ask their own questions.

Looking beyond the text

- Children can be put into groups of two or three and asked to devise one question about the story (illustrations included).
- Encourage the children to focus on how the illustrations might be telling a different story to the pictures.
- Look carefully at the body language of the participants.
- Follow the actions of one character throughout the whole story. Use this tracking as a basis for studying character, motive and plot!

Looking beyond the text is especially exciting, as, even with numerous readings of the same text, the children always spot something new. This was demonstrated when I discussed *This Is the Bear* with a class of five-year-olds. Briefly, this is the tale of a teddy bear who is pushed into the dustbin by a dog and mistakenly taken to the dump. He is found, after a long search, by the same dog, and driven home to a hero's welcome! Questions devised about the story included:

- Why did the dog push the bear into the bin?
- How does the bear feel about being in the bin?
- How would you feel if you lost your teddy and couldn't get it back?
- Do you think that the dog is jealous of the bear?
- Do you think that the bear likes the dog?
- What's that dog thinking, Mrs. Bromley?

I think that it is important to note that there were no questions of the 'What colour is the van?' type. All of the questions generated by the children looked deep into the story to try and find out more about the characters in it.

Games and play

Whenever I have carried out such activities with my class, I have always told the children that it is part of a game; sometimes them against me, sometimes a collaborative guessing game. For example, individual words can be covered up with a small piece of card, while the children close their eyes. When they open them, they have to guess which word is covered. This promotes close scrutiny of the text and finger/voice match. Then, when the large-group session is over, I always suggested that if they wanted to play the games themselves, later, then they could do so. All that needs to be provided is a big book, clipped to an easel, four chairs placed in a semi-circle around it and something to be used as a pointer.

This game was a particular favourite with Eleanor, Hannah and Rebecca, who would often take the opportunity to persuade other members of the class to come and take part as pupils, whilst they operated their own version of team teaching. Rebecca, the most experienced reader in the group, would ask questions like 'Can you find "the" on this page?' Eleanor, who was particularly skilled at memorising texts, would read the book to the rest of the group, pointing with the ruler as she did so. That left Hannah, who had an excellent grasp of initial sounds and was able to devise questions such as 'Can you find a word on here that begins with the same sound as "apple"?' I think that the pupils in the game were getting some excellent teaching from three young experts.

From watching the children play what in my class has become known simply as 'schools', it is apparent that the children reproduce and therefore reinforce the types of behaviour demonstrated by the teacher. Each time the game is played it is never an exact copy of the previous game: new ideas are added and children negotiate and discuss the questions and the answers.

Developing children's awareness

The children in my class have also had the opportunity to share the Big Books available with their reading partners, children from a Year 2 class. At one session, I asked the children to reflect, in their pairs, on how Big Books might help them with their reading. Here are some of their comments:

'I like Big Books because you can always see the writing.'

'I think and my friend thinks that a Walker Big Book is good because you can see them better than you can see an ordinary book and you can see the pictures better.'

'Big Books help you to read properly because they have big words to help you read.'

'It will help you write better. Reading will help you think better. It will help you to learn. It will help you think about the pictures.'

As you can see, the children are very much aware of how the large format of the books encourages them to become participants in the shared reading process, allowing them to become even more involved than in a normal storytelling session. Talk is central to all of the activities outlined above. They are operating in the zone of proximal development (Vygotsky, 1986) alongside a more experienced reader, and their own knowledge and learning potential will only become apparent if they are allowed to explore their knowledge through conversation. Through role play (such as the game of 'schools') they are able to have the opportunity to act as the more able other, in the company of their peers. Self-esteem and confidence is built up this way, and there is room for errors to be made away from the watchful eye of an adult.

THiS IS The
BEAR

BIY NiiJKi
ahɒ KeLLJKi
aʌɒ PaUL

BIɬ BOOKS

Heip you to YeD PoPey
Bekey Tay HaF BIG WUS.
To HLP uoy riɒ.

Figure 9.3 *'Big Books help you to read properly because they have big words to help you read'*

Group reading

Big Books are not the only way in which children can be encouraged to play with their reading. Group reading around multiple copies of the same text provides similar opportunities if the right atmosphere for learning and risk-taking is created.

Maisie Middleton is the story of an ordinary little girl who gets up one morning and, despite attempting to rouse her parents, eventually has to prepare breakfast for herself. It is a story which appealed to all the children in my class, possibly because they too would like to share some of Maisie's independence, however transitory. It was because of the popularity of the book that I chose it as a subject for group reading. All four children in the group had heard the story an equal number of times and could therefore bring some previous knowledge to the group situation.

During the session, the children first listen to the story read out loud, joining in if they wish. They then take it in turn to ask questions about each of the pages of the book, either to each other or to the adult present. I was surprised at how involved the children became with this particular text. I soon realised that I had underestimated its potential. The first page shows the exterior of Maisie's house, framed in an arch with a flower on the top. Eleanor began. 'I wonder who sleeps behind the blind with the stripes on?' she asked, and immediately the others joined in, speculating on the possible occupants of the house. Brooke was trying to imagine herself at the front door, stroking the cat and bringing in the milk. What to me had appeared to be a fairly simplistic picture provided the children with a rich source of discussion for at least 15 minutes. I thought that we were never going to get any further into the book! Much knowledge was revealed in this discussion and many questions asked and answered. It's wrong to assume that it is always the adult that provides the answers. Thomas wanted to know why the milk was still on the doorstep; he was worried in case the sun turned it sour. It was Brooke that pointed out to him that as the blinds were still down, it must still be early in the morning. Eleanor also pointed out that the stars were still in the sky, so 'That's why the milk hadn't been taken in.' This discussion clearly demonstrated the children's speaking and listening skills, as well as their powers of reasoning and their ability to apply their knowledge of the real world to the imaginary world of the book. It also allowed them to develop ways of taking pleasure from the text that were in addition to those intended by the author.

Whilst we were still considering the first two pages of the book, the children started to do something that I can clearly remember doing as a child: they began to pretend that they were in the book themselves. They began by deciding which room was which in Maisie Middleton's house and divided them up amongst themselves. Space was also made for siblings and pets, ensuring links between the real world and the imaginary one.

I felt that this incident demonstrated an enormous amount, not only about the children's understanding of the book, but also of their awareness of the possibilities that exist for any reader. (Another description of a child talking about Maisie Middleton can be found in Barbara Jordan's 1992 article 'Good for any Age'.) I feel strongly that these lessons are as important as the lessons of sight vocabulary and decoding of text. It was very rewarding when, a few days later, Eleanor asked 'Can we play that pretending game again? You know, that one when we were in the book. That was really good.' Following the success of this activity, I built it into further group-reading sessions, although the children did not need much direction from me. It was as popular with non-fiction texts as with stories, with children taking on the roles of knights and soldiers in one particular book.

Some tips for group reading:

- Try to provide a range of texts for this activity: include non-fiction, comics, etc.
- Use groups of texts by one author/illustrator, so the children can identify similar features.
- Promote discussion about the characters. Who would the children most like/not like to be?
- Encourage and promote the use of puppets and props with the books: a group of zoo animals with *Dear Zoo*, for example.

'Reading out'

This activity was actually devised by my class themselves, and was to provide a source of pleasure to them for many weeks, as well as giving me the opportunity to listen to them read, checking their sight vocabulary, acquisition of known texts and their understanding of what they were reading. Reading standards in the class improved dramatically, as did listening skills and concentration spans. It was such a worthwhile activity that I shall definitely introduce it to any new group of children that I teach.

The activity began when Rebecca came in one morning and asked if she could read *Daley B*, her favourite book of the moment, to the rest of the class. It was agreed that she could, and later in the day she read the book, with great expression and obvious understanding. The reaction from the rest of the class was extremely positive. Not only did they all, including the most restless children, listen attentively and with keen interest, but many of them offered to read out too. In fact, the whole activity snowballed. Children were allowed to 'read out', on their own, with a friend or in a small group. This was to allow some of those children who were not quite brave enough to read by themselves to have the opportunity to participate in what became a very highly regarded activity.

The most popular grouping for the activity was a trio. Within this group there would be one child who knew the text extremely well, one who knew it quite well, and one who was in the group to gain confidence and add to their knowledge of that particular text. This was a very good example of how children are able to achieve more when in the company of others than they could possibly achieve on their own. It provided great opportunities for the rest of the class to practise texts that were known to them already and add new texts to those that were familiar. Because the children were copying behaviour that they had seen in adults, many of them became adept at reading with the book held next to them, teacher-style, showing the pictures and questioning their very attentive audience.

I tried not to appropriate this activity, although I found this difficult as I desperately wanted everyone to have a turn. One child in particular, Alyck, could not be encouraged to read out, however hard I tried to persuade him. This situation changed when his friend Sebastian wanted someone to read out *Each, Peach, Pear,*

Plum with him. He chose Alyck, who found it impossible to refuse his friend, even though it had been quite easy to refuse my requests. Alyck did read the book out with Sebastian, extremely well, and this provided an enormous boost to his confidence and self-esteem. After this occasion, he frequently read out to the class.

Although I was involved in the activity as a non-participant observer, the children regulated the whole of the sessions themselves. Everyone who wanted to read out would leave their chosen book, with a named post-it note on the front, on a special chair, waiting for reading out time. They would question each other about the books that were read out and would comment on each other's reading. This was delightful to hear, and was only ever positive. Comments such as 'Your reading's coming along very well, Hayley', were never patronising, but well meant.

The teacher's role

It is important to realise that the three activities outlined above should not be young children's only experience with good quality picture books. They should exist as part of a well thought out set of experiences designed to give children myriad opportunities to engage with the literacy heritage that surrounds them. As educators, we have the power to excite and inspire the children in our care and this should not be underestimated. Early years educators should make good use of, and familiarise themselves with, the rich variety of books that are published for young children, developing favourites of their own in order to be able to demonstrate to children that it is OK to have tastes and preferences that are different from one another.

I believe quite passionately that the picture books of today will provide far more 'good friends' for the children that I teach than the *Happy Venture Series* ever did for me. However, in order to become known to children, these friends must first be invited into classrooms and introduced to children in ways that make them want to 'play with them', time and time again. As Henrietta Dombey (1992) states:

> All children need the skilled help of informed and sympathetic adults, who appreciate their strengths and weaknesses, have a clear idea of the goal ahead and engage the children's interest and commitment. They also need to encounter texts that are involving, manageable and satisfying, and give them a clear sense that they are making progress. If all this occurs in ways that are exciting and inspiring, then young children will certainly acquire many 'friends for life'. (p. 20)

Pointers to supporting the emergent reader

- Take the time to get to know a wide range of children's books yourself.
- Act as a role model for the children, demonstrating enthusiasm for and an interest in books and other reading materials.

- Encourage children to talk about what they have read, to you and each other.
- Plan for a wide range of reading experiences which include incorporating reading into children's play experiences (puppets, props, etc.).
- Develop effective and informative ways of monitoring the children's progress that truly reflect all aspects of the reading process, not merely the acquisition of sight vocabulary.

References

Dombey, H. (1992) *Words and Worlds: Reading in the Early Years of School.* Sheffield: NATE.

Holdaway, D. (1979) *The Foundations of Literacy.* Sydney: Ashton Scholastic.

Jordan, B. (1992) 'Good For Any Age: Picture Books and the Experienced Reader.' In M. Styles, E. Bearne, & V. Watson (Eds.), *After Alice.* London: Cassell.

Lewis, C.S. (1982) *On Stories.* New York and London: Harcourt Brace Jovanovich.

Vygotsky, L. (1986) *Thought and Language.* Cambridge, MA: MIT Press.

Waterland, L. (1992) 'Ranging Freely: The Why and What of Real Books.' In M. Styles, E. Bearne, & V. Watson (Eds.), *After Alice.* London: Cassell.

Children's books mentioned in the text

Ahlberg, J. & A. (1980) *Each, Peach, Pear, Plum.* London: Picture Lions.

Beck, I. (1991) *The Teddy Robber.* London: Picture Corgi.

Blake, J. (1992) *Daley B.* London: Walker Books.

Burningham, J. (1984) *Granpa.* London: Cape.

Campbell, R. (1985) *Dear Zoo.* London: Puffin.

Hayes, S. (1995) *This Is the Bear.* London: Walker Books.

Holmelund Minarik, E. (1957) *Little Bear.* New York: Scholastic Book Services.

Schonell, F.J. (1958–) *Happy Venture Reader* [series]. Edingurgh: Oliver & Boyd.

Seuss, Dr. (1965) *Fox in Socks.* London: Collins.

Sowter, N. (1994) *Maisie Middleton.* London: Diamond Books.

Waddell, M. & Benson, P. (1991) *Farmer Duck.* London: Walker Books.

Waddell, M. & Oxenbury, H. (1992) *Owl Babies.* London: Walker Books.

The wider curriculum

CHAPTER 10

'We are passing the smile around'

PERSONAL, SOCIAL, HEALTH AND EMOTIONAL
EDUCATION IN THE EARLY YEARS

Sue Bingham

Introduction

When a young child starts in school, becomes a member of a class or goes out into the playground, before they can even begin to take in any 'formal' learning, a huge amount of new personal, emotional and social learning has to occur. The child will be bringing with them their *home* experience of acceptable and unacceptable behaviours and they will have already developed some sense of right and wrong. Although, obviously, the more aligned the values and attitudes are between the home and school, the smoother the child will find the transition, in a sense, the child needs to 'start again' within this different social group called school.

Fundamentally the child needs to feel comfortable with, to get to know, and relate to one or more key adults. They need to become familiar with their surroundings, finding their way around strange buildings and rooms, with new routines and rules. And they have to become used to being with lots of other children, most of whom are likely to be unfamiliar at first. These are all new experiences for the child and require speedy accommodation of particular 'rules':

*   Rules for behaviour within a group: Why do I have to wait? Why can't I have my turn on the scooter right now?
*   Rules for behaviour within a classroom: What does 'tidying up' mean here and why can't I run inside when I want to?
*   Rules for behaviour within a school: What is 'assembly' and why do I have to put my hand up?

In essence, these 'rules' form a basic framework for ways of behaving generally in life, within any group of individuals, where the needs and desires of others, as well as oneself, have to be taken into account and reflected in behaviour. Early Years practitioners are pivotal in shaping a young child's first experiences in being in a society outside the family and in scaffolding their personal learning to adapt, cope and succeed in emotionally and socially demanding situations. There is much to be learned from the many studies of interaction between *parents* and children within a home environment, which provide a strong starting point for the sensitive practitioner to build upon in supporting the child's personal, social and emotional needs. Such pointers include:

- Often, parents are in a 1:1 situation with children, or at least in a small group – so there is *frequent interaction*.
- Parents explicitly demonstrate their love and care for their child – this is reflected in signs of *genuine interest* in their actions, thoughts and development.
- Parents operate in the *real world*; they are surrounded by a panorama of visual, aural and tactile stimuli – authentic sights and sounds which continually fascinate children and cause them to ask what, why and how.
- In most situations, parents *respond* to their child's initiatives for interaction, rather than deciding beforehand what the child needs to learn.
- Within the informal learning environment of the home, parents give their children *time* to learn – time to pose meaningful questions, time to form own hypotheses, time to try things out, time to make mistakes, time to leave things be – time to return to them later when the time is right.

What is 'social and emotional learning' (SEL)?

Social and emotional learning (SEL) has been defined as the process through which emotions are recognised and managed, healthy relationships are established, positive goals are set, ethical and responsible behaviours are developed and negative behaviours are avoided (Payton et al., 2000). Only some of this learning takes place within school environments, of course – but over recent years a persuasive body of research on ways to support young children's emotional and social behavioural self-regulation in educational establishments has emerged in the form of SEL programmes to guide professionals. Many of these programmes break down emotional and social concepts into a framework of curriculum content, to be 'transmitted' in lessons but not necessarily starting from the interests, experience and choices of young children within their individual social contexts. Hence, in this chapter I argue that the provision of a mere PHSE 'curriculum' is inadequate for children in Early Years. A more holistic and balanced approach is required for young children in these crucial years of development. A 'pedagogy' is required – a broader concept than 'curriculum', in that it takes into account the wider everyday physical and social environments of young children, placing equal value upon their care, physical development and learning. The aims of such a pedagogy are not so much content-related but process-related; there needs to be an emphasis upon supporting the learning of skills and the acquiring of dispositions towards personal, health and social and emotional well-being that will be useful to the child in their life-long learning.

So, even though current best practice recommends that SEL programmes should begin in the pre-school and continue through the school-age years, within this chapter there is a strong emphasis upon practitioners supporting children's emotional and social skill development _through the weaving of activities throughout the regular school day in a way that encourages meaningful incremental learning and consolidation_, rather than 'stand alone' lessons delivered in isolation as part of a timetabled PHSE curriculum. The development and maintenance of a safe, supportive learning environment in which children feel respected and cared for, and the adults model social and emotional skills appropriately, provides opportunities for children to practice and apply them both in class, throughout the school and into the home environment. There is persuasive evidence that 'whole-school' approaches, involving changes to the school environment, personal skills development in class, and parental participation, are on the whole more effective than purely classroom-based programmes (e.g. Barlow, Parsons, & Stewart-Brown, 2005).

The development of whole-school approaches

The development of a 'whole-school' approach involves consideration of all associated individuals' personal responses to questions about ethos and values that guide their behaviour and interpersonal relationships within school. Such consideration leads into discussion and agreement amongst everyone in the setting, including catering staff, playground supervisors, parent helpers, secretarial support staff, caretakers, classroom assistants, practitioners, parents – and, of course, children. Such discussion takes time, but is crucial in building consistency in approach between every member of the school in every activity throughout the school day. In essence, responsive adults build respectful, caring relationships with children through:

- treating the children as equal partners in conversation;
- following the child's lead; and
- negotiating meanings and purposes.

The messages related throughout every aspect of school life need to project a consistent ethos of respect, consideration, inclusion and equality. The notices on the wall, the letters home, the manner in which all families are treated and the way in which children are spoken to in the playground are all part of this work. It is the motivation, energy, enthusiasm and positivity of all the adults that energises a school into a hive of productive and creative activities and which builds an environment perfect for learning and development.

Social and emotional learning programmes (SEL programmes)

Within Social and Emotional Learning programmes, social and emotional skills are explicitly taught, practised and applied to diverse situations. Examples of such classroom-based programmes include _Zippy's Friends_ (Clarke & Barry, 2010), PATHS

(*Promoting Alternative Thinking Strategies*) (Domitrovich & Greenberg, 2000) and, in use in many UK primary schools, the DCSF's *Social and Emotional Aspects of Learning* (DCSF, 2005) teaching programme, implemented in many maintained schools with children aged 3 to 11 years. The overall intention of these programmes is that children internalise the specified skills, strategies and attitudes, integrating them into their repertoire of behaviours. It is intended that they should help children feel motivated to succeed, to believe in their success, to communicate well with their practitioners, to set academic goals, to organise themselves to achieve these goals and to overcome obstacles.

However, PHSE programmes need careful planning across the year groups so as to avoid over-repetition or the introduction of emotional concepts that are too advanced for the developmental stage of the children for whom the lesson is prescribed. Further, the dominant methods within many of the PHSE resources rely upon a capacity and willingness on the part of the child not just to recognise and manage feelings, but to talk about them as well. For many personalities, a repeated focus on introspection and self-evaluation may be at best uncomfortable and, at worst, even distressing. Moreover, due simply to immaturity, young children may not have the skills of articulation required by this approach. The introduction of issues such as the recognition and management of emotions and the use of regulation strategies by the child need to be handled with great sensitivity by practitioners in today's settings, as we deal with children from a wide range of backgrounds with associated diversity in their experience of cultural, emotional and social behaviours and 'norms'.

The real-life emotional-regulation strategies required in adulthood encompass abilities to assess socially and emotionally challenging situations and decide whether to join in, avoid them or try to modify them. We *should* be encouraging even young children to acquire and practise such strategies for coping with their own feelings and others' behaviour, but in *naturally occurring situations* within the setting. As with all *real* learning, emotional and social 'lessons' have to be personally experienced to be properly learned. Children need to make mistakes and learn from them; where better to learn this than in the safe environment of their setting with their friends? The *ways* in which practitioners can most successfully focus upon elements of personal, social, emotional and health education with children – building upon children's naturally developing competencies in self-control, recognising and managing feelings, and in interpersonal problem-solving – by weaving them into everyday, naturally occurring classroom 'episodes', are examined in the following sections.

Self-determination theory

Self-determination theory (SDT) offers a useful description of three areas of focus that underpin continuing personal development not just for children, but for all individuals, throughout life. SDT is a theory of motivation that assumes that all learners, no matter how young or inexperienced they might be, are guided by a set of innate psychological needs, namely relatedness, autonomy and competence, which shape their self-motivation, their building of self-esteem and their healthy personal development. The theory holds that, from the very earliest stages of development, children have an inbuilt, proactive motivation to explore and understand aspects of their environment. From a practitioner's perspective, finding ways to support this active motivation in children is the key to facilitating their optimal learning, engagement, constructive emotional development and social well-being (Ryan & Deci, 2000).

Personal and health education

Competence

The concept of 'self' starts to develop early in life. By the time a child starts in the foundation stage they have a relatively sophisticated understanding that they have knowledge, experiences, preferences and desires that may be quite different from those of other children. The practitioner can build upon this emerging understanding of 'self' in many ways to support healthy psychological development.

Building self-esteem

When children feel good about themselves they are more likely to approach tasks in a positive way and learn to accept disappointments. Practitioners can support the building of positive self-esteem through:

- showing an interest in what the child is doing and learning;
- providing encouragement and praise for things they have done well, and also for trying new things; and
- avoiding jumping in too early to do things for children and introducing simple tasks the child can do by themselves.

Autonomy

Practitioners who support children's autonomy believe it is important for them to initiate behaviours, to learn from both their successes and their failures and to try to solve problems for themselves rather than relying upon the practitioner to tell them what to do. The child's developing 'I can' approach towards learning experiences must be nurtured. Their inner motivation to try new activities and 'have a go' can be built upon by the sensitive practitioner through recognising the children's natural inclinations, finding ways in which to build teaching activities around their interests, preferences, and sense of fun, and through providing challenge and choice-making. A child's growing sense of autonomy may be enhanced through the environment, in tandem with the adults' practice:

Figure 10.1 *'Oh yes! My turn! My turn!'*

- positioning learning resources and seating arrangements in such a way so as to encourage activity rather than passivity;
- giving children options both in the context of practitioner-planned activities and during free choice time;
- providing opportunities for children to talk and to work in their own way;
- agreeing rules and routines with children that are clear but flexible; and
- allowing children appropriate responsibilities, such as finding and putting away materials, trying to solve problems before going to the practitioner, having class-room 'jobs'.

Encouraging children to become 'masters' of themselves

Many of the child's natural motivations to become competent and to 'master' their world can be built upon through a setting's approach to personal and health education. Children naturally want to do what adults do, by themselves – how many times have we heard the phrase 'I can do it myself!' as we go to help a child put on their own coat or shoes? This desire to self-regulate in physical ways can be built upon by practitioners through everyday routines and activities within the setting which reinforce self-help skills and promote the development of children's gross and fine motor skills. It may mean that some basic routines initially take longer than if the adults were doing the acts for the children, but just think of all that burgeoning self-esteem, as the children become increasingly competent!

Figure 10.2 *'I'm not going to spill a single drop!'*

- Self registration upon arrival
- Putting on own shoes, coats, gloves, aprons
- Pouring own drinks (see Figure 10.2)
- Encouraging basic 'good manners' such as holding the door open for others to pass through; closing, not slamming doors; offering others a piece of fruit before taking a piece oneself; wiping up spills at the snack table ready for others.

Getting into healthy routines

Routines are also a natural way to implement healthy habits into the setting's everyday activities. In many cases, pictures or photos on the wall near where the routine takes place can remind the child of the sequence of actions they need to carry out.

Keeping clean

Good hygiene habits are an essential part of daily care and are important for protecting children against illnesses. Practitioners can teach children *when* to wash their hands and *how* to do so – for example, how to use a tissue to blow their nose and then 'bin it'.

Dressing skills

Practitioners can support the tricky habit of putting on a coat before going outdoors by modelling how to put the arms in and do up the zip. Rather than deflating a child's self-esteem after attempting to put on their own shoes or plimsolls, practitioners can think about how to address the fact that they are on the wrong feet by gently asking whether their feet 'feel funny?' or 'look funny?'

Practitioners can encourage children to become 'sun aware' by encouraging them to take responsibility for themselves in protecting their skin from sun damage before going outdoors by:

- wearing sun protective clothing – covering up as much of the skin as possible and wearing a hat that covers the face, head, neck and ears and by wearing sunglasses;
- applying sunscreen; and
- seeking shade – on sunny days, making use of trees or built shade structures.

Healthy eating

Children's growth and weight are mainly influenced by the food and drinks they eat and drink and the amount of activity they do. So, within the setting, helping children to set up healthy eating and activity habits is important for normal growth and a healthy weight. The habits they develop now may influence their future health.

Food is a common frustration for practitioners working with young children. While they are still learning about food, tastes, textures, using cutlery, table manners and eating routines, food is one way they express their new found independence. Practitioners can support children by making healthy foods available at regular meal and snack times, setting an example and keeping such times relaxed.

It is common for healthy children to be very hungry some days and not eat much on other days. It is normal that a child's appetite varies from meal to meal and day to day. When children are offered nutritious food they are actually very good at knowing how much they need to eat. A regular meal pattern will help children form healthy eating habits. Try to serve meals and snacks around the same time each day. A break between eating gives the body a chance to feel hungry. It is also good for teeth. Try to share snack and mealtime decisions with the children. Practitioners need to put thought into the healthiness of meals and snacks – and their timings.

- Let the children decide if they want a snack, and offer choice between a limited range of healthy options.
- Let the child decide when they have had enough and remove leftovers without a fuss. Avoid offering alternative snacks if the child does not eat much.
- Provide an end to the snack time – such as leaving the table – to help the child learn that eating has finished until the next meal or snack.

- Phrases like 'Good girl for eating everything' are not helpful because they teach the child to clean their plate or continue to eat when full. Many adults find it hard to break this habit, often because they themselves were told as a child to finish everything on their plate.

Water is the best drink to quench thirst. Tap water and milk are the best drinks for healthy teeth. Encourage the children to drink tap water: a jug can be kept in the fridge in hot weather, or ice cubes, straws and a slice of orange can be used to add interest. Serve tap water or milk (or watered down fruit juice) with meals and snacks.

Talking about weight

Weight is a sensitive issue for parents and children, even as young as four years old. Practitioners should focus on the things that influence weight, not weight itself, encouraging children to eat well and be active through:

- promoting a positive body image by encouraging and praising what the child's body can do, for example learning to ride a bike or doing a somersault; and
- avoiding commenting on body weight (even your own weight) in front of the children;
- never promoting dieting or suggesting weight-loss to the child.

Encouraging children to explore and yet keep safe

Children need opportunities to practise using their body in a safe environment so that they develop confidence in their own skills – for example in bike riding, climbing and digging. They naturally love to run around inside and outside, climbing over and under obstacles and trying to do things that are just above their ability. This will cause some tumbles, bruises and scratches as they test their skills and judgment. It is important to let them explore, but four-year-olds are adventurous and do not always understand danger. In encouraging a 'have-a-go' approach to new experiences, practitioners should resist being over-protective, but make sure that learning areas are safe and that children have appropriately sized equipment for their age and size. Safety rules might include:

- We don't climb up the slide, in case someone decides to slide down!
- We wear a helmet when we play on the bikes!
- Keep away from electric sockets!
- Keep scissors closed in your hand!
- When we cross the road with an adult, we hold hands.

Emotional development

Relatedness

The social environment influences the way in which children's responsiveness and relatedness develop. In particular, the modelling provided by important people in the young child's environment, including very specific types of parental and practitioner behaviours, have been found to be associated with the development of pro-social behaviours in young children. These practitioner behaviours demonstrate strategies of co-operation and negotiation rather than coercion, and have been found to include:

- Modelling pro-social and altruistic behaviour to children within the class; with young children actions may be more powerful than words
- Empathetic care and teaching; a warm and responsive relationship between the practitioner and children may be the most effective promoter of pro-social behaviour. The social 'climate' in which young children grow has a major influence on the child's feelings about others
- The provision of clear rules and boundaries are more likely to foster pro-social behaviours in children, with explicitly detailed consequences of actions. For example, say 'We never kick people; it hurts!' Prohibitive instructions such as 'Stop that!' do not help a young child, as there is no principle to be transferred to a different situation. Moreover, a rule needs to be delivered with emotional conviction so that the child realises the significance of the cognitive message.
- The use of descriptive praise is important. When you praise a child, describe precisely what it is that you like.
- The attribution of positive qualities to the child. When children are repeatedly recognised for pro-social attributes, such as helpfulness and kindness, they internalise these attributions and they become intrinsic motivators for action.

Acknowledging and accepting children's negative emotions

When a practitioner communicates their acknowledgement and acceptance of the fact that sometimes children will not want to conform to classroom practices and rules, for example, they reveal an understanding and support of the children's perspectives and rights to express their sometimes negative emotions as a valid reaction to some of the classroom demands and structures. By 'containing', or accepting children's sometimes negative emotional responses, the practitioner guides children in ways to manage these emotions productively, thus supporting rather than undermining their sense of autonomy and social and emotional competence.

Within Attachment Theory (Bowlby, 1988), the capacity and sensitivity of the primary caregiver, and their ability to understand negative emotions in a child triggered by uncertainty or fear, for example, is a significant aspect of early attachment experience. Bion (1967) linked this to learning and thinking, describing the way in

which the infant, with no experience of the outside world or of the future, experiences some events or needs as 'overwhelming'. However, the sensitive parent or
caregiver understands the child's extreme negative emotion and takes on the bearing
of it, responding in a way that communicates this understanding to the child – in
the early days, perhaps this is communicated through physical contact such as cuddling, or stroking. Bion calls this act *containment* (p. 45). The infant is reassured by
the parent or carer's understanding response and their negative emotion is moder-
ated through the experience of being understood. As the child enters toddlerhood
and beyond, words come to play a role in the adult being able to diminish the child's
negative emotion, and their fear or frustration is therefore reduced through language and thinking. The concept of *containment* of negative emotion can, of course,
be extended to use by practitioners in the setting.

Further, practitioners can scaffold children's emotional development within the
setting through the sensitively timed 'handing back' of elements of the *containment*
process to the child. In other words, the practitioner can support the child's learning of strategies to cope with those negative emotions that seem so overwhelming.
This may begin with introducing children to the language of emotions to help them
identify their feelings. Identifying feelings and 'labelling' them is the first step in
understanding them and learning about their expression, so gives the child a sense
of control over these 'overwhelming' experiences. Eventually, the child becomes
able to think about their negative emotions independently, transforming fear or
disappointment into bearable, thinkable thoughts, tolerating their frustrations or
sadnesses and mediating them through words and reflection. This is the beginning of emotion regulation, the controlling of aroused feelings and the expression of
them in appropriate ways – both important aspects of self-regulated functioning by
young children and important in forming social skills, with implications not only for
friendship and peer status but also for academic competence, self-image and emotional well-being (Denham & Burton, 2003).

Building upon children's natural motivations to relate

Practitioners who think about the language they use in communication with children in the setting are able to build and maintain respectful, trusting relationships
with individual children through:

- listening carefully and being keen to imbue the child's words with meaning;
- treating children's perspectives with respect, empathising with the learner's
  point of view, using straightforward, non-controlling language;
- giving sincere answers to children's questions;
- providing timely, positive feedback, praising progress and encouraging effort
  when it occurs, offering encouragement and giving progress-enhancing hints; and
- keeping behaviour issues brief and non-disruptive, often involving explanations
  or assisting children in their own problem-solving.

Establishing places and times to talk about learning and feelings:
Circle-time

One of the modes through which practitioners support children reflecting on appropriate emotions in specific situations, and ways to manage them, is through the use of circle-time. Jenny Mosely (1996), in her book *Quality Circle Time in the Primary Classroom*, provides a model for a democratic and creative approach used to support practitioners in managing a range of issues that affect the whole learning community. Mosely promotes QCT as part of a whole school approach, with every class participating in their own meeting. QCT has proved successful in promoting better relationships and positive behaviour, two of the most effective improvements to both learning and the smooth and harmonious running of a school (see Figure 10.3).

More generally, a circle-time approach can be used by practitioners for group discussion and to address arising issues for children of almost any age: feelings, how we can be kind to one another, friendships, negotiation skills and how to manage frustration are all commonly debated within the safe confines of circle-time 'boundaries'. It is important that practitioners focus on authentic issues that have arisen in relation to the children's specific real-life social and emotional contexts, at home or in the setting, in order to make such discussions genuine and meaningful for the children, rather than theoretical and abstract.

Figure 10.3 *'We are passing the smile around'*

Citizenship and involvement

In time, the children will come to learn that they can make a difference and that their contribution to the group, their little community, counts. This in turn leads to an understanding that everyone has a responsibility towards the social setting and the peers around them, throughout life.

Practitioners can support children in taking part in discussions with others, encouraging all to become knowledgeable, have an opinion and to take part in simple debates about topical issues. In so doing, practitioners will be supporting children to recognise the choices they can make, and recognise the difference between right and wrong. Children come to:

- realise that they belong to various groups and communities, such as family and school;
- realise that people and other living things have needs, and that *they* have responsibilities to meet them (see Figure 10.4); and
- understand what improves and harms their local, natural and built environments.

The ways in which practitioners can further support *relatedness* in the setting are discussed in the section on social development, below.

Figure 10.4 *'Wow, look at them eating that weed!'*

Social development

Other peers within the setting have an important role in the development of a child's social control and competence (Dunn, Cutting, & Fisher, 2002). Success in establishing friendships is a central issue in development during the Early Years period and depends upon a child's ability to develop an attitude of negotiation and mutual respect, to regulate emotions and control behaviour appropriately in relation to their peers. Simply *being* with other children is not enough to create social competence and so practitioner support in building constructive peer relationships and modelling ways of interaction is important, since the effects of peer neglect are so enduring (Ladd, Herald, & Andrews, 2006), and inadequate, unsuccessful or aggressive patterns of interaction may continue through primary and into secondary school.

Foundation stage children still frequently require practitioner assistance to inhibit impulses, solve social problems and strengthen pro-social attitudes, as well as to accommodate peers' individual differences, other children's desires, suggestions or needs and cope with frustration. The Year 2 child, with a greater appreciation of the perspectives of others, learns to negotiate more actively and independently as peers become increasingly important. Success in establishing friendships is a central issue in development during this period, since access to the teacher is often more limited in larger classes and therefore dependence upon peers for emotional and academic support increases. Moreover, children who participate in social interactions with peers develop more advanced cognitive, linguistic and social skills and develop effective strategies for communicating (Wentzel & Asher, 1995). Peer rejection is associated with both 'externalising disorders', such as aggression, hyperactivity or inappropriate behaviour, and 'internalising disorders' such as excessive negative emotionality and withdrawal behaviours (Eisenberg, 2002). It seems that a lack of peer interaction skills may be related to difficulties in establishing peer relationships in middle childhood years; this in turn appear to predict adjustment problems in adulthood.

Creating a child -oriented setting

The practitioner is key to establishing the physical framework to support social learning within the setting and promote co-operation, negotiation and social competence.

Welcoming children

Most settings have a 'settling in' policy for working with children and parents new to the setting. In many cases practitioners will visit the child in their home environment, reflecting the importance, particularly in the child's Early Years, of the partnership with parents. Such a visit can establish a strong link with home and acknowledges the child's prior experiences as being an important starting point for their new 'school' experiences.

Practitioners can make the environment particularly welcoming through:-

- greeting the child personally each session;
- using a variety of the children's home languages to greet everyone each session;
- establishing a regular system for registering the children, so that they know they are expected and part of the 'whole' group (see Figure 10.5); and
- making sure every child has their own 'space', perhaps with their photograph to identify whose it is – a coat peg, place for their shoes and PE clothes, a tray for their pictures or book bag, for example.

Agreeing rules

In order to feel a sense of safety and security within the setting, as well as relating to others within it, children need to know the 'boundaries' in which to operate. Having this knowledge provides the child with some sense of 'belonging',

Figure 10.5 *A simple self-registration system*

predictability and control, thereby diminishing feelings of threat. If the children are able to be part of the devising of the 'rules' shaping their own behaviour and that of the other members of their little community, then they are far more likely to 'buy into' them. Many practitioners find the time spent in discussing the desired and undesired behaviours for the classroom (or playground, or outdoor area) well worth the effort – and it is useful to do this at the beginning of the academic year, as everyone is getting to know each other and becoming used to sharing the space. Such discussions with the children might include ideas for how we want to move, speak to each other, share resources, treat each other, and look after each other. With young children, the resulting ideas might best be encapsulated in drawings or posters, or the practitioner might couch the ideas as reminders phrased in simple and positive terms, for example:

- We listen to each other.
- We use gentle hands.
- We use kind voices.
- We take turns and share.
- We use 'walking feet' indoors.

Of course, such messages become more naturally ingrained into behaviours if they are repeated with consistency and fairness throughout the whole setting and at different points of the daily routine, such as when lining up, going outside, or having lunch in the dining hall.

Setting organisation: layout and resources

Sadly, in many parts of the UK, parents have become averse to risking letting their children play unsupervised – so they tend to play indoors, in their gardens, or in specially designed play areas, often with safety surfaces to prevent injury from falls. Young children's free time is increasingly closely micro-managed by adults who timetable activities for them, such as music or sports lessons, or – preferring to know the exact whereabouts of their child at all times – encourage them to spend time in isolated activities such as watching TV or DVDs, or playing on computer games (Lester & Russell, 2010). There is clearly a danger that, with less time for engagement in co-operative play and an increase in the reliance upon adults for supervision and direction, there is likely to be a negative effect on children's developing social competencies both in the short and in the longer term. To support their social experiences and learning, Early Years practitioners have an important role in providing opportunities within the setting to encourage collaboration and co-operation between children.

Seating and grouping arrangements

Practitioners can encourage interaction through:

- seating arrangements around tables or on the floor, so that children are in close proximity and can share talk together and ideas;
- keeping large areas of indoor and outdoor space available for block play, construction kits, rail-track building, or large puzzles which encourage problem-solving between children;
- large equipment, such as water trays, sand boxes and wendy houses, being positioned so that children can move freely around them in play as they co-operate in play;
- provision of a comfortable book corner and communal listening spaces for sharing stories indoors and out;
- social snack and meal times, where conversation is encouraged; and
- provision of facilities for drama or joint music-making, such as a stage or a puppet theatre (see Figure 10.6).

The role play area

Role play provides exciting opportunities for socio-emotional development, as skills such as turn-taking, sharing and negotiating are required. Since children are highly motivated to play, practitioners have an influential role in creating role play areas that support such learning. They can scaffold not only through the provision of specific resources and props (such as dressing-up clothes and objects), but also, since children show more advanced imagination when they imitate the pretence of others, through the adults' own role play (Lindqvist, 2001).

Figure 10.6 *'Once upon a time . . .'*

Figure 10.7 *'Five little speckled frogs . . . '*

Firstly, it is interesting to highlight that pretend-play may not really be 'free play' at all, contrary to how it may at first appear upon casual observation. As Vygotksy (1978) pointed out, it is precisely in pretend-play situations, and of their own choice, that children acting within a role put aside their innate desire to act impulsively (e.g. seizing the desired toy, or holding tight to something they want) in favour of 'rule-based' behaviour. He termed this 'the paradox of pretence' (p. 100) – where the child subordinates his or her immediate desires (e.g. to dress up in one particular 'princess dress') in order to conform to the rules of the play, (e.g. to join in with the older children's make-believe drama), which then become the child's 'new form of desire' (p. 100). Several studies (for example, Elias & Berk, 2002) have revealed that pretend-play with other children supports the child's development of self-regulation, since in such role play with peers children learn to check their impulses and manage their behaviour. Role play requires a recognition of and adherence to rules, and this aids the development of self-regulation, particularly inhibition (see Figure 10.7).

Secondly, 'socio-dramatic' play helps a child to understand emotions (Lindsey & Colwell, 2003) and others' mental states and perspectives. These psychological capacities are important for the child in coming to understand their own and others' behaviours and motivations. This emerging psychological capacity is often seen in young children's socio-dramatic play; as the child becomes able to 'read the mind' of another 'character' in the imaginary world or drama being created in play, they may engage in a 'mental state dialogue', taking on the voice tone or vocabulary of their play 'character'. Evidence suggests that the constructions of shared imaginative play with another child and the discourse about inner states that is a key part of this play depend on the quality of the relationship between the children. Several studies (including Singer & Singer, 2005) have demonstrated that frequency of friends' shared pretend-play depends upon the quality of the relationship, together with smooth and successful communication, social competence and pro-social actions, low levels of conflict and divergent thinking.

Resources and activities to promote social competence

- *Games with rules* help children understand the nature of 'rules' and encourage socio-emotional learning which arises from sharing time and space and seeing events from others' perspectives. A range of simple turn-taking board games with dice or sand-timers to regulate the taking of turns can be made available within the setting for children to access easily and play without the need for adult supervision. Large scale games are fun for the outdoor area (see Figure 10.8).
- *Physical play* is also effective in supporting children's emotional and social development, where 'boundaries' of physical force and acceptable types of contact can be tested within the 'safety net' of the setting context and with adult monitoring (see Figure 10.9). Parachute games, climbing-frame play and scooter, bike and trike play all require children to control their motor movements, co-operate and take turns.
- Team games and sports can reinforce the benefits of working together with peers towards a common goal (see Figure 10.10).

Helping children learn strategies for co-operation with peers

A practitioner can positively reinforce friendly actions 'spotted' in the setting, such as acts of kindness, children showing gratitude, or children offering their toy to another, for example, through highlighting the behaviour and using genuine praise and encouragement. However, some social lessons need to be explicit and reinforced. Through observation of children facing social 'challenges' within the setting, the

Figure 10.8 *Large scale games are fun for the outdoor area!*

Figure 10.9 *'Wheeeeeeeeeeee!'*

Figure 10.10 *'Come on, green team!'*

practitioner can 'teach' and model strategies to promote empathy:

- requesting permission to join in with others' play: phrases can be practised with the child if they are shy or reluctant to 'break in' to others' play (see Figure 10.11);
- sharing: modelling the sharing of materials by adults can demonstrate to children that when resources are finite, there is a need for compromise;
- waiting and taking turns: the use of a sand-timer or other device, if necessary, to measure the length of 'a turn' can promote the idea of respecting others' rights;
- recognising that there are different types of teasing and how to spot when someone is being deliberately 'unfriendly' or not: practitioners can support children in differentiating between when to 'ignore' unfriendly behaviour and when the behaviour is unacceptable and how to get help; and

Figure 10.11 *'One, two, three, hup there!'*

- helping children practise ways of 'saying sorry' and to understand that it means 'I'll try not to do it again'.

Co-operation: developing a model for children self-regulating in conflict situations

Consider the following two everyday situations and the actual learning that takes place.

Scenario A

One child hits another in an argument over whose turn it is to have the 'digger' in the sandbox, and the aggrieved party ends up crying loudly. The practitioner approaches, takes hold of the toy and holds it up, out of reach, saying 'That's not very nice! Say sorry, Jack! Stop crying Joseph! You need to share and play nicely boys! You can have the first turn, Joseph, and you can have a go in a minute, Jack!

Scenario B

One child hits another in an argument over whose turn it is to have the 'digger' in the sandbox, and the aggrieved party ends up crying loudly. The practitioner approaches, bends down to the children's eye level, and asks 'What is happening?' as she gently removes the toy into neutral territory. She listens attentively to both children's points of view, one at a time, preventing each from interrupting the other if they interject, and nodding as they each speak. She describes and acknowledges the emotions each child displays as she perceives them, if they are unable to label their feelings themselves. She asks each child to look at the face of the other and describe what feelings they see on their friend's face. She asks, 'Why is Jack/Joseph feeling like this?' She asks how they can make each other feel better and how they can 'sort out the problem of sharing the digger'.

In Scenario A, the children are learning that loud shows of emotion produce results in terms of attracting a practitioner's attention – Joseph has not learned that he needs to express his distress in a more appropriate way. They are both learning that they need an adult to sort out their problem, rather than trying to find a solution to the sharing issue independently. Both boys are learning that they have done something wrong, for which Jack is expected to apologise (insincerely?) but it is not made clear what 'playing nicely' means. Joseph is made to feel that crying is unacceptable. Opportunities are missed for the boys to make choices and solve problems; they simply follow the adult's instructions.

In Scenario B, the children are given an opportunity to distance themselves from their raw emotions of anger and frustration over whose turn it is – and they are given time to express their feelings in alternative, more socially acceptable ways. They are led to identify their own and their peer's feelings and to think about the causes. The practitioner leads the children to take a degree of responsibility for having caused these negative feelings and, at the same time, provides an opportunity for them to demonstrate their independence in planning to do something to make them both feel better. She also asks them to think about what they will do next time to share, so that the same negativity may be avoided in the future.

Pointers for PSHE in the Early Years

Children learn as much, if not more, from the way in which we behave with them as from the content of lessons and activities. The approaches we use and the respect and care we show children in their Early Years will affect their ability to learn and their development into effective citizens. In planning for PSHE in early childhood education we must keep in mind the following key points:

- The links between children's personal, social and emotion learning and their cognitive competencies has been well established by research.
- The quality of the relationships between the adults and the children is pivotal.
- The partnership between the family and school is significant.
- The benefits of a whole school approach to social and emotional learning is fundamental.

References

Barlow, J., Parsons, J., & Stewart-Brown, S. (2005) Preventing emotional and behavioural problems: The effectiveness of parenting programmes with children less than three years of age. *Child: Care, Health and Development,* 31 (1), pp. 33–42.

Bion, W. (1967) A theory of thinking. In *Second Thoughts: Selected Papers on Psychoanalysis.* London: Karnac.

Bowlby, J. 1988 *A Secure Base.* London: Routledge.

Clarke, A.M. & Barry, M.M. (2010) *The Link between Social and Emotional Learning and Academic Achievement.* London: Partnership for Children.

Denham, S. & Burton, R. (2003) *Social and Emotional Prevention and Intervention Programming for Preschoolers.* New York: Kluwer-Plenum.

Department for Children, Schools and Families (2005) *SEAL: Social and Emotional Aspects of Learning for Primary Schools.* Nottingham: DCSF Publications.

Domitrovich, C.E. & Greenberg, M.T. (2000) The study of implementation: Current findings from effective programmes for school aged children. *Journal of Educational and Psychological Consultation,* 11, pp. 193–222.

Dunn J., Cutting, A., & Fisher, N. (2002). Old friends, new friends: Predictors of children's perspectives on their friends at school. *Child Development,* 73, pp. 621–635.

Eisenberg, N. (2002) Emotion-related regulation and its relation to quality of social functioning. In W.W. Hartup & R.A Weinberg (Eds.), *Child Psychology in Retrospect and Prospect: In Celebration of the 75th Anniversary of the Institute of Child Development,* 32, pp. 133–171. Mahwah, NJ; Erlbaum.

Elias, C.L. & Berk, L.E. (2002) Self regulation in young children: Is there a role for socio-dramatic play? *Early Childhood Research Quarterly,* 17, pp. 1–17.

Ladd, G.W., Herald, S. & Andrews, K. (2006) Young children's peer relations and social competence. In B. Spodek & O. Saracho (Eds.), *Handbook of Research on the Education of Young Children,* vol. 2 (pp.23–54). New York, NY: Macmillan.

Lester, S. & Russell, W. (2010) *Children's Right to Play: An Examination of the Importance of Play in the Lives of Children Worldwide.* The Hague, Netherlands: Bernard van Leer Foundation.

Lindqvist, G (2001). When small children play: How adults dramatise and children create meaning. *Early Years,* 21, pp. 7–14.

Lindsey, E.W., & Colwell, M.J. (2003). Preschoolers' emotional competence: Links to pretend and physical play. *Child Study Journal,* 33, pp. 39–52.

Mosely, J. (1996) *Quality Circle Time in the Primary Classroom,* vols. 1 and 2. Wisbech, UK: LDA.

Payton, J.W., Wardlaw, D.M., Graczyk, P.A., Bloodworth, M.R., Tompsett, C.J. & Weissberg, R.P. (2000) Social and emotional learning: a framework for promoting mental health and reducing risk behaviour in children and youth. *Journal of School Health,* 70 (5), pp. 179–185.

Ryan, R.M., & Deci, E.L. (2000). Self-determination theory and the facilitation of intrinsic motivation, social development and well-being. *American Psychologist*, 55, pp. 68–78.

Singer, J. & Singer, D. (2005) Pre-schoolers' imaginative play as a precursor of narrative consciousness. *Imagination, Cognition and Personality*, 25 (2), pp. 97–117.

Vygotsky, L.S. (1978) *Mind in Society*. Cambridge, MA: Harvard University Press

Wentzel, K.R., & Asher, S.R (1995). The academic lives of neglected, rejected, popular, and controversial children. *Child Development*, 66, pp. 754–763.

CHAPTER 11

'How do I do this better?'

FROM MOVEMENT DEVELOPMENT INTO PHYSICAL LITERACY

Patricia Maude

How do you like to go up in a swing

Up in the air so blue?

Oh, I do think it is the pleasantest thing

Ever a child can do!

(Robert Louis Stevenson, 1945)

Introduction

The Early Years are exciting times both for children's physical development as they grow, changing in shape and size, and for their movement development as they gain in body awareness and as they explore the vast range of available movement experiences within their environment. Through experimentation, trial, error and success, young movers progress towards co-ordinated, mature movement knowledge and performance. Not only is movement the main medium of exploration for the young child, but physical activity is essential for normal growth, providing the necessary stimulus for optimum development and learning. As young children develop other abilities including language, observation skills, knowledge of the environments in which they live and understanding of movement contexts, so they also become increasingly physically literate.

We, as educators, are charged with ensuring that the children with whom we work are encouraged and enabled to experience the widest available world of movement. This world of movement includes not only a range of indoor and outdoor environments, but also a varied programme of physical activity which balances the demands made on different parts of the body and takes into account the maintenance and enhancement of strength, mobility and endurance, helping to ensure the development of sound physique, posture and an active lifestyle. Providing young children with frequent opportunities for active play, and nurturing worthwhile movement experiences in a range of environments with a rich provision of resources, helps to develop their motor competence, enhance movement confidence and capitalise on creativity in movement. Confidence in movement is vital for self-expression, and articulate co-ordinated movement ability greatly enhances the development of self-esteem. One of the challenges for the Early Years educator is to build on the vast movement experience that most children have accumulated throughout infancy and prior to starting school by exposing them to a rich and rewarding movement vocabulary from which they can increase physical competence, knowledge and skill, and progress along their physical literacy journey. Physical literacy can be defined as the motivation, confidence, physical competence, knowledge and understanding necessary to value and take responsibility for maintaining purposeful physical pursuits/ activities throughout one's life-course.

In this chapter we examine some of the processes of physical development from birth through infancy and early childhood, including sensory and neuro-motor development in the brain. We explore physical competence by looking at ways in which acquisition of movement patterns and movement experiences are achieved by the young child. We also consider the role of the child as a movement learner through play and the role of the educator as a facilitator of physical literacy and a provider of movement experience and knowledge. Suggestions will be made as to what might constitute quality movement learning for children in their first years at school. In exploring physical literacy in the life of the young child, we also consider some of the aims and content of the physical development and physical education curriculum in the Early Years, including the Foundation Stage and Key Stage 1 of the National Curriculum in England.

Readers are encouraged to:

- review their knowledge of children's early physical and movement development;
- consider ways of extending children's movement vocabulary and movement memory;
- extend their ability to observe and analyse children's movement in order to enhance movement quality by giving informed feedback on performance;
- provide an appropriate curriculum which emanates from children's active play, and which includes a variety of environments, equipment, apparatus and other resources and which raises standards in children's movement competence; and
- guide children in their entitlement to physical literacy.

Some principles and processes of physical and movement development

First and foremost is the fact that one purpose we have for possessing a brain, is in order to move! Physical activity provides the vital stimulus for brain development as it promotes neural connections between the billions of cells in the brain. Daniel

Wolpert (2012, p. 35) states that 'movement is the only way we have to affect the world around us'. Ratey and Hagerman (2008, p. 4 and p.245) state that 'exercise cues the building blocks of learning in the brain' and exercise is 'the single most powerful tool to optimise brain function.' They also remind us that 'to keep our brains at peak performance, our bodies need to work hard.'

Also pertinent to the learner and teacher of movement are three key factors in the early physical development of infants, namely the principles of:

- cephalo-caudal development;
- proximo-distal development; and
- differentiation.

These three principles not only provide us with many insights into the process and rhythm of development of the infant, but also underpin many aspects of child development. They are particularly relevant as we consider the movement development of young children. Movement is the lead area of functioning for the infant in exploring and acquiring information about the environment and in learning about the self.

Cephalo-caudal development

This first principle of physical development is so named because it stems from the Greek word for 'head', which is 'kephale', and the Latin word for 'tail' which is 'cauda'. It denotes the principle that development occurs from the head downwards towards the feet. This seems obvious, since the head houses the brain which is the chief controller and regulator of all bodily functions. The brain also regulates the growth and development of the body. The head is the most developed part of the body at birth, whereas the lower limbs are relatively undeveloped and of relatively little importance, lacking in musculature and function.

Movement development, such as the development of locomotion, follows the same principle of cephalo-caudal development, commencing at the 'head end' and working downwards to the 'foot end'. The journey towards standing up and walking begins with the development of strength in the neck and shoulder muscles in order to push up from front lying to raise the head. This precedes strength and control of the spine and hips, enabling the infant to learn to achieve a sitting position. Working on downwards, the muscles around the hips, knees and ankles, and later the feet, develop the strength required for weight-bearing on the feet and for achieving a standing position. Upright posture is the gateway to locomotion through first steps, towards walking, toddling, jogging, jumping, hopping, skipping, running, galloping and leaping.

This principle of 'top-down' development influences planning and teaching as we seek to ensure that children acquire essential movement patterns to enable them to be physically competent and articulate movers, particularly in the lower limbs. For example, the ankle joint, upon which efficient locomotion is dependent, is at the greatest distance from the brain. Helping children to know and understand about efficient use of the ankle joint, as a joint capable of extension, flexion and rotation, is of paramount importance in the promotion of efficient and lifelong mobility. In the Early Years the use of vocabulary that is lucid, succinct and fit for purpose when communicating about movement is invaluable in facilitating movement learning. Directing learners' attention to focus on named joints helps them to embed appropriate movement information and knowledge from the brain to the functioning joints. For example, asking learners to straighten, stretch or extend the ankle, rather than to 'point the toes', enables the transfer of neural information from the brain directly to the point of operation, namely the ankle joints. As another example, if learners are being tasked to make a shape that shows straight legs, asking them to 'make straight knees' helps them to direct their movement attention to the key operational joint.

Proximo-distal development

The second principle refers to development from the centre of the body outwards towards the extremities, 'proximo' being near to and 'distal' being far from the centre. The central nervous system, which controls all messages from the brain, runs down the spinal column and manages all the life functions of the infant. The vital organs, essential to survival, are housed in the centre of the body, with maximum protection given by the surrounding bones of the chest and pelvis. These central elements are the most active at birth and throughout life. By comparison, the early activity of the distant and peripheral elements – such as the hands, being the most distal of the upper limbs – is relatively insignificant and functionally limited in early life. Indeed, at this stage they are not structurally ready for action, due to lack of musculature, and also, for example, because the bones in the wrists have not yet differentiated. Before the wrists are fully prepared and ready to service the complex variety of movement demands that will be placed upon the hands, their cartilaginous structure must mature into a complex arrangement of bones and then, through frequent activity and exercise, must develop sufficient musculature.

As with cephalo-caudal development, proximo-distal development is important for the educator in creating a movement programme that takes account of the length of time necessary to achieve movement competence in those parts of the limbs that are relatively more distant from the centre of the body. Classroom learning is also significantly dependent upon this principle, as, for example, learners may not have achieved the moment of readiness to hold a pencil with the pincer or tripod grip (between the thumb and index finger) and feel more comfortable using the palmar or power grasp (pencil gripped between the palm and the fingers). The product of work produced using the palmar grasp is usually less accurate than that of the pincer grip, with which it is possible to achieve greater control. However, the muscles of the wrists and hands must be sufficiently strong to enable the child to sustain the more demanding pincer grip. Physically active play involving the shoulders, elbows, wrists and hands, in activities such as climbing, swinging, gripping and releasing, greatly assist this development.

Differentiation

The third principle is that whereby the new-born child offers an apparently global response, whereas the more mature child is more discriminatory in response. For example, in response to a pin-prick on the hand, the infant cries, pulls the limb away, and generally thrashes about; the older child will withdraw the limb and may cry; and the adult is unlikely to do more than consider withdrawing the affected limb if necessary. As neurological development takes place and the child matures, so the ability to differentiate responses grows. This ability to discriminate responses with increasing maturity is an important element of learning for the Early Years child in school.

The sequence of growth and development

This leads us on to consider the sequence of growth and development including motor development. This sequence is invariable, but the pace of progression is variable from one infant to another. Normally, in the development of locomotion, for example, infants learn first to roll over, then to sit, and later to stand before learning to walk (see Figure 11.1).

Figure 11.1 *The regular sequence of motor development in infants. From Rathus 1988, p. 202*

Gross and fine motor skills

Linked with the three preceding principles of motor development is another invariable and not surprising feature of child development, that of 'gross' and 'fine' motor skills. The child achieves greater control in large (gross) body movement before managing control in smaller (fine) movements. For example, the gross motor skills of walking, jumping and running are more advanced in their performance and control at a relatively younger age than are the child's drawing, cutting or colouring-in, where detailed involvement of the developing muscles of the wrist and hand can be extremely challenging and tiring for the young child. Since much learning activity in the classroom involves drawing, painting, writing, measuring, cutting and sticking, etc., the more mature the child's wrist and finger development and thus the stronger the musculature, the more successful will be the practical elements of the product, with least inhibition and muscle fatigue. Sometimes it is assumed that when children are 'off-task' or lacking concentration they are failing in behavior management. However, lack of postural strength might be making it difficult to sit up and keep still for sustained periods and immaturity in the structure and functioning of the wrist and hand, resulting in weak musculature of the wrist, may be limiting maximum participation. Since gross motor competence serves as a springboard for developing efficient fine motor skills, it is incumbent upon educators to provide frequent opportunities for young children to engage extensively in active play involving gross movement activity.

The importance of active play

How better can provision for frequent gross and fine motor activity be made than through active play? The British Heart Foundation (BHS 2012), concerned to reduce the amount of sedentary activity, proposes a minimum of three hours of active play, spread through the day, and defines four types of play for young children, namely:

- unstructured play – free exploratory play without adult support;
- child-initiated play – with appropriate adult enabling, in the form of scaffolded support offered at the child's moment of readiness;
- focused learning play – adult guided; and
- highly structured play – planned and adult directed.

In developing a movement curriculum for young children, the notion of building upon play is a compelling aim. Active physical play is important for:

- encouraging discovery of movement abilities;
- allowing for creativity and exploration of the movement environment and the varied apparatus, resources and equipment therein; and
- offering practice time to enhance movement competence and strengthen the cardio-respiratory and musculature systems.

The provision of stimulating environments, both for children's pre-school play and for developmental play during and after the school day is a matter for detailed planning for parents and other educators of young children. In providing for developing physical competence, environments might include:

- a hard area with wheeled toys including trucks, go-carts, scooters, tricycles, balance bikes, bicycles and other ride-on and push-along toys;
- a playground with suitable markings to encourage challenge in movement;
- an indoor space with soft-play and other gymnastic-type equipment;
- grass and hard areas with balls of various sizes and textures, beanbags, hoops, bats, velcro-catchers, targets, skipping ropes, ribbons and scarves;
- safe footpaths;
- an adventure playground;
- a secret garden;
- a wooded area; and
- water for wading, paddling, floating and swimming.

These and other home, school and community provisions significantly enhance the movement-learning experience and movement-maturity potential for young children.

The importance of play involving gross and fine motor skills is of paramount importance in children's movement development and must underpin the physical development and physical education curriculum. Indeed, the school curriculum should be founded upon the natural movement vocabulary of the playing child.

We rely on children arriving at school already articulate in movement, with mature movement patterns already established in the fundamental motor skills. On arrival at school, with a wealth of pre-school movement experiences, children should expect to draw from their existing movement vocabulary, using established and efficient movement patterns to enable them to participate fully in the activities on offer, to enjoy their learning and to be successful. My experience suggests that even where articulate movers arrive in school, reinforcement of mature movement patterns should continue to be a part of the curriculum. As the child grows, as body levers lengthen, strength increases and body awareness is enhanced, the child is in a state of readiness to become even more skilful and to acquire an even greater movement vocabulary and movement memory.

Towards an appropriate movement curriculum for young children

As a starting point for devising a movement curriculum we may ask ourselves what constitute the most useful movement skills that children bring with them to school. Efficiency and confidence in all daily living tasks, including feeding, toileting, dressing and moving safely around the environment, enable the child to operate independently in school. Additionally, most children bring a range of gross and fine motor skills that are needed for full participation in class-based and outdoor activities. Where children arrive at school with poorly developed postural muscles, poor co-ordination and balance and inefficient locomotion, it is essential to provide programmes to remedy these, so that children can more readily access and benefit from the curriculum content.

Many children bring with them a rich movement vocabulary developed through play. The importance of play as a basis for all aspects of Early Years education cannot be overestimated.

Aims of the physical development curriculum

Before deciding on the content of the physical development curriculum, we should explore what we might consider to be the aims of that programme. In order to enhance children's learning opportunities and to ensure that, as the educator, you offer the best possible provision for them, the following broad curriculum aims should be considered. These relate to physical and movement development, movement skill acquisition and confidence in movement as physical literacy develops.

Physical development

- to stimulate growth;
- to enhance physical development; and
- to provide healthy exercise.

Movement development

- to build on existing movement vocabulary;
- to develop co-ordination, body tension and control;
- to build a rich movement vocabulary;
- to improve movement memory through building phrases and sequences of movement; and
- to enhance movement quality.

Movement skill acquisition

- to develop fundamental motor skills to the mature stage;
- to introduce new motor skills;
- to increase knowledge of dynamics of movement;
- to develop posture, balance, co-ordination and control; and
- to teach accuracy and efficiency in movement.

Movement confidence development

- to teach movement observation skills;
- to develop movement experimentation and expression;
- to enhance self-expression; and
- to enhance self-confidence, self-image and self-esteem.

Other aspects of provision in promoting physical literacy might be to:

- teach appropriate vocabulary for describing, explaining, discussing, questioning, assessing and improving the quality of movement;
- stimulate thought processes that feed into movement development and physical competence;
- set high expectations and expect high quality work from children, according to their experience, progress and ability;
- encourage independence, confidence and ownership of learning;
- learn respect in co-operation and competition;
- enhance positive attitudes towards health-related exercise and active lifestyles;
- provide experiences that teach children to plan, perform and evaluate their movement learning; and to
- sustain feelings of enjoyment and well-being in physical activity.

Are there other aims that should underpin a curriculum plan for Early Years children in movement development and physical education, such as providing stimulating, challenging and imaginative learning experiences for children? These can then be built into the curriculum, to ensure children's entitlement to be physically educated and to be physically literate.

The physical development curriculum therefore, should contain an extensive, broad and generic movement vocabulary of learning experiences for all children, from which, specialization can later develop most successfully.

The development of skilled movement

A route to the acquisition of skilled movement has been plotted by Gallahue and Ozman (2006). They name three progressive stages in skill learning:

1   *The initial or rudimentary stage.*
    This is the emergent movement pattern, or early experimentation stage.
2   *The elementary stage*
    At this stage, in which co-ordination is improved, the movement is still incorrectly performed and incomplete, perhaps lacking in strength, mobility, balance or speed.

3   *The mature stage*
     Finally the child achieves the mature stage in which all the elements of the move-
     ment pattern are integrated and in which the movement includes appropriate
     preparation, followed by accurate action and ending with efficient follow-through
     and recovery. At this stage the movement pattern also becomes integrated into
     the movement memory, to be called upon with ease.

Watch a professional cricketer throw the ball in from the boundary and compare that
action with the overarm throw of the average five-year-old (see Figure 11.2) and your
mind's eye will no doubt provide ample evidence of potential for further development in the young child's achievement: you will have observed the forward trunk
flexion in the elementary thrower rather than trunk rotation which is essential in
successful throwing.
   Figure 11.3 illustrates the movement development between a beginning and an
advanced runner. With the advanced runner there is a much fuller range of leg
motion and the thighs and arms drive forward and back in opposition, rather than
swinging out to the sides.
   When one bears in mind that the elementary and mature movement patterns are
normally achieved during the primary school years, the educator has considerable
responsibility for recognising the three stages in the various fundamental movements of locomotion (e.g., walking and running, jumping [including taking off and
landing on two feet and, later, on one foot) and projection [throwing and kicking,
accompanied by receiving and catching)] and for analysing the child's achievements
in order to improve performance.

Figure 11.2 *A beginning thrower. From Haywood 1993, p. 145*

Figure 11.3 *A beginning and mature runner. From Haywood 1993, pp. 128–9*

What is skipping?

Can you describe skipping in three words?

It has sometimes been said that boys can't skip. Is this really so – and, if so, why? Skipping ought surely to be as readily accessible to boys as it is to girls, particularly when appropriate feedback is given to learners. It seems that this relatively straightforward sequence of movements often becomes overcomplicated by the use of complex vocabulary to describe the action and by lack of a clear role model for children as they learn to skip. In three words, skip is 'step forward, hop'. It is a repeated sequence of one forward action followed by one upward action.

What is involved in hopping? What progressive activities are the building blocks that can assist children's learning? We could say:

- being able to jump and land on two feet;
- gaining sufficient strength to fix the pelvis so that it remains horizontal when transferring the body weight over one foot;
- achieving efficient balance and co-ordination to stand without wobbling on that foot; and
- taking off and landing on the same foot.

When children first start to master hopping they often travel forwards before discovering how to hop on the spot. Quality in the technique includes an upright body position, height, a clear shape in the air, a resilient, controlled landing and a rhythmic series of steps and hops, on the right foot as well as on the left.

What is biking?

Is it a matter of attaching trainer (outrider) wheels to maintain the bike in an upright position, or the patience of an adult who holds the back of the saddle and walks or runs along behind the bike, growing ever more exhausted, as the child tries to stay upright and pedal? The short answer is a resounding 'NO!' Biking is first and foremost about balancing, with steering and pedaling as useful adjuncts in achieving locomotion.

In Figure 11.4 we see Jack, aged two years, on a balance bike. He became an independent and proficient cyclist at the age of three. His balance bike gave him independence from the outset. He quickly learnt how to get on and off and to sit on the saddle with his feet on the ground. Then he began walking the bike along, turning round at the end of the path and walking back. Next he started jogging, trotting and then running. Throughout, he was in control of all decision-making in respect of going, stopping and turning and was gaining experiences necessary to master the essential component of balance. As he became more confident in his ability to balance, he started to lift his feet off the ground momentarily and then put them down again, until he achieved longer sequences of gliding along, the bike upright, with his feet off the ground. Not many months later he was happily biking in the park with his family, fully proficient.

Figure 11.4 *Jack on a balance bike (aged two)*

Kicking

The child illustrated in Figure 11.5 has acquired, by the age of six, a sophistication of skill in kicking that is rarely seen in Key Stage 1.

Leaping

The child seen in Figure 11.6, who is also aged six years, has achieved a quality of body and spatial awareness in leaping that should be our aim for all children in Key Stage 1. Are all the children in your class able to leap? What is involved and what activities make useful progressions? Perhaps:

- jumping and landing on two feet;
- landing on one foot as in hopping;
- stepping from right to left foot and from left to right foot;
- stepping over lines marked on the floor;
- taking off from one foot and landing on the other foot; and
- leaping over lines.

The physically competent leaper pushes off high into the air, maintains an upright posture, extends both knees and ankles in flight, extends the elbows, wrists and fingers in flight – and lands with resilience and control on one foot.

For the normal child there need be no constraints beyond those imposed by the limitation of the developing body and brain, the confidence of the learner, and the bounds of reasonable safety imposed by the environment, the equipment to be used and the other children sharing the same space.

Figure 11.5 *A six-year-old shows a mature kick*

Figure 11.6 *Leaping*

Figure 11.7 *'I am catching'*

Learning to catch

If it is clear that the child cannot catch the object being thrown, then, rather than by leaving him or her to repeated experiences of failure, it is better to use a range of progressions. Progressions can be considered in at least two aspects:

1 missile used–its size, weight, texture, shape, surface; encourage the child to choose a missile that is easy to catch, such as a velcro catcher, a soft bean bag or a foam ball.
2 receiving activity: progressions can include:

- passing a ball from hand to hand, around the body, under one leg and then the other;
- rolling a ball to a rebound surface such as a wall and collecting it as it returns;
- sending up and catcing scarves, beanbags and other easily controlled objects;
- sending up and catching a variety of balls;
- sending up and clapping before catching the object;
- receiving a ball into two hands when rolled slowly along the ground towards the two waiting hands of the receiver;
- catching from an underarm feed with bounce, so that the ball comes up to the waiting hands of the receiver;
- catching a self-bounced ball;
- catching a ball self-fed to a wall; and
- catching from an underarm throw.

The technique of the catch involves three phases:

- **the preparation:** including the stance, arms extended towards the missile, the open-palmed ready position of the hands and the eyes watching the missile rather than the sender;
- **the action:** the hands closing around the ball, the arms bending or recoiling to control the impact of the missile; and
- **the recovery:** in which the catcher regains a controlled position.

Learning to forward roll

The forward roll is made up of at least 17 flexions and extensions of joints of the body, making it quite a complex series of actions to perform! Can the children in your class name all of them?

As with the catch, there are many progressions that can precede doing the full forward roll:

- building a vocabulary of simpler rolls on the floor, on mats and along appropriate apparatus, such as the sideways roll in a straight shape to the right and the left;
- practising sideways rolls in a tucked shape to right and left;
- trying out varieties of starting and ending positions, such as on both knees or one knee;
- using an incline such as a foam ramp and rocking forwards to place the feet on the mat and stand up;
- developing the ending of a forward roll by lying on the back in a tuck shape and rocking forward to place the feet on the mat near the seat, reaching forwards with the hands to add momentum to stand up;
- rolling forwards down a soft, gentle incline such as a foam ramp, reaching forwards to help transfer the weight from the seat to the feet;
- rolling forwards from a low platform by starting in front-lying or kneeling, then taking weight through the arms by placing the hands flat on the mat to control the descent of the body onto the back of the shoulders, then rolling down the back to end standing on the feet;
- rolling forwards from a straddle shape (i.e., wide legs, thereby lowering the body and making space to tuck the head under, in order to transfer the weight from the feet to the hands and to the shoulders); and
- forward roll from standing, by bending the knees into a tuck shape, transferring the weight from the feet to the hands, tucking the head in (chin on chest) to transfer the weight to the back of the shoulders, rolling down the spine and ending as above.

In the selected activities described above, we can see some of the main teaching points and examples of some progressions that can provide learners with guidance in becoming fluent, articulate and skilful movers.

Recognising the moment of readiness in the child, the moment at which intervention to enhance learning and performance has the greatest potential for success, is a skill in itself for the educator. The moment of readiness depends, for example, upon the child's stage of physical development, physical competence and experience. Moments of readiness also depend upon acquisition of knowledge, application of spatial and body awareness and appropriate maturing of the body structures and brain functioning. The frustration of anticipating readiness too soon is outweighed by the satisfaction of helping a child to be successful in enhancing a partially learnt skill or in acquiring a new skill!

Physical development and physical education curricula

So, what should we include in our physical development curriculum that will meet our selected aims and provide satisfaction and rich movement experience for our young learners? In England, the curriculum guidance for the Foundation Stage (2012) shows children learning through movement in almost every area and also focuses on physical development as one discrete area in seeking to develop children's physical competence. The emerging physical literacy curriculum (www.physical-literacy. org.uk) promotes physical competence in the form of the development of generic movement ability and skill for children in the Early Years. At Key Stage 1, physical education in the National Curriculum currently promotes experience in activities that in Key Stage 2 lead to dance, games and gymnastics. These activities seem entirely appropriate for children whose Early Years physical development and movement experience has been made up of broad-based and varied active play.

One approach to the physical development curriculum in the Early Years and Key Stage 1 is the Youth Sport Trust's (2012) Start to Move Programme, in which the approach taken is to develop physical competence around three key aspects, namely *locomotion, stability and object control*. The movement vocabulary for *locomotion* is made up of the myriad ways a person can travel from one place to the next, such as along the ground, up, down, along, through, over and under apparatus, on feet and foot, hands and feet, seat, front and back, by stepping, rolling, jumping, sliding, pulling and pushing, the right way up and upside down, for example. *Stability* is made up of static and dynamic balance and extends from normal standing posture through a vast vocabulary of ways to balance in still shapes and ways to maintain control of the body in flight and when travelling and using equipment such as balance bikes or climbing and balancing apparatus. *Object control* involves developing hand–eye and foot–eye co-ordination and control when manipulating and managing equipment such as beanbags, balls, bats and balls that are more usually related to games-playing, and scarves, ribbons, hoops and ropes which feature in dance and gymnastics.

Learners can extend their movement vocabulary, movement memory and movement quality through drawing on past experience and increasing their knowledge and understanding of movement by applying locomotion, stability and object control in a variety of contexts that lead to dance, games and gymnastics. Through this approach, learners can achieve the mature stage in fundamental movement patterns and can explore and apply movement ideas; be creative; push out the boundaries of past experience; derive challenge; and experience enjoyment, increased confidence and motivation, as well as knowledge and understanding of physical competence. In addition to promoting competence, confidence, agility, balance, co-ordination and challenge, the Key Stage 1 National Curriculum also promotes the playing of co-operative and competitive games and creation of movement patterns in dance.

For me, the Early Years programme must be one of discovery and achievement, of valuing the learner, with evidence of excitement, challenge, enjoyment and satisfaction in learning. Can you recall an experience similar to that quoted at the start of this chapter, by Robert Louis Stevenson? Do you remember the effort of getting the swing started and then of discovering the knack of leaning back and then forward to increase the height of the swing and then the fear of going over the top, having seemingly swung too high? Do you also remember the pleasure derived from such play activities as are recalled here by A. A. Milne:

> He played with his skipping rope,
>
> He played with his ball.
>
> He ran after butterflies,
>
> Blue ones and red;
>
> He did a hundred happy things –
>
> And then went to bed.
> ('Forgotten' , Milne 1927)

Perhaps it is here, in the young child's physical play, that we should start observing in an attempt to discover the 'life-world' of physical literacy for young children. If we are to provide worthwhile learning experiences that challenge children, give them ownership of their learning and enable them to build on pre-school play experiences, we must seek out appropriate starting points. From these we can build upon:

- the fantasy and exploratory expressive play that can become dance, as in twirling, galloping, leaping, reaching up and away and pausing;
- the games-like play that involves chasing, dodging, catching, throwing, kicking and hitting; and
- the gymnastics-like play that involves rolling, jumping, climbing, swinging and balancing.

The role of the educator

As we proceed to influence children's development through the pedagogical framework that we provide, we may need to take a closer look at what children actually do when they engage in physically active play and, as a result of that observation, put ourselves even more in touch with the nature of children's physical development. Through initial training and inservice education, teachers can increase their technical knowledge, can draw on personal experience, build a bank of progressions that lead to skilful performance, develop observation techniques in order to analyse what they see and provide appropriate developmental feedback to learners.

Satisfying the 'skill-hungry' years is a constant and often insatiable challenge for the educator which involves addressing a key question often asked by children: 'How do I do this better?'

This need not be an insurmountable challenge. Teachers and parents who observe, study and build on the life-world of physical activity experienced by young learners engaged in natural movement development are well on the way to success. When children are put at the centre of the learning experience, the joy of exploring and indulging in a wide range of physical activities can be sustained and enhanced – such that as they mature they can participate ever more skilfully and knowledgeably towards becoming independent learners.

Pointers for physical and movement development, physical literacy and physical education in the Early Years

An effective physical development and physical education curriculum helps to cultivate in children movement that is skilful, creative and satisfying in establishing a life-long commitment to a physically active lifestyle. In order for young children to acquire the physical competence that enables them to be confident and articulate movers and to develop their physical literacy, they need teachers and carers who have:

- acquired knowledge of the physical development of young children in relation to movement development and physical competence, including the achievement of mature movement patterns;
- learnt and understood the exploratory stages in movement acquisition, along with progressions and techniques for developing maximum movement potential;
- developed observation skills to facilitate assessment of progress and the giving of appropriate developmental feedback on each child's performance;
- built the physical development and physical education curriculum from natural movement and play; and
- provided children with rich and frequent opportunities to explore movement and to practise and increase their movement vocabulary, enhance their movement memory and the quality of their movement.

The Early Years Foundation Stage curriculum and the new National Curriculum for Physical Education both provide the basis for ensuring that all children attain their potential in physical competence and physical literacy and thereby achieve the optimum physical and movement development to which they are entitled, and from which they can progress successfully along their lifelong physical literacy journey.

References

Haywood, K.M. (1993) *LifeSpan Motor Development*, 2nd ed. Champaign Illinois: Human Kinetics.

Milne, A.A. (1927) *Now We Are Six*. London: Methuen.

Ratey, J. & Hagerman, E. (2008) *SPARK: The Revolutionary New Science of Exercise and the Brain*. New York: Little Brown & Company.

Stevenson, R.L. (1945) *A Child's Garden of Verses*. Kenosha, Wisconsin: John Martin's House.

Wolpert, D. (2012) A Moving Story. *Cambridge Alumni Magazine*, 66 (Easter).

Further reading

By the author

Maude, P. (2001) *Physical Children, Active Teaching*. Buckingham: Open University Press. Available at www.observingchildrenmoving.co.uk

Maude, P. (2003) *Observing Children Moving*. CD Rom.

Maude, P. (2010) Physical Literacy and the Young Child. In M. Whitehead (Ed.), *Physical Literacy Throughout the Lifespan*. London: Routledge.

Maude, P. & Pickard, A. (2014) *Creative Teaching of Physical Education in the Primary School*. London: Routledge.

Movement development

Department of Health (2011) *Start Active, Stay Active: A Report on Physical Activity From the Four home Countries' Chief Medical Officers*. Available at www.gov.uk/government/publications

Drew, S. (2007) *Including Children with Dyspraxia in the Foundation Stage*. London: A.C. Black.

Gallahue, D. & Ozman, J. (2006) *Understanding Motor Development: Infants, Children, Adolescents, Adults*, 6th ed. Boston: McGraw Hill.

Goddard-Blythe, S. (2012) *Assessing Neuro-Motor Readiness for Learning*. London: Wiley-Blackwell.

Macintyre, C. (2000) *Dyspraxia in the Early Years*. London: David Fulton.

Rathus, S.A. (1988) *Understanding Child Development*. New York: Holt, Rinehart and Winston.

Physical development and physical education

British Heart Foundation (2012) *Early Movers: Helping under 5's Live Active and Healthy Lives*. Available at www.bhf.org.uk/children's-resources/babies-and-nursery.aspx

Davies, M. (1995) *Helping Children to Learn through a Movement Perspective*. London: Hodder Headline.

Hopper, B., Grey, J. & Maude, P. (2000) *Teaching Primary Physical Education*. London: Falmer.

International Physical Literacy Association (n.d.) Available at www.physical-literacy. org.uk

Portwood, M. (1999) *Developmental Dyspraxia*. London: David Fulton.

Youth Sport Trust (2011) *Start to Move*. Loughborough: Youth Sport Trust. Available at www.youthsport.org. Email info@starttomovezone.com.

CHAPTER 12

'I've got a song to sing'

CREATING A MUSICAL ENVIRONMENT FOR CHILDREN IN THEIR EARLY YEARS

Linda Bance

Introduction

Music in the Early Years can be a highly pleasurable area of learning for both children and teachers. Most young children love music-making and singing and are curious about how rhythmic and tuneful sounds are made. However, many teachers and practitioners lack confidence when engaging with music in the nursery or reception class, deeming themselves 'un-musical' or 'un-tuneful'. Despite this, given encouragement, training and support, most are able to provide a broad and exciting musical environment for all young children; a curriculum that is based on current theories where the children are at the heart of planning; and a place where children are able to learn, not only through adult-led activities, but through their own social interactions, self initiated play and explorations.

What is music in the Early Years all about?

Research consistently highlights the key contributions of music to the learning of young children. The direct link with language development and its impact on relationships, emotions and communication makes it all the more important that we include it in our curriculum and that we celebrate it as 'an important element of the traditions of early childhood education' (Pound & Harrison, 2003, p. 1).

This chapter will help readers to develop a broad vision of what musical activity in the Early Years can look like. For most young children, music is about singing and the emerging melodic contour of their developing voices. It is about heightening the awareness of pulse and beat though movement and play and about encouraging young children to be 'explorers of sounds', curious to find out about all musical instruments, what they sound like and how they can be played in different ways. Most importantly, it is about encouraging creativity, with process being at least as valuable as outcome.

This sounds like a tall order when considering the myriad demands and pressures on educators, yet if we are creative in our planning of a musical environment then the activities developed will embrace all areas of learning and, at the same time, have a positive effect on children's well-being. Dr Sue Hallam (2008) suggests that 'there is growing evidence that active involvement in music making can have positive benefits for children's intellectual and social development' (p. 1).

Why music?

Children need to experience the world in lots of different ways in order to make sense of it and draw from it what they like best. Because sound-making and rhythm is such a source of enjoyment to children, music is an excellent pathway into areas of the curriculum which they might otherwise see as difficult or irrelevant.

(Ouvery, 2004, p. 11)

Of course, singing and music-making can be seen as support for language development, maths and numeracy, the development of physical awareness, and the acquisition of our knowledge of the world. It also enhances social and emotional development and allows children to be expressive and creative. But music in its own right can be seen as a powerful tool that can uplift, unwind, refocus, relax, reinvent and reflect as children become increasingly comfortable and confident in the world around them. What would life be without music, dance, artwork and poetry in our lives?

I frequently hear music's place in Early Years settings justified because 'It is fun' or 'They love it', by which I take to mean this understanding of music's value is because it is pleasurable and uplifting.

(Young, 2009, p. 9)

What could music look like in an Early Years setting?

Depending very much on your setting, music can happen in many different places and at many different times, acting as a thread that weaves its way through the day. Music can, for example:

- be an element of free-flow time when children can make their own music inside and out;
- be the focus of shared time together for singing, music-making, sound stories, listening to music;
- support everyday routines through simple songs: lining up, tidying up or washing hands;
- enhance celebrations, assemblies and special occasions; or
- be a spontaneous activity for small groups in a role play or story corner.

Whichever way is relevant, access to music should be for everybody and, as far as possible, a daily occurrence.

Our own musicality

Many people question their own musicality, thinking 'I love music but I'm not musical'. This can cause worries: 'I have been given the role of music coordinator but I cannot play an instrument', 'I can't sing a note', 'I'm tone deaf', 'I can't read music', 'I don't play an instrument', or 'I'm just not musically gifted' (Pound & Harrison, 2003 p. 5). The list of concerns is endless.

Negative perceptions such as 'I can't sing' or 'I'm not good enough' will be quickly communicated to children and colleagues, but a 'Let's have a go' attitude will enable you to begin to develop a broad and creative approach to the musical activities that can be organised for your setting (Bance, 2012).

The idea of taking up the playing of a musical instrument might seem a little too demanding for a busy Early Years teacher, but understanding more about how music 'works' will nevertheless allow music to become more rewarding. This understanding can be developed through a range of activities including those described in the following paragraphs.

Your voice and singing

A good start to the improvement of a singing voice is to become more aware of breathing. Take plenty of breaths and do not try to sing loudly, as maintaining a quiet, strong voice rather than a high-pitched loud one will encourage children's listening (Street & Bance, 2006). Practising songs will develop the confidence to 'sing out' with the children and other staff.

Awareness of beat and pulse

When listening to music, become aware of the beat (the underlying pulse of the music). Practise picking out patterns in the music and memorise them by repeatedly singing the tune or by clapping or tapping the rhythm.

Exploring timbre

Take time to explore the musical instruments in your classroom, making sure that they are all in working order, no pieces are missing and that the sounds the instruments make are of good quality. Try out rhythm patterns on instruments of contrasting types and materials, exploring the different possibilities of sound making.

Listening to and appreciating music

Music is listened to for many different reasons: to set or change a mood, to distract, to relax or maybe just to make the day go with a swing. Listening to music with a

concentrated focus can develop understandings of the elements of music, the feelings evoked, and the rhythms, melodic shape, phrasing, tone, colour and texture.
Ask yourself:

- What can I hear?
- What does the music sound like?
- When does it change?
- How are the sounds made?
- How does it make me feel?

Enjoy this experience and share it with children, watching for non-verbal responses
and encouraging them to talk about how they are feeling, or what they are hearing.
Musical listening is a certain and distinct kind of listening, very different from, for
instance, speech listening (Odam, 1995, p. 24).

Playing a musical instrument

So many who have played musical instruments in the past dismiss the experience as
having no current relevance. Young children love to hear different types of musical
instruments, so reviving a talent – even if it is only to play simple melodies – can be
both a great personal achievement and the basis of a wonderful learning experience
for the children.

And finally . . . be creative

Developing your creativity should help you to be creative about your delivery of
music. Immerse yourself in the experience and question everything you do. Research
and discover new ways of delivering music, and when you do not know how to do
something, find somebody who does. Spend time imagining how it could be and
let your dreams run wild. Become a good role model with your approach: 'If we are
serious about wanting children to develop a creative attitude to life . . . we have to
start displaying to them our own creativity' (Claxton, 2003, p. 3).

Understanding the musical development
of young children

Before we begin to plan provision for music, it is wise to explore how children
develop musically. What can they already do as they begin their time with us?

Around the age of four years old, children develop a great sense of creativity
and imagination. They are open-eared and beginning to sing songs, both those
that they have learned from others and those that they have made up themselves.
They are capable of controlling beats, are becoming aware of patterns, and enjoy

moving to music. Most importantly, they are expert explorers of sounds and producers of their own spontaneous compositions, repeating, transforming, combining and developing their own or borrowed musical ideas into increasingly complex structures (Young, 2003).

This is indeed an exciting world for children, so ready and open to new ideas, and, as discussed, this can also be a creative and exciting time for teachers. The ideas below will help teachers to develop emergent musical skills to allow our children to become confident singers, movers and composers. The aim is to develop a good balance of adult-led and child-led activities that ensure a musically rich environment (Bance, 2012).

Children's singing voices

Singing is undoubtedly one of children's most natural means of musical expression. As previously discussed, by the time they enter school young children are typically able to match pitches as they sing, and frequently they sing songs and melodies of their own invention (Shehan Campbell, 2010). In considering approaches to developing and nurturing the emergent musicality of children, the value of nursery songs and folk songs from our own cultures should not be underestimated. 'Children learn these songs with the same ease as they learn their mother tongue and the playful repetitive melodies are the most suitable basis for children's singing and improvisation' (Forrai, 1985, p. 20).

The range of notes for children's songs should be quite short as very young voices have a limited range. This range is normally that shown in Figure 12.1, from middle C to B (a sixth above). Repetition is of course key to successful group singing and limiting the amount of words for each song will help everybody. (These repetitive games can be used as the basis of many activities, as we will see later.) Some children feel happy to sing along with others, or even to sing alone, but there will be many who find this activity just too worrying or unachievable to attempt. Where there is reticence, allow children to listen; this will encourage confidence to grow. Forcing a child to sing is unlikely to result in positive results or satisfaction for either teacher or child.

Each little voice is unique and special, with great potential, and the context most likely to encourage the development of vocal competency is one that affords frequent

Figure 12.1 *The normal range of children's voices*

opportunities for vocal play and encourages both vocal exploration and accurate imitation (Welsh, 2006).

What can children already do?

In order to identify an appropriate starting point for singing activities you will need to assess the children's ability to match pitch, the extent to which they can cope with text or language, their confidence in singing at speed and their awareness of other children. Observation of children's responses as they engage in some of the singing games below will help you to gain insights into these areas of development, allowing you to make singing a fruitful and enjoyable experience for everybody.

Starting a song

When starting a song it is a good idea to give children a 'starting note' by singing 'ready steady off we go'. This will help children to pitch their singing to the starting note and will also help to focus the group.

Playing around with the voice

Here are two examples of songs that can be used to encourage confident participation and good singing voices.

> *Copy Kitten*
>
> Copy Kitten, Copy Kitten
>
> Miaow! Miaow! Hiss!
>
> Copy Kitten, Copy Kitten
>
> Sounds like this.
> > (Street & Bance, 2006)

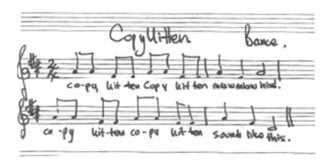

Figure 12.2 *'Copy Kitten'*

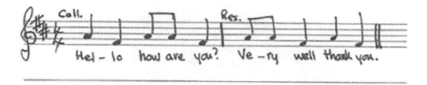

Figure 12.3 *'Hello! How are you?'*

Sit in a circle with a group of children. Pass around a toy kitten as you repeatedly sing the song. As each rendition ends, encourage the person with the kitten to make a sound with his or her voice (most sounds are acceptable). Everybody else listens and then copies the sound.

Sing the first phrase in Figure 12.3 to the children and encourage them to respond with the second. If the children find this difficult to start with, model the game using a puppet. The starting note suggested is a guide, but using a lower 'starting note' might help those children for whom singing with a high voice is a challenge. The game can also be varied by:

- splitting the group into two and encourage the children to play the game independently;
- changing the emotions of the song to sing happily, sadly, quietly, loudly, with a cross voice or with a kind voice;
- imagining how it would sound if sheep, tigers, or mice(for example) were singing this – ask the children for their ideas.

There are many songs available that are appropriate for our young singers (see Resource list).

Rhythm and pulse

> As children move and dance through their lives, there is rhythm and phrasing in their movement.
>
> (Young, 2009, p. 107)

Children are, of course, natural movers, and encouraging action songs, finger rhymes and lots of movement with music will allow children to move naturally to a beat and become aware of patterns within the music. To heighten awareness of beat and rhythm, the following strategies are useful:

- encourage as much large and small movement as possible in musical games and songs;
- introduce rhythm activities with body percussion, made sounds and percussion instruments;

Figure 12.4 *Children are natural movers*

- play around with patterns (see activities below); and
- use vocabulary that describes movements made to the music, e.g., fast, slow, quickly, slowly, short, long.

Keeping a steady pulse

Figure 12.5 is an example of how you can introduce and develop a simple activity to heighten the awareness of keeping the pulse.

> *Peter Taps*
>
> Peter hammers with one hammer, one hammer, one hammer.
>
> Peter hammers with one hammer all day long.
>
> (Traditional)

This is a versatile song that can be adapted to suit different contexts. Begin by familiarising children with the words and tune, and encourage them to keep the beat by clapping, tapping, or slapping thighs. Adapt the song by adding musical instruments and changing the words. For example: 'Julie plays a drum song, drum song, drum song . . . '

By matching syllables with sounds you can alert children to rhythm patterns in a playful way.

Figure 12.5 *'Peter Taps'*

Old Mister Woodpecker

Old Mister Woodpecker sitting in a tree

Hey Mister Woodpecker play a tune for me.

Say the poem with the children, modelling how to clap the rhythm as the words are said (each clap matches a syllable). Once the children are familiar with the poem, introduce some claves or musical instruments which can be tapped or banged. Children can then recite the poem together and join in with their instrument tapping the rhythm. At the end of the poem, one person plays their own piece, prompted by the words 'Off we go'. This allows for children to play their own piece and, as they become confident about their patterns, they will begin to play their own patterns which can then be copied by others.

Caterpillar Crunch

Crunch! Crunch! Crunch! Crunch!

Here comes a caterpillar for his lunch

Walking round on his many feet then stops for a green leaf to eat.

(Bance, 2012)

This song can be used in conjunction with other learning on the theme of mini-beasts or after reading Eric Carle's well-known *The Very Hungry Caterpillar* (Carle, 1969/2002). Recite the chant and at the same time try keeping the pulse by slapping thighs or even using percussion instruments. Let the children decide what the caterpillar will eat and use their ideas for rhythm pattern awareness.

Make some rhythm pattern cards using the images in Figure 12.6. Allow the children to choose one of the playing cards. Say the word on the card. Clap the word and play the word as a rhythm pattern. Two cards can be placed together so that the activity can be extended to match the children's ability, e.g. 'cherry cake, green leaf'. To focus on listening skills, change the use of the cards so that children are challenged to spot the card that matches the pattern played or clapped by teacher or pupil.

Figure 12.6 *Rhythm pattern cards*

Playing and exploring with musical instruments

Young children are natural sound-makers, from body sounds and sounds found all around us to choosing and playing from the selection of musical instruments offered in our settings. Sound-making is often a favourite activity. Ideally children should play freely, explore sounds, and be curious, playful and creative in finding out how sounds are made and how they can be used for experimenting with musical ideas. Within the classroom or Early Years setting, and particularly as children reach full-time schooling, it might be also appropriate to introduce some group music time where adult-initiated activities can be explored and extended. This balance between child-led and adult-initiated activities will allow a creative musical approach that is worthwhile for everybody.

Free-play music area

> The opportunity to play freely with instruments is absolutely essential if children are to develop skills and understanding in using them. There is no substitute for having quiet uninterrupted time in which to explore and absorb a detailed knowledge of the instrument's potential and how it feels to play it.
>
> (Young & Glover, 1998, p. 147)

This type of provision needs time and thought and will be influenced by space and practical issues. A musical free-play area could include:

- cushions, floor mats and low benches which allow both adults and children to work together;
- photographs and pictures on musical themes, to inspire activity;
- a variety of improvised sound-makers, such as hanging saucepans or chimes;
- a varied selection of tuned and untuned percussion instruments;
- a CD player accessible to children;
- props such as puppets , scarves and hats;
- a stage, partition, or curtained areas for those who prefer not to 'perform' – and mirrors for those who do.

Whilst working in this free-play area the children will have the opportunity to explore the sounds that instruments can make (see Figure 12.7) and to:

Figure 12.7 *Exploring the sounds that an instrument can make*

- play spontaneously using their own ideas;
- play imaginatively;
- explore sounds;
- express themselves emotionally;
- discover how sounds are made;
- realise a variety of audio sensory experiences; and
- realise that music is for everyone.

Whilst supporting this area, the practitioner can:

- observe;
- listen;
- offer positive reinforcement, verbally and non-verbally;
- encourage those who would normally be hesitant about exploring new things;
- play with and take instructions from the children;
- play a 'your turn, my turn' game;
- be expressive and creative alongside and with the children;
- offer extensions to their play, based on reflective practice;
- understand the musical development of a young child; and
- use observations when planning a group activity.

Adult-initiated group-work with musical instruments

As mentioned earlier, in addition to child-initiated free-play musical activity, small group-work with musical instruments can be effective in developing particular skills of playing or learning how to control the volume or tempo of sounds made (Young, 2009). The children can develop confidence in handling and using musical instruments, learning how to control them and use them to accompany stories or songs. Encourage children to take turns and listen to each other enjoying sharing their ideas with the others in the group. The development of musical skills and confidence requires much patience and self-discipline from both adult and child.

Small group activities enable the adult to extend ideas that have been seen in the free-play music area. Ideas of rhythm and patterns can be modelled and specific learning can be reinforced and extended. Useful strategies include providing a starting point for children to take on and lead, and encouraging everybody to join in together. You might channel children's ideas to create a performance or help the children to create sound pictures and stories, or invite the children to use musical instruments to accompany their songs and musical activities.

The following specific ideas of how to work in a group situation might also be helpful:

- *Stop and start*: ensure that all the children have an instrument, and encourage them to play as a 'band'. Through playful activities, familiarise the children with signals for stopping and starting. Once these are securely understood, allow one child to be the conductor.
- *Patterns*: sitting in a circle, encourage the children to listen to each other as sounds are explored. Take ideas you hear and use them to reinforce and extend. Ask 'Who can make up a pattern?' When one child plays a pattern, model a copying process and encourage others to join in.
- *Music to movement*: invite one child or supporting adult to dance and move in the middle of the circle whilst everybody plays. Encourage a variety of movement including, for example, running, walking, bouncing or curling up. Allow the children to make some music to accompany this movement, extending descriptive vocabulary by talking about playing slowly, fast, quietly loudly, happily, or 'growly'.
- *Creating a mood*: use a variety of instruments with a story to create an atmosphere – for example, music for rain, for wind, for running fast, or for being scared.

Music and ICT

Digital technologies have become an integral part of our lives and the lives of young children. The familiarity of digital sources of music can support musical learning in the Early Years by facilitating collaboration with a context of shared experiences (Rinta, Purves, & Welch, 2011). They offer the potential for self-teaching and imaginative thinking, and offer sounds and experiences which could 'bring with them all kinds of hitherto unimagined new possibilities' (Young, 2008, p. 333).

What kinds of digital music resources are suitable for use in the Early Years?

- *CD and MP3 players* offer children the opportunities to make their own choices and to control and lead activities.
- *Karaoke players* provide young singers with extend opportunities for performance, which contributes to confidence and self-esteem.
- *Voice recorders and microphones* help children understand the quality of their own voice. They allow them to hear what they sound like and to make self-evaluations, which is very important in assisting language and communication. They can also be an instant and valuable resource for teachers to provide sound files which can be compared over time as part of formative assessment processes.
- *Keyboards* can allow children to play around with pitch and to explore and compose their own unique pieces of music. This way of working within a free-play area can work well, especially when a pair of headphones is made available.
- *Video recorders* have become so child friendly that they can be used by the children to make up their own stories and performances or just record everyday experiences which can then be revisited for discussion.
- *Computer software and Internet-based resources* allow endless possibilities for multi-modal experiences using pitch, rhythm, timbre, layers of music and textures which in turn encourage imaginative and independent thinking and expression.

Media and technology provide unlimited musical resources from the multicultural and globalized culture for children to plug into, which affect the musical taste of children dramatically. The task of teachers is to remain open and receptive to these large scale impacts and to sort out which music can be effectively used in school – and how. The retention of traditional songs of children's experience and heritage songs and other music made live and in person, is a noble goal for teachers in schools, even as the music of meditated and technological sources provided a parallel sound stream in children's lives.

(Shehan Campbell & Lum, 2009, p. 328)

Listening activities

Sounds, noises and events fill our lives – but do we really listen? Is it possible to tune in to just one sound and really pay attention to it, allowing it to take precedence and transform the moment? Experience reveals that even very young children can be sensitive to sounds and alert and ready for listening, and this is at the heart of learning. When allowing children the opportunity to listen and respond both verbally and non-verbally to music, children are 'at their most spontaneous. The whole child is involved. The whole of this activity involves cognitive psychomotor responses which help to produce creativity' (Gardener, 1994). Giving appropriate opportunities to listen to music can also allow children to experience a calmness which leads to relaxation and focus. These experiences help to develop aural memory, and regulate emotions and feelings.

When deciding how to introduce this aspect of music learning, think about using a broad range of musical genres which reflect the tastes and cultures of everybody within the community of your setting. Draw on classical music, folk music, popular music or music from other countries and cultures. Talk to the children about their experiences of listening to music, thus forging links between the home and school environments.

Live musical performances offer multi-sensory musical experiences for young children. Invite musicians from among friends, parents, governors or older school children to perform for you. The opportunity to look carefully at an instrument and to listen to the sounds it makes will expand knowledge and understanding and offer a unique learning experience. Recording such a special event in sounds and pictures allows the children to revisit this experience again and again.

Listening to recorded music should also not be underestimated. Our world holds a rich tapestry of music which can be accessed through recorded music 'instantly available' in our settings. From jazz to Bollywood, folk to classical, a broad range will expand children's vision of what music is and will offer opportunities to discuss and develop preferences and choice. The use of cyber-performances through online resources can also provide children with high quality visual and musical experiences.

Planning a listening activity

It is a misconception that listening to music requires children to sit still. To ensure the effectiveness of this activity, adapt it to the children's knowledge and the particular learning environment and its challenges, and ensure that you as teacher are a good role model. Possible places and situations for listening could be the story corner, a corner of the hall or large area ready for movement and dance. Sometimes a quiet outside area can be suitable, or indoors during rest and relaxation time.

The choice of music to be played will clearly have an impact on the outcomes of the activity. Big band music will uplift and energise whilst gentle folk tunes might provoke calm and quiet. A tune from a well-known film will allow the imagination to flow whereas something new and different, for example African drummers or an Indian piece, will broaden the children's musical ideas. The length of the piece is crucial to ensure concentration and focus. Repetition will allow the children to become familiar with the piece of music, thus developing aural memory and enriching the learning experience, as children remember, anticipate and respond.

Preparation for this activity will involve careful listening on the teacher's part. Are there contrasts in the music – for example, loud and quieter sections, fast and slow? Are there familiar sounds or musical instruments or special effects? What was the mood of the music and did it 'spark' emotions? How might children respond to this piece? Are there other activities that could be linked to this music?

Whilst listening to the music with the children, watch them nonjudgmentally. Ask open-ended questions, such as:

- What did you hear?
- What happened to the music then?
- How did it make you feel?
- What could we do to this music?

Drawing children's attention to elements within the music will promote the effective development of listening skills and sensitivity, and will encourage the making of links with children's lives outside the setting. These, in turn, will provide children with tools for musical creativity. As confidence develops, children will become more able to represent their responses to music in a variety of ways. As ideas flow, children will enjoy responding through movement and dance, from playing air guitar to dancing like fairies. Similarly, children will enjoy drawing or painting whilst the music is played. Our aim is to encourage open-minded children listening intently, sensitively and with meaning, resulting in a very special experience.

Conclusion

Whether the teacher is a musical specialist or non-specialist, music in the Early Years can make an effective contribution to the development of well-rounded, inspired and creative young children. The opportunities to build on children's ideas provide endless possibilities for making this area of learning increasingly exciting, enriching the learning experiences of children and providing practitioners with a source of great enjoyment as they observe the positive outcomes of both children's developing musical appreciation and their own music-making.

Key pointers for music in the Early Years

- Depending very much on your setting, music can happen in many different places and at many different times.
- Understanding what music means to us as adults is a good starting point for planning a musical environment.
- Less is more when planning and repetition is key to effective learning.

(Continued)

(Continued)

- Music is not just about singing but about moving, dancing, exploring, creating, making, and listening, and can be woven into everyday activities to enhance and support all areas of learning and development.
- A balance between adult-led and child-led musical activity will ensure that everybody gets to be creative and inventive in their musical expression.
- Sharing songs and activities with other members of staff beforehand can help us as teachers to deliver more confidently, in the knowledge that the other members of staff are supporting you.

The author wishes to thank all those who have helped make this chapter possible, including Taylor & Francis/Routledge for excerpts from Music for Early Learning, and the families of Brunswick Nursery, Cambridge.

References

Bance, L. (2012) *Music for Early Learning: Songs and musical activities to support children's development*. Abingdon: Routledge.

Carle, E. (1969/2002) *The Very Hungry Caterpillar*. London: Puffin.

Claxton, G. (2003) *Creativity: A Guide for the Advanced Learner (and Teacher)*. Available at: http://www.guyclaxton.com/documents/New/A%20Guide%20for%20the%20Advanced%20Learner.pdf (accessed 11th October 2013).

Forrai, K. (1985) *Music in Pre-School*. Budapest: Corvina.

Gardener, H. (1994) *The Arts and Human Development*. New York: Basic Books.

Hallam, S. (2008) Music Education around the World 14. *International Society for Music Education Newsletter*, October /November.

Odam, G. (1995) *The Sounding Symbol: Music Education in Action*. Cheltenham: Nelson Thornes.

Ouvry, M. (2004) *Sounds Like Playing: Music and the Early Years Curriculum*. Early Education: The British Association for Early Childhood Education.

Pound, L. & Harrison, C. (2003) *Supporting Musical Development in the Early Years*. Buckingham: Open University Press.

Rinta, T., Purves, R., & Welch, G.F. (2011) Usability of a Jamming Mobile with 3–6-Year-Old Children for Enhancing Feelings of Social Inclusion and Facilitating Musical Learning. Paper presented at Proceedings of the 5th Conference of the European Network of Music Educators and Researchers of Young Children, Helsinki, Finland, 8–11th June, pp. 275–286.

Shehan Campbell, P. (2010) *Songs in Their Heads: Music and Its Meaning in Children's Lives*, 2nd Edition. New York: Oxford University Press.

Shehan Campbell, P. & Lum, C.-H. (2009) Live and Mediated Music Meant Just for Children. In K. Smithrim & R. Upitis (Eds.), *Listen to Their Voices* (pp. 319–329). Waterloo, Ontario: Canadian Music Educators' Association.

Street, A. & Bance, L. (2006) *Voiceplay: 22 Songs for Young Children*. New York: Oxford University Press.

Welsh, G. (2006) Singing and Vocal Development. In G. McPherson. (Ed.), *The Child as a Musician*. Oxford: Oxford University Press.

Young, S. (2003) *Music with the Under-Fours*. London:Routledge Farmer.

Young, S. (2008) 'Digital Technologies, Young Children, and Music Education Practice'. In K. Smithrim & R. Upitis (Eds.) (2007) *Listen to Their Voices: Research and Practice in Early Childhood Music* (Research to Practice Series, Vol. 3). Edmonton: Canadian Music Educators' Association.

Young, S. (2009) *Music 3 to 5*. Abingdon: Routledge.

Young, S. & Glover, J. (1998) *Music in the Early Years*. London: Falmer Press.

Further reading

Duffy, B. (2006) *Supporting Creativity and Imagination in the Early Years*, 2nd Edition, Maidenhead: McGraw Hill.

Geoghigan, L. (2000) *Singing Games and Rhymes for Early Years*. National Choir of Scotland.

Macgregor, H. (1998) *Tom Thumb's Musical Maths*. London: A&C Black.

Macgregor, H. (1999) *Bingo Lingo: Supporting Literacy with Songs and Rhymes*. London: A&C Black.

MacGregor, H., Gargrave, B., Roberts, S., & Shulman, D. (2001) *Let's Go Zudie-O*. London: A&C Black.

Nicholls, S., Roberts, S., & Breeze, L. (1992) *Bobby Shafto Clap your Hands*, London: A&C Black.

Waterhouse, C. (1998) *How Can I Keep From Singing!* South Croydon: British Kodaly Academy.

Whitlock, V. & Court, S. (2009) *Singing Sherlock*, Vol 3. London: Boosey & Hawkes.

Useful Websites

www.youthmusic.org.uk
www.singup.org
www.musicaleyes.org.uk
www.soundconnections.org
www.meryc.eu.
www.musicmark.org

CHAPTER 13

'Once there was someone who walked on the sky'

CREATIVITY IN THE EARLY YEARS

Kate Cowan and Miles Berry

When discussing creativity in teaching and learning, the strongest associations are often with traditional 'creative arts' areas of the curriculum, such as music, dance, art and drama. Consider, however, the creativity and innovation that can be demonstrated in solving mathematical problems, or the imagination and adaptability necessary to make scientific inventions. This chapter suggests that creativity can, and should, be part of all areas of learning in the Early Years, and that through creative teaching, this can be an embedded and holistic approach rather than an addition to the main curriculum. Drawing upon examples from two Nursery schools influenced by the creative approach in Reggio Emilia, suggestions are made as to how projects might be started, sustained and documented creatively, presenting the rationale for a creative pedagogic approach, and what is needed from a creative educator.

What is creativity?

> Imagination is more important than knowledge. Knowledge is limited. Imagination encircles the world.
>
> (Albert Einstein)

Definitions are disputed and varied, but creativity might be considered to encompass qualities such as innovation, imagination, adaptability, problem-solving, expression and originality. Creativity has been defined as 'connecting the previously uncon-nected in ways that are new and meaningful to the individual concerned' (Duffy, 1998, p. 18). This has links with constructivist theories of learning, which suggest that experiences confirm and strengthen what is known already, or challenge and extend understanding further, giving rise to creative processes. Creativity can therefore be considered a way of thinking, where existing knowledge and understanding are used to identify similarities and differences, and to generate new connections.

Creativity is sometimes associated with several unhelpful misconceptions, for instance, that being creative is an innate talent or gift, possessed by some and lacking in others. Instead, a definition of 'little "c" creativity' has been offered, suggesting creativity can be life-wide and life-long (Craft, 2002). In this way, creativity is not seen as extraordinary or sacred, something only great artists, authors or composers might achieve, but as a powerful way of making meaning which is open to all. The consequence for educators is to position every child, and every adult, as having valuable creative potential.

This has much in common with the image of the child held by the Reggio Emilia infant-toddler centres and preschools of northern Italy, attended by children from three months to six years of age. The schools have gained prominence and popularity in response to their child-centred, discovery-based approach to learning, which offers a particular understanding of creativity:

> Creativity should not be considered a separate mental faculty, but a characteristic of our way of thinking, knowing and making choices.
> (Malaguzzi, cited in Edwards, Gandini, & Forman, 1998, p. 75)

The distinctive pedagogy of Reggio Emilia was developed after the Second World War, with citizens investing in early education settings as democratic places to teach children to think for themselves. Within this approach, every child is accredited with rights, and recognised as an inquisitive, sociable, creative agent in his or her own learning. Rather than viewing children as empty vessels to be filled with facts, Reggio educators emphasise the ability and potential of all children to create and construct their own theories and understandings about the world around them. Whilst this approach has gained particular international interest, it builds upon a longstanding tradition of progressive education, influenced by theorists such as Froebel and Dewey, and is not considered a model to be simply copied, but an approach to prompt dialogue and reflection in an educator's own context.

Adopting a view of children as powerful, expressive, social and creative inevitably has implications for the role of the teacher in the Early Years. Rather than being seen as experts, adults are also considered learners, accompanying and supporting children's enquiries. Educators are not viewed solely as 'programme deliverers', but as independent thinkers and learners, rich in their own creative potential. The role of the adult might therefore be to offer encouragement, clarify or challenge ideas and provide complimentary experiences which help children to build connections. Such a creative pedagogy also necessitates a shift in emphasis from creative output to recognition of the importance of creative processes, and the potential of a creative environment to act as an additional 'teacher'.

Why adopt a creative approach?

The creative adult is the child who survived.

(Ursula K. Le Guin)

Creativity, imagination and play are important qualities of the deepest learning, when children are intrinsically motivated to make connections, take risks and hypothesize. Creativity as a starting point for teaching and learning might therefore enable children to take the lead in their own enquiries, actively following their fascinations and becoming independent, self-regulating learners. The school and the educator play a vital role in fostering the 'creative ecosystem' (Harrington, 1990) which supports, or prohibits, this type of learning. Robinson suggests that all too often, 'schools kill creativity' by educating children *out* of their creative capacities through over-emphasis on a knowledge-based curriculum (2006). Robinson considers this particularly worrying given the changing world around us, where creativity might be essential to adapt and innovate in an unpredictable future.

One particularly important social change is within communication, with digital technology changing the way information is represented. The rules of the page, which historically have been dominated by the linguistic mode of writing, are increasingly being reshaped by the rules of the screen, where writing is likely to be just one part of a multimodal ensemble. Such ensembles might include still and moving image, sound effects, music and layout, in addition to speech and writing. A creative curriculum, which recognizes and supports children's multimodal design in visual, embodied and spatial modes, as well as linguistic, can therefore be seen as vital in supporting all children making and expressing meaning in a 'changing landscape of communication' (Kress, 1997).

Such an approach has connections to the Reggio Emilia concept of 'the hundred languages of children', a theory linking thought and expression. In young children, these 'hundred languages' might manifest themselves in drawing, construction, music, shadow-play, dance and storytelling, to name just a selection, and the theory is considered 'a declaration of the equal dignity and importance of *all* languages, not only writing, reading and counting' (Rinaldi, 2006, p. 175). Within his famous poem, 'No Way. The Hundred Is There', Reggio founder Loris Malaguzzi celebrates the expressive and inventive capabilities of children and urges educators to recognize these as valuable and vital capacities:

> The child has
>
> a hundred languages
>
> (and a hundred hundred more)
>
> but they steal ninety-nine.
>
> The school and the culture
>
> Separate the head from the body
>
> (Malaguzzi, 1996, p. 4)

It is therefore suggested that carefully attending to the full array of children's 'languages' can support vital expressive and communicational skills for representing and making sense of the world. Researchers have suggested that a multimodal pedagogy can be particularly empowering and inclusive in recognizing the learning of children who may find it difficult or prefer not to express understanding or experiences in the verbal or written modes often prioritized in education (Pahl, 1999; Flewitt, 2006; Stein, 2008), and that Reggio children demonstrate impressive levels of communication, symbolic skills and creativity relative to their age (Cadwell, 2003).

In Reggio, creative inquiries are carried out through *progettazioni*, roughly translated as 'projects', but with a distinct emphasis on projecting forward possible directions, rather than adhering to a fixed or predetermined model. The examples in this chapter come from settings inspired by the child-led project approach found in Reggio Emilia, outlining some considerations in adopting a project-based creative practice to support children's creativity in the Early Years.

Starting projects creatively

Creativity takes courage.

(Henri Matisse)

Ethos

Embedding creativity at the heart of teaching and learning is not only about tangible changes, such as resources and classroom layout, but also concerns the fundamental aims and values at the heart of practice. Taking the view of all children as inquisitive and capable agents in their own learning, the starting point must be something that truly matters to children. This positions children as key protagonists, with adults adopting a supportive and collaborative role in maintaining creative enquiry.

Beginning child-led projects can have an element of uncertainty, not knowing at first what the focus will be, whether interests will diverge or meander, or where the project will end up. In contrast, it can feel as if there is security in planning projects *for* children, deciding upon a focus, mapping out progression and structuring activities which lead to a finite end point and outcome. For all its good intentions, this approach is unlikely to be based in the children's true fascinations, or to have the flexibility to change and evolve *with* the children and their interests. As Reggio *pedagogista* Rinaldi suggests, 'The potential for every child is stunted if the endpoint of learning is formulated in advance' (cited in Bancroft, Fawcett, & Hay, 2008, p. 5).

Reflecting upon her teaching of a Reception class, author and educator Bernadette Duffy recalls a well-meaning activity she initiated about Springtime, carefully preparing a background of hills and showing children how to sponge-print grass and make egg boxes into flowers. Noting that her class worked hard but had little interest in the finished piece, she realised that this scene did not resonate with the children's own experiences of Spring in an inner-city school: 'It was not an example of the children's creativity but of mine. Creativity is about representing one's own image, not reproducing someone else's' (Duffy, 1998, p. 10).

True creativity takes courage, both on the part of the child and the practitioner. Safe and procedural activities, leading to a single answer or outcome, are unlikely to allow space for real innovation. In contrast, tasks with an element of ambiguity and risk, which are carefully balanced and supported by the educator, can encourage true creativity and generate deep understanding. In this way, the role of the adult is not passive, but a responsibility 'to provide, to organise, and to value' (Drummond, 1996). Beginning a project which is child-led and open-ended may feel like a challenge, but can be an opportunity for learning and true creativity for children and educators alike.

As well as practitioner courage, it is also vital to cultivate children's creative confidence. Children must feel able to test out ideas and take risks without fearing that mistakes will be criticised. It is as they make predictions, and realise something they thought would work does not, that understanding moves on, with errors forming a fundamental part of the creative process. An ethos that emphasises ideas and hypotheses over correct answers and fixed outcomes establishes an atmosphere supporting limitless individual possibilities, rather than simply being right or wrong.

Crucially, children may not always be able to, or choose to, verbalise their understanding, so the educator must be alert to the many other 'languages' they may use in their meaning-making and expression. It is the educator's duty to cultivate an atmosphere where creations are recognized and valued in all their multimodal forms, supporting children to develop creative confidence.

'Just running?'

During a Nursery woodland project, some children experienced the space by running fast and running far. This posed several challenges. There was initially concern related to 'running away' and it was sometimes dismissed as 'just running', while adult attention often focused on slower, quieter or more settled exploration. There was also a practical difficulty in listening to and accompanying the children without disrupting their experience. A conscious effort was made to attend to the embodied exploration of the running children, whose physical experiences were valued just as much as those expressed verbally, graphically, or in other symbolic modes. Using video as a helpful observation tool, the children's running games were recorded, re-viewed and interpreted by the educators and developed throughout the course of the project, revealing a game of 'magic tricks' which explored ideas of invisibility, disappearing, reappearing, being lost, being found, and being in control.

Environment

The ethos of the setting and values of the educators ought to shape the routines, structure and layout of creative practice. To elicit children's fascinations, the environment should prompt interest and wonder, with ample time for play, exploration and discovery. Settings with limited space can still adopt such an ethos, and the many possibilities of trips into the local environment multiply opportunities for exploration. The physical space is just one aspect of the environment, alongside the emotional climate created by educators. The emotional environment needs to support children's freedom to explore and pursue ideas, knowing that the adult will take their interest seriously, supporting and accompanying their inquiry.

As creativity occurs when children are deeply absorbed, it is important that they are given ample time to carry out and continue their investigations, whether this is from morning to afternoon, day to day, or over weeks and months. It is therefore important to provide spaces where creations-in-progress can be kept safely, and to ensure that educators are not rushing exploration to get onto the next topic, unit or project. Time can seem a luxury in Early Years settings, but placing a creative ethos at the centre of practice can enable a unified, holistic approach to learning rather than the juggling of several unconnected initiatives, directives and events.

Bringing the woodland into the classroom

Class visits to the local woodland happened weekly, but the project formed the basis of all teaching and learning for the Nursery children throughout its duration. Notes, photographs and video created by parents and educators in the woods provided observations to aid planning, and to make assessments about children's learning, identifying 'next steps' which would be explored in future woodland trips. An interest in digging in the woods, for instance, led to a collection of underground 'treasures' being brought back to nursery and proudly displayed, then reflected upon further through drawing and telling stories about the found objects. The children were active in planning their future visits, deciding they would like to take digging equipment, such as trowels and sieves, on future visits to the woods. The ongoing exploration formed the basis of classroom displays, and a curriculum evening for parents described the woodland exploration, showing things the children had discovered, re-telling their stories from the woods, and linking this to the Early Years curriculum. In this way, the trips to the woods were not an extra activity to be accommodated alongside existing topics and obligations, but formed the basis of all teaching and learning for the duration of the project, ultimately creating more time to deeply explore the children's interests.

Making children's fascinations the basis of projects demands careful and committed looking and listening from the educator, informing a cycle of observation, reflection and planning. This necessitates a planning system which makes space for flexibility, uncertainty, and the children's own input. As such, it is unlikely that detailed long-term plans will effectively identify and accommodate children's interests. Short-term planning instead requires the educator to draw on their professional understanding of the learning potential offered by different projects as interests emerge, whilst overseeing and recording children's achievements as the project develops. This requires a further element of space, in the need to make room in the practitioner's day for reflection, ideally in collaboration with colleagues, parents and, often, the children themselves, to reflect on what is happening, identify learning and plan where the project may go next.

The central position of creativity and imagination in the Reggio approach can be found in the organisation of their schools, which feature an *atelier*, or studio, in each setting, and *mini-ateliers* in each classroom. Supported by an *atelierista*, who may have expertise in the visual arts, dance, music, photography or other expressive skills, these spaces contain specialised equipment and resources for creative exploration and expression. Linked deeply to the concept of the 'hundred languages', the *atelier* reflects Malaguzzi's vision to create schools made up of many 'laboratories' in which children can imagine and discover. The emphasis is on providing children with creative possibilities daily – what they call 'rich normality' – rather than as an exceptional opportunity. Whilst an *atelier* may not be replicable on this scale in every context, the 'spirit of the studio' might still incorporated in terms of its ethos, shaping aspects of the environment and available materials (see Gandini, Hill, Cadwell, & Schwall, 2005).

Materials

What is on offer in the environment will determine the ways in which children are able to research, represent and communicate their ideas creatively. Having certain materials available every day allows children the time to explore and get to know their properties, developing competence and independence. Reggio Emilia places particular emphasis on the use of natural, reclaimed and open-ended materials as sources of creative potentials. This is also advocated by Steiner-Waldorf kindergartens and underpins the philosophy of heuristic play and the use of treasure baskets with infants (Goldschmied & Hughes, 1992).

Such materials are rich in potential because they offer diversity and sensory interest, particularly in comparison to the manufactured plastic toys often provided to children. Hughes suggests plastic can be 'dull and disappointing' (2006, p. 21) and that such toys can be limited in their creative possibilities: 'Whilst they are often attractively complicated and "educational" from an adult perspective, they are woefully limited in their "potential for discovery" from the [child's] point of view' (Hughes, 2006, p. 4).

In contrast, it is suggested that the best materials for exploring and representing creatively are intriguing, flexible and open-ended in their use. Such resources have been called 'intelligent materials' by Reggio educators, rich in their simplicity and versatility. Pebbles, for instance, might be used to explore fundamental concepts of quantity, as pretend food in role play, to explore rolling and motion, or arranged in a trail to be followed. In contrast to products designed with limited functions for specific tasks or topics, intelligent materials are generous in their potentials, prompting multiple imaginative and creative uses.

Such materials are often easily and cheaply obtained. In partnership with local businesses, some regions run 'scrap-stores' or creative recycling centres offering large quantities of materials to educators for very little charge. Investment in some more expensive open-ended resources, such as simple wooden blocks, musical instruments, a light projector or a digital camera, may also be worthwhile for the versatile creative potential they offer, usable time and time again for different projects.

Possible 'intelligent materials' for continuous provision

- paper and mark-making materials of various types (eg. pencils, pens, crayons, chalk, paints, lined paper, plain paper, coloured paper, newspaper)
- natural materials (eg. pine cones, conkers, feathers, pebbles, shells, dried herbs, seed pods)
- recycled materials (eg. lids, tubes, fabric, boxes, plastic bottles, cotton reels)
- made materials (eg. pipe cleaners, bolts, hinges, buttons, treasury tags, paperclips, magnets, magnifying glasses, mirrors)

Clay and wire are often used in the *progettazioni* of Reggio Emilia, valued particularly because of their transformational and flexible properties. These materials encourage development of not only fine motor skills, but also the creative and imaginative possibilities afforded by their malleability. Rather than introducing materials for a limited time or duration of a topic – for instance, a week 'doing clay' or a one-off activity creating watercolour portraits – it is important to provide opportunities to revisit materials regularly, with different prompts and in different contexts. This supports children to fully come to know the properties of different materials, consolidate and develop new skills, and to draw upon these in making creative connections.

Reggio educators place great importance upon the presentation and organisation of materials, so that children can access what they need in a calm and ordered environment. Resources arranged accessibly and attractively help foster an appreciation of beauty and order, as well as of the materials themselves as valuable and full of creative potential.

Figure 13.1 *'Intelligent materials' organised and displayed in the Nursery classroom*

Focus

With rich resources, materials and experiences on offer, observations of children's play are likely to identify several different interests and potential directions of creative enquiry. How, then, might the educator decide which to follow as the basis of a project? It will certainly not be possible to explore every avenue of every interest, but there is still value in the practice of exploring *something* of real significance to the children through in-depth creative inquiry.

One strategy may be to revisit observations and ephemera collected over time to identify recurring fascinations, prominent themes, or interests shared by several groups of children. Interests might be explored at face value or as manifestations of 'big ideas'. A recurring interest in dinosaurs, tigers and sharks, for instance, might be explored on the surface as an interest in animals, or indicate that the underlying interests concern power, force, fear, and the boundaries between good and bad.

First Hand Experience (Rich et al., 2005) outlines an 'alphabet of learning from the real world', taking purposefully 'big' ideas such as 'Enemies', 'Nothing' and 'Yesterday' and exploring how these might become extended inquiries. As Rich and colleagues demonstrate, using a single word to describe a project can be helpful in providing a focus in an initial 'prologue' stage of project-planning, whilst maintaining open-ended creative possibilities. Their book provides many suggestions as to how educators might use this model as a springboard to create their own projects and learning stories based on what matters to the children in their own settings.

Exciting the imagination

The 'Pink Project' developed its focus from practitioner observations relating to children and their ideas about colour. It was noted that several children were unsure about naming colours, and that many also held some associations between gender and colour, with comments such as 'boys don't wear pink'. The 'Pink Project' was planned with children to involve sustained exploration of the colour pink in different forms – for example light, wax, food, paint and natural materials. Creatively exploring and challenging these associations between pink and gender led to the construction of pink role play resources to feature in typically boisterous play involving knights and castles, as well as exploring cultural colour connotations through looking at pink clothing, decoration and artwork from around the world.

A further strategy for identifying a project focus is making use of children's questions, seeing these as their serious and meaningful work at making sense of the world. Children's questions or hypotheses – such as 'When does the future start?' (Rich et al., 2005, p. 72) or 'Everything has a shadow except ants' (Reggio Children, 1999) – present opportunities to creatively test or explore ideas and predictions. It may be helpful to keep a notebook or create a designated display space in the setting to collect and keep the children's questions prominent, making the evolution of the project visible.

Projects might also develop out of interesting events that have happened in the setting. The project 'Catness', for instance, focused upon a mother cat and her kittens living in the grounds of a preschool (Reggio Children, 1995). Events as the initial stimuli for projects may be unexpected, or might sometimes be offered by the adult as 'provocations'. For instance, a selection of mysterious keys could be hidden for the children to discover, or an event such as a performance from a musician might be organised. Whilst it is the adult who facilitates these experiences, it must still be the children's own interests which drive the project forward. The adult may imagine or hope, for instance, that keys could prompt discussion of houses and homes, but the children may be more captured by the idea of finding and collecting hidden treasures. If provocations are used to initiate projects this must be done with careful attention to the children's responses, and still allow scope for the unexpected and for children to creatively take the lead.

Whichever approach to finding a focus is used, it is particularly helpful to discuss emerging interests with colleagues and parents, who can bring additional perspectives and insights. In Reggio, children discuss ideas for potential projects with educators, deciding upon a shared focus. The duration and 'end product' of the *progettazione* are not decided at the outset, and might involve many children or just a small group, continuing for days, weeks, months or even from year to year. Rich et al. describe a zig-zag route from project to project, evolving in response to children's changing, or deepening, interests (2005). Projects, therefore, will be different shapes and sizes, and may have projects within projects, appealing to different children's interests at different stages.

Sustaining projects creatively

Conditions for creativity are to be puzzled; to concentrate; to accept conflict and tension; to be born every day; to feel a sense of self.

(Erich Fromm)

Creative questioning

Having identified an important fascination, and choosing to make it the basis of a project, the educator's responsibility is to provide and organize the sustained inquiry that will support children making new connections and extend their thinking creatively. Questions and discussion will, of course, happen at every stage in a project, but can be particularly useful for understanding the meanings and ideas children already hold, helping the educator to plan and support the inquiry.

With children positioned as the protagonists in their own creative investigations, it is important to resist the temptation to give quick answers or teach facts about emerging interests. Questions are often used to test what children know or do not know, with a 'correct' answer already in the adult's mind. This can stifle creativity if children become concerned or embarrassed about getting questions wrong. A more helpful starting point might be to instead pose questions designed to elicit children's existing thoughts and ideas. Open-ended questions can be especially effective in supporting creative thinking, particularly when these are 'big questions' to which the educators do not themselves know the answers.

Questions are also a useful way of modelling creative thinking processes, helping children to reflect and take the lead in planning and carrying out enquiries. For example:

- What would happen if . . . ?
- I wonder why . . . ?
- What could we try next?
- How do you know?
- What do we need to help us find out?
- What could we do differently?
- How did you feel?
- What do you think?

Questions of this kind support what has been called 'possibility thinking', through encouraging children to critically evaluate what they have done, justifying their choices and reflecting on what they might do differently (Burnard, Grainger, & Craft, 2006). When these questions are used routinely, children can be supported to constructively ask such questions of themselves and each other, developing independent and collaborative learning skills as well as individual aesthetic and emotive responses to their own and their peers' creations. However, as some children may not choose to or be able to express their understanding verbally, it is important that the materials on offer, as well as the attention of the supporting adults, are organised to attend to children's communication and representation in all its forms.

Magic questions

Having observed the children performing 'magic tricks' and telling stories about magical characters, such as witches, fairies and dragons, in the woodland project, the exploration was sustained through asking 'big' questions about magic. The questions had no predetermined answers, inviting children to share their own experiences and use their imaginations to puzzle things out. These helped to understand the ideas and interests the children already held, and to give shape to developing the project further. Some of the questions included:

- What is magic?
- Where does magic come from?
- Can anyone be magic or do magic?
- Can you be not magic and still do magic tricks?
- What does it feel like when you do a magic trick?
- What does magic sound like?

Representations

Questions can also be used to invite children to undertake representational challenges. Representing ideas and experiences requires children to think symbolically. Words can be used as symbols, as can creations such as pictures, models, gestures and sounds, standing for something in the real world and developing the facility for abstract thought. Moving between symbolic modes, for example from words into pictures, or from a picture into a model, strengthens and deepens creative connections. As well as requiring an understanding of the concept or experience itself, it also demands an understanding of the properties, or affordances, of the modes available. In Reggio, children are routinely encouraged to make drawings of their ideas and experiences, and might then be provided with the materials to move from 2-D representation into 3-D, and potentially also into forms such as music and dance. In this way, supporting children to represent ideas in their 'hundred languages' not only amplifies the range of children's creative expression but also the opportunity for deepening understanding.

'Do you want to see my magic trick?'

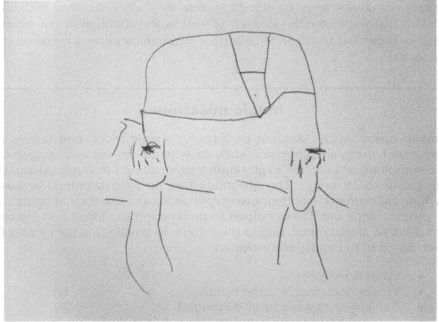

Figure 13.2 *Zack draws his magic trick*

During the woodland project, Zack explored the winding pathways through the densely wooded areas and asked, 'Do you want to see my magic trick?' He pointed at a place to wait, running in a big circle, disappearing behind trees before reappearing where he started. The magic spread, and several children then demonstrated their own variations on the trick.

As a representational challenge, Zack was invited to draw his trick. He created the illustration shown as Figure 13.2, and explained, *'That's me, and that's me, and that's my magic trick.'*

This simple but sophisticated drawing demonstrates his understanding of orientation in the woods, and his ability to represent motion and perspective. Other children then experimented with depicting their tricks as maps and diagrams, reinforcing the idea that mark-making can create lasting records of physical exploration. As well as challenging the children's means of expression, it also deepened the exploration of tricks as differentiated knowledge between the magic trick runner and the audience, and of shared imagination.

In addition to what is continuously available to children, inquiry might be extended and deepened through offering additional materials for representation in line with children's interests. This includes materials which are particularly sympathetic to children's existing interests, or which pose a particular conceptual challenge. In the magic trick project, wax crayons and candles were provided alongside dark paint to respond to and build upon the children's interests in appearing, disappearing and invisibility. The materials themselves might not be new to the children, but might be presented in new ways or unusual combinations to challenge expectations or assumptions. For instance, sponges placed in a sand tray might challenge the expectations of children who had been exploring the properties of water 'disappearing' through absorption.

Whilst the emphasis in these projects is on children creating their own representations, the adult still plays an important role. Careful instruction and modelling from the adult can help children to see the potentials of new or complex resources, such as woodwork tools and digital cameras, encouraging them to persevere with challenges, developing skills and confidence. Adult instruction can also help develop habits which ensure materials are used safely, carefully and with respect. The educator must maintain a delicate balance between providing materials and experiences which are new, interesting and puzzling, and those which resonate sufficiently with what the children know and understand already. Too little challenge, and the children will not be interested. Too challenging, and the activity may create anxiety. It is the educator's task to carefully observe and interpret the children's learning, making considered and reciprocal offerings which achieve this balance and strengthen new creative connections.

Provocations

Whilst provocations may be used at the outset of a project to generate initial interest and exploration, offerings from the educator also play a vital role in sustaining and deepening investigations initiated by the children. Questions and materials can be provocations, as can visits, visitors, objects, stories, performances, works of art and sources of information. Provocations throughout the project can be seen as 'donations' from the educators which deepen and extend inquiries.

A story from the sky

During the woodland project, one group showed particular fascination in shadows, darkness, and the woods at night. The practitioners responded to this interest in the Nursery by offering a light projector layered with acetate photographs children took in the woods, including the sky, the trees and the ground, along with collected items such as sticks, bark and feathers. The children were invited to manipulate the images and objects to create their own shadowy woodland on the walls of the classroom.

(Continued)

(Continued)

It was while investigating the objects on the projector in this way that Ollie imagined and narrated a story of giants and birds, with the opening line giving the title to this chapter: '*Once there was someone who walked on the sky*'.

The resources were purposefully provided to complement an existing interest in light and dark, materially echoing experiences in the woods, but also offering a prompt for ideas to be extended into new imaginative dimensions.

Figure 13.3 *A light projection of natural materials creates shadowy images*

Visits can be particularly rich as they provide opportunities for children to connect their learning in the setting with the outside world, researching their environment first-hand. Visits need not necessarily be whole-class trips, and might be to places we as adults would consider very ordinary. Even visits within the school site, for example to the kitchen or caretaker's shed, can offer rich potential for making connections and deepening learning when linked to children's interests and inquiries. Rather than organising the same visit for all children, it may be more appropriate for a small group to make a visit so they can follow up a particular interest or problem, reporting back and sharing the experience with the whole group.

There is sometimes an uneasy sense that we ought to offer children identical educational experiences. However, a creative approach might consider how we can tailor educational experiences to individuals and groups, recognising their creative capacities and interests. Reggio educators place a strong emphasis on the child's place within communities of learners, with many projects structured around smaller groups within a whole class. In the initial stages of a *progettazione*, adults and children might collaboratively decide how different groups will proceed with various aspects of an inquiry. Duckett and Drummond describe a Nursery project centred around construction, in which the children formed distinct groups such as 'the builders', 'the decorators' and 'the path makers', each with its own role and sense of identity within a larger group (2009). Groups might form as children work together on part of a larger collaborative project, or may emerge based on children's similar interests and underlying 'big ideas'.

A project may also be supported by inviting visitors to share something of particular interest. This could be a parent or family member, or someone not known to the children, sharing their own skills, experiences, memories or sources of expertise with the children to extend their meaning-making. *Creative Partnerships* have documented several projects involving collaboration between educators and creative enablers, such as artists, architects and scientists, as has the work of 5×5×5 = *Creativity* (Bancroft, Fawcett, & Hay, 2008) and the Sightlines Initiative (Duckett & Drummond, 2009).

Works of art, pieces of music, stories, maps and inventions could all be shared as provocations to stimulate and further creative enquiry. Sharing examples of the creative arts with children also develops an aesthetic appreciation of different forms of representation, as well as a sense of their own culture and the cultures of others. The possibilities are endless, but should be carefully chosen to deepen interest and support children to make their own creative connections, rather than as exemplars to copy.

A simple but effective way to both extend and reflect on learning might be to revisit the children's own creations and experiences, for instance, rephrasing their hypotheses as questions, re-reading their stories aloud, or re-watching video clips of an experience or visit. Such revisitings deepen the learning experience and prompt children to consider new possibilities, supporting them to take a lead in extending or altering the direction of their inquiry. This can become a cyclical part of creative practice, and is an important role of project documentation.

Documenting projects creatively

> If we believe that children possess their own theories, interpretations, and questions ... then the most important verb in educational practice is no longer to talk, to explain, or to transmit, but to listen.
>
> (Carlina Rinaldi)

Practitioner as researcher

Reggio educators position both themselves and children as 'full time researchers', a concept explored in the 5×5×5 = *Creativity* project, *Researching Children Researching the*

World (Bancroft, Fawcett, & Hay, 2008). As a researcher of children's learning, a key task for the educator is to collect as many sources of information as possible to better understand children's thoughts, feelings and ideas. This involves what the educators in Reggio call a 'pedagogy of listening', where listening is an active rather than passive verb, giving value and attention to the many modes children use to create and express their thoughts and ideas.

Documentation is central to this process, as it is a way of making children's learning visible, incorporating a record of the educator's 'listening' which includes interpretation. In this way, documentation might consist of a combination of written notes, children's transcribed speech, photographs, videos, audio recordings and children's creations. It should be carried out at every stage of a project, informing each level of the continuous cycle of observing, interpreting and planning. Documentation is not only a report of how a project progressed, but also an intrinsic part of the inquiry itself.

For the educator, it is a way of planning and recording learning, and a professional development tool for reflecting on practice. For children, documentation can recognise and value their creativity in its many forms, and provide an opportunity to revisit and reflect on learning. For parents and carers, documentation gives an insight into what their children do on a daily basis, as well as an understanding of how they learn. For the wider educational community, documentation can prompt dialogue with other educators, provide lasting evidence of important learning experiences and become part of the history of the setting.

Documentation is not just an accumulation of ephemera related to learning, but its power and purpose is in how it is drawn together and carefully interpreted by the educator. These interpretations, carried out at every stage of the project, highlight creative processes in addition to creative outcomes. These will be both formative interpretations, such as how to focus and develop a project creatively, as well as summative interpretations, retrospectively identifying the learning that occurred during a project. Explicit links to the curriculum help develop a robust argument for teaching through creative practice.

Authoring experiences

Documenting the woodland project generated discussion amongst the educators involved about the purpose of observation, and how it is recorded. We reflected that for the purposes of Early Years assessment, there is often an emphasis on 'objective' descriptions of things children have said, done or created. We questioned how objective we can ever really be in what we choose to record and how we depict it, as the authors of children's experiences. This generated discussion of the place of interpretation in observation. Whilst it was agreed that educators should remain open-minded about what is happening when observing, we also discussed the in-depth knowledge educators develop about children and their learning, and how we might co-author these experiences with parents and the children themselves. We considered developing confidence and trust in our interpretations, which might provide a valuable insight into children's learning beyond simple description.

Sites of display

Given these powerful purposes of documentation, it is important to consider how we document and what forms it can take. Wall displays are a common site for sharing documentation and children's creations, enabling records of projects to become part of the learning environment. Whilst it is important to value children's creations and display them in attractive ways, the prime purpose of a wall display is not merely decoration. A display will carry important messages about how children's creativity is viewed within the setting. If it consists of thirty near-identical collages, for instance, each made using the same limited materials chosen by the adult, this carries an equally limited notion of creativity and creative potential, and the role of the child in relation to the group.

An alternative way to make use of wall space might be to use it to plan and document a project in-progress, as a 'working wall', incorporating transcribed speech, photographs, drawings, diagrams and practitioner reflections as a theme develops and deepens. Such a display is likely to consist of a variety of creative interpretations on a theme, for instance, drawings, collage, weaving, light exploration, sculpture work and children's quotes all exploring different aspects of a central theme such as 'pink'. The displayed documentation can show progression and deepening of ideas, brought together by practitioner commentary highlighting the learning that took place. On a large display board, it can be difficult to clearly show development and the passage of time. Arranging the space into panels or a timeline may be a way to depict the project's evolving journey.

The idea of a 'learning journey' or 'learning story' can be a helpful one when drawing documentation together, thinking of the project as beginning, deepening, and perhaps concluding or leading onto future projects. Project books can be a useful format for following this idea, which can then be handled by the children and easily shared with others. Projects documented on wall displays can later be converted into books, creating a lasting record of the inquiry and avoiding duplication of material whilst freeing up space for another display. In Reggio, wall panels of past projects remain on display permanently as records of learning, becoming part of the fabric and identity of the schools. Project books may be created and collected in this same way, building a library of projects, enabling children to see and discuss their learning and the various projects of children that attended the setting before them.

There will be some material which it is difficult to document in wall displays and project books. 3-D creations such as clay and wire sculptures may be best appreciated in their original form, rather than as 2-D photographs. Modes which are embodied, enacted or aural, such as running, dancing, role play and singing can pose particular challenges in documentation. Whilst these might be transcribed into different modes – for instance, role play depicted as a series of images and written speech – there may be qualities such as gesture and intonation which were important to the original creative expression. Video can be a particularly valuable resource for creating lasting records of these instances in all their multimodal richness, which can be re-watched time and time again. With support, the children themselves can become camera operators, editors and film-makers, making choices about how this material is re-presented. Digital technology such as interactive whiteboards and monitors can be used as sites to display material such as video, animation and slideshows, retaining much of the detail of the original experience, enhanced by educator's commentary.

The 'Pink Project' book

The 'Pink Project' was documented as a photo book, containing chronological images of the children exploring, investigating and discovering as well as depicting the things they created. This documentation of process, not just product, became a resource for practitioners, acting as visual evidence for skills such as fine-motor control and mark-making (see below). The prominent use of images enabled the children to access the documentation independently, to see the project unfolding over time, and acted as a prompt for reflection, discussion and future project planning. The project book also became a valuable resource for the setting as a means of creating a record of an important creative investigation, sharing practice with children's families, with colleagues and with other settings, and becoming part of the history of the Nursery.

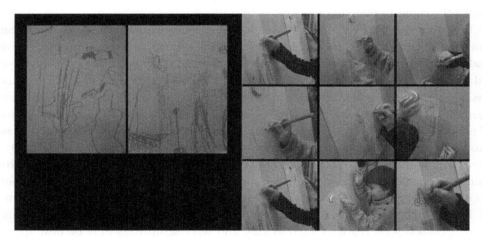

Figure 13.4 *A spread from the 'Pink Project' book*

A further affordance of digital technology is the shareable nature of material. Whilst this must be carefully considered in terms of safety and protection of the children, formats such as blogs can provide a way of widely sharing projects with others. This might be useful for involving parents or relatives who are unable to visit the setting, or fellow practitioners, locally and globally, who are interested in sharing and reflecting on practice. These can also be regularly updated with new posts, offering 'diary-like' documentation of a project, with the possibility for others to add their own comments online.

Although it is important not to have a predetermined end-point in mind, and to value creative processes as much as creative products, there may be occasions when a project culminates in a particular celebration, event or creation. This may be on a grand scale, like the collaborative artwork of the *Theater Curtain* project (Reggio Children, 2002), or may be a small-scale event inviting parents and families to share and reflect on a project. As the woodland project drew to a close, families were invited to watch a slideshow and extracts of film demonstrating the children's magic tricks, and an evening event was organised to share the stories the children had told in the woods. These stories and their comments and illustrations, accompanied by practitioner commentary, were made into a small book, a copy of which was given to every family as a memento of the project, and of their child's year in Nursery. The possibilities for what, and how, to document are rich and exciting, inviting the educator to employ their own creativity in considering how learning is recorded and shared.

Conclusions

Once children are helped to perceive themselves as authors and inventors, once they are helped to discover the pleasures of inquiry, their motivation and interest explode.

(Loris Malaguzzi)

The project approach outlined above and examples from Reggio Emilia show that all learning and thinking can be creative, and that creativity can be embedded, running throughout the whole curriculum. As Rinaldi notes, creativity is a process of generating new connections, and so ought to be at the heart of all learning processes: 'In schools, creativity should have the opportunity to be expressed in every place and in every moment. What we hope for is creative learning and creative teachers, not simply a 'creativity hour' (Rinaldi, 2006, p. 120).

This requires creative practice that values children as inquisitive, imaginative, self-regulating protagonists in their own learning. If we view children in this way, then it is the educator's responsibility to support, sustain and recognise children's learning through attentive listening, interpreting, offering and providing. This involves developing not just the children's creative courage, but also the educator's creative confidence to move beyond prescribed programmes, instead becoming a collaborator on projects led by children's own interests and fascinations.

Creativity and imagination are vital to development, in early childhood and throughout life. We do not know what kind of world today's children will come to inhabit, but we can support them in developing the essential skills needed to adapt, innovate, express and make meaning in an unpredictable future.

Key points for creativity in the Early Years:

- Creativity can, and should, be part of all areas of teaching and learning in the Early Years.
- Creativity can be considered a way of thinking, and we can view every child and adult as having valuable creative potential.
- Look and listen carefully to identify children's interests and fascinations, using these as the starting points for projects in which children can take the lead.
- Adults can adopt the role of co-learners, helping children create connections by taking their interests seriously, offering support and encouragement, clarifying or challenging ideas and providing complementary experiences.
- Ask children open-ended questions without predetermined answers to uncover the 'big ideas' they hold, and to model creative thinking processes.
- Use a planning system that makes space for flexibility, uncertainty, open-endedness and the children's own input.
- A creative environment acts an additional 'teacher'. Ensure it prompts interest and wonder, with ample time for play, exploration and discovery.
- Support children's creative confidence by recognising and valuing creativity in all its multimodal forms, such as movement, mark-making, music, construction and language.
- Equip the setting with a range of open-ended creative materials which are available to the children every day, and value creative processes as much as creative products.
- Consider creative ways of documenting experiences, for instance through displays, project books and digital media, to record, deepen, share and reflect on creative inquiries.

References

Bancroft, S., Fawcett, M., & Hay, P. (Eds.) (2008). *Researching Children Researching the World: 5×5×5 = Creativity.* Stoke-on-Trent: Trentham.

Burnard, P., Grainger, T., & Craft, A. (2006). Documenting possibility thinking: A journey of collaborative enquiry. *International Journal of Early Years Education, Special Issue on Creativity and Cultural Innovation in Early Childhood Education,* 14 (3), pp. 243–262.

Cadwell, L. B. (2003). *Bringing Learning to Life: The Reggio Approach to Early Childhood Education.* New York: Teachers College Press.

Craft, A. (2002). *Creativity in the Early Years: A Lifewide Foundation.* London: Continuum.

Drummond, M. J. (1996). Play, learning and the national curriculum: Some possibilities. In T. Cox (Ed.), *National Curriculum in the Early Years.* London: Falmer Press.

Duckett, R. & Drummond, M. J. (2009). *Adventuring in Early Childhood Education.* Newcastle upon Tyne: Sightlines Initiative.

Duffy, B. (1998). *Supporting Creativity and Imagination in the Early Years.* Buckingham and Philadelphia: Open University Press.

Edwards, C., Gandini, L., & Forman, G. (1998). *The Hundred Languages of Children – Advanced Reflections.* Greenwich, Connecticut: Ablex Publishing.

Flewitt, R. (2006). Using video to investigate preschool classroom interaction: Education research assumptions and methodological practices. *Visual Communication,* 5 (1), pp. 25–50.

Gandini, L., Hill, L., Cadwell, L., & Schwall, C. (2005). *In the Spirit of the Studio – Learning from the Atelier of Reggio Emilia.* New York: Teachers College Press.

Goldschmied, E. & Hughes, A. (1992). *Heuristic Play with Objects* [Video]. London: National Children's Bureau.

Harrington, D. M. (1990). The ecology of human creativity: A psychological perspective. In Runco, M. A. and Albert, R. S. (Eds.), *Theories of Creativity.* London: Sage.

Hughes, A. M. (2006). *Developing Play for the Under 3s – Treasure Basket and Heuristic Play.* London: David Fulton.

Kress, G. (1997). *Before Writing: Rethinking the Paths to Literacy.* London: Routledge.

Malaguzzi, L. (1996). The hundred languages of children. In T. Fillipini, & V. Vecchi (Eds.), *The Hundred Languages of Children: Narrative of the Possible.* Reggio Emilia, Italy: Reggio Children.

Pahl, K. (1999). *Transformations: Meaning Making in Nursery Education.* Stoke-on-Trent: Trentham Books.

Reggio Children (1995). *Catness.* Reggio Emilia, Italy: Reggio Children.

Reggio Children (1999). *Everything Has a Shadow Except Ants.* Reggio Emilia, Italy: Reggio Children.

Reggio Children (2002). *Theater Curtain.* Reggio Emilia, Italy: Reggio Children.

Rinaldi, C. (2006). *In Dialogue with Reggio Emilia – Listening, Researching and Learning.* Abingdon: Routledge.

Rich, D., Casanova, D., Dixon, A., Drummond, M.J., Durrant, A., & Myer, C. (2005). *First Hand Experience – What Matters to Children.* UK: Rich Learning Opportunities.

Robinson, K. (2006). *TEDTalks: Ken Robinson says schools kill creativity.* [Video] Retrieved August 19, from http://www.ted.com/talks/ken_robinson_says_schools_kill_creativity.html

Stein, P. (2008). *Multimodal Pedagogies in Diverse Classrooms: Representation, Rights and Resources.* London: Routledge.

CHAPTER 14

'How many toes has a newt?'

SCIENCE IN THE EARLY YEARS

Penny Coltman

Rich in first-hand explorations, science can be seen as one of the most dynamic areas of the Early Years curriculum. The intention of this chapter is to consider some of the factors which can support the development of secure scientific concepts and process skills in young children. The desirability of accessing and building upon existing ideas and understandings will be discussed, together with some practical implications of this approach. The aim of the chapter is to endorse the value of both real and imaginary contexts in promoting learning, as they encourage children to see both purpose in their activities and usefulness in their new-found knowledge and capabilities.

Entering an Early Years classroom to observe a science lesson, it was unexpected to find twenty or so children draped in various pieces of fabric and seated in a large circle. The initial reaction was to suppose that a mistake had been made; the class was not carrying out a science activity after all, but was engaged in a rehearsal for some sort of performance. A closer look, however, revealed that this was a lesson about observing and describing the properties of materials. The children were absorbed in a role play activity in which they had been carried away to a distant land by a magic carpet. In true Arabian Nights fashion they had been transported to the palace of a king who had been cursed. Unable to see or feel beautiful objects, the king was dependent upon the children to tell him about the wonderful things which they had brought for him. Only by helping the king to sort the materials they had brought into various enchanted circles (each labelled with different, descriptive vocabulary) could the children help to lift the dreadful curse.

This lesson, planned and led by a talented trainee teacher, was magical in more ways than one. It showed a rare appreciation that, although science may be viewed as a progression towards an understanding of perceived realities, the teaching of science in the Early Years can and indeed should adhere to those principles which are understood to promote any effective learning in young children, not least of which is a substantial use of imagination.

Working with children's ideas

If we accept a holistic model of learning in the Early Years, then the notion of science as an independent curriculum subject becomes somewhat spurious. As children learn in a wide-ranging, multi-disciplinary manner, they constantly explore the phenomena and workings of their world and make increasing sense of their findings. The interpretations which children make may be anomalous, based on literal constructions or idiosyncratic connections, but nevertheless such ideas are remarkably resistant to change, and children will hold onto them even when subsequent experiences provide conflicting evidence (Driver 1983).

This awareness of the potential variety of ideas which young children may bring with them to the classroom leads to a constructivist approach to the teaching of science, which involves a constant cycle of accessing and modifying children's ideas. Harlen (1999) describes constructivism as a model in which learning is seen as changing pupils' own ideas into those consistent with the scientific view. A key element of teaching any aspect of science through this approach is consequently the range of strategies used in eliciting responses from children which illuminate existing understandings.

Amy Arnold discusses some of the ways in which children's ideas can be accessed in Chapter 4, but it is worthwhile here to consider some additional strategies for gaining insights into children's thinking. Conversation is certainly a powerful tool, especially when children feel comfortable in the company of the interviewer. It can be even more enlightening to place children in role for the purposes of assessment. When in role, children respond with confidence. In role, anything is possible. In a realm of fantasy there are no right or wrong answers – anything goes. The children on the flying carpet at the beginning of this chapter were at that boundary beyond which imaginative worlds become at least a temporary 'reality', so intense was their captivation. Such scenarios allow and encourage children to venture ideas within a safe context: the bounds of possibilities are known to become elastic, as anything goes in a fantasy world.

Similarly, children can be placed in role as directors. Such devices are now commonplace in mathematics lessons in which children correct the counting errors made by a cuddly but inept puppet, thus demonstrating their own proficiencies. It is not hard to see how this strategy could be transferred to science as the same character, for example, plans his meals or plants his garden. In Chapter 7, Lesley Hendy describes a similarly effective lesson in which children give advice to Mrs Pig about the relative merits of the various materials her children have chosen to use to build their houses. The skilful presentation of this context gives an urgency to the response reminiscent of the 'It's behind you!' moments in a pantomime, guaranteed to motivate and enthuse young learners.

Collaborative storytelling can be used in much the same way. In a recent lesson the class teacher started to tell a class of six-year-old children a story about themselves.

They had gone on a school trip and become hopelessly lost, eventually finding themselves in some dark and mysterious caves. Each member of the class was woven into the story, delighting the audience as references were made to their own characteristics. The storytelling then became much more interactive, with children confidently adding details to their own adventures, and at this point the assessment purpose of the activity became clear. The teacher was exploring children's ideas about the variety of light sources. As the story progressed through the gloomy tunnels, each child in turn was encouraged to find new ways of providing light:

Teacher: As the children turned around the corner they could hardly see their way, but luckily Robert found a . . . ?
Robert: A torch!
Teacher: This made all the difference, but unfortunately the batteries in the torch were not strong, and the children had not gone far when the torch went out. Fortunately Elli found a . . . ?
Elli: A candle!

Language and science

One of the difficulties in making assessments about children's understandings is that conceptual development and language development may not be in step. Science is a discipline which is heavily dependent on precise definitions; indeed one of the indicators of progression in science is the use of increasingly sophisticated and refined vocabulary. In the Early Years, children's attempts to describe or explain a phenomena may well be open to misinterpretation as they search in vain for the most appropriate language to use. An example of this is often encountered when young children, playing outside on a sunny day, use the word 'reflection' to describe the shape they see on the ground. It may indeed be the case that there is some confusion of concepts, and that children have the idea that the ground is somehow behaving as a mirror. Alternatively, it may be that in the search for a word to describe the observation, children have used one which they have found useful before in describing 'an image of themselves'. In other words, use of inappropriate language cannot always be assumed to indicate a genuine misconception, but may be more indicative of the problem many will have faced when trying to order a drink in a foreign language. We use the best word available in our limited vocabulary – and it may not prove to be quite as accurate as we would like! Such difficulties are evidence not of *mis*conceptions, but rather of concepts which are still unrefined. Further experience of both mirrors and shadows will be needed before the two words are understood to relate to distinct and unrelated phenomena.

Further illustrations of children's ideas can be found in the reports published by the SPACE (Science Processes and Concept Exploration) project, which was a joint project between the Centre for Educational Studies, King's College, London, and the Centre for Research in Primary Science and Technology, Liverpool University (SPACE 1990–94). Many examples are cited, and often the source of misconception or confusion is explored. Young children, for example, frequently expressed the idea that an object is seen because of something coming from the eyes. Osborne (1995) describes how this idea is extended by children to imagine that the eyes direct some ray towards objects to make them visible and goes on to cite examples of everyday speech which implicitly reinforce this notion: we 'look at' books, 'cast our gaze', 'have looks thrown at us' or even 'look right through people'. We might also speculate on the effect of cartoons such as those in which superheroes send laser beams from their eyes in order to see in the dark or zap the enemy.

Another example is commonly found as young children describe materials and appear to demonstrate misconceptions over the use of the words 'soft' and 'smooth'. If we try to clarify the meaning of the word 'smooth' the difficulty becomes apparent. This is a problem of definition. An explanation, for example, of the word 'smooth' is almost certain to focus on negatives. A smooth surface does not have bumps, it is not rough and it is not creased or crumpled. This is a confusion which only experience will resolve. As children handle hard pebbles which are smooth or soft knitted fabrics which are soft but textured, the distinction between the two terms becomes less ambiguous. So, as questioning reveals a greater insight into children's understandings, the importance of language development in Early Years science becomes ever more apparent.

Rosemary Feasey (2000) lists three major challenges of language development in the Early Years which are relevant to science:

Figure 14.1 *May explores materials as she makes a batch of dough*

- 'to introduce language that is directly related to immediate, concrete, everyday, hands-on experiences;
- to move children on, so that they are able to use the same scientific language in a wider range of contexts that are removed by time and space; and
- to develop scientific language that is conceptually based, that is, linked to ideas which may be difficult to understand, for example the movement of particles in dissolving and changes of state.'

If children are to move from concrete to abstract in their thinking, or from generic to specific language, they must be given the opportunity to manipulate and experience objects, materials and phenomena and to talk about them. The basic words of naming and describing become the tools of the future. The everyday contexts of making a collage of shiny, curly or transparent materials, or of using paints of different textures and thicknesses, provide rich contexts for the development of this vital language. As adults talk about activities, explaining or questioning, the use of new language is modelled in an appropriate and secure context. As vocabulary is introduced it is helpful to draw attention to it, encouraging children to repeat and enjoy the new words. Using new language in questions then helps to consolidate and ensure understanding: *Can you think of something which is shiny to use for the robot's buttons? What sort of material do you think we should use for the baby fairy's bed?*

Developing skills

Science is a subject with two complementary aspects. The exploration of areas of knowledge encountered – materials, natural sciences or physical processes – provides the contexts for the development of skills, such as observation, questioning, communication and using measurement, which in turn will facilitate the acquisition of knowledge. Later in the primary phase the skills of science will be combined to form investigations, but in the Early Years they will largely be developed independently. An analogy can be made with the way in which children learn to play a team game such as football. Skills such as kicking and aiming a ball, passing and receiving, must be practised before a team game can be played. Eventually these will all be drawn together, but only with a great deal of adult direction. It will be some time before children are ready to organise themselves into coherent teams. In the same way, the skills related to scientific exploration, which will eventually be woven together, need to be separately honed. Later they will be brought together as children carry out their first investigations, but the structure of these will be heavily teacher-directed. Careful teacher guidance, gradually involving greater degrees of pupil initiative, will allow the investigation process to become internalised, until, by the end the primary phase, or thereabouts, children are ready to plan and carry out fair tests, with independence and confidence.

The first stage in the field of measurement, for example, is language which categorises by size: big, little, thick or thin. Progression is seen as children begin to use comparative vocabulary; smaller, taller, etc. By the end of their reception year, most children have begun to use arbitrary units, introducing a quantitative aspect to their measuring skills. The length of a table can be measured in toy cars and the weight of a teddy can be determined by counting the conkers which will balance it. Stories such as that of the king whose new bed is measured by the strides of carpenters of vastly differing sizes are used to help children to understand the limitations of such methods, and the conkers and shells will soon be replaced by uniform units, such as plastic cubes, counters or dominoes. This is then the precursor to the introduction of standard units. Over the remaining primary years children will then become adept in measuring, using increasingly sophisticated resources to ever finer degrees of accuracy.

Daisy (see Figure 14.2) is four years old. She is able to count small numbers fairly accurately and knows something about measure. The newt, pictured with her, was perhaps unfortunate enough to be discovered during an outside play session. Daisy gently held the animal on her hands, carefully examining it from every perspective and expressing great delight as she noticed its tiny feet. 'I can see its toes', she said. 'I am going to count them.' Then she spotted a cardboard teaching clock on the ground nearby and carefully placed the newt in the middle of it. 'Look,' she announced emphatically, 'The newt weighs ten!'

Figure 14.2 *Daisy investigates a newt*

The role of questioning

The brief interaction described demonstrates that Daisy is confident in making observations. She is able to look closely and to talk about what she sees. In addition she is confidently exploring the idea of quantifying her observations. She is also able to apply the knowledge she has already gained of animals to inform her exploration of the newt, looking for legs, toes, eyes, and, less successfully, ears. As Daisy makes such connections between new and previous experiences she will gradually develop and refine her understandings and will begin to be able to make reasoned assumptions.

Early years curriculum guidance tends to place great emphasis on the importance of encouraging children to ask questions. The thinking behind this is presumably to foster the sense of enquiry which will lead to cognitive and conceptual developments as illustrated by Daisy. However, children need no encouragement to be curious; they spend their lives in exploration and experimentation. Observation in an Early Years setting, however, generally provides fewer instances of children asking questions than might be anticipated. Part of the reason for this may be that the concepts which children are encountering and developing, are, by reason of their newness, rarely within their confident linguistic grasp, as previously discussed. To formulate a question also requires a degree of familiarity with possibilities gained by experiences which are as yet beyond young learners. So the role of questioner in the Early Years classroom could be described as one predominantly to be adopted by the educator rather than the children.

We now have to accept that children's explorations alone are not going to result in the acquisition of secure and accurate concepts. We can take a child to water, but that will not make him learn!

> Sand and water play is often promoted and justified as supporting children's learning in science, but we can easily overestimate what young children learn through these activities. In fact our expectations are often contradictory. While we fail to recognise the quality or significance of the child's observational skills in their day-to-day interaction with the world, we nevertheless expect them to discover phenomena whenever we make the relevant resources available to them.
>
> (Siraj-Blatchford & MacLeod-Brudenell 1999, p. 33)

Learning in relation to specific objectives will only occur when the adults supporting an activity are clear about the learning intentions of that activity, and promote relevant conversations, rich in carefully framed questions. This questioning can support learning in a number of respects:

- It presents a linguistic role model, showing children how to frame appropriate questions: '*I wonder what would happen if* . . . .' '*How could we* . . . ?'
- It can present a model of autonomous learning which is characteristic of science. If we want to find something out, then we can do something about it. Children are shown how to be pro-active learners: '*What do you think the snails would feel like?*'

- It directs children's attention to those activities and aspects of activities which will lead to teaching opportunities: *'Where do you think the water has gone?'*
- It can reinforce new vocabulary: *'What else do you think the magnet might be attracted to?'*
- It can promote thinking and problem solving skills: *'How could you change the bubble mix?'*
- It can help children to make connections between new and existing experiences:
- *'What do you think has happened to the chocolate? Think about the ice cubes we used yesterday.'*

Questioning is also one way of introducing ideas which gently challenge children's existing cognition, leading children towards new understandings. This is sometimes described as creating 'dissonance', and it is particularly effective when the new thinking opens up, in a manner which is clear to the learner, new possibilities and/or explanations (Harlen 1999).

Here is an example to illustrate this. Daniel was attempting to balance a short, flat piece of wood on top of three cones. He carefully lined up the three cones in a row and placed the piece of wood on the top of them. When the wood immediately fell down, he checked that the linear arrangement of the cones was as straight as could be, and then tried the balance again.

Figure 14.3 *Inviting curiosity: Why does the picture disappear when I stand here?*

Daniel's teacher then replaced the piece of wood with a cube and asked Daniel whether he could use the cube and cones to build a model rocket. Both the chosen context and the constraints of the blocks available now strongly suggested that the cones should be arranged in a group under the cube rather than in a line. As Daniel arrived at this conclusion, and successfully balanced the cube on the cones, he discovered the concept of a tripod. His previous understanding, that linear arrangements are generally more likely to be successful, was challenged and found wanting. Armed with his new discovery, he returned to the original piece of wood, arranged the cones in a tight group and successfully managed the balance. As Daniel showed an awareness of his learning and its potential usefulness, a further element of meta-cognition was seen: he was later observed taking great delight in applying the idea of tripods made from cones or pyramids to the constructions he created during free play. New possibilities had been created not only for methods of achieving balance, but for the cones and pyramids themselves which had previously been used exclusively to decorate or punctuate the tops of towers. (For more details, see Coltman, Anghileri, & Petyaeva 2002.)

The importance of purposeful science

Writing about ways of helping children become confident mathematicians, Whitebread (2000) cites the observation that mathematics is often bereft of any real, meaningful or supporting context as a prime feature contributing to difficulties experienced by young children. Children complain that mathematics 'isn't about anything'. Sadly, in many instances the same criticism could be levelled at the teaching of science. Too often, children are taught procedures or pieces of knowledge, but are not presented with opportunities to use them in any meaningful way. They consequently have little or no appreciation of the value of their learning or the possibilities for its use. There is no notion of the model of teaching and learning suggested by a popular brand of electrical goods: 'The appliance of science.'

Failure to provide opportunities for children to use their learning prevents them from demonstrating anything other than superficial understanding. The development of secure concepts is manifest when children are able to show metacognition, transferring learning to new situations, as Daniel used the tripod. Annie, aged six, demonstrated this beautifully when she announced after a lesson on simple circuit building: 'I know what I could do – I could put landing lights on that plane I built.' (see Figure 14.4).

Creative tasks can also support learning by providing a focus for relevant conversation. As children weave with fabric samples they will discuss texture, colour, thickness, flexibility and appearance. The selection of materials for a woven seascape or tapestry of autumn colours invites discernment and gives real purpose to discrimination. As they make salt dough models of faces, children will use the vocabulary of features and expressions and will describe the feel of the dough as

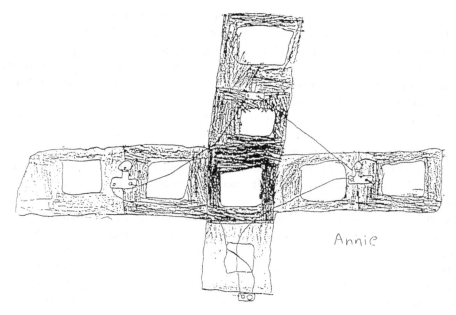

Figure 14.4 *Annie's drawing shows how she used her knowledge of circuits to add landing lights to a plane made from a construction kit*

they manipulate it in their hands and the forces used as it is stretched, flattened and squeezed. Motivation and engagement and consequent meaningful learning are again promoted by the goal of the finished artefact.

The manufacture of artefacts is an underrated route to assessment. As children make things they demonstrate their knowledge not only by the conversation elicited by the task, but also by their representations. A child constructing an imaginary animal, for example, will happily discuss the location in which it might be found, the appearance of its legs, head and wings and whether or not it can run, swim or fly. Less obvious ideas are explored: Can this animal talk or sing? What other animals might it like to live with? Would you want one in your garden? In this way children are not only demonstrating an appropriate use of subject-related vocabulary as they name and describe features, but are also communicating a broader understanding of interrelationships, structure and function.

Using the outdoor environment

One particularly encouraging aspect of Early Years curricula is the developing emphasis on the use of the outdoor environment. By exploring the natural world around them children encounter a wealth of constantly changing phenomena illustrating an infinitely diverse range of concepts. Science is firmly placed within a real, relevant and vibrant context which is familiar and yet constantly changing and endlessly fascinating. It is through such explorations that the attitudes of responsibility and respect towards both the living and non-living environments can be engendered, as children learn to look closely, to 'not disturb' and to handle with care.

Simple trails can be set up which encourage children to develop awareness of a range of environmental features, and the use of different senses and methods in making observations. Sensory trails have stations which encourage children to explore experiences: 'Shuffle the leaves with your feet. What can you hear?' 'Rub a leaf between your fingers. Enjoy the lovely smell.' Other trails invite the use of apparatus: 'Use a mirror to look around the corner. Can you see the spider's web?' 'Look at the moss through a magnifier.' The joys of such discoveries are compounded by opportunities to share findings with others, and it is not hard to imagine how such ideas can be built into opportunities for children to plan and make trails for others to enjoy.

As schools develop ideas of the 'outdoor classroom', many are including permanent and semi-permanent features to encourage children to enjoy and care for school grounds. Many schools now have gazebos and outdoor working tables to facilitate outdoor learning, and mazes, tunnels and huts made from living willow wands are sprouting in profusion. Wildlife areas vary from formally designated sites, with fences, pond, and seats to a log in an unmown patch of grass with a tree swathed in knitting wool: 'What can you add to the weaving tree?'

But, desirable as these may be, environmental education is not dependent on anything so structured, and as always it is often the simplest of ideas which are the most effective. The construction of a 'playground for a mouse' or a 'rain shelter for a fairy' are examples of the types of activities which foster imagination and creativity and remain in memories for a very long time. Intense concentration is evident as children select natural materials for their tasks, supplementing them by sequins, twisted aluminium foil goblets or a smooth, round pebble placed as a throne, and rich and relevant conversation flows. These are 'materials chosen for their uses' in the real sense, with a purposeful context leading to autonomous and self-directed learning as children meet their own self imposed challenges.

The following passage is taken from the book *The Hundred Languages of Children*, which accompanies a remarkable touring exhibition presenting a series of projects carried out by children in Municipal Infant/Toddler Centres and Pre-schools in Reggio Emilia, Italy. It epitomises a pedagogical approach which is based on an enquiring and aesthetic appreciation of the natural world, and the importance of listening to children. Both uncertainty and amazement are valued as integral to any learning and especially to learning in science. The smallest of everyday contexts is seen as rich in opportunities for scientific enquiry and deduction. The excerpt describes what happens when a group of children explore a puddle:

> The children's excitement . . . becomes astonished and vociferous when they notice the play of light, of colours, of transparencies in the puddle and the reflection of their images and that immediate part of the world around them which the puddle mirrors back at them. From that moment on the game opens up and

expands, changes level, and draws in all the children's intelligence. And this intelligence stimulates children's observations, thoughts, and intuitions, and leads the children closer and closer to convincing laws of physics and perception, even when – and perhaps above all – they use their intelligence playfully to contemplate situations and even worlds that are turned upside down, with everything this implies.

(Malaguzzi 1996)

Key points for Early Years science

- Science is a creative area of learning which can be taught through rich imaginative contexts.
- Educators must take into account the diversity of children's previous experiences and the consequent variation in their understandings
- Language development is a crucial consideration in effective science teaching
- Each of the process skills related to scientific investigation has its own strands of progression and should be separately addressed
- The educator has a vital role in promoting scientific enquiry through questioning
- Children should have opportunities to use newly acquired skills and knowledge in practical and purposeful contexts.

References

Coltman, P., Anghileri, J., & Petyaeva, D. (2002) Scaffolding learning through meaningful tasks and adult interaction. *Early Years* 22(1): 39–49.

Driver, R. (1983) *The Pupil as Scientist?* Milton Keynes: Open University Press.

Feasey, R. (2000) *Primary Science and Literacy*. Hatfield: The Association for Science Education.

Glauert, E., Heal, C., & Cook, J. (2008) Knowledge and understanding of the world. In Riley, J. (Ed.), *Learning in the Early Years*, 2nd edn. London: Paul Chapman Publishing.

Harlen, W. (1999) *Effective Teaching of Science: A Review of Research*. Edinburgh: SCRE Publications.

Johnston, J. (2005) *Early Explorations in Science*. Maidenhead: Open University Press.

Malaguzzi, L. (1996) Puddle intelligence. In Filippini, T. & Vecchi V. (Eds), *The Hundred Languages of Children*. Italy: Reggio Children.

Osborne J. (1995) Science from a child's perspective. In Atkinson, S. & Fleer, M. (Eds.), *Science with Reason*. London: Hodder and Stoughton.

Siraj-Baltchford, J. & MacLeod-Brudenell, I. (1999) *Supporting Science, Design and Technology in the Early Years*. Buckingham: Open University Press.

SPACE Project (1990–1994). A Science Processes and Concept Exploration project between King's College London and the University of Liverpool. Various publications. Liverpool: Liverpool University Press.

Whitebread, D. (2000) Teaching numeracy: helping children become confident mathematicians. In Whitebread D. (Ed.), *The Psychology of Teaching and Learning in the Primary School*. London: Routledge/Falmer.

CHAPTER 15

'How many shapey ones have you got?'

NUMBER AND SHAPE IN THE EARLY YEARS

Sue Gifford and Penny Coltman

NUMBER

Playing with early number: the big ideas

A nursery child asked her teacher, 'How do you write three-and-a-half?' Her attempt was to draw three crosses: + + +. Perhaps she thought the crosses looked like halves, and so did three of them.

Two boys in a reception class were supposed to be drawing their favourite story-tale character. Instead they drew two columns, wrote 'Esdmat' above one and 'TOT' above the other. In the 'Esdmat' column they wrote '1003', '76776', '303030' and '21268710'. Under TOT they wrote 7, then 8. The previous day they had filled in a sheet requiring them to estimate then count numbers of pencils and crayons. These boys had obviously enjoyed the activity and had chosen to do it again, but this time with ridiculously huge estimates. 1003 was their attempt at writing one hundred and three, by combining 100 and 3.

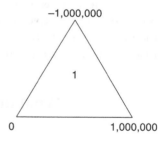

A seven-year-old was asked to put a total number in the middle of a triangle, then put numbers at the corners to add to it. He chose one as his total and then said he would have 'minus a million' and 'a million and one going upwards' at the corners. Zero was his third number.

All these children were using creative logic to investigate the number system, using reasoning to push boundaries, and enjoying fractions, large numbers, and the paradox of using big numbers to make a tiny one. The third child was used to playing with numbers on a calculator. For many adults, especially those for whom the mention of mathematics creates anxiety mounting to panic, it is hard to see numbers as things to play with, as these children do.

Young children can be creative and investigative mathematicians – but how do they get to be this way? What are the key ideas which develop number sense and how do children learn them?

In countries where children start school later than in the UK, they achieve more highly, pointing to the importance of informal early learning and of deferring written arithmetic (Aubrey et al. 2000). Children know a lot about number before they come to school: young children can tell whether there are more or fewer objects, usually know some number words, and can recognise small numbers of objects without counting. They know that numbers give status in terms of age. They learn that number symbols are significant, on doors, cars, football shirts or party invitations. They also find that counting earns praise and large numbers are exciting. However, understanding the meaning of numbers and the structure of the number system is a complex and gradual process: researchers have pointed out that children need a lot of repeated experience over time (Fuson 1988; Munn 1997).

Children learn a lot at home: however, this will vary according to family circumstances. One child may experience a lot of talk about time and learn to recognise number symbols from clocks and calendars. Another may learn their door, car and phone number, and possibly their height and weight too. Older siblings may sit around doing homework with impressive 'sums'. For some three-year-olds, learning to count, whether stairs or spoons, will be part of daily life: grandmother may sing number rhymes or an older brother teach them to write numbers. Some will pick up number skills incidentally. New Zealand researchers concluded that children were number 'experts' or 'novices' dependent on the amount of number experience they had at home. Research has also shown that the strongest predictor of mathematical achievement is parents' socio-economic status (SES), suggesting that children from poorer homes are also likely to be disadvantaged mathematically (Gersten, Jordan, & Plojo 2005). Children who start behind tend to stay behind: however, an effective home learning environment is not always determined by income, and a number focus in pre-school settings can make a difference, as UK research has shown (Sammons et al. 2002).

What do we know about how children learn about numbers?

Recently, neuroscientific research has suggested the importance of different kinds of memory for learning. In learning to count, children use verbal memory for the word sequence, kinaesthetic and spatial memory for keeping track of which ones they counted, and working memory to ensure each is only counted once and to remember the final number. Children's working memory expands considerably after the age of about six, so learning to count is challenging, especially for young children who are also developing co-ordination skills. Spatial memory is usually stronger than verbal memory for younger children, which explains why some respond to 'how many' questions by holding up the right number of fingers, while saying the wrong word.

Subitising

Young children often learn to recognise numbers up to five on dot dice, without counting. Using visual patterns like this is called subitising. For numbers over five, the symmetrical doubles seem more memorable, perhaps because we are symmetrical beings.

In many cultures, children will be taught to recognise numbers of fingers, and, since ten is the basis of our number system, this is very useful.

Part-whole relationships

'When I see six, I see three and three'. Children who make remarks like this can see numbers as made up of other numbers, showing an awareness of part–whole relationships. Some children learn that seven can be made up of five fingers on one hand and two on the other (and also four fingers and three fingers). These visual and kinaesthetic finger images help children learn addition facts, making use of spatial memory rather than taxing verbal memory.

Linking images with symbols

Children need to learn that number words and numerals can represent a range of number images, collections of objects, sounds and actions. Munn (1997) concluded that learning numerals, for instance when labelling a box of things, helped young children to understand number concepts, even before they understood counting.

One-more-than relationships

Four-year-olds, when asked if they would rather have five or four sweets, often cannot pick the larger number. It seems that comparing numbers which are close together is difficult, even when children have learned to count. Researchers found that middle-class children starting kindergarten in the USA could do this, but most from poorer families could not: 96 per cent compared with 18 per cent (Gersten, Jordan, & Plojo 2005). This underlines the importance of home experience and also of working with parents.

When young children learn to count, they do not realise that counting numbers are connected by size in a _one-more-than_ relationship. The staircase image of the number system represents this: children enjoy constructing staircases from numbered sticks of cubes. Muddling them up and re-ordering helps children to realise that five is one more than four.

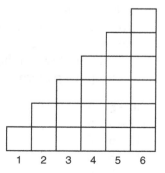

Gersten, Jordan and Plojo (2005) suggest that failing to connect counting and relative size may inhibit children's number sense and that 'creating such linkages early may be critical for the development of proficiency in mathematics'.

Using counting as a thinking tool

Whether a five-year-old could count out five pencils from a potful predicted how good they would be at mathematics when they were nine, according to New Zealand researchers (Young-Loveridge 1991). In order to understand the purpose of counting, children have to realise that the final number word gives the number in the collection.

Young children need to *use counting as a thinking tool* to solve problems, according to Nunes and Bryant (1996). Children who count to get the number of plates for the table, or to check they have the right number of counters in a collecting game, understand the purpose of counting. The most challenging problems are those which require children to count to compare, for instance to see if sweets have been shared fairly. This requires children to reason about the results of their counting.

Beginning to calculate mentally

Connecting counting with number size leads to being able to add and subtract. It helps to know that one more will give the next counting number and taking away one gives the preceding number. Early subtraction experiences are provided by number rhymes like 'Five Little Ducks', which encourage children to predict. The importance of episodic memory, for significant personal experiences, also suggests the power of drama and stories for helping children to learn mathematics.

Some older children and even adults rely on their fingers to calculate. They may add eight and two on their fingers by counting on from eight: 'Nine, ten'. Children who know that eight and two are ten may see that eight and three will be one more. If children see numbers as made up of other numbers, and are used to playing around with relationships between numbers, they are more likely to reason like this. Deriving unknown facts by reasoning from known facts is behaviour typical of higher achievers.

This was the method used by Daniel, who was working out the number of hidden bears: his teacher had started off with ten bears, of which five were visible. He said five were hidden, so she got eleven bears, with five visible, which he readily said was six, so then she got twelve, then thirteen. When they came to fourteen bears, he said, 'Last time it was eight, so this time it has to be nine!' This practical game helped Daniel to spot a pattern.

$$10 - 5 = 5$$
$$11 - 5 = 6$$
$$12 - 5 = 7$$
$$13 - 5 = 8$$
$$14 - 5 = 9$$

Implicit in this pattern is a rule: if you increase the starting number by one, but take the same number away, then the result will increase by one. Some children will spot such short-cuts, especially if they are led to them by a 'chain' like this. Teachers can help by focusing children's attention on the recorded pattern and asking 'What do you notice?' Children can go on to spot other patterns from $10 - 5 = 5$:

$10 - 5 = 5$	$5 + 5 = 10$	$10 - 5 = 5$
$10 - 6 = 4$	$6 + 4 = 10$	$11 - 6 = 5$
$10 - 7 = 3$	$7 + 3 = 10$	$12 - 7 = 5$
$10 - 8 = 2$	$8 + 2 = 10$	$13 - 7 = 5$
$10 - 9 = 1$	$9 + 1 = 10$	$20 - 15 = 5$

Asking 'If you know this, what else do you know?' is a good way of generating and spotting such patterns and helping children to become flexible with numbers.

Groups as units

Number sense includes the ability to see numbers of objects as units. Some young children can count pairs of socks, while others insist on counting single socks. Being able to talk about three pairs leads on to answering 'How many twos in six?' and understanding multiplication and division. Children from Asian cultures who are taught to count in threes by using the segments of their fingers may have a head start in multiplying and dividing by three. Being able to count groups of ten, as with fingers (and toes), is vital for an understanding of place value.

Place value

The boys at the beginning were not yet aware of the significance of place value. For this, children need to understand that the value of individual digits in a number is determined by its position relative to the others, so that in 13 the 1 is worth ten, whereas in 31 it is only worth one. In writing 1003, the boys did not realise that they were placing 1 in an invisible 'thousands' column, by writing three digits to its right. To begin to understand tens and units, children need experience of representing objects grouped in tens, such as fingers or sticks of cubes. Scenarios which involve objects packed in tens, like boxes of pens, are useful to help children think in numbers of tens. Fosnot and Dolk (2001) describe a teacher's story about a seed merchant sending out orders of expensive seeds, ten to an envelope. The children 'helped' by representing orders for different numbers: they did this in their own ways, moving gradually from drawing seeds and envelopes to representing by written numbers. They then progressed to 'packing' hundreds of seeds by grouping ten envelopes to a box. The story context helped to develop place value understanding because it generated repeated activity and provided an opportunity to develop recording which was meaningful to the children. The extremely gradual development of abstract understanding is revealed when children record activities in their own way, because they only adopt symbols when they understand them. Some contexts like this offer simple, structured images, whereas others (for instance stories involving groups of children) will lead to distractingly detailed pictures.

Later, children can spot and describe patterns with two digit numbers, discovering, for instance, that adding ten to a number alters the tens digit, but leaves the units digit the same:

$$5 + 10 = 15$$
$$15 + 10 = 25$$
$$25 + 10 = 35$$
$$35 + 10 = 45$$

They enjoy generating their own patterns involving place value:

$50 + 50 = 100$	$500 + 500 = 1,000$
$60 + 40 = 100$	$600 + 400 = 1,000$
$70 + 30 = 100$	$700 + 300 = 1,000$
$80 + 20 = 100$	$800 + 200 = 1,000$
$90 + 10 = 100$	$900 + 100 = 1,000$

Children can explore larger numbers with calculators: for instance, if challenged to find different ways of making 5, they will produce patterns like the following:

$$10 - 5 = 5$$
$$110 - 105 = 5$$
$$210 - 205 = 5$$
$$310 - 305 = 5$$
$$1,010 - 1,005 = 5$$

Conclusion

Young children are ready to spot patterns and to recognise the significance of numbers in their everyday lives. Some need more help from number experts; all of them need time and encouragement to make the connections which will help them develop a feeling for number. If adults can also feel that numbers are interesting to play with, this will help children develop the positive dispositions which are vital to mathematical learners.

Key pointers for number in the Early Years

- Young children learn about numbers in a variety of ways from their everyday lives, (including playing games outdoors).

- They need to link counting skills to the meaning of numbers.
- Young children are excited by large numbers and are keen to spot patterns.
- Adults can help children to play with numbers.

SHAPE

Getting into shape

In recent years the strong focus on developing number skills in the Early Years has tended to place initiatives and innovation related to early studies of shape rather on the educational back burner. Anecdotally, practitioners tend to perceive shape as relatively straightforward, with well established approaches to teaching. Indeed, a browse through an Early Years resource catalogue offers little evidence of new thinking as materials to support the teaching of shape remain familiar and traditional. This part of the chapter aims to show how a fresh look at shape might offer new insights into children's developing understandings, and suggest some new approaches to supporting this development.

Looking at 2D shapes

Before further discussion about pedagogy, there is one issue linked to early experience of shape that must be addressed. When giving children experience of two dimensional shape, most practitioners are unwittingly guilty of underpinning a key misconception. We cheat. A two-dimensional 'flat' shape, by its nature, only exists as an image – a drawing or a picture that cannot be picked up. Any object that can be handled must be three dimensional. Yet in most settings one of the most widely used resources for exploring the way in which 2D shapes 'behave' is a box of mosaic blocks. This would not be a problem if children were encouraged to look for a shape with a 'square face', but it is much more likely that as verbal shorthand creeps in both adults and children discuss the fact that the 'triangles' will fit together. It is similarly not unusual for even published texts to recommend that 'feely bag' activities can be used to encourage children to identify triangles, squares and circles. Again, this is a nonsense that merely serves to supports confusion.

The key property of any 2D shape is its border. In recognising a shape as a triangle, the attributes that identify it are its three straight sides and three pointed corners, and it would be an expectation that in describing a triangle children would draw attention to these features. So it is only sensible in the Early Years to ensure that children gain plenty of experience designed to establish and consolidate understanding of this vocabulary. What do we mean by a 'straight' side? Does this have any relation to other uses of the word: 'Do it straight away', 'That picture is not straight', or 'My hair is straight'. In other words, the ability to describe 2D shapes must begin with an ability to talk about *lines* – wiggly lines, wavy lines, zig-zag lines, lines that go around and around, lines that curve, lines that turn corners, lines that squiggle and wriggle and, yes, lines that are straight. Explorations with paint, rope, ribbons on sticks and fingers in sand, wet clay or foam will all help to familiarise children with these basic building blocks of language.

The use of interactive software can make a real contribution to activities relating to flat shapes. This is a context in which children really can manipulate 2D images as they rotate, flip and drag them around the screen, finding dissimilar shapes that fit together in tilling patterns, or working with multiple copies of the same shape to explore tessellation. Here there is no 'cheating': the shapes remain exactly what they are – two dimensional images that cannot be picked up.

One of the prime mysteries in relation to shape in the Early Years must be the almost exclusive emphasis on regular geometric shapes (which applies to both flat and solid shapes). Important as the ability to describe a triangle may be, is it really so much more important than the ability to describe the shape of a butterfly's shadow or the edge of a leaf? Developing a broad experience of shape and line through rich, practical and playful activities using real examples enables children to later work with a wealth of diverse and exotic shapes, confidently drawing on a bank of vocabulary to describe their observations.

Learning about the faces of 3D shapes

The need to manipulate 3D shapes is absolutely fundamental. Without extensive concrete experience of handling, turning and examining objects children cannot develop the ability to imagine shapes as they begin to work in more abstract contexts. When any geometric object is placed on a table, for example, a child who has had inadequate first-hand experience cannot possibly be certain of the shape of any faces that are hidden from view (Clements & Battista 1992). The implication for practice is that it is essential to give children time to explore the properties of different shapes as they make their own constructions using wooden building blocks, or recycled 'box modelling' materials. These activities may involve children setting their own agendas and goals or may centre on a problem posed by an adult. Observations of children absorbed in such tasks will reveal them to be engaged in both discovering and exploring properties of shapes and using the language of shape for their own real purposes as they discuss progress and share ideas (Coltman 2006). The quotation from a child used as the title for this chapter – 'How many shapey bits have you got?' – comes from a transcript of children's conversations as they collaboratively used wooden blocks to create a large house for a toy dog, Paws (see Figure 15.1). One group of children collected shallow cuboids to tile a 'carpet', whilst others used prisms, cylinders, arches and cones to decorate the exterior. In both instances the group used their own words to describe the kinds of blocks that they were collecting. Shallow cuboids were referred to as 'flats' and the blocks being used for decorative purposes were referred to as 'shapey' ones. This coding system in which children

Figure 15.1 *Reception class children work together as they build a house for a large toy dog, Paws*

use self generated language can only be effective when there is a shared understanding of meaning (Lampert & Blunk 1998). In this instance the words also indicated awareness of some key attributes of the blocks being described. The shallow cuboids were indeed 'flat', and the term 'shapey' could be interpreted as meaning essentially 'non-rectilinear'.

Julia Anghileri and Sarah Baron (1999) recognised that the development of secure understandings of 3D shapes is a complex process and pursued this idea using traditional wooden blocks. Working in classrooms, they explored some of the most common tasks that young children are asked to complete. They found, for example, that children frequently experienced difficulties in correctly orientating a 3D shape so that it stood on a simple outline of one of its faces, or in reaching into a feely bag to find a given shape such as a cylinder. Building on this work, Coltman, Petyaeva and Anghileri (2002) studied individual children as they approached such tasks, identifying the particular difficulties they encountered. Findings were used to inform the design of problem-solving activities which would effectively support teaching and learning about shape in the Early Years.

Figure 15.2 shows a nursery exploration of the properties of 3D shapes using a light box. The stack made on the side of the light box shows a range of understandings. The bottom two layers of the stack show equivalence as two smaller shapes are aligned to match one longer one. Notice how carefully the edges are aligned. Above that, a tricky shape with sloping sides is re-orientated to lay flat, making it much easier to stack other blocks above it. The shape with the curved surface has presented additional problems, illustrated by the position of the child's hands and the intense

Figure 15.2 *Exploring the properties of 3D shapes by stacking*

expression of concentration and pleasure in achievement. Finally, notice how the transparent coloured fillers of the shapes highlight the silhouette of the block when it is placed in the light box.

In one investigation, observations were carried out of children undertaking the face recognition activity described by Anghileri and Baron (1999). Children were given a card of simple geometric outlines, and asked to look at each in turn and to find a block with a face that exactly matched it. The activity was essentially a work-card version of the classic 'shape sorter' toy in which children post blocks through shaped holes. Incorrect responses included the matching of shape but not size, or a failure to orientate a correctly chosen block in such a way as to match the face to the outline. In a few cases, an encouragement to pick the blocks up, turn them, look at and feel the edges of faces was sufficient to prompt children to 'see' matches.

To support the skills of matching faces to outlines, children were shown how to print 'footprints' with the blocks in soft dough, making impressions of recognisable shapes. They were encouraged to run their fingers around the edges of the impressions and to then feel the edges of the face of the block that had made them. The strong story context built around matching footprints to blocks gave the activity purpose and relevance.

Finally, children were invited children to help to pack a selection of blocks into a home-made 'shape sorter' toy lorry. The crucial adaptation was that the shaped openings into the lorry were packed with foam underneath, so that correctly chosen blocks were held in the shaped recesses. This was done to address a perhaps under-recognised problem with many commercial shape sorters: that when a shape has been posted it disappears. There is no opportunity to talk about what has happened. Did the shape chosen go through the hole by sheer luck, or was there some careful looking and matching? Preventing the blocks from falling through the lorry holes allowed tactile and visual reinforcement of the link between the orientation of the block and the shape of the corresponding hole in the lorry.

Interestingly, when this work was repeated in Moscow, it was found that Russian children showed a greater inclination to pick blocks up and turn them around in their hands to find faces that matched 2D outlines. One suggestion to explain this came from comparing the activities routinely presented to the different groups of children. In UK settings common problem-solving shape activities are jigsaws. In order to solve these puzzles children need to turn jigsaw pieces around, looking at the shapes of edges and the pieces of picture visible on the upper surface. There is rarely any need to pick pieces up to examine other faces. Russian children, by contrast, are frequently offered 'picture block' puzzles that take the form of covered cubes. In order to complete a picture, each cube must be picked up in turn and rotated in all directions as each face is individually explored.

Using feely bags

Feely bag games are widely used not only in the study of 3D shape, but also in language and science activities designed to develop the use and understanding of descriptive vocabulary. Children explore a hidden object, feeling and describing it before it can be withdrawn for 'checking'. Children may be asked to identify the 3D shape 'hiding' in the bag, or to locate a given shape from a selection in the bag. The activities are seen as enjoyable and challenging.

And in many ways they are.

But their popularity belies the challenges they present to children. When feeling shapes that cannot be seen, children need to make constant translations between the tactile sensations experienced and remembered or imagined visual images. Again, for children with insecure concepts due to a lack of first-hand experience, this procedure becomes increasingly complex, rendering the task inaccessible.

To support children in early feely bag activities, it is a good idea to ask children to 'find another block like this'. Children are encouraged to manipulate a cube, for example, before reaching into the feely bag to find another. Thus they are matching like with like; two tactile experiences. Providing the children with a block to hold in one hand whilst reaching in the bag to find a matching one takes this support one step further.

Identifying 3D shape 'families'

There is another hurdle in developing the skills of naming 3D shapes. This is associated with the properties of individual shape 'families'. If a group of people are asked to think about cubes, all the imagined shapes will be more or less the same. Regardless of size, the proportions and shape-related properties of cubes remain constant.

Once children have met one cube, in many ways they have met them all. Similarly, one sphere is much like another. But this is not true of all shapes. A cylinder, for example, might look like a wheel, a grocery tin or a drinking straw. A triangular prism might resemble a roof or a portion of well-known Swiss chocolate. How can we help children to recognise members of these more complex shape 'families'?

A useful approach is to identify the key characteristic properties shared by all shapes which share the same name. What makes a cylinder a cylinder? Children who were observed by Coltman, Petyaeva and Anghileri (2002) sorting cylinders from a selection of shaped wooden blocks were frequently seen to select blocks that met their own criteria based on partial understandings of cylinders. Blocks were chosen, for example, that were 'tall'.

To develop understandings, key knowledge was placed in a memorable story context. The children were told about a mother 'cylinder bird' who was able to recognise her babies using two key pieces of information. Drawing on the printing strategy previously discussed, it was explained that cylinder bird babies like to jump in muddy places (represented by dough) and whether they jump on their heads or their bottoms they leave the same round shape in the mud. Secondly, young cylinders love to roll down slopes, and are good at it, rolling quickly straight down to the bottom. Again, this is readily illustrated using a tipped tray. Using these two key clues, and with access to the appropriate 'testing' resources, children were later able to confidently identify cylinders of several different proportions from a selection of blocks that included cones, brick-shaped cuboids and cubes.

Conclusion

In thinking about why strategies of the type described in this chapter can be so effective in supporting learning about shape, it is useful to consider the factors shown by research to enhance young children's learning in any context. Referring back to Chapter 1 in this book will remind readers of the evidence supporting the importance of using playful, imaginative contexts where possible, so that tasks are perceived by children as having both purposeful and relevance. Similarly, the involvement of adults in 'scaffolding' learning, in the manner described by Bruner, can guide the learning experience to the point where children found solutions for themselves. These principles apply throughout the mathematics curriculum, whether the context is counting, number problems or acquiring knowledge of shapes.

Key pointers for shape in the Early Years

- The complexities of shape as an area of mathematics are often underestimated.
- An ability to describe 2D shapes is founded in an ability to talk about lines.

- Children need to manipulate 3D shapes, reinforcing visual observations with tactile experiences.
- Approaches to supporting the development of mathematics, as much as any other area, should be embedded in the principles known to enhance learning in young children.

References

Anghileri, J. & Baron, S. (1999) Playing with the materials of study: Poleidoblocs. *Education 3–13*, 27 (2), pp. 57–63.

Aubrey, C., Kavkler, M., Tancig, S., & Magauna, L. (2000) Getting it right from the start? The influence of early school entry on later achievements in mathematics. *European Early Childhood Education Research Journal*, 8 (1), pp. 75–85.

Bruner J. (1983) *Child's Talk*. New York: Norton.

Clements, D.H. & Battista, M.T. (1992) Geometry and spatial reasoning. In Grouws, D.A. (Ed.), *Handbook of Research on Mathematics Teaching and Learning*. New York: Macmillan Publishing Company, pp. 420–464.

Coltman P., Petyaeva, D., & Anghileri J. (2002) Scaffolding learning through meaningful tasks and adult interaction. *Early Years*, 22 (1), pp. 39–49.

Coltman P. (2006) Talk of a number: Self-regulated use of mathematical metalanguage by children in the foundation stage. *Early Years*, 26 (1), pp. 31–48.

Fosnot, C. & Dolk, M. (2001) *Young Mathematicians at Work: Constructing Number Sense, Addition and Subtraction*. Portsmouth, NH: Heinemann.

Fuson, K. (1988) *Children's Counting and Concepts of Number*. New York: Springer Verlag.

Gersten, R., Jordan, N.C., & Plojo, J.R. (2005) Early identification and interventions for students with mathematics difficulties. *Journal of Learning Disabilities*, 38 (4), pp. 293–304.

Lampert, M. & Blunk, M. (1998) (Eds.) *Talking Mathematics in School*. Melbourne: Cambridge University Press.

Munn, P. (1997) Children's beliefs about counting. In I. Thompson (Ed.), *Teaching and Learning Early Number*. Buckingham: Open University Press, pp. 9–19.

Nunes, T. & P. Bryant (1996) *Children Doing Mathematics*. Oxford: Blackwell.

Sammons, P., Sylva, K., Melhuish, E., Taggart, B., Elliot, K., & Siraj-Blatchford, I. (2002) *Technical Paper 8a: Measuring the Impact of Pre-School on Children's Cognitive Progress over the Pre-school Period*. London: Institute of Education, University of London.

Young-Loveridge, J. (1991) *The Development of Children's Number Concepts from Ages Five to Nine*. Hamilton, New Zealand: University of Waikato.

CHAPTER 16

'But what does it do?'

INFORMATION AND COMMUNICATIONS
TECHNOLOGY (ICT) IN THE EARLY YEARS:
AN EMERGENT APPROACH

John Siraj-Blatchford

Information and Communications Technology (ICT) continues to change the ways in which we interact with each other. It has profound effects upon the way in which we conduct our lives, upon our learning, our work, and our leisure. Inevitably our acceptance of many of these changes involve us in making value decisions and sometimes we *all* feel as if things are moving too fast and we are being left behind. A child who recently received a teddy bear for her birthday is reported to have spent several moments prodding and squeezing it with a confused look upon her face before asking 'But what does it do?' It may have been that the child thought the cuddly toy was broken, or that the batteries were flat. In any event many readers will relate to the consternation of the grandmother who had given her the toy and witnessed this event.

Socio-constructivist perspectives in early childhood education (Sayeed & Guerin, 2000) recognise the importance of viewing play as an activity where children are developing their confidence and capability for interacting with their cultural environment. ICT is a major part of the environment in which the child is growing up. If we are to provide for an appropriate, broad and balanced education in the Early Years we must first think about children playing: but then we must also think about the particular subjects of that play. We must recognize that in recent years the application of information and communications technology (ICT) has brought about fundamental changes to our culture and society, and the legitimacy of its place in the curriculum should not be doubted.

Since computers were first introduced into UK primary schools in the early 1980s, an ever wider range of ICT products have been developed for use by young children. Some of these have been found appropriate for use in preschools, and other new products have been developed specifically for this age group (Siraj-Blatchford, 2006). But given the relatively high cost of ICT and of ICT software, and the even greater investment that is often required in the training required to use them effectively, it is important that we make critical and informed choices regarding their use. One crucial aspect is for us to begin to empower children to make their own informed choices in the future.

There are six commonly cited benefits in applying ICT in the Early Years. It has been argued that:

- Computers offer a means of teaching basic (literacy and numeracy) skills more efficiently.
- Computers have been widely employed in schools, business and industry, and it is therefore important for children to begin to develop the computer keyboard and mouse skills that will increasingly determine their future success in these new technological environments.
- Children working at the computer benefit from the experience of collaborative learning with their peers.
- Programmable toys and screen images provide motivating real and virtual objects for the child to 'think with' (Papert, 1982).
- Early play and experience with ICT supports the development of technological literacy and an enduring positive disposition toward the subject.
- Technology provides a range of powerful compensatory tools to be applied in educating children with special educational needs.

Learning 'the basics'

A range of software products have been developed to support early learning in a wide range of subject areas. These include drill and practice programs designed to support the development of number and letter recognition and basic phonic skills. A good example of a popular early 'drill and practice' program that has been used in preschools for many years is *Millie's Math House* (Riverdeep). This includes 'Make a Bug', 'Number Machine' and 'Bing/Bong', a program that encourages children to complete patterns; the program makers claim this will 'empower children to recognise other patterns in music, mathematics, art, and science and to make better sense of the world'. While an optional free-play mode is included in this program, it also provides a very clear demonstration of a behaviorist teaching approach (a learning approach based on behavior modification) that is inherent in many of the programs of this genre. If the child gets a right answer they are rewarded by some amusing action sequence and/or tune. If they make a mistake the options are gradually reduced until they are forced to make the 'correct' response. This is an approach that is widely considered inappropriate in British early childhood settings as it runs against the grain of the dominant 'play and discovery' philosophy of early childhood education.

A much more recent iPad 'app' that involves a very different playful learning experience is *CHIMES* (SRRN Games), which may be used to support children in developing sorting and sequencing skills. It's a musical activity that requires perseverance, concentration and problem-solving. At the first stages the game is very simple: five coloured spheres have to be tapped to clear like-coloured obstacles that flow across the screen. Siraj-Blatchford and Parmar (2011) report on research that suggests that the *AlphaBlocks* series of activities that have been developed to support the UK's CBeebies television channel can be used effectively to support young children's emergent literacy.

When children interact with high quality computer and handheld 'app' software their interaction is often especially absorbing and extended. But products should be carefully reviewed to ensure that they are suitable. There are flaws even in some of the most popular programs. Most significantly, many are designed for solitary play even though we know that child development in the Early Years is more effectively supported through encouraging the child's co-operative and collaborative verbal engagement with adults and peers (Sylva et al., 2010, Sabol et al., 2013). One software product explicitly designed for use by a child collaborating with a more capable peer or adult is the *Land of Me*. *The Land of Me* provides a series of animated adventures involving three main characters, Eric, Willow and Buddy – a racoon, a bird, and a large bear, respectively. Adults are provided with prompts to guide their dialogue with the child in fruitful directions, and in the desktop version the advanced software functions are controlled through the adult's use of the mouse while the child is engaged in applying his or her own control through the use of the space bar and return key.

As the US National Association for the Education of Young Children (NAEYC) *Position Statement on Technology* suggests: 'Educators should use professional judgment in evaluating and using technology and media, just as they would with any

Figure 16.1 *The Land of Me*

other learning tool or experience, and they must emphasize active engagement rather than passive, non-interactive uses' (NAEYC, 2012, p. 12).

The use of an inappropriate teaching method can have a devastating effect upon a child's learning dispositions. There is evidence to suggest, for example, that excessive early drill and practice in the teaching of reading can undermine a child's dispositions to be a reader (Katz, 1992). Yelland (2007) usefully cites Negroponte (1995) in this context:

> In the 1960s, most pioneers of computers in education advocated a crummy drill-and-practice approach, using computers on a one-to-one basis, in a self-paced fashion, to teach those same God-awful facts more effectively. Now, with the rage of multimedia, we have closet drill and practice believers who think they can colonise the pizzazz of a Sega game to squirt a bit more information into the heads of children, with more so called productivity.
>
> (Negroponte, 1995, pp. 198–199)

Computer keyboard and mouse skills

Many Early Years teachers prioritise the development of basic mouse and keyboard skills, and software such as *Switch on Original: Picture Building* (Brilliant Computing) is often used specifically for these purposes. School suppliers and toy shops provide a range of other apparatus and equipment designed to satisfy the same needs. Yet, if we look back to the early days of educational (or industrial) computing, one of the most obvious changes has been in precisely these areas. The first computer introduced into many schools was the Sinclair ZX81 (see Figure 16.2). Programs were stored on cassette tapes that took a long time to load. None of the early computers had a mouse and written commands in the BASIC programming language had to be typed onto the screen – the 'drag and drop' facility that was first developed by Xerox and Apple had yet to be introduced. We have come a long way since these early days. . .but they weren't actually that long ago, and that is something we really need to think about. Future developments are difficult to predict but, looking back on the manner of developments so far, it is clear that computing in the future will be much faster and easier to access.

Touch-sensitive screens have already replaced other means of control in a variety of hand-held devices including tablet computers and smart phones, and the likelihood of the infants of today operating a 'mouse' in their future employment is extremely doubtful. New technologies are constantly being developed and voice recognition systems are becoming increasingly sophisticated. The future of the QWERTY keyboard seems even bleaker. The odd layout of the QWERTY keys was initially designed to slow down the typist to avoid the typewriter 'hammers' colliding and locking together as they were thrown against the ribbon and paper. That keyboard is already a technological anachronism . . .

Figure 16.2 *The Sinclair ZX81*

Children do need to access the technology that is currently available, and the point that I am making here is not that we shouldn't support them in initially gaining that access. We should provide them with the best possible access to the technological tools currently available. But what we shouldn't do is present that as a central objective of Early Years ICT education.

Most new desktop computers arrive with an instruction book that warns the user about some of the ergonomic difficulties associated with extended exposure to the screen and in operating the keyboard and mouse. The dangers of developing repetitive strain injuries (RSIs) and carpal tunnel syndrome have been well documented. The recommendations for appropriate posture should therefore always be followed as far as possible. Yet this is often extremely difficult to achieve in a classroom, and in preschools the difficulties may actually be insurmountable. Young children vary greatly in height and the provision of suitable furniture is often beyond the resources of playgroups and nurseries. In these circumstances, the identification of alternative technology, such as laptop computers, tablets and smart phones, and alternative patterns of usage and means of access, become crucial.

A major advantage of using a touch-screen is that children's interactions with the computer are often relatively short, and the equipment may be set up to be accessed by the child from a standing position. This overcomes many of the ergonomic problems alluded to above. A very good example of what is possible is the *Noodle Words* iPad app from NoodleWorks. The app is designed to offer emerging readers a playful place to develop word recognition and comprehension – and it really works.

Figure 16.3 *Noodlewords*

Collaboration

While the extended use (e.g., in excess of 40 minutes or an hour at a time) of desk-top computer keyboards is therefore not to be recommended in early childhood, there are still a great many Early Years programs available that can be used to encourage collaborative activity (see Figure 16.4).

As Light and Butterworth (1992) argue, 'joint attention' and 'children learning to share' and/or 'engage jointly' is a cognitive challenge for young children. In collaboration children articulate their thinking, sharing their understandings and bringing to consciousness many ideas that they may still be only beginning to grasp intuitively (Hoyles, 1985). Collaboration is also considered important in providing opportunities for cognitive conflict as efforts are made to reach consensus (Doise & Mugny, 1984), and it has been recognised as important in facilitating the co-construction of potential solutions in the creative processes of problem solving (Forman, 1989). The best of these provide context for work away from the screen. In *The Land of Me*, off-screen extension activities are specifically provided to encourage socio-dramatic and small-world play beyond the screen. But any on-screen 'design' created in a paint program such as *TuxPaint*, or a construction designed in *SoupToys* (Figure 16.5) may be subsequently constructed off screen using play dough, construction kits or other found materials. This provides additional motivation for collaborative activities and has the additional benefit of introducing the children to another very important and influential application of ICT, Computer Assisted Design (CAD). Research in South Wales (Morgan & Siraj-Blatchford, 2014) has now demonstrated the effectiveness of

Figure 16.4 *Good Early Years software encourages collaboration and joint attention*

Figure 16.5 *Souptoys*

preschools using ICT to support the development of the children's home learning environment. In many homes and preschools, parents and professional educators are already building upon established, or developing/new, 'shared reading' and playful learning practices at the computer screen. Free-to-download programs such as *TuxPaint* and *SoupToys*, along with many free apps, have a great deal of potential as they are easily distributed to parents and can be applied to support such parent partnership activities (Morgan & Siraj-Blatchford, 2014).

Adventure games such as *Lili* (iOS) and simulations like *Souptoys* (Windows) have enormous potential for supporting dialogue and collaboration with an adult or older child and there are also excellent software products available that allow a young child and an adult to sit together and create an animated picture story; examples include 2Simple's *2Create a Story* (Windows) and the Open University excellent (free) app *Our Story* (iOS). There are also a wide range of graphics programmes on the market that can be applied collaboratively, including *TuxPaint* (Windows/Mac OSX).

'Manipulables'

At one time it was thought that many of the activities associated with computers would not encourage creativity, and in fact required only that the child press buttons. The manipulation of virtual objects on a screen was seen as a weak substitute for the manipulation of real 3-dimensional objects, artifacts and toys. But as Yelland (2007) argues, the potential of computers to enable children to encounter and play with ideas has been increased, and products such as those produced by 2Simple, *The Land of Me*, *TuxPaint* and *Noisy Things* (Windows/Mac OSX) have for many years provided a means by which children can create and manipulate objects, playing with them in a variety of ways. In such environments the children often spontaneously discover mathematical ideas and engage in interactions with other learners that would not have been possible without the technology.

Most early childhood educators believe that young children learn best by investigating with their senses, but a common concern among early childhood educators has been that children are not ready to work with computers. In discussing developmental issues surrounding the use of computers in childhood education, Silvern and McCary (1986) suggested that two conditions should be met for an activity to be considered 'concrete'. The first is that the material used in the activity should be easily manipulated and the second is that 'the results of the manipulation must be directly verifiable by the manipulator'. Using these criteria, concrete uses of the computer may be identified and effectively applied by children. But, as Clements and McMillen (1996) have stated, in any event 'What is concrete to the child may have more to do with what is meaningful and manipulable than with its physical nature' (p. 273).

Clements (1994) has also highlighted the unique characteristics of computer manipulatives, and suggests that they include:

- flexibility;
- the ability to change arrangement or representations;
- the storage and availability of configurations;
- recording and replaying children's actions;
- linking the concrete and the symbolic and providing feedback;
- dynamic linking of multiple representations; and
- focusing the children's attention and increasing motivation.

While most of us are very much aware of the ways in which ICT has revolutionised *communications*, its parallel effects in *control* technology is often forgotten. This is unfortunate because it's probable that the vast majority of the computers that we interact with on a day-to-day basis are dedicated to these purposes alone. Microprocessors are now routinely incorporated in a vast range of devices. They are also incorporated in a growing number of children's toys. In the UK, programmable toys are now commonly available to children as 'symbolic objects to think with' (Papert, 1982). A floor 'turtle' such as the TTS *Bee-Bot Programmable Floor Robot* is controlled by the child by giving it program instructions: Forward, Back, Left, Right. These instructions make the turtle move and, in the process, children use their thinking skills to explore, take risks and apply their prior knowledge in new and creative ways. Many experts believe this can enhance their cognitive development. *Bee-Bot* is exceptionally simple to control and provides a very good starting point as an 'object to think with'. TTS also supply software that provides a means of programming the Bee-Bot on-screen, which is an interesting development from other popular screen turtle applications such as the 'Jelly Bean Hunt' in *Trudy's Time and Place House* (EDMARK) (see Figure 16.6), and *2Go* from the 2Simple *Infant Video Toolkit*. All of these programs support young children in the development of their co-ordination and spatial awareness, and in learning about mapping and directions.

Symbolic play, and socio-dramatic play in particular, is seen as a characteristic mode of activity for this age group, and by inference the most appropriate vehicle for learning (Vygotsky, 1978; Wood & Attfield, 1996; Anning & Edwards, 1999). Early childhood ICT research has shown that the manipulation of symbols and images on the computer screen may actually represent a new form of symbolic play, which the children seem to treat as every bit as 'concrete' as the manipulation of any alternative blocks and small-world toys:

> On-screen images were 'grabbed', scolded, fingered and smacked, with dramatic effect, as part of the small-group interaction with the software. In some instances, they took on an off-screen life of their own, as children continued the game the computer had initiated, away from the machine. 'Food' items were one of the favourite symbols . . . These three, and other girls, frequently 'grabbed' apples and pears from the screen, begged each other to share them, and licked their lips appreciatively after pretending to eat them.
>
> (Brooker & Siraj-Blatchford, 2002, p. 267)

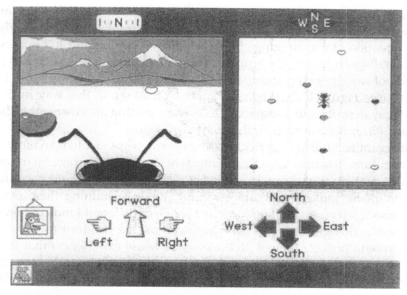

Figure 16.6 *The 'Jelly Bean Hunt' in Trudy's Time and Place House*

Developing technological literacy and positive dispositions to ICT

'I'm a rocket scientist', one engineer complained to me. 'I design missile systems, but I can't figure out how to program my VCR.'

(Norman, 1995)

As Norman (1995) has argued, it is inevitable that as technology has developed we have all come to know less and less about the inner workings of the systems that are under our control. This is as true of adult experiences of technology as it is of children's experience. In the face of these changes, we need to consider carefully what our educational priorities should now be. We also need to consider what it actually means to 'understand' a technological product. When technology was mostly mechanical we could see the internal workings and we could see the effects of our actions on machines. But increasingly their operation and design are invisible and abstract, so that, if we are not to be entirely alienated from the technology around us, we need to redefine what it means to be technologically literate. It is this sort of argument that has provided the rationale for developing a new curriculum for ICT in schools that is based on computer science and emphasises more strongly the 'uses of technology' in the Foundation Stage Curriculum.

Many early childhood applications provide a parallel with adult applications. Children are now introduced to a wide range of computer software and apps in addition to all of those referred to above; they soon come to apply software encyclopedia and a range of word processors, spreadsheets and databases in school. Hardware and software applications have also been developed specifically for the Early Years with the intention of encouraging children to 'play' within adult ICT contexts. For example, the *Playskool Store* (Hasbro) checkout unit clips on to the keyboard providing a point-of-sale shopping simulation that incorporates a 'working' till, barcode reader, etc. (see Figure 16.7). When we apply technology in this way in the Early Years, we may describe our perspective as one supporting an 'emergent technology curriculum' (Siraj-Blatchford & Siraj-Blatchford, 2006)

An 'emergent technology curriculum' is in many ways just like an emergent literacy curriculum. Teachers who teach emergent literacy encourage 'mark-making' as a natural prelude to writing. In emergent technology we should encourage the 'application' of technology and support the child in sustaining them over time. Teachers who teach emergent literacy *read* a range of different kinds of text to children. In emergent technology we should introduce the children to 'new applications'. We should provide them with the essential early experiences that they must have if they are to go on to understand and be empowered by technology in their later lives. These early experiences will include playing with a range of different

Figure 16.7 *The Playskool Store checkout unit*

technological artifacts and software products (real and pretend telephones, cameras, computers, etc.). They will also include drawing children's attention to the uses of technology in the world around them. We can also encourage 'technology play' in the nursery, setting up office-play environments, supermarket checkouts and bank cashpoints for children to integrate into their play. Teachers who teach emergent literacy provide positive role models by showing children the value they place in their own use of print. In emergent technology education we can do the same by talking about technology and involving children in the development of our own collaborative technological applications. We can set up a computer database to keep a check on the books and other resources that we use. We can use the computer for our own purposes, sharing our experiences of its use with the children. In doing so, we will encourage children to develop an emergent awareness of the nature and value of these resources as well as a positive disposition towards the kind of technological applications that they will experience in the future.

Many of those promoting emergent literacy see parent and teacher 'modelling' – that is, teachers and parents providing good role models – to be the most important factor in developing children's capability. They therefore encourage parents to read to their children and ensure that the children see them reading for their own purposes. This is backed up by numerous large-scale research projects that show that the single most influential factor in determining children's future academic success in the Early Years is parents reading to children and taking them to the library regularly (Sylva et al., 2010). This in turn is related to social class and other factors, but the primary determinant has been shown to be the parent's behavior (see Morgan & Siraj-Blatchford, 2014): change that and it will compensate for social class differences in academic achievement! So the real challenge is to provide children will strong models of technology so that they develop positive attitudes and beliefs about the importance of the subject. That, more than anything else, is what will influence their motivation to engage in it in the future.

Play is a 'leading activity' (Leontiev, 1981; Oerter, 1993), and, as van Oers (1999) has suggested, when children consciously reflect upon the relationship between their 'pretend' signs and 'real' meanings they are engaged in a form of semiotic activity that will provide a valuable precursor to new learning activities:

> [L]earning activity must be fostered as a new special form of play activity. As a new quality emerging from play activity, it can be argued that learning activity has to be conceived as a language game in which negotiation about meanings in a community of learners is the basic strategy for the acquisition of knowledge and abilities.
>
> (van Oers, 1999, p. 273)

From this theoretical standpoint I want to argue that we should be providing opportunities for children to play with technology and to play at being technologists. It is commonplace for children to play at being Mummies and Daddies, as well as a wide range of traditional roles, such as Soldiers, Doctors, Nurses and Firemen. In the UK, preschool suppliers and toy shops produce 'dressing-up' clothes to promote this kind of play. All we need to do is to provide the props and encouragement to include the technology in all of this as well. For some practitioners this may seem to be prescriptive, but, as Vygotsky argued, 'In one sense a child at play is free to determine his own actions. But in another sense this is an illusory freedom, for his actions are in fact subordinated to the meanings of things and he acts accordingly' (Vygotsky, 1978, p. 103).

Special educational needs

Experience in the UK and abroad suggests that the use of ICT may actually be maintaining, and may even be exaggerating, educational inequalities. Some children benefit from having frequent use of computers in the home, and boys tend to be encouraged to use them much more than girls. Girls' and boys' software preferences differ and it is all too easy for the children who have the most experience and capability to dominate the computer's use. ICT provides no panacea for educational inequality; everything depends upon the choices that are made to provide technology that is appropriate to each child:

> For children with special needs, technology has many potential benefits. Technology can be a powerful compensatory tool – it can augment sensory input or reduce distractions; it can provide support for cognitive processing or enhance memory and recall; it can serve as a personal 'on-demand' tutor and as an enabling device that supports independent functioning. The variety of assistive-technology products ranges from low-tech toys with simple switches to expansive high-tech systems capable of managing complex environments. These technologies empower young children, increasing their independence and supporting their inclusion in classes with their peers. . . . Yet, with all these enhanced capabilities, this technology requires thoughtful integration into the early childhood curriculum, or it may fall far short of its promise. Educators must match the technology to each child's unique special needs, learning styles, and individual preferences.
>
> (NAEYC, 1996)

Research has shown that ICT can provide accessible language forms that are supported through visual cues and animations:

> The computer often provided a shared focus and experience for children who didn't share the same spoken language, and this undoubtedly contributed towards the development of the very positive, collaborative, and language enriched multicultural learning environment that we observed.
>
> (Brooker & Siraj-Blatchford, 2002)

Conclusions

We began the chapter by identifying six reasons that might be given for introducing the computer into early education: they might be used to teach basic skills more efficiently; prepare children for the future in schools and employment; encourage collaboration and positive disposition towards ICT; provide objects for the child to 'think with'; and/or provide for special educational needs.

The evidence shows that when they are given the freedom to play with appropriate software, young children are active in constructing their own learning at the computer, and in scaffolding each other's learning. As I have argued above, there can be few places better to start this process than in early childhood sociodramatic play.

We all have a contribution to make in providing a better ICT education for young children, and in doing so we should always be acutely aware of the influence of the wider environment, and of role models, in particular, on young children. In our work and interactions with children we should demonstrate confidence and competence with technology. As Pluckrose (1999) has suggested, young children learn a great deal from the models that are provided for them:

> Watch a nursery child put on a pair of high-heeled shoes and a Sloane Ranger hat and toss a giant sized handbag over her shoulder. Listen to the language. Admire the walk. Then, take time to reflect upon the interpretation of her world through her eyes, marvelling that one so young is able to 'read', so meticulously, the adults who people her world. . . .
>
> (Pluckrose, 1999)

If we show that we value the new technology and confidently control it then children will be encouraged to develop the same attitudes. But if we present them with models that are disempowered and helpless in the face of technology, we take the risk of encouraging just the same in them.

Pointers for Early Years ICT

- Beware of over-using drill and practice software with young children.
- How children access software (QWERTY keyboard; mouse) will change and should not be a central objective of the curriculum.
- Ergonomics are important; consider using touchscreens, laptop computers and tablets with the children.
- Use software which encourages collaboration and verbal interaction.
- Manipulating objects on-screen in a meaningful context provides valuable opportunities for symbolic play.

(Continued)

(Continued)

- Using computers should be part of a wider 'emergent technology curriculum'.
- Children should be provided with opportunities to engage in socio-dramatic play with all kinds of technology.
- Teachers should positively model their use of technology.
- Used thoughtfully, technology can empower children with special educational needs and support their inclusion.

References

Anning, A. & Edwards, A. (1999) *Promoting Young Children's Learning from Birth to Five*. Buckingham: Open University Press.

Brooker, E. & Siraj-Blatchford, J. (2002) 'Click on Miaow!' How children of three and four years experience the nursery computer. *Contemporary Issues in Early Childhood*, 3 (2), pp. 251–273. Available at http://www.wwwords.co.uk/pdf/freetoview.asp?j=ciec&vol=3&issue=2&year=2002&article=7_Brooker_CIEC_3_2

Clements, D. H. & McMillen, S. (1996) Rethinking concrete manipulatives. *Teaching Children Mathematics*, January, pp. 270–279.

Clements, D.H. (1994) The uniqueness of the computer as a learning tool: Insights from research and practice. In J.L. Wright & D.D. Shade (Eds.), *Young children: Active Learners in a Technological Age*. Washington: NAEYC, pp. 31–50.

Doise, W. & Mugny, G. (1984) *The Social Development of the Intellect*. Oxford: Pergamon Press.

Foreman, E. (1989) The role of peer interaction in the social construction of mathematical knowledge, *International Journal of Educational Research*, 13, pp. 55–69.

Hoyles, C. (1985) What is the point of group discussion in mathematics? *Studies in Mathematics*, 16, pp. 205–214.

Katz, L.G. (1992). *What Should Young Children Be Doing?* ERIC Digest. Urbana, IL: ERIC Clearinghouse on Elementary and Early Childhood Education, University of Illinois.

Leontiev, A. (1981) *Problems of the Development of Mind*. Moscow: Moscow University Press.

Light, P. & Butterworth, G. (Eds.) (1992) *Context and Cognition: Ways of Learning and Knowing*. Hemel Hempstead: Harvester-Wheatsheaf.

National Association for the Education of Young Children (NAEYC) (1996) Developmentally appropriate practice in early childhood programs serving children from birth through age 8. A position statement of the National Association for the Education of Young Children. In Bredekamp S., and Copple, C. (Eds.), *Developmentally Appropriate Practice in Early Childhood Programs*, rev. ed. Washington DC: National Association for the Education of Young Children.

National Association for the Education of Young Children (NAEYC) (2012) *NAEYC Position Statement: Technology and Interactive Media as Tools in Early Childhood Programs Serving Children from Birth through Age 8.* Adopted January 2012. Available at http://issuu.com/naeyc/docs/ps_technology_issuu_may2012?e=2112065/2087657#search

Negroponte, N. (1995) *Being Digital.* Rydalmere, NSW: Hodder Stoughton.

Norman, D. (1995) Designing the future. *Scientific American,* September, p. 159.

Morgan, A. & Siraj-Blatchford, J. (2014) *Using ICT in the Early Years: Parents and Practitioners in Partnership,* revised edn. Salisbury: Practical Preschool Books.

Oerter, R. (1993) *The Psychology of Play: An Activity Oriented Approach.* Munich: Quintessenz.

Papert, S. (1982) *Mindstorms: Children, Computers, and Powerful Ideas.* Brighton, Sussex: Harvester.

Pluckrose, H. (1999) *The Caring Classroom: Towards a Learning Environment.* Nottingham: Education Now Books.

Sabol, T., Soliday Hong, S., Pianta, R., & Burchinal, M. (2013) Can rating pre-K programs predict children's learning? *Science,* 341 (6148), pp. 845–846.

Sayeed Z, & Guerin, E. (2000) *Early Years Play: A Happy Medium FOR Assessment AND Intervention.* Abingdon: David Fulton Publishers.

Silvern, S. & McCary, J. (1986) Computers in the educational lives of children: Developmental issues. In J. L. Hoot (Ed.), *Computers in Early Childhood Education* Englewood Cliffs, NJ: Prentice-Hall, pp. 6–21.

Siraj-Blatchford, J. (Ed.) (2006) Developing New Technologies for Young Children. Nottingham: Trentham Books.

Siraj-Blatchford, J. & Parmar, N. (2011) Knowledge, learning processes, and ICT in early childhood education. *He Kupu,* 2 (5).

Siraj-Blatchford, I. & Siraj-Blatchford, J. (2006) A Curriculum Development Guide to ICT in Early Childhood Education. Nottingham: Trentham Books with Early Education.

Sylva, K., Melhuish, E., Sammons, P., Siraj-Blatchford, I., & Taggart, B. (Eds.) (2010) *Early Childhood Matters: Evidence from the Effective Pre-school and Primary Education project.* London: Routledge.

van Oers, B. (1999) Teaching opportunities in play. In M. Hedegaard & J. Lompscher (Eds.), *Learning Activity and Development.* Aarhus: Aarhus University Press.

Vygotsky, L. (1978) *Mind in Society: The Development of Higher Psychological Processes.* Cambridge, MA: Harvard University Press.

Wood, E. & Attfield, J. (1996) *Play, Learning and the Early Childhood Curriculum.* London: Paul Chapman.

Yelland, N. (1999) Reconceptualising schooling with technology for the 21st century: Images and reflections. *Information Technology in Childhood Education Annual,* 1, pp. 39–59.

Yelland, N. (2007). Shift to the Future: Rethinking Learning with New Technologies in Education. New York: Routledge.

Useful websites

http://www.bbc.co.uk/cbeebies/alphablocks/watch/alphablocks-watch/
http://busythings.co.uk/cd-rom-noisy-things.php
http://www.2simple.com
http://www.hasbrotoyshop.com
http://www.souptoys.com
http://www.tts-group.co.uk
http://tuxpaint.org/
All of the iPhone/iPad apps mentioned in the chapter are available in the iTunes store.

CHAPTER 17

'So what is long ago and where is far away . . . ?'

A SENSE OF TIME AND PLACE

Jayne Greenwood and Holly Linklater

In this chapter we outline what is known about children's historical and geographical knowledge and understanding of the world, and what teachers can do to support and extend their learning in this area. We argue that it is important to recognize young children as interactive in their own learning, and that this is particularly relevant to developing a sense of what is meant by 'history' or 'geography', and why history and geography are important parts of the curriculum. When thinking about how best to support and enhance children's learning, we argue for the importance of teaching that has been specifically planned to start with the ways in which children make sense of their lives, and that first-hand experiences will be central to this.

In the first section, we offer a review of educational theory that helps us to understand what historical and geographical knowledge is, and the core ideas that teachers should be looking to help children learn. In the second section, we focus on the practicalities of what teachers can do, presented as a series of case studies. These cases reflect what young children are capable of when they are supported by thoughtful and imaginative teachers in their Early Years. The examples are intended to help you to gain a sense of the teachers' thinking throughout the process of planning and teaching, as well as how children responded – in different ways, but all developing their historical and geographical skills, knowledge, and understanding. For each case, we give practical suggestions of how the activities could be easily adapted. We also suggest resources that could be used as a stimulus for teaching. All cases are intended to be starting points to inspire teaching and learning, not definitive instructions on 'how to'. We hope that these ideas will encourage many new ways to develop rich opportunities for learning about history and geography.

What is historical and geographical knowledge?

The world-renowned educational philosopher John Dewey suggested that the curriculum should lead children, in a purposeful and gradual way, outward in time and space from their immediate experiences. This perspective of how children learn has had a particularly keen impact on our understanding of how children learn historical and geographical skills, knowledge, and understanding in their early education. For example, typically children in school settings will already have a keen sense that they were aged three once, but now they are four (and they will be five). This knowledge of time might be related to their experience of the world with memories of when they were too small to reach the light switch in the bathroom, or that they are now too big for their 'old' car seat. Similarly, they are likely to have an understanding of the place where they live, but also other places that are different. This may have been learned from the experience of visiting grandparents, or going on holiday. Using the idea that effective teaching and learning must start with the child (and that there is no other place for the child to start), the responsibility of the teacher might be thought of as that of 'expanding horizons'. However, young children may also often demonstrate a fearless interest in learning *all* there is about dinosaurs, the arctic, the story of Robin Hood, or what sharks like to eat. Children readily show us that their first-hand experiences are not the only point from which learning can occur – imagination matters, too. History and geography are perhaps two of the richest sources of enchanting stories about how we understand ourselves and our world.

It is important to recognise that the child who knows all about dinosaurs has not necessarily developed what might be thought of as a *historical* appreciation. Similarly, we should not assume that children understand their immediate surroundings and experience in a conceptually meaningful way. One of the challenges for educational curricula is to structure, or scaffold, the way that people learn how to fit concepts and the content together. As the old saying goes, fish don't discover water. Rather than reviewing the details of particular curriculum documents, in this chapter we have focused on identifying the concepts and contents that might be thought to define the idea of 'history' and 'geography'.

Historical skills, knowledge, and understanding

A distinct vocabulary accompanies historical skills, knowledge, and understanding: age, era, period, time, century, decade, ancient, modern. Usually these terms reflect an understanding of people's experience of time and its measurement, and a sense of chronology. History is also recognizable by the way in which it informs and develops our sense of identity and place within society. In the first instance this might be in relation to our family and locality and how change affects us over time.

Geographical skills, knowledge, and understanding

Geography can be thought of as the relationship between the Earth and its peoples. This relates to an understanding of location (both physical and human features) and the interaction of people with the environment. The study of geography is valued for the way in which it encourages and sustains a sense of wonder about the world, develops an informed concern about the quality of the environment, and encourages a sense of responsibility for the care of the Earth and its people. Distinct geographical skills are the reading, using, and making of maps, globes, and atlases.

Common approaches to historical and geographical inquiry

The process of historical inquiry or geographical fieldwork involves a combination of observing, raising questions, hypothesizing, describing, investigating, communicating, sequencing, recording, and explaining. Depending on the purpose of historical inquiry, the resources being used, and who is doing the investigating, all of these skills may be required and used at different points. The process of doing and learning about history and geography involves exploration, investigation, or problem-solving. For this reason, both history and geography are recognized as developing skills that are relevant across the curriculum.

Historical and geographical study is perhaps most easily identifiable by the types of questions that are asked along the way. These questions are usually about the relationships between people over time or in relation to particular places. For example:

- When/how did people live?
- Where do people live?
- Why do they live there?
- How do we know?
- Why/how did things change?
- What was similar/different?

In the process of answering these sorts of questions about ourselves, or others, we learn about how we connect to our world and how changeable and diverse this process is. Because of this, history and geography have been thought to represent the way in which we construct our own contexts for the present (Hoodless, 2008). Hoodless goes onto argue that children should 'do' history, as well as learn about it. This argument links with the idea outlined in the introduction to this chapter that both first-hand experiences and imagination will be important to children's learning. Effective teachers will think seriously about how the children they work with are assembling knowledge. Often, the topics we associate with both history and geography and the relevant resources such as people, pictures, objects, and books, provide a rich and cohesive context and content for cross-curricular learning.

Practical case studies

In this section, we present a series of short case studies that exemplify the arguments presented above. To make both teachers' thinking and children's learning clear, each section has been structured according to an understanding that the characteristics of effective learning for young children are:

- Exploring and playing – children use all their senses and imagination to investigate and experience things, independently and collaboratively.
- Being actively engaged – children are actively engaged in first hand experiences, people, places, objects, materials etc. They concentrate, persevere with challenges, and enjoy their achievements.
- Thinking critically and being creative – children have regular opportunities to put experiences into words. They develop their own ideas, make links between ideas, and develop strategies for doing things.

The following case studies exemplify how each of these aspects were encouraged and developed in classroom settings with young children.

A sense of time case study: baby Harvey's story

We all have our own way of interpreting and understanding the past, and the most effective way of demonstrating this to young children is by an exploration of their own personal history. A list of resources on the theme of babies or growing up can be found at the end of this chapter.

Background

The visit of baby Harvey was part of a half-term topic focus about clothes entitled 'Dressing Up.' Within this Year 1 classroom a role play area was created entitled 'The Magic Changing Room' (based on the old television series *The Extraordinary Adventures of Mr Benn*). Much of the storytelling, drama, and literacy activities were based on this too. The visit of baby Harvey introduced the idea of the past and the changes that occur over time. Amy, Harvey's mum, introduced her baby by explaining how old he was, what he liked to eat, what he could do now that he could not do when he was first born. She also brought with her a set of photographs that documented Harvey's development and growth, his favourite toys, and clothes that he had worn since birth but had now outgrown.

Exploring and playing

- The children played with Harvey and his toys and discussed how they were different from the toys they play with and why that might be.
- Children compared photographs of Harvey at different stages with those they had brought in of themselves.

Being actively engaged

- Children examined the photographs and the clothes and made a timeline of each.

- They gave a commentary about their timeline with an explanation of why they had chosen to place items in a particular place.
- They used language relating to the passage of time: 'When Harvey was first born he wore this tiny baby-gro. Next he wore . . . After that . . . ' etc.
- The opportunity to handle actual objects, in this case clothing, actively engaged the children in their learning and sparked their interest and curiosity.

Thinking critically and being creative

- An old baby gown was then added within the clothing timeline as baby Harvey had worn this at his christening. It belonged to the family and had been passed down.
- The children were challenged to think why this old item was in the line. 'Is it new?' 'Who might have worn it before?' 'Why do you think baby Harvey wore it?' 'Do you think it would fit him now?'

The children were then given the opportunity to think about a time even further in the past. The Victorian baby gown was discussed. The children were invited to handle this and to make comparisons with Harvey's own clothing. The main points for consideration were:

- Different materials: the Victorian baby gown was white cotton and, although well-worn, not as soft as Harvey's clothing.
- Construction and decoration: Harvey's clothing was colourful and could be fastened in different ways. The Victorian baby gown was white and had lacy decorations of the same colour.

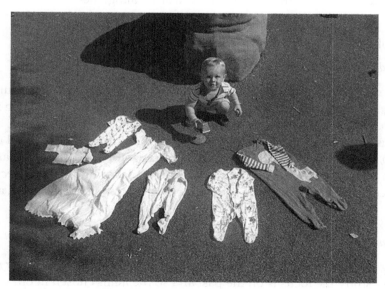

Figure 17.1 *Baby Harvey with an heirloom in a timeline of his clothes*

- The effects of time: some old objects appear worn, tatty, or torn, etc.
- How people viewed the world in the past: the children were fascinated by the fact that both boys and girls would have worn this baby gown. There was also speculation about the length of the gown. Were children much longer/taller a long time ago to account for the excessive length?

Exploring and playing

- In small groups the children passed around the baby gown and were asked to say something about it using one of their senses. There were comments such as 'It doesn't smell as nice as baby Harvey's clothes.'

Being actively engaged

- To encourage careful observation of the old gown, a photograph was taken, cut in half and stuck onto the centre of a piece of drawing paper. This was then photocopied and the children encouraged to look very carefully at the baby gown and to draw the missing half to make a complete picture.
- Comparisons of the old baby gown and a newer baby-gro were made. Spotting the differences consolidated earlier learning and reinforced vocabulary.

Thinking critically and being creative

- There was then a show and tell time (at which the children were used to asking a where, when, what, why or how question) with Amy, Harvey's mum, in the hot seat. This stimulated questions such as 'Who did the baby gown belong to first?' 'How old is it?' 'How many babies have worn it altogether?'

A sense of time case study: the story of the lost bag

Background

This is a rich cross-curricular activity that provides plenty of opportunities for observing, handling objects, speaking and listening, predicting, and using imagination. It can successfully be used to support learning about places, the past, or as part of religious education (for example, to introduce Hinduism the bag could contain a diva lamp, story of Rama and Sita, pictures of rangoli patterns etc.). It can also be used with any age group. For activities to support learning about a specific place the items could be souvenirs from the country, a guide book, map, or flag, as well as coins, etc.

Preparation

Pack a bag with objects that give clues about the type of person the owner might be. In this case study the focus is on the past and so the items chosen in our case study supported this and were from when the class teacher herself was at school. If possible,

Figure 17.2 *A satchel of treasures*

the number of items in the bag should match the number of children in the group who will be unpacking it, so everyone has equal turn to speak. Ideally, the final item that is unpacked should reveal the identity of the owner and answer some of the children's questions; perhaps use either a named object or a photograph of the person. The scene was set for the story by explaining that a lost bag had turned up and that the owner could not be found as there was no luggage label. Then the children were invited to become detectives and try to work out the type of person to whom the bag may belong. The teacher explained that she was unsure if the bag had been lost recently or is from a long time ago.

Exploring and playing

- This activity began with the teacher modelling how to describe the bag itself before the children had their turn. This encouraged the children to look carefully and gave them an understanding of the type of information they might include when it was their turn. For example: 'This bag is quite small; it is brown in colour; it is made of two types of material, canvas and plastic; it has a long handle that you might carry over your shoulder; it fastens with a buckle that is made of metal.'
- The children then took turns to remove an object from the bag. They were encouraged to talk about the item they selected, describing to the rest of the group the colour, size, feel, or possible smell of the item and what it was made from – and to identify what it was, if they knew.

Being actively engaged

As the objects were unpacked, a story developed about a person and their life. Good detective work can be encouraged by asking and answering questions:

- How old do you think the owner might be?
- What do they use this bag for?
- Is the owner a boy or a girl? How do you know?
- Does this bag belong to a young or an older person? How do you know?
- Are the objects in the bag new or old? How do you know?
- Can you guess who this bag belong to?

Thinking critically and being creative

- Once the owner of the lost bag was identified, the children were set the challenge of identifying the objects we might use now for the same purpose.
- Comparisons were made between these old and new objects, e.g. the old school exercise books and our current ones.
- The activity was followed up by writing a postcard or letter to the person explaining that their lost bag has been found.

The activity could also be followed up by further work on the theme of bags: owners and users of bags (doctor, postman, hiker); bags for different functions (sleeping bag, tea-bag, handbag, book bag); or edible bags (ravioli, samosa, pasties). Some resources on the theme of bags can be found at the end of the chapter.

A sense of place case study: porridge and postcards

Developing an awareness of our place in the world helps us to make sense of it. At the heart of this is a focus on people and places through active exploration of the immediate environment. The growing sense of a child's 'own special place' and a natural curiosity about 'other places' is influenced by a range of experiences through film, television, stories, music, and computer games, as well as first-hand exposure through a visit.

Background

This case study exemplifies a specific teacher-directed or teacher-imagined activity, informed by conversation within the class. It also illustrates how one task interrelates to various aspects of the curriculum, as well as shared experiences at school and outside school.

'Once upon a time' was chosen as a place to start the new spring term in this Reception class. It offered so many possibilities, building in particular on the children's enthusiasm for their stories and shows, as well as being reassuringly 'familiar' – all children would be able to contribute some level of experiential expertise.

Exploring and playing

- We began by reading and comparing different versions of the story of Goldilocks and the three bears.
- We looked at books and websites about real bears, and the children worked 'in teams' writing either factual or fictional texts. Where do real bears live? Can we find these countries on a world map?
- We learnt about directional language by retelling the story and describing how Goldilocks got to the three bears' house.

Being actively engaged

- The children started to build their own house for the three bears out of cardboard pallets. They painted pictures illustrating the story for a classroom display that showed the sequence of the story.
- The children began to use the house as the setting for telling their own stories (one about a Daddy, Mummy, baby tiger, and lion), paying homage to the traditional tale we had been playing with.
- We made and ate porridge and sampled different toppings. Data was collected about the most popular porridge topping.

Thinking critically and being creative

- The three bears' role play house was used and the children described what was inside the house using positional language.
- Maps were made showing the location of the house within three bears' wood.
- The route that Goldilocks took through the woods was shown on the map by a series of cut-out black footprints. This allowed the storyteller to change the route if desired.
- What would Goldilocks see or pass on her way to the three bears' house? Did she take the same route out of the wood when she ran away at the end?

To sustain a pace of interest in our explorations, activities were planned around a different text: Little Red Riding Hood. A conversation about the story had led to thinking about our grandmothers and a kind thing that we could do for them. Tales of long car journeys, or even needing to go on a plane, established that many grand-parents lived far away. The idea of sending a postcard was suggested. A few children had sent or received them before. All seemed enthused by the idea of making their own: drawing pictures on the front, writing a short message on the back along with 'the address', and going to the Post Office to buy a stamp and posting it.

Exploring and playing

- A collection of postcards from many different places, along with a magnifying glass for close examination, were investigated. Children discussed the various types of handwriting, stamps, and pictures showing the place it had been sent from.

 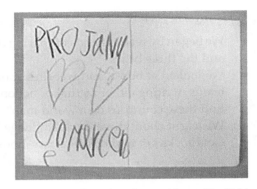

Figure 17.3 *Marlene's postcard with writing in Czech 'because Grandma does not know English'*

- Blank postcards were provided for children to practise using in readiness for making their own special postcards.

Being actively engaged

- The purposeful nature of this activity made it highly engaging. One little boy, Will, worked solidly and determinedly in a way only seen when he plays fire-fighters. He sat for ages thinking about what to write. When asked to imagine what his granny might like to know, he wrote 'I have learnt to write'!! Some children wrote in their own language knowing that this was the best way to communicate with their grandparent.
- We decided to not only write some 'news' but also to ask Gran a question – that way, she would have a reason to reply.
- The choice of picture for the postcard generated plenty of discussions. Should it be our school, here where we live, or where Grandmother lives?
- When walking along the streets to the Post Office we read the numbers on doors, matching the numbers to those painted on wheelie bins.
- We each bought our own stamp and learnt where it should be stuck on the postcard. We spent time reading the sign on the postbox stating the collection time. What time is it now? How long before they will be collected? When do you think the postcards will get there?

Thinking critically and being creative

- We looked at street maps of where we had been on our journey to the Post Office.
- The children drew their own maps of where they had been and what they had seen, from a new perspective – a bird's eye view . . . which included what was not seen but the children thought was there (lots of pipes and wires under the road).
- The children looked on maps to see where their postcards would be going. Which route might they take to get there? Did some need to go on a boat, a train or even an aeroplane?

- In the weeks that followed several children brought in postcards they had received from some *very* grateful grandmas. It was very gratifying to have been able to facilitate with such ease so many conversations about their learning and what they have been doing beyond the standard home–school link.

A sense of place case study: landscapes for growth

Background

The aim of this project was to devise a set of plausible designs and concepts that reinterpreted the traditional idea of the playground – to become a place of interaction to stimulate the imaginations and learning potential of young children. Even if there is no play-area makeover imminent, this is a worthwhile project as, by encouraging pupil voice, small additions can be made to the outside area that give children ownership of their space.

Exploring and playing

- The project began by observations of the children at play in the existing outside space. Photographs were taken that revealed several surprises . . . the bushes were actually a bat cave and the long grass was a special place 'to work in'.
- What potential was there in a space that had been designed by the children with their interests specifically in mind?
- An exploratory expedition was arranged where the children would make a journey across their own city of Cambridge, gathering information along the way. Cameras were provided for ease of recording of ideas.
- Likes and dislikes of features were discussed along the journey, some of which was undertaken on foot and some by bus, which gave the children another perspective – that of looking down from the top deck.

Being actively engaged

On return to school, the children's photographs were used in a variety of ways:

- To identify the location of the photograph on a map.
- The photographs were sorted using happy and sad face symbols into those features the children liked or disliked. The children then went on to explain why they had made their decisions.
- The photographs were ordered according to the route of the children's journey and the 'story' of their day was told.
- The children used red cubes/counters to place on photographs they considered to be dangerous or unsafe places and green cubes/counters for safe areas.
- The photos of run-down or dilapidated buildings or features were photocopied and the children encouraged to 'improve them' by drawing over them the features they would like to see (graffiti painted over with works of art, flower tubs, etc.).

Thinking critically and being creative

Using the children's own ideas, a collaborative plan was drawn up for an ideal outside play area. These ideas incorporated many of the features seen in the city streets – for example the creation of a variety of paths linking the different spaces, using slabs, bricks, and pebbles as found around the city. There were also ideas for tunnels and landscaping – but one of the most important was the idea for a 'gallery wall':

- This would be a place where artwork could be displayed.
- A series of concrete tiles or slabs would be created. These would have objects embedded in them that reflected the children's own interests and hobbies, or simply said something important about an individual child. The finished result would be a sort of 'time-capsule'.
- The children were asked to think carefully about what they would like to include in the tile. Discussions were had about the fact that once embedded there was no chance of getting the object back. Also important was the material and the importance of its resilience to weathering.

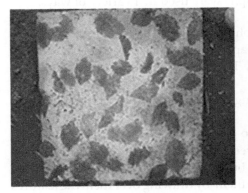

Figure 17.4 *Concrete slabs/tiles with embedded objects selected by the children*

- Moulds were created and the children added their objects, which included toy cars, an old cochlear implant from a partially-hearing child, old toothbrushes, marbles, sea shells, hama beads, autumn leaves, and plastic flowers.
- These tiles personalised the space and provided a great talking point. The children enjoyed revisiting to reflect on their past work and to see what each new class had made.

Pointers for teaching and learning about time and place in the Early Years

The following key points are important to recognise and remember when planning for activities in Early Years classrooms:

- Be aware of the contribution history and geography make to the growth of personal and social identity.
- It is important to explore why places and people are important to us personally as well as learning about different or new places and events.
- Ensure that activities and discussion promote investigation and enquiry.
- Provide opportunities for young children to explore known and unknown worlds and times through play, stories, maps, photographs, etc.
- First-hand experiences are central – especially, though not exclusively, through fieldwork investigations.

References

Hoodless, P. (2008) *Teaching History in Primary Schools*. London: Sage.

Further reading

Cooper, H. (2002) *History in the Early Years*, 2nd edition. London: Routledge Falmer.
Drummond, M.J., Myer, C., & Rich, D. (2008) *Learning: What Matters to Children*. Rich Learning Opportunities.
Edwards, C., Gandini, L., & Forman, G. (1998) *The Hundred Languages of Children*, 2nd edition. Westport CT: Ablex.
Palmer, J.A. & Birch, J.C. (2004) *Geography in the Early Years*, 2nd edition. London: Routledge Falmer.
Rich, D., Casanova, D., Dixon, A., Drummond, M.J., Durrant, A., & Myer, C. (2005) *First Hand Experience: What Matters to Children: An Alphabet of Learning from the Real World*. Rich Learning Opportunities.

Resources on the theme of babies or growing up

Once There Were Giants by Martin Waddell
Peepo! and *The Baby's Catalogue* by Janet and Allan Ahlberg
The stories about Alfie and Annie Rose and Lucy and Tom by Shirley Hughes
The Elephant and the Bad Baby by Elfrida Vipont
Charlie and Lola by Lauren Child
Mirror by Jeannie Baker
The poems and performances of Michael Rosen: start with 'Boogy Woogy Buggy';
    'Me and My Brother' is great too.
Music that we listen to at different times of life: lullabies, school songs, pop songs . . .
Art: 'The Graham Children' by Hogarth; Mary Cassat's paintings of children and
    parents; Norman Rockwell; Carl Larsson's depictions of family life
The Bethnal Green Museum of Childhood
Sudbury Hall National Trust Museum of Childhood

Resources on the theme of bags

My Granny's Purse by Paul Hanson
The Paper Bag Princess by Robert Munsch
The Shopping Basket by John Burningham
The Lighthouse Keeper's Lunch by Ronda and David Armitage
Handa's Surprise by Eileen Brown
Don't Forget the Bacon by Pat Hutchins
The Huge Bag of Worries by Virginia Ironside and Frank Rogers
Burglar Bill by Janet and Allan Ahlberg
Mary Poppins' bag; Paddington's suitcase; Tintin's rucksack
Bags for different professions (doctor; vets; district nurse; builder)
Artwork: Alexander Calder's suitcase filled with elements from Calder's circus

Resources on the theme of letters or postcards

The Jolly Postman by Janet and Allan Ahlberg
Dear Greenpeace by Simon James
Dear Daddy by Philippe Dupasquier
Postman Pat by John Cunliffe
Meerkat Mail by Emily Gravett
Katie Morag Delivers the Mail by Mairi Hedderwick
This Is the Night Mail, the poem by W.H. Auden as performed by John Grieson
Paintings of people posting /reading letters – e.g., posting a letter to Father Christmas.
    What might the letter say? How do you know?
Artwork: 'Souvenir of a journey to Courbron' by Jean-Baptiste-Camille Corot

Resources on the theme of journeys

We're Going on a Bear Hunt by Michael Rosen & Helen Oxenbury
Owl Babies by Martin Waddell
Window by Jeannie Baker
Where the Forest Meets the Sea by Jeannie Baker
Dinosaurs and All That Rubbish by Michael Foreman
The Little Boat by Kathy Henderson
Rosie's Walk by Pat Hutchins
Elephant Dance: A Journey to India by Theresa Heine
Don't Forget to Write by Martina Selway
The Wonderful Journey by Paul Geraghty
Dick Whittington (traditional)
We All Went on Safari: A Counting Journey through Tanzania by Laurie Krebs and Julia Cairns
Music and songs such as 'We're all going on a summer holiday' or 'The wheels on the bus'
Artwork such as that by Richard Long or Edward Bawden

CHAPTER 18

'Why is she all yellowy, Miss?'
'Why have you got two mums?'
'You can't use the pink – you're a boy!'

EMBRACING DIVERSITY AND DIFFERENCE
IN THE EARLY YEARS

Natalie Heath

Why does it matter that we reflect on issues of difference and diversity in Early Years practice given the diverse demands on us as educators? Behaviour management, assessment, curriculum, planning, child-centred teaching, special educational needs, and the outdoor learning environment: the list goes on when training to teach. This chapter aims to illustrate why, in order for us to be genuinely inclusive as teachers, it is vitally important that we consider children's home cultures, gender, ethnicity, and an array of other factors and influences which children bring with them into the classroom. As you will see, education has the very real potential to be an additional source of exclusion and disadvantage for many children, hence the urgent need for us as practitioners to critically consider diversity and difference and the ways in which we can strive to make the Early Years as open, accessible, fair, and inclusive to all children as we possibly can.

We have long known from research evidence that certain social, cultural, and ethnic groups are persistently underachieving and seem disadvantaged in a range of ways within our education system from the Early Years onwards. There has also long been concern over girls' experiences in education which has now been joined by popular concern over the underachievement of boys. So what does this mean for us as practitioners? The research evidence that we will consider in this chapter (e.g. Gillborn 2008) clearly suggests that schools must in some ways be implicated in the perpetuating of inequalities and disadvantages for some groups of students. Therefore there is an urgent need for us as Early Years practitioners actively to engage with these issues. We need to explore and address our own roles in relation to the perpetuation of such inequalities and find ways in which we can challenge them.

In the following pages we will explore how a genuinely child-centred approach, combined with critical engagement and reflection by practitioners, can allow all forms of difference and diversity to be embraced in positive ways which will hopefully, at the very least, enhance the experiences of all the children in our settings.

Ethnicity, educational experiences and achievement: what's the story?

From Foundation Stage Profiles, SATs, GCSEs, and A-Level results we are able to see and compare how boys and girls, children in receipt of free school meals, and children from different ethnic groups are doing within the English education system.

With regard to ethnicity, data shows that some ethnic groups perpetually underachieve throughout their schooling. African Caribbean students, especially boys, and Roma gypsy/ traveller children are at the most at risk of achieving considerably below the national average. For example, in 2011/12 pupils from a black background achieving five or more GCSEs at grade A* to C or equivalent including English and Mathematics were 4.2 percentage points below the national average. There was an even larger gap of nearly 10 percentage points for Black Caribbean students, and Roma gypsy/ traveller children were nearly 40 per cent below national average at GCSE attainment (DFE 2013, p. 4).

The possible reasons for these inequalities are complex given that it is difficult to isolate ethnicity from both gender and social class. However, research by Gillborn and Mirza (2000) clearly suggests that even when you control for gender and class effects there are significant inequalities linked to ethnicity. Research suggests that teacher expectations and stereotypes may be related to these inequalities. Gillborn's work (2008) shows that underachieving ethnic groups score less well on the current Foundation Stage Profile (FSP) than they did on the previous Baseline Assessment. This is interesting given that the Baseline Assessment was much more prescriptive and relied less heavily on teachers' own observations and personal judgements. This implies that practitioner expectations and stereotypes may shape the behaviour of children in their care or colour the ways in which practitioners perceive the ability and educational progress of children from different groups. Again this was supported by DFES research (2006) which showed that teachers gave children with English as an Additional Language (EAL) lower national curriculum levels for their work compared with the levels they gained in externally marked tests. Youdell's work (2003) identifies the ways in which teachers are likely to see certain students, in this case African Caribbean boys, as presenting a challenge to authority and being generally problematic for the teacher.

The data here is powerful and suggests that we as practitioners may, in some ways, be implicated in continuing, rather than challenging, inequalities. Gillborn (2008) argues that teachers, schools, and the education system may all be implicated in maintaining a 'normative sense of whiteness' rather than challenging what we are doing in our classrooms. Certainly, in the 1970s and 1980s there was discussion of the ways in which the school curriculum was colour-blind. It continues to be argued that education policies have a tendency to be colour-blind, where ethnicity is not explicitly addressed, as the education system is viewed to be largely fair and equitable for all children (Gillborn & Ladson-Billings 2004). This, however, means that inequalities can be ignored as irrelevant to schooling, which is highly problematic given the very visible inequalities in attainment that we can see in the data.

Reflection

Reflect for a moment on your own stereotypes. Picture a high achieving, motivated child who is always on task, keen to engage with the adults and children in the setting, attends well on the carpet, doesn't challenge your behaviour expectations and so on…

- Are they male or female?
- What ethnicity are they?
- Is English their first language?
- Are they receiving free school meals?

When teaching, we need to reflect on our responses, attitudes, and stereotypes to the children in our classes. Do we have different expectations for different children, and, if so, why? How might these differing expectations shape and influence the children's experiences in the setting? We also need to think about our classrooms and teaching in relation to all the children in our classes. Does the curriculum engage all children, or does it only focus on white traditions? Do children from a wide range of cultures and ethnic backgrounds and with different levels of English find things in the setting to identify with and which can act as bridges between their familiar home cultures and the different world which they find themselves in at school?

How do we embrace ethnic diversity in our settings without being tokenistic?

The idea of embracing multiculturalism in the classroom is not a new idea and most schools aim to value multicultural ideas and acknowledge a range of religious traditions and beliefs. There is a danger with this strategy, however, in that it can lead to a piecemeal approach to engaging with diversity. The school and practitioners may celebrate a number of religious and cultural festivals with the children, such as Eid, Harvest, Easter, Hanukkah, and Diwali, in a fun and colourful but ultimately tokenistic fashion. It has the potential further to isolate children if their home culture, ethnicity, or religion is only addressed through specific cultural festivals or on certain days. Engaging with diversity in your classroom is not just about celebrating Eid or Diwali, but is about reflecting all year round, day in, day out on:

Figure 18.1 *Chopsticks and bangles: a wide range of resources from different cultures for children to explore*

- **The curriculum**: What are we teaching and why? Is it appropriate and accessible to all our children? Do we reflect on the content and what it means for all our children?
- **Everyday practice**: Do our stereotypes, words, and actions advantage or disadvantage certain children? Are we providing real links between home and school cultures?
- **Resources**: Do our resources allow children to embrace diversity through their play?

Practical ways to address ethnicity: hints and tips

Curriculum: Think carefully about what the children are learning about. Can you find ways to embrace difference?

Role play area: Have a range of resources reflecting a diversity of cultures available all the time for children to use, rather than just when celebrating a particular festival. For example, chopsticks in the home corner, a range of clothes from lots of cultures in the dressing-up box.

Displays: Show that text can be communicated in a range of languages. For example at a writing area you can display different alphabets and key words in languages spoken by the children in your class and school.

Resources: Provide and share books with stories and characters from many cultures and countries. Have available to the children dual language books and dolls and small-world people from a range of cultures/ethnicities.

(Continued)

(Continued)

Music: Make sure that the classroom repertoire of songs and music embraces as many cultures as possible. Sing songs in different languages and listen to different styles of music as part of everyday classroom practice. Have instruments from around the world available at all times for the children to use.

Involving parents/community: Encourage parents to come into the setting to share their home cultures with the children as often as you can. Also reflect carefully on whether all parents feel equally able to access your advice as their children's teacher. Is there a language barrier for some parents due to low levels of English or not being able to read? How is your school addressing this?

Gender and education

'The gender gap is widening.' 'Girls out-perform boys yet again.' The popular media is rife with social comment about gender and achievement. Every summer as GCSE and A-Level results are published the differences in performance between boys and girls are analysed and reflected on. The available data shows that there are some differences in achievement between the genders. In 2011/12, 86.3 per cent of girls achieved 5 or more GCSEs at grade A* to C compared to 79.8 per cent of boys, with a wider gap when you include English and Maths GCSEs of 63.6 per cent of girls achieving the 5 A* to C grades compared with 54.2 per cent of boys (DFE 2013, p. 2).

There is currently much concern over the disengagement of boys within the education system. The lack of male role models in the early and primary years has been highlighted with schools now actively recruiting men. There has also been debate about the potentially different learning styles of boys and girls which need to be catered for in the classroom.

Whilst the attainment gap in relation to gender is relatively small, there is no escaping the fact that many children from a very young age already have very stereotypical ideas about gender. One only has to look in toy shops and at television adverts aimed at children to see that alarmingly stereotyped gender roles are still being relentlessly transmitted to children. Many toys and other products for children are colour coded along a pink/blue divide and the large majority of toys are designed with a specific gender in mind. Anything pink, fluffy, creative and involving home-based activities is packaged to appeal to girls, who are inculcated into a culture where to be female you have to like pink, and vice versa for boys. Whilst with the introduction of GCSE exams we saw girls and boys being more likely to take subjects once seen largely as the preserve of one gender or another, we only have to look at course choices in further and higher education and at the labour market to see that women and men are still often playing very different roles. Work by Reay

(1998) and Younger and Warrington (2008) demonstrate ways in which such gender role stereotypes and inequalities are perpetuated in educational settings.

As Early Years practitioners it is important to consider our own views on gender, the stereotypes we may unconsciously draw on, and the kinds of messages we are explicitly and implicitly transmitting to children about what it means to be male or female.

Reflection

Reflect for a moment on a summary of two children from their reception class teacher:

Alex is five in the last term of reception. Alex loves the colour pink and was very excited to share at news time getting a pink scooter at the weekend. Exploring the dressing-up box is a favourite activity and Alex's favourite outfit to wear is currently the wedding dress. Alex loves to line up all the teddy bears to listen to stories. Alex has very good levels of concentration, is always the first child on the carpet, and takes great pleasure in showing finished work to the teacher and bringing in pictures and arts and crafts made at home.

Frankie is one of the youngest in the reception class. Frankie struggles to listen at carpet time, liking to distract the other children by making funny noises. It takes much persuasion to get Frankie to sit down at a table in the classroom to do a written activity, which Frankie clearly finds difficult. Holding the pencil correctly is especially tricky. Frankie is happiest outside, digging in the sand, practising ball skills or den building with sticks and sheets of fabric.

What gender do you think Alex and Frankie are?

Drawing conclusions about gender based on stereotypes is very difficult to avoid as we automatically group things that are similar together. Alex appears to be a girl given the love of pink and so on, whereas Frankie appears to embody many of the qualities we associate with boys in the classroom. However, the teacher's comments above were referring to a boy called Alex and a girl called Frankie. Did you assume that Alex was a girl and Frankie a boy? The cameos described above illustrate many of the commonly held assumptions about boys and girls in the Early Years. It is often argued that girls are more likely to have good fine-motor skills, enjoy sitting and concentrating on tasks, be imaginative, and so on. On the other hand, there is the assumption that boys find concentration harder, find fine-motor activities more demanding, and prefer to manipulate real-life materials on a larger scale in the outdoors. Whilst these arguments are useful to evaluate the provision we offer and to consider whether we are meeting the needs of both boys and girls, they may also in some ways continue to perpetuate stereotyped approaches to gender.

What should our role as Early Years practitioners be with regards to gender?

In the Early Years children need to feel free to explore the world around them, pursuing their own interests. Inevitably children are largely shaped by family cultures and other forces which impinge on childhood, such as television, media, and toy manufacturers. But, ideally, the Early Years classroom, if following a child-centred approach, needs to allow children freely to explore a range of masculinities and femininities. If we base our teaching around each child's own unique learning journey we also avoid grouping all boys and all girls together in relation to the stereotypes discussed above. Children need to play and explore with a wide range of materials and to have the opportunity to access many different kinds of learning approaches. The classroom needs to be a place where we challenge traditional gender roles and assumptions which the children may hold. For example, the little girl who is quoted in the title of this chapter telling a boy that he can't choose to use a pink crayon because pink is only for girls needs to be challenged in her thinking on this. We need to consider gender when we think about:

- **The curriculum**: What are we teaching and why? Does the content appeal to all children? Does it favour girls or boys in some ways? How do we make what we teach accessible to all the children?

Figure 18.2 *Putting out the fire: role play areas allow the children to challenge assumed gender stereotypes*

- **Everyday practice**: Do our stereotypes, words, and actions advantage or disadvantage certain children? Think about the language we use with the children: do we ask for strong boys to move the PE equipment and some kind girls to help a child who is lonely? Many of these things we do without even thinking about it!
- **Resources**: Do our resources reflect the challenging of stereotypes or do they perpetuate them? Do we have books where children and adults of both genders engage with a wide range of activities in non-stereotyped play? Do small-world toys in the classroom allow children to act out many different roles for boys and girls? Do we encourage children to access and try a wide range of activities, materials, and resources?

Practical ways to address gender inequalities: hints and tips

- **Language we use with children and our own expectations**: Critically consider your own views of boys and girls within your classroom. Think about the ways in which you may inadvertently shape children's behaviour by the language that you use. Do you convey to the children particular views of what boys and girls should be doing. Do you say 'What a kind boy' as often as you say 'What a kind girl'? And the same for the word 'strong' – do you use it in relation to girls as well as boys?
- **Curriculum content/ activities that are accessible for all children**: Does the curriculum contain particular gender messages? For example, do you consider important women in history as well as men? If there are particular activities and tasks which certain children do not want to engage in, try changing the setting and context of where, when, and how these activities take place in order for them to appeal to a wider range of learning styles, be they gender related or otherwise. For example, if you have children who have trouble with fine-motor skills provide activities in a range of locations indoors and outside which would help with this, e.g., tweezers and a pot of tiny interesting items, different textures of play-dough to push and pull, screwdrivers and items with screws to undo.
- **Role play area**: Use the role play area to allow children to try out a wide range of activities exploring all kinds of gender roles. A role play florist's shop, space station, or fire station, for example, allows the children to take on lots of different roles and challenges gender stereotypes.
- **Literature**: Try to make sure that there are plenty of stories showing children and adults engaging in a wide range of roles.
- **Role models** - Try to use parents and other adults to model a wide range of jobs and interests that people have. Try to encourage both male and female carers to be involved in classroom activities.

Social class and poverty

As Early Years teachers we very rarely explicitly address social class in relation to our teaching. For many it is seen as a controversial or challenging idea best avoided. However, the current evidence shows that children in receipt of free school meals (FSM) are the most disadvantaged within our education system. The inequalities for children in receipt of FSM compared to those not on free school meals are stark at all levels of schooling. In 2011/12, at GCSE level 36.3 per cent of children known to be eligible for FSM achieved five A* to C GCSEs including iGCSEs compared with 62.6 per cent of all other students (DFE 2013, p. 5).

The gaps here are consistently much wider than for gender and ethnicity. The data we have is limited as we do not know how children from each social class fraction do within education. Instead we have to make do with comparing children in receipt of FSM with those who are not. We assume that children in receipt of FSM are growing up with a degree of poverty and their parents may be working-class, in the sense of having low levels of academic qualifications. So why do these children fare so much worse in our schools, despite having been a huge focus for government support and intervention over the last decade?

Research evidence suggests that it is not the case that parents of children in receipt of FSM do not care about their children's education. In fact, quite the opposite appears to be the case. However, these families face so many additional challenges that they are not as successful in supporting their children as their middle-class counterparts (Crozier 2000; Reay 1998; Vincent 1996). Bourdieu's ideas of cultural and social capital (1997) are helpful here in explaining and understanding the potential causes of these inequalities. As both Lareau (2003) and Reay show, some parents are more able to advantage their children within the education system than others. Cultural capital refers to the dominant forms of culture in a society which are valued by the dominant groups within that society. School expectations reflect those of the dominant groups in society. Hence whether or not families have access to these dominant forms of cultural capital affects how well children are able to engage with schooling. In the Early Years setting there will be some children whose parents have had the time and financial resources to provide all kinds of enriching experiences for their children from a very young age. These children may well find the expectations of school easier to cope with if they have already been to pre-school music or gym groups, story times at the local library and so on. All these activities will have taught the children how to follow instructions, perform complex tasks, and listen carefully.

Children who have not had these pre-school experiences may find certain aspects of school life much harder. If children come from a home where parents cannot read or do not have the resources to buy or borrow books, then these children will be disadvantaged from the beginning in a classroom where listening to stories and engaging with books is central. Social capital is also important here. It refers to the social networks which individuals have and how these social relationships may advantage or disadvantages individuals. Families which have a wide range of social relationships and high levels of social skills are successfully able to engage with the teacher and to support their children's navigation of the education system.

In contrast, members of some families may have had negative experiences of schooling themselves and may feel threatened by the institution of the school. They are less likely to be able to engage with and seek support from the teacher to help their children within the education system. Hence, as Reay argues, parents care deeply about their children's success but some parents are much better placed to engage with the school and teachers, and also to help and enrich their children's learning through help with homework, listening to reading, trips, holidays, and extra-curricular activities.

There is also a whole range of practical issues which families living in poverty often face which may impact on children's engagement and progress in the Early Years and beyond. Simple aspects like not having access to breakfast, or living in unsuitable temporary accommodation with no space or resources for play, or family uncertainty about housing, employment, or asylum status may all play a part.

What is our role in addressing these social and financial inequalities?

The fact that such stark inequalities persist in relation to social class implies that schools are not adequately addressing the issues and barriers which some children face when engaging with education. Obviously schools are not the only influences on children and may not be able to overcome all inequalities, but at the least it is vital to reflect on potential difficulties which children face in light of family background and cultural capital.

- **Classroom routines**: Find a range of ways to introduce Early Years children to classroom routines and bear in mind that not all children will have had access to the same resources and experiences prior to entering school.
- **Broadening experiences**: Consider ways in which you can provide opportunities to enrich children's experiences if there are experiences which they are not able to access outside of school. Can you organise a class trip or visitors to the classroom to support children with topic work if they have not had prior experience of an activity? Can you provide extra books, story sacks, or paper and pens to allow parents to do learning activities with the children? Reflect on the different experiences of children in your setting and the different support they might need to access different areas of learning.
- **Genuine engagement with parents**: Consider any barriers which parents/carers may face in accessing the school and engaging with practitioners. If parents have had negative experiences of education themselves, how can you engage them? Remember that parents will have very different skills and resources when it comes to engaging with the institution of the school. Speaking to teachers may

be a source of great anxiety for parents, particularly if they have only had negative experiences from their own schooling. They may feel threatened or anxious and may not know the appropriate channels to go through when they have worries or concerns about their children. Think about ways that you can put parents at ease and help them to voice and explore their concerns with you. Building good relationships with all carers is critical here, and in the Early Years, where we have easier access to parents and carers, this can be as simple as sharing a quick positive word with as many carers as possible at home time. Remember that writing in home–school diaries and reading records is not easy for all families if they have low levels of literacy or English as an additional language.

- **Valuing home and school cultures and raising expectations**: Try to find ways to engage positively with aspects of children's home cultures, seeing them as different rather than deficient. Also consider ways in which your own stereotypes and expectations of certain children may influence their experiences.
- **Be sensitive to the needs of the children**: Be aware of the additional needs which children living in poverty bring with themselves to your setting. Lupton (2006) talks about the ways in which some primary schools in disadvantaged areas are often unpredictable places due to the wide ranging issues which children may bring with them to the classroom. You need to consider this in order to ensure that all children are equally able to access the classroom experiences you are providing.

But it's not just race, class, and gender . . .

As you can see, there is no straightforward answer to addressing the inequalities we have considered so far. Each child's situation is unique, with very particular gender, ethnicity, health, social and educational needs, family culture, and so on, all of which will affect their learning experiences.

When we reflect on diversity and difference in the classroom we need to be aware that gender, ethnicity, and class/poverty are not the only sources of difference and inequality which the children are shaped by and experience. Difference and diversity come in a whole range of forms. There are many other factors which may affect how children engage with education and which also need to be addressed in the setting if we are to genuinely embrace difference and diversity with the children.

Special educational needs and specific physical limitations/ disabilities, behavioural or emotional needs

It is as vital to address the individual-level needs of children as the broader categories. Young children are often very aware of differences but at the same time are often very accepting and accommodating. As a teacher you have a key role in helping children to be accepted by their peers and finding ways to allow all children to fit into their class and form positive relationships. Inclusion is the key idea here, but one that raises lots of questions. Firstly, there are the practical aspects of how you fit children with specific needs into your setting. How do you give them equal access to learning activities, and how do you empower them to engage with things which may be challenging? Children with a wide range of physical, emotional, and behavioural needs must be included fully within the life of the classroom and school. So how do other children view their peers with additional needs? As a teacher it is important to model inclusive practice by showing the children how you can find ways to include those children who need additional support. At the same time, children in your setting may be very aware of the ways in which some children differ to them or appear to be treated differently by staff and need help to understand why this is.

Having a wide range of learning resources is vital to allow all children access to learning regardless of physical or psychological challenges. You also need to think about how best to arrange and manage the classroom space and routines in order to give all children access to the activities and to make the classroom as comfortable as possible. For example, you may need to make a calm, neutral uncluttered space for an autistic child, or adapt resources so that a child with a physical disability can access all areas of learning. It is also important to have resources that model differences to all the children in a class – for example, small-world toys which include children in wheelchairs and books which reflect and explore the range of needs children can have.

Families as enormously diverse and often reconstituted (one-parent, two-parent, step-families, extended families, and same-sex parents)

In the last thirty years we have seen a huge divergence away from the nuclear family with increasing numbers of children living with one biological parent, living in a step family or with two parents of the same gender. Hence there are a number of ways in which children may find themselves with two mums or dads, or with other family structures different from those of their peers. Young children often comment on such differences, so it is useful to reflect in advance on ways to enter into dialogue about these issues. There is a growing range of useful children's books which specifically engage with these differences in age-appropriate ways.

Additional aspects to consider, which may be a source of difference for children in the Early Years setting include:

- Very different home cultures and religions.
- Growing up in care.
- Being a young carer for a sibling or parent.
- Having a family member in prison.
- Bereavement or physical or psychological health difficulties of close family members.

Why do challenging questions always happen at home time? Answering children's questions

It is often assumed that individual differences and inequalities pass young children by, but as anyone working with young children knows they are astute observers of the social world and will often ask very complex questions about social affairs. As one three-year-old asked me, 'Jack's Daddy made bad choices. Is that why he doesn't live with him?' This was followed by 'Why do some children only live with one grown-up?' I also vividly remember two children in a nursery sitting next to each other in the cloakroom. One child turned to the other and asked, directly, 'Why is your skin all yellowy coloured?'

Early years practitioners need to be able to respond carefully and sensitively to children's questions like those above and in this chapter's title. If children are to be independent learners then questioning and thinking ideas through is a central part of this and through the very nature of children's questions we can understand further how they view the world and social experiences around them. So the challenge is what to do when faced with these big questions, which are guaranteed to be asked at the most awkward moments, like at 3.15 pm when the bell has rung for home time and you are trying to get thirty impatient children into their coats.

Young children want to feel valued and listened to, and that their views and ideas are taken seriously. Sometimes it will be appropriate to answer a question with the whole class, whilst at other times a very specific question may be best discussed quietly with an individual or small group of children. Regardless of the context, it is important to genuinely engage in discussion with the children about the issues and concerns which they themselves experience. Again, having a wide range of children's books which sensitively address issues of diversity is important for helping children to accept differences between individuals that they experience.

Teachers need to model positive interactions with all children and to acknowledge and embrace aspects of diversity and difference which children bring with them.

Conclusions

So how do we in the Early Years setting address all the issues raised in this chapter? Ultimately, as educators we want to create learning environments where all children are fairly treated, are able to reach their true potential, and are not held back by prejudice in any form. We also want to ensure that the children learn to respect one another and the differences between them. In our currently diverse society and increasingly globalised world it is vital that we prepare children to accept differences and to learn to be fair and tolerant of others who may hold very different views, beliefs, and values.

Do we give up now with this seemingly impossible task? What does this overarching inclusion really look like in practice? A genuinely child-centred approach to education starting from the children's own positions can allow difference and diversity to be embraced in positive ways which will hopefully enhance and benefit the experiences of all the children in the setting. Our primary task as teachers is to be constantly reflective on our own practice, our influences on the children, and our interpretations and expectations of the children. Are these disadvantaging any children, are we creating stereotyped gender expectations or assuming that the African Caribbean boy in our setting is going to have challenging behaviour? Are we considerate of individual needs and of the fact that some home cultures may be at odds with the expectations of the school?

We also need to consider the practical functions of our classroom and ways of working with the children to encourage an understanding and respect of difference whilst also fostering a sense of community and intrinsic values for all human beings.

Pointers for diversity in the Early Years

- **Reflect**, reflect, reflect on your role as a teacher and your own prejudices and stereotypes, which may shape how you view and respond to children in your setting.
- **Evaluate** what your setting offers for children from diverse ethnic backgrounds.
- **Focus** on how gender roles are portrayed and transmitted in your classroom.
- **Look** for ways in which you might make active links for children between their home and school cultures and consider the ways in which poverty may adversely impact on learning experiences for children in your class.
- **Expand** the range of strategies you use to include all children within your setting who may have a wide range of special individual needs and come from very diverse families with distinct cultures.
- **Challenge** the assumptions and stereotypes about underachievement, encouraging all children to succeed.
- **Talk** sensitively and honestly with the children in your setting in age-appropriate ways, to answer their acknowledgements of, and questions about, diversity and difference.

References

Bourdieu, P. (1997) 'The Forms of Capital.' In A.H. Halsey, H. Lauder, P. Brown, & A. Stuart Wells (Eds.), *Education, Culture Economy and Society*. Oxford: Oxford University Press.

Crozier G. (2000) *Parents and Schools: Partners or Protagonists?* London: Trentham Books.

DFE. (2013) *SFR 04/2013: GCSE and Equivalent Attainment by Pupil Characteristics in England, 2011/12.* London: Department for Education.

DFES. (2006) *Research Topic Paper: Ethnicity and Education: The Evidence on Minority Ethnic Pupils Aged 5–16.* Available at http://www.education.gov.uk/research/data/uploadfiles/DFES-0208-2006.pdf

Gillborn, D. (2008) *Racism and Education: Coincidence or Conspiracy?* London: Routledge.

Gillborn, D. & Ladson-Billings, G. (2004) *The Routledge Falmer Reader in Multicultural Education.* London: RoutledgeFalmer.

Gillborn, D. & Mirza, H.S. (2000) *Educational Inequality: Mapping Race, Class and Gender – A Synthesis of Research Evidence.* London: Office for Standards in Education. Available at http://www.ofsted.gov.uk/content/download/1779/12012/file/Educational%20inequality%20mapping%20race,%20class%20and%20gender%20(PDF%20format).pdf

Lareau, A. (2003) *Unequal Childhoods.* Berkeley: University of California Press.

Lupton, R. (2006) 'Schools in Disadvantaged Areas: Low Attainment and a Contextualised Policy Response.' In H. Lauder, P. Brown, J. Dillabough, & A.H. Halsey (Eds.), *Education, Globalization and Social Change.* Oxford: Oxford University Press (pp. 654–672).

Reay, D. (1998) *Class Work: Mothers' Involvement in Their Children's Primary Schooling.* London: Taylor and Francis.

Vincent, C. (1996) *Parents and Teachers: Power and Participation.* London: Falmer Press.

Youdell, D. (2003) 'Identity Traps or How Black Students Fail: The Interactions between Biographical, Subcultural, and Learner Identities.' *British Journal of Sociology*, 24 (1).

Younger, M. & Warrington, M. (2008) 'The Gender Agenda in Primary Teacher Education in England: Fifteen Lost Years?' *Journal of Education Policy*, 23 (4).

The way forward

CHAPTER 19

Whatever next?

FUTURE TRENDS IN EARLY YEARS EDUCATION

Mary Jane Drummond

In this chapter I explore the proposition that the ways in which we think and talk about young children can and do affect the ways in which we provide for their learning and support their development. To put it another way, what we know about children, or think we know, shapes what we do for them in the name of education. I examine some ways of thinking about children, and children's learning, taken from recent accounts of Early Years classrooms (and other settings) and try to show how we might take steps to re-organise and re-shape our thoughts, our assumptions and our expectations. Future developments in Early Years education will, I believe, spring from the efforts of educators who prioritise the serious work of thinking for themselves about children's learning, and thereby achieve an enhanced understanding of children and childhood.

Teachers teaching and children learning

One of the most challenging and entertaining books I have ever read about children's learning is *GNYS AT WRK: A Child Learns to Write and Read* (Bissex 1980). It is a detailed, vivid, first-hand narrative account of how five-year-old Paul became an accomplished writer and reader; what makes it unique is not just its puzzling title (taken from a notice Paul pinned over his workbench-desk at the age of five years six months) but its insider's viewpoint: the author, Glenda L. Bissex, is Paul's mother. She was also, when the story began, a teacher studying for her master's degree in education. One afternoon, when she was trying to read, Paul wanted to play with her. Frustrated in his attempts to make her put down her book, Paul disappeared for a few minutes, returning with a piece of paper, on which he had printed, with rubber stamps from his printing set, the letters RUDF ('Are you deaf?') His mother was dumbstruck and, in her own words, 'Of course I put down my book'.

The bulk of the book comprises Bissex's regular observations of her son's acts of writing and reading, illustrated with copious extracts from the written material that Paul produced over the six years of the study: there are excerpts from stories, lists, notices, books of jokes, report cards for his pets (including marks for PEING) and, in due course, when he started school (at 5 years 10 months) his first written texts from the classroom – sadly stilted, after the richness of his earlier output. For example, at 6 year 10 months he writes at school 'This is my reading book', whereas 3 months earlier, at home and in just one day, he had written four newspapers, complete with cartoons, news, advertising and weather (THE SAFTERNEWN IT'S GOING TO RAIN).

Bissex's commentary and conclusions are based on her privileged position as both mother and teacher. With a kind of binocular vision she sees some disconcerting truths about how educators intervene in children's learning. In one memorable passage she writes:

> We speak of starting with a child 'where he is', which in one sense is not to assert an educational desideratum but an inescapable fact; there is no other place the child can start from. There are only other places the educator can start from.
>
> (Bissex 1980, p. 111)

I hope I am not alone in finding this insight an uncomfortable one. Bissex seems to me to be suggesting, all too credibly, that educators do (sometimes? often?) start in 'other places', and that the consequences for children's learning are frequently undesirable. Furthermore, this suggestion seems to be an alternative version of the proposition with which I began: that how we think and talk about children – or 'the child' – is of crucial importance in how we educate them, or him, or her. And this proposition, however we phrase it, raises questions worth worrying about. If Early Years educators do not, as Bissex suggests, start 'where the child is', with a coherent and principled understanding of the child's learning, then where do they start? And why? Can we learn to move closer to a more desirable starting point? What would it look like? What do we really mean by this 'educational desideratum', or a principled understanding of children?

My conviction that Bissex is telling us something important about teaching and learning is based on two distinct sources of evidence: first, my own experiences as an educator and observer in Early Years classrooms and other settings for young children, and, secondly, written accounts and research studies of what Early Years educators actually do, and how they conceptualise the relationship between teaching and learning.

My own first-hand experience tells me that – all too often – my carefully prepared activities, my lovingly drawn-up topic webs, my finely adjusted schemes of work, have failed to connect with children's pressing intellectual and social concerns, or with their energetic and enquiring minds. My observations in other classrooms have, over the years, confirmed my awareness of what I think of as 'the curriculum gap', the distance, sometimes a hair's breadth, sometimes a yawning chasm, that stands between what educators teach and what children learn.

If there is such a gap, and I am certain that there is, at least some of the time, in every setting for young children, I am equally certain that it cannot be attributed to malice or apathy in the hearts and minds of Early Years educators. Nor do published studies of children's early experiences at school (Wells 1987, Hughes 1989, or Brooker 2002, for example) resort to the language of blame to account for what they see in classrooms. These authors do not mince words in identifying the mismatch between the educators' benevolent and educational intentions and the children's learning. But nor do they suggest that educators deliberately disable learners, or consciously create dysfunctional learning environments. So what is going wrong? And what can we do to put it right?

Some of the evidence suggests that part of the problem lies in the weakness of the language in which we describe and justify our work. In an early study of infant teachers' thinking (or, rather, a study of what infant teachers are prepared to say about their work to investigative sociologists), Sharp and Green (1975) report an interview with 'Mrs Carpenter', a teacher of a vertically-grouped class of rising-5s to rising-7s. The discussion turned to the need for structure in teaching, and proceeded as follows:

Interviewer: How do you mean?

Teacher: I mean we all, well, I have a little plan but I don't really ... I just sort of, mmm, try and work out what stage each child is at and take it from there.

Interviewer: How do you do this? How does one notice what stage a child is at?

Teacher: Oh we don't really know, you can only say the stage he isn't at really, because you know when a child doesn't know but you don't really know when he knows. Do you see what I mean? You can usually tell when they don't know (long pause). (There was a distraction in the interview at this point.) What was I talking about?

Interviewer: Certain stages, knowing when they know –

Teacher: – and when they don't know. But even so, you still don't know, when they really don't (pause) you can't really say they don't know, can you? ... That's why really that plan they wanted wouldn't have worked. I wouldn't have been able to stick to it, because you just don't ... you know when they don't know, you don't know when they know.

Interviewer: How do you know when they don't know?

Teacher: How do I know when they don't know? (pause) Well, no, it's not so much that you don't know. I know when they're not ready to know, perhaps that's a better way of putting it.

(Sharp & Green 1975, p. 168)

The disarming candour of these statements should not blind us to the poverty of the understanding they express. This teacher, for all her good intentions, which I am willing to take for granted, is unlikely to be able to start 'where the child is'. She does not, on the evidence of this interview, have a way of explaining, even to herself, what it is that the educator knows when she or he knows where a child is, or what it is that the educator must then do with that knowledge.

Sharp and Green's work has been succeeded by other enquiries, less ideologically driven, but reaching similarly worrying conclusions. For example, Bennett et al. (1984) investigated the match between tasks and pupils, and identified a chronic weakness in educators' skills of diagnosis. In this carefully planned and cautiously quantified study of 'the quality of pupil learning experiences', the researchers found that more than half of the observed tasks were badly matched to the child's level of understanding and achievement. High attainers were regularly underestimated and low attainers overestimated (p. 65).

The diagnostic skills of a group of 17 experienced infant teachers were studied in detail. As part of an inservice course, they were asked to examine transcriptions of some of the mismatched tasks recorded in the early part of the study. They were invited to discuss what seemed to be going on, to hypothesise about the children's understanding, and to explore any questions raised by the observations. The authors report that the teachers were extremely unwilling to respond to the classroom material in this way. 'They saw all problems as self evident . . . (they) made no use of the notion of hunch or hypothesis . . . all problems were to be solved by direct teaching' (p.197). It seems as though these teachers' prime concern was with the quality of teaching, and that they had correspondingly little interest in learning.

Evidence from studies such as these suggests that there is indeed a serious problem. The professional language of the Early Years educator does not seem to be robust enough to frame adequate or effective descriptions of children and their learning. It is, I believe, not just the looseness and vagueness of the words we use that let us down, but a more fundamental issue. Starting 'where the child is', for all its familiarity as a slogan, as an 'educational desideratum', is simply not the best place to start; it is not an effective way of conceptualising the enterprise of Early Years education.

'To have' and 'to be'

I am influenced in this argument by the work of Erich Fromm, sociologist and psychoanalyst, who suggested in *To Have or To Be* (1976) that the human condition in general is suffering from the dominance of western society's desire 'to have', at the expense of our understanding of what it is 'to be'. Applying this distinction to Early Years education, to its curriculum, its pedagogy, and its most idealistic aspirations, suggests to me that there is a need to re-emphasise our understanding of what children are, rather than where they are, or what we want them to have. Since, as Fromm says, 'there is no being that is not, at the same time, becoming and changing,' it follows that, if we know what we want children to be, in the first four or five years of their educational lives, then we are likely to be effective in helping them to become the well-educated seven or eight-year-olds who will move into the next stage of their education. We will be well placed too, during their years of early education, to support to the utmost their present 'powers to be' – another of Fromm's memorable phrases (in *Man for Himself* 1949).

Since reading and re-reading Fromm, I have been drawing on his concept of children's 'powers to be' in my thinking and writing, and I am slowly becoming convinced of the strength of this starting point in thinking about the future of Early Years education. This vital phase of education has, until recently, straddled the statutory/pre-statutory divide. Now the years from birth to five are known as the Early Years Foundation Stage, and educators are being encouraged to think of this period as a distinct phase of education. By the time they enter Key Stage One, 'Foundation Stage children' will have been living and learning for five solid years, in their homes and in a bewildering variety of other settings. But both before and after the children's fifth birthdays, we, their educators, are still at liberty to think about them in ways that match our philosophy and our principles. Whatever new official frameworks are prescribed for us in the future by successive Departments of Education, we can still choose to think about learning and learners for ourselves, using the categories and concepts of official policy documents as a support, not a substitute, for our own thinking work. And my argument is that we cannot do better than to think in terms of what we know for certain about children's powers – their powers to do, to think, to feel, to know and understand, to represent and express. There is no requirement for us to think of children in the Early Years as students of numeracy, literacy and so on. If children's learning is our priority, there are more effective ways to be their educators than by surrendering our own powers to think to the volumes of guidance we have so generously been offered.

By way of encouragement, we would be wise to turn to the Early Years curriculum document in use in New Zealand (Ministry of Education 1996), which sets out guide- lines for the education of children from birth to age six (the age of starting school). The Maori title of this bilingual document, *Te Whāriki*, refers to a traditional hand- made mat which can be woven in an infinite variety of patterns; it represents the idea that the planned curriculum, based on commonly agreed goals and principles, can have a different pattern for every kind of Early Years service, in every individual Early Years centre. This, in itself, is a stimulating approach from the perspective of this country, but even more challenging is the set of ideas embodied in the five goals that constitute the heart of the guidelines.

These goals are:

1 **well-being** (the health and well-being of the child are protected and nurtured)
2 **belonging** (children and their families feel a sense of belonging)
3 **contribution** (opportunities for learning are equitable and each child's contribu- tion is valued)
4 **communication** (the languages and symbols of their own and other cultures are promoted and protected)
5 **exploration** (the child learns through active exploration of the environment)

Early years educators in New Zealand, in whatever kind of setting, are invited to commit themselves to these goals for children; some of them may seem to go almost without saying, but others are well worth thinking about more carefully. The goal of well-being fits securely within the English tradition; we are still proudly conscious of our legacy from the great pioneers of early education: Rachel and Margaret McMillan, for example, working in the back streets of Bradford and Deptford to bring health and hygiene into the lives of young children (Steedman 1990). The goal of communication is equally likely to receive general assent from Early Years educators here, though it may be some years yet before our Department for Education publishes its curriculum guidelines in two languages. But the goals of belonging and contributing are radical departures from our familiar ways of thinking.

In these goals, it seems to me, the New Zealand educators are boldly articulating their aspirations for children's 'powers to be'; they are explicitly prioritising the principle that children can, and should, be members of a harmonious community, in which they have a place, to which they can make a contribution. This is a way of thinking about young children, and the education they deserve that, I believe, we might enthusiastically try for ourselves.

The New Zealand representation of children's powers set out in *Te Whariki* reads easily enough across onto a model of children's learning that is proposed in a series of questions set out in *Making Assessment Work: Values and Principles in Assessing children's Learning* (Drummond, Rouse & Pugh 1992). In this discussion pack, the authors argue that effective assessment is predicated on the educator's principled understanding of the purposes of Early Years education. Practitioners are invited to ask themselves about their aspirations for children. What do we want our young children:

- to do?
- to feel?
- to think?
- to know and understand?
- to represent and express?

Answering these questions, is, I believe, part of the way forward for Early Years education in this country. And there are, fortunately for us, many sources to which we can turn to support us in our thinking. In this volume, too, other authors have written of their personal experiences of children's powers, and the versatility and enthusiasm of children's learning in appropriately structured environments. There is a healthy emphasis, throughout this collection, on the range of children's powers, and an accompanying emphasis on the context – children's play – in which so many of these powers are exercised.

Play and imagination

This emphasis on play is an important element in the argument to be made for a distinctive approach to Early Years education. But it is also a particularly challenging part of the task that lies ahead. Every Early Years educator, it is safe to assume, has at some time been made painfully aware that the importance of play in educational settings is not universally acknowledged. Although numbers of recent publications have taken up the challenge, and defended the educational value and outcomes of play, perhaps we have put too much professional energy into defending the contentious verb 'to play', which in some quarters is used as the polar opposite of the verb 'to learn'. Perhaps we would do better to emphasise 'play' in its noun form, and to construct our arguments around a full description of what, in the context of play, children think, feel, do, understand and express. What kinds of important thinking and feeling characterise play? Should we not be making a case for these, for imagination, for empathy, for experiment and exploration? (Just some of the acts of mind and will that can readily be seen whenever children play.)

In making such a case as an in-service educator, working with practitioners from settings across the Early Years Foundation Stage, I have found it salutary to see the confidence and the zeal with which other educationalists, outside the Early Years community, argue a position that I find thoroughly convincing. Mary Warnock, for example, moral philosopher as well as educational reformer, argues in *Schools of Thought* (1977) that the imagination is good in itself. Being more imaginative, like being more healthy, needs no further justification (p. 153). In *Imagination* (1976), Warnock makes even bolder claims:

> I have come very strongly to believe that it is the cultivation of imagination which should be the chief aim of education, and in which our present systems of education most conspicuously fail, where they do fail . . . In education we have a duty to educate the imagination above all else.
>
> (Warnock, 1976, p. 9)

She characterises imagination as the human power 'to go beyond what is immediately in front of (their) noses', and, in a telling phrase she has borrowed from Wordsworth's *Tintern Abbey*, as the capacity to 'see into the life of things'. It is a power which is not only intellectual: 'its impetus comes from the emotions as much as from the head'. Imagination is both necessary and universal; as part of human intelligence, it needs educating, and this will entail 'an education not only of the intelligence but, going along with it, of the feelings' (1976, p. 202).

The need for high expectations

Warnock's aspirations for the human condition, even in this briefest of summaries, seem to me to illuminate some exciting possibilities for children's early learning. If we can recognise, as I believe we can, the young child's powers to think and to feel, we can see clearly the weight of our responsibility to educate, to exercise and strengthen those powers.

In recent years, there has been considerable interest in an approach to Early Years education practised in the Emilia-Romagna district of Northern Italy. A touring exhibition of their work, The Hundred Languages of Children, which has visited the UK three times in recent years, testifies to the extraordinary richness of their early educational provisions. 'The cornerstone of our experience', says Carla Rinaldi, until recently the Director of Services to Young Children in the region, is an understanding of children as 'rich, strong and powerful'. She spells out what this means:

> they have . . . plasticity, the desire to grow, curiosity, the ability to be amazed, and the desire to relate to other people and communicate . . . Children are eager to express themselves in a plurality of symbolic languages . . . [they] are open to exchanges and reciprocity as deeds and acts of love which they not only want to receive but also want to offer.
>
> (Edwards, Gandini & Forman 1993, pp. 101–2)

There are interesting parallels here, I think, with the New Zealand educators' categories of belonging and contributing. But the Italian educators are not exclusively interested in the social dimension of learning; a central feature of their provision is the atelier, a creative workshop, rich in materials and tools, in which children from birth to six years old become masters of the 'plurality of symbolic languages' (such as painting, drawing, dancing and working in clay). In the atelier, 'children invent autonomous vehicles of expressive freedom, cognitive freedom, symbolic freedom and paths to communication' (ibid., p. 120) In the atelier, surely, they are exercising the powers that Warnock describes: 'to see into the life of things' – and not just to see, but to represent and express what they see.

The Emilia-Romagna approach to early childhood provision has, I am arguing, much to teach us in this country. I am not suggesting that we should follow their prescriptions to the letter, or that we should swallow, wholesale, their priorities and perceptions. But I am convinced that their way of seeing children, from birth, as strong to do and feel, skilled in learning and powerful in communicating, has profound effects upon the curriculum they provide, a curriculum that is sensitively and challengingly matched to the children's developing 'powers to be'. Their expectations of what children can do, and think and feel, are, to English eyes and ears, extraordinarily high. But the children in their settings rise to these expectations, as they explore both the world that is opening out in front of them and their own interior worlds of feeling and imagination. As one reads the detailed accounts of their cross-curricular projects, given in Edwards' book and in a growing number of other publications (for example, Comune di Sant'Ilario d'Enza 2001, Vecchi 2002), one wonders what these Italian educators would make of some of the experiences provided in Early Years settings in this country.

My own observations of four-year-olds in their first terms in primary school in several local authority areas suggest that in some classrooms children's powers are seriously undervalued. The demands made on the children – to follow instructions, to complete worksheets, to cut and stick and colour in, as required by their educators – do not do justice to the children's energetic and enthusiastic minds. In one classroom, as part of a local authority evaluation programme (Drummond 1995), a child was observed using a template to draw a shape representing a T-shirt on a square piece of wallpaper. The T-shirt was one of twenty similar cutouts, destined for a frieze of teddy bears who were being changed from their winter outfits to their summer clothes as part of the classroom topic on 'the summer'. The child followed his teacher's directions as best he could, but the scissors were far from sharp and the wallpaper prone to tear. After some frustrating minutes had passed, the child looked up at the teacher who was leading this activity and said 'I can sew, you know'. I take this child's comment seriously, as a gentle – even forgiving – admonition to his educators. It is as if he was telling them to think again, to question their motives in asking him to perform this meaningless and unrewarding task. It is as if he were pointing out, most politely, that his powers to think, and do, and feel, were not being nourished or exercised by a curricular diet of templates and teddy bear friezes.

Bennett et al. (1984), we have already noted, found evidence that teachers both overestimated and underestimated children's abilities to complete language and number tasks. One particularly interesting finding from this study is that the problem of underestimation, when the task set was too easy for a child, seemed to be 'invisible to teachers in classrooms' (p. 49). The teachers in the study did not identify any tasks as beneath the child's current level of achievement, or not challenging enough, or as a waste of a child's time. Bennett et al. explain this finding by reference to the emphasis placed on procedure, rather than product, in literacy and numeracy tasks. When teachers saw children correctly following these procedures (using full stops in their writing, for example, or carrying a ten in an addition task), they 'did not compare the child's product with his actual level of understanding' (p. 63) They appeared to be satisfied with the children's compliance with the procedures they had been taught. This explanation seems reasonable enough, but it may only be half of the story. If one piece of the puzzle is excessive concern for procedures as defined by the educator, then another, equally important, element in the picture is a serious lack of concern for what children can do for themselves. It appears that the teachers in this study were not interested in the possibility that the children could do more than was required of them. They seemed to be blind to children's inventiveness, their individual ways of seeing, their personal explorations into the unknown.

By contrast, in another classroom in the evaluation study cited above (Drummond 1995) a group of young children spent 25 minutes absorbed in water play. The nursery nurse had, at their request, added some blue dye to the water, and the children were intrigued by the different shades of blue they could see: paler at the shallow margin, and darker at the deepest, central part of the water-tray. One child was even more interested in another, related, phenomenon. He spent nearly ten minutes of this period of water play observing his own shoes and how their colour appeared to change when he looked at them through the water and the transparent water-tray. The child seemed to be fascinated by what happened when he placed his feet in different positions; he leaned intently over the tray to see what colour his shoes appeared to be at each stage. He did not use the words 'experiment' or 'observation', but that was what he was engaged in, nonetheless. After each trial, he withdrew his feet into the natural light of day, as if to check that they retained their proper colour. Had the dye stayed in the water, where he had seen it put? Or had some of it seeped out, into his shoes?

At the end of the morning session, the teacher and nursery nurse announced that it was time to tidy up. The children worked together to empty the water-tray of the sieves, funnels and beakers they had been using. They took out the jugs, the teaspoons and the ladles, emptied them, and put them away. When they had nearly finished, the boy stopped and asked aloud, of no-one in particular, 'How do we get the blue out?'

I think this is a remarkable question, showing, as it does, this young scientist's mind at work. Only further conversation with him would reveal his present understanding of the concepts of light, colour, and reversibility, but his question is incontrovertible evidence of his urgent desire to find out how the world works, how its regularities and unpredictabilities can be accounted for. It is evidence too of his already firmly established knowledge that, as an active member of the world, he can experiment with it, act on it, question it and reflect on it– on the way to understanding it.

This powerful child's question offers his educators exciting opportunities for development, but only if they respond to what he can do, and is doing. If they focus on what he does not know, or does not fully understand, they will miss the chance to feed and exercise his growing powers to hypothesise and experiment. The way they conceptualise this child's question – as genuine enquiry, or unthinking ignorance – will directly affect the experiences they go on to provide for him.

Conclusion

I have been arguing that the way forward for Early Years education is in a re-examination of some of our taken-for-granted assumptions and expectations. If educators, without any ill-will, choose to think of young children as immature, incapable, illiterate or ignorant pupils, then the experiences and activities they provide will not give children opportunities to prove themselves for what they really are – rich, strong and powerful, as Rinaldi argues: accomplished learners, passionate enquirers, loving companions. The primary classroom and its predefined tasks, the Early Years setting and its learning goals, will simply not be spacious enough for the exercise of children's powers to be: to be scientists, artists, citizens, dramatists, moralists, constructing and reconstructing the world.

But if Early Years educators can free themselves from any notion that because the children they work with are the youngest children in the system, not yet ready for the academic demands of Key Stage One, they are therefore the least capable, and least competent, then the future looks bright. There is then a real possibility that we can provide experiences, time and space, food and exercise, for learners who are already, long before they start school, capable, competent, imaginative and eloquent.

The co-founder and, for many years, Director of the Reggio Emilia programme is the late and much revered Loris Malaguzzi. In a long interview about the principles underpinning their developing pedagogy he describes how, in Italy too, pressure from later stages of education threatens to distort and deform Early Years practices.

If the school for young children has to be preparatory, and provide continuity with the elementary school, then we as educators are already prisoners of a model that ends up as a funnel. I think, moreover, that the funnel is a detestable object, and it is not much appreciated by children either. Its purpose is to narrow down what is big into what is small. This choking device is against nature.
(Malaguzzi, in Edwards, Gandini & Forman 1993, p. 86)

But Malaguzzi is optimistic, visionary even, in his determination that Early Years education will not choke or be choked. His fundamental position is a succinct summary of the argument I have proposed here: 'Suffice it to say that the school for young children has to respond to the children'. I have suggested that for settings for young children to do this, our starting point must be a thorough understanding of what children are, in order that we can support their being and becoming. And if we can achieve such an understanding, we will be well placed to share in the glory of Malaguzzi's vision of the future. 'The continuing motivation for our work', he claims (p. 88), is 'to liberate hopes for a new human culture of childhood. It is a motive that finds its origin in a powerful nostalgia for the future and for humankind.'

References

Bennett, N., Desforges, C., Cockburn A., & Wilkinson B. (1984) *The Quality of Pupil Learning Experiences*, London: Lawrence Erlbaum Associates.

Bissex, G. L. (1980) *GNYS AT WRK: A Child Learns to Write & Read*, Cambridge, MA: Harvard University Press.

Brooker, L. (2002) *Starting School – Young Children Learning Cultures.* Buckingham: Open University Press.

Comune di Sant'Ilario d'Enza (2001) *The Future Is a Lovely Day*, Reggio Emilia: Reggio Children.

Drummond, M. J. (1995) *In School at Four* [Hampshire's earlier admissions programme Final evaluation report]. Spring. Hampshire: Hampshire County Council.

Drummond, M. J., Rouse, D., & Pugh, G. (1992) *Making Assessment Work: Values and Principles in Assessing Young children's Learning*, Nottingham: NES Arnold/ National Children's Bureau.

Edwards, C., Gandini, L., & Forman, G. (1993) *The Hundred Languages of Children: The Reggio Emilia Approach to Early Childhood Education*, Norwood, NJ: Ablex Publishing Corporation.

Fromm, E. (1949) *Man for Himself*, London: Routledge & Kegan Paul.

Fromm, E. (1976) *To Have or To Be?* London: Jonathan Cape.

Hughes, M. (1989) 'The child as learner: The contrasting views of developmental psychology and early education.' In Desforges, C. (Ed.), *Early Childhood Education*, British Journal of Educational Psychology Monograph Series No. 4, pp. 144–157.

Ministry of Education (1996) *Te Whāriki: Early Childhood and Curriculum*, Wellington, NZ: Learning Media.

Sharp, R. & Green, A. (1975) *Education and Social Control: A Study in Progressive Primary Education*, London: Routledge & Kegan Paul.

Steedman, C. (1990) *Childhood, Culture and Class in Britain: Margaret McMillan, 1860–1931*, London: Virago.

Vecchi, V. (Ed.) (2002) *Theatre Curtain: The Ring of Transformations*, Reggio Emilia: Reggio Children.

Warnock, M. (1976) *Imagination*, London: Faber & Faber.

Warnock, M. (1977) *Schools of Thought*, London: Faber & Faber.

Wells, G. (1987) *The Meaning Makers*, London: Hodder & Stoughton.

INDEX